Battleship

Also by Dorothy Ours

Man o' War

Battleship

A Daring Heiress,
A Teenage Jockey,
and America's Horse

Dorothy Ours

St. Martin's Press

New York

www.stmartins.com

Design by Phil Mazzone

ISBN 978-0-312-64185-6 (hardcover)
ISBN 978-1-250-02132-8 (e-book)

St. Martin's Press books may be purchased for educational, business, or promotional use. For information on bulk purchases, please contact Macmillan Corporate and Premium Sales Department at 1-800-221-7945 extension 5442 or write specialmarkets@macmillan .com.

First Edition: April 2013

10   9   8   7   6   5   4   3   2   1

For all kinds of family

Throw your heart over [the fence], and your horse will follow.
—Thomas Assheton Smith, Esq.
Master of the Quorn Hunt, 1806–1816

A ship in port is safe. But that is not what ships are built for.
—Rear Admiral Grace Hopper, U.S. Navy

Prelude

TWO HOOVES, TWO ANKLES, TWO CANNON bones swathed in thick cotton lead the way over the five-foot hedge at Becher's Brook, aiming for a secure landing spot on the bank beyond the deep-cutting stream. The legs belong to a small horse, airborne, then slanting toward earth, reaching for the right angle to save himself. Atop the horse, a boy balances like a pendulum, tipped back and forth by muscular motion and unforgiving gravity.

The horse's leading forefoot nears the turf, committed like an airplane wheel about to touch tarmac. His neck pitches down, his hips jerk up. The boy, braced for anything, lets his own tall body lean parallel with the little horse, his shoulder blades almost meeting the steeply raised haunches, his long legs nearly vertical. His arms extend low and straight toward the horse's mouth, releasing every possible bit of freedom to the plunging head and neck; his hands, gripping the last inch of reins, are the emergency brake.

A hoof nears earth—a chance already taken many hundreds of times by this horse, thousands of times by his young rider. Ten years before, another hoof had gone wrong, landing in a rabbit hole during a foxhunting gallop, flinging the boy into unconsciousness. To this day, his mother can't stand to watch him ride jump races. His father, seemingly fearless on horseback, trusts their son to handle the most perilous course but thinks that this particular horse is too small and quirky to safely jump it. The boy thinks the whole thing can't be any worse than his early childhood hunting runs, when he was expected to keep up with his father, going like "a bat out of hell" over formidable obstacles, while mounted on a pony.

The horse is propelled by his own instincts, while responding in each moment to his rider. He knows nothing, of course, about the human reckonings that put him in *this* race. And yet his attitude and movements speak his history, springing from everything he was bred to be, showing all he has learned and failed to learn, deciding the remaining course of his life.

A hoof touches earth; a nose jolts toward the turf. A tremor races through two bodies, with all the possibilities that burst open whenever *I* becomes *we*.

1

BRUCE HOBBS WAS SEVEN YEARS OLD when he opened his eyes and saw nothing at all. Blinking, staring, straining, but nothing changed. Only darkness, beyond his control—a sudden loss he could not understand. At first, the only things assuring Bruce that his friendly world still existed were his mother's voice, his mother's hands. Her voice promised Bruce that he hadn't lost his eyesight. He had hit his head very hard and suffered a concussion. While his head healed, he would have to protect himself by staying in the blacked-out room.

Bruce's mother, Margery, blamed his father, Reginald. Taking crazy chances on horseback and making their boy do the same. Ponies might be all right, but not the way Reg made Bruce ride, following the quickest grown-ups in one of England's most challenging foxhunts. Reg Hobbs saw things another way: doing everything possible to make his boy as good as himself. That's how Reg had learned from his own father, Tom Hobbs, one of the most respected huntsmen and horse dealers in England.

Reg knew how destiny could suddenly stretch, even take you across an ocean and back. He had seen it at age fifteen. One day he had been a gifted young rider, winning a cross-country race in Leicestershire with a horse that his father might sell. The next morning, in his father's office, he had met a wealthy American client—and learned that his father was, in a sense, selling him as well.

"Mr. Clark has bought your little horse, Reg," Tom Hobbs told his son. "He wants you to take the horse over to America and to stay with him over there, helping with his stud."

At first glance, Frederick Ambrose Clark didn't look like much. Not very tall, a hump between his shoulders, a habit of talking "down his nose." His appearance disguised a bold athlete. A man bent but not defeated by many broken bones, a man once upon a time described by the *New York Times* as "one of the most skillful and daring amateur steeplechase riders of the metropolitan turf."

Tom Hobbs knew. His boy was going to land at one of the grandest estates on Long Island, New York. His boy would handle some of the finest foxhunters, show horses, and polo ponies that money could buy. And beyond those material benefits, his boy would report to a kindred spirit. Like Tom Hobbs, Brose Clark knew the best and would not settle for anything less. In every way, working for him would reinforce what Tom wanted Reg to be.

Everything that had followed that morning in his father's office weighed on Reg while his own son lay in the blacked-out room. That room was provided by Brose Clark and his wife. It belonged to a cottage at Warwick Lodge, Leicestershire, where the Clarks foxhunted every winter and Reg managed all aspects of their impressive stable. A day of sport might even include the prince of Wales—and at the same time, Reg had the satisfaction of knowing that his own riding and appearance were second to no one. He also knew that his wife enjoyed a more than comfortable home and his child went to school with sons and daughters of landed gentry. For Reg, top-notch horsemanship yielded rare privileges. If Bruce only would persevere, he might enjoy the same.

But that pathway required physical risk. Working with horses, there was no way to eliminate danger. For two weeks, while Bruce existed in the dark, his mother hoped that when he eased back into the world her boy would choose a safer course. His father treated the accident as a temporary setback, best brushed away. Their fighting peppered Bruce's daily life.

Underneath it all, the young boy felt a deep sense of security. If his parents fought this hard over him, clearly he mattered a lot. On the other hand, no matter how he tried, he couldn't please them both. Somewhere between his mother's protection and his father's relentless drive, Bruce would have to find his own identity.

He wanted normal childhood pleasures. But even at age seven, Bruce Hobbs could sense a great reward waiting somewhere beyond the edge of comfort and safety. He could begin to feel that hard work and courage might bring this reward within his reach. Bruce could not yet understand how this pressure from his father was affecting his own character; he could only hope that, eventually, his father would be satisfied. But he did not see just how far his father wanted to go.

Reg Hobbs's wildest ambition centered on a racecourse near the English village of Aintree, a few miles north of Liverpool, its horizon haunted by active factory smokestacks, its boundaries partly drawn by a railway line and the Leeds and Liverpool Canal. At this place where ancient met modern, more than a quarter million people gathered in late March every year to experience a horse race called the Grand National.

The Grand National was well named: it dwarfed everything. The winner would gallop nearly five miles and leap thirty obstacles. Most of the brush-covered fences stood at least five feet high. The only short hedge marked a broad jump over water. Reg Hobbs, who had won steeplechases in his youth, still imagined riding *that* course and winning the National someday.

In another decade, Reg would find his moment. During the time it would take for his boy to grow up, he would discover his own greatest role. But first, a distant person had to grow into the same dream. Someone else's dawning ambition had to start stretching toward his own.

A catalyst came in 1928, the year of Bruce's accident. A record number of Grand National contestants circled within Aintree's saddling paddock. At the call for "Riders up!" forty-two men settled onto racehorses' backs. A hand touched one horse's throat, pulling the plug from the silvered tracheotomy tube worn by hundred-to-one shot Tipperary Tim. Being tubed, a common treatment for English cart horses who developed upper airway constrictions, was a last resort for racehorses. Unplugging the metal cylinder before hard exercise let in a full stream of air, but harmful substances could rush in, too. Tipperary Tim's rider probably carried a cork in his pocket, an emergency stopper if they happened to fall in water.

Forty-two horses paraded onto the rain-soaked course. Most of them came from the British Isles and several from France. Nine raced for American owners. Two American entries actually had been bred, born, and raced in the United States. One of these had attracted an American entourage, hundreds of Yankees now waiting in Aintree's chilly grandstands and many more gathered in downtown Baltimore, Maryland, where a transatlantic telephone hookup from Aintree to Sun Square would let fans follow the race as it happened. The horse drawing so much attention was a rather plain, dark brown gelding with a checkered past. As he stepped onto the Aintree course, he deserved a greeting given to his namesake in a Louisa May Alcott book: "Why, Billy Barton, how in the world did you get here?"

Five years earlier, this unassuming-looking horse had made a bad scene at Baltimore's Pimlico Race Course. Rearing and kicking at his handlers in the saddling paddock, then trying to kick spectators as he headed out to the track, five-year-old Billy Barton had hardly seemed like the same performer who had won the Cuban Derby at age three. His latest owner was trying to make him win a claiming race–an event where each horse was for sale at a small price—for the second week in a row. But when Billy reached the track, he bolted, tearing along at racing speed for half a mile. Wrangled to the starting barrier, he began the race, then couldn't keep pace. All wagers on him were wasted. He finished last.

After nearly fifty races and a steep downward trend, Billy Barton decided to quit. His trainer sent him back to school at the starting barrier, but Billy refused to run when the webbing stretching across the track sprang into the air. His determination must have been immense. Assistant starters, assertive men charged with motivating reluctant horses, often made their point with buggy whips. But the long lash didn't change Billy's mind, and the racing officials had no choice: they banned him from competition. In racing's earn-your-keep economy, he was worthless.

And yet Billy Barton also was young, athletic, and sparky. That spring of 1923, a Baltimore steel factory executive named Howard Bruce saw him at Pimlico and paid $2,000 for the ordinary-looking colt with strong shoulders and sturdy legs. Bruce had him gelded and gave him plenty of time to learn a noncombative lifestyle. Out in the countryside north of Baltimore, Howard Bruce served as Master of the Elkridge Hounds. He needed a bold, fast horse to keep him up front during a fox chase.

Billy Barton, the racetrack rogue, loved his new job. Monotonous circles around a dirt track gave way to diverse miles of meadows and woodlands, hills and streams. He always would have a feisty streak, greeting his handlers with pinned ears and bared teeth. Billy Barton was nobody's pet. And yet, in the hunt field, Bruce found him an extraordinarily willing partner. Whatever obstacle confronted them, Billy jumped.

He excelled so greatly that Howard Bruce got curious. Three years after his Pimlico meltdowns, Billy Barton entered a cross-country jumping race; three miles later, he had won easily. The sour, banned flat racer had become a 'chaser so fit, gifted, and willing that he won Maryland's Grand National, the Maryland Hunt Cup, and the Virginia Gold Cup— three classics totaling eleven miles—during three consecutive weeks. By the autumn of 1927, Billy had won seven of his eight steeplechasing starts, some in record time. With nothing left to prove in his home country, Howard Bruce shipped Billy to one of the best trainers in England to prepare for the world's greatest jump race.

In 1928, Billy Barton reached Aintree with a new identity: a cross-country champion who had never refused when his rider asked him to jump. Now, he might become the first American-bred horse to win the world's greatest steeplechase for an American owner. British bookmakers, however, gave him little chance. Earlier that winter, Billy Barton had uncorked a dazzling win for his first English race, but he had fared badly in two later starts. Thinking that the American was in well over his head, the bookies set his National odds at thirty-three to one. Also, most of his opponents were quite literally over his head. A Maryland sportsman watching the field parade to the starting post noticed that Billy Barton— despite his good height of 16.1 hands, or five feet five inches, at the withers—was one of the smallest horses in the race.

Then again, being lighter might count for something today. Overnight and early-afternoon showers had waterlogged the turf, making it heavy underfoot as the field lined up at the far right end of the course, their backs to the grandstand, their faces aiming toward the long, distant backstretch known as "the country." Clouds sailed overhead, threatening to rain again, unblocking random spots of sunshine. A mist had settled over Aintree. The first fence made a blur about four hundred yards ahead. Some people high in the stands near the start could see the second fence. Beyond that, fog hid everything.

Two false starts wasted several minutes, prolonging the tension. Finally, the crowded field leaped forward together. Surprisingly, everyone cleared the first fence. Then the fog began swallowing the galloping forms, and most of the quarter million spectators had no idea what was going on. Hoofbeats sounded through the mist, the only proof of an invisible race.

For several minutes, the grandstand crowd waited for the field to reappear. How many would handle the big drop on the landing side of Becher's Brook? How many would navigate the abrupt left-handed Canal Turn, with a ninety-degree swivel to avoid diving into the Leeds and Liverpool Canal—then hurdle Valentine's Brook and three more hedges five feet high? How many would pass the grandstand with riders still on their backs, completing the first half of the National?

Finally, hoofbeats drew near. At the head of Aintree's long homestretch, six horses with riders charged into view. Less than halfway through the race, thirty-six had disappeared. In the stands, a French countess turned her back to the track and began saying the Lord's Prayer. Other voices overlapped hers. "That's the Yankee horse leading." "Come on, Billy Barton!"

Six horses leaped the water jump in front of the stands, the one-time-only broad-jumping challenge. Billy Barton stepped in the flat-bottomed pool but sprang out with unusual agility. Six horses passed the finish line for the first time, then turned left and passed their starting point. Billy Barton led five others back into the mist while scattered groups of Americans cheered.

Again the vast crowd listened for hoofbeats, waiting one, two, three minutes for the runners to return. At last, three horses appeared: Billy Barton, Great Span, and Tipperary Tim. Two fences stood between them and the quarter-mile gallop to the finish line.

Great Span looked as if he might be going best of the three. Moments later, as he launched over the next-to-last fence, that didn't matter. Great Span's saddle slipped sideways, spilling his rider into the ditch. With the loose girth draped over his back and the empty saddle flapping underneath his belly, Great Span galloped onward. He had become what one horseman called "the greatest terror of Grand Nationals—a loose horse." With no rider guiding him, a loose horse moved unpredictably. Great Span decided he wanted to be near Billy Barton.

Three horses rose as one to the final fence. Billy Barton held the inside position; close to his right side, nearly leaning into him, came the riderless Great Span. Far to their outside came the only horse other than Billy Barton who could win this Grand National: the hundred-to-one shot from Ireland, Tipperary Tim. With each stride, Tim produced a whistling sound: air rushing through his tracheotomy tube.

Three horses rustled across fence thirty, a four-and-a-half-foot hedge. The race would come down to two survivors, each with one perfect quality. The winner would be either the long shot attempting the National only because, his trainer said, "He never falls down," or the American star who, his owner said, had never refused a jump. Tipperary Tim, not very fast but unusually steady, landed well. Billy Barton, crowded by the riderless horse and looking weary, landed awkwardly and flipped like a fish on a line, throwing his jockey off toward the inside rail. Barrel rolling on his right side, Billy stood up as his feet touched earth and let a spectator who rushed under the rail catch his reins. Other spectators helped jockey Tommy Cullinan to his feet and boosted him onto Billy's back, nearly sending the dazed rider all the way over. Meanwhile, Tipperary Tim opened an insurmountable lead. He was pulling up, an easy winner, as Billy Barton slogged past the finish line, accompanied by astonished murmurs and boisterous Irish cheers.

The only tubed horse to win the Grand National, Tipperary Tim had found salvation through his seeming disability. Kept to a far outside path so that other horses wouldn't kick debris into his breathing tube, Tim had enjoyed a trouble-free trip. Billy Barton, on the other hand, had won a moral victory even greater than the grandstand crowd had seen. Billy had been severely tested because Easter Hero, the fast but inexperienced horse who led the pack over the first several fences, had a bad habit.

Instead of aiming straight ahead when he jumped, Easter Hero sometimes angled his body to the right. Leaping a simple fence, this might not matter. But the Canal Turn at Aintree presented complications: an open ditch two feet deep yawning in front of a hedge five feet high. Furthermore, the hedge fanned forward to the right, angling into the course's hard left-hand turn.

Well after the race ended, spectators returning from the distant, foggy Canal Turn described what the grandstand crowd had missed. Easter Hero, taking off too far ahead of the open ditch and jumping to the right, not knowing that the fence line angled forward, had stuck on top of the hedge. While Easter Hero struggled in the brush, gradually sliding backward, waves of horses behind him misjudged their leaps or refused to try. An American reporter noted that, as Easter Hero thrashed and slowly dropped, "others bumped and sideswiped everything within reach," many of them landing in the ditch. An English reporter said it looked as if a machine gunner was attacking the fence, taking almost everyone down.

A horse named Eagle's Tail found himself standing in the ditch, parallel to the hedge, his jockey still in the saddle, while Billy Barton galloped straight toward him. Billy had two choices: slide to a stop and a likely collision, or jump over the standing horse and rider as well as the massive hedge.

Billy jumped.

When Billy Barton emerged from the mist to complete the first lap, few people knew what a prodigious effort had brought him that far. More than two miles later, when he rose to the final fence, few guessed how much heart had brought him to that place beside the leader, his rider still upon his back. As the word spread, Billy Barton became known as more than a talented cross-country horse. He represented a young nation itching to show its parent that it measured up. He showed that an American might be the real thing. But according to British horse-racing authorities, American racehorses weren't actually Thoroughbred.

Connoisseurs don't take kindly to substitutes. Champagne should come from a single region of France. Thoroughbred horses should come from Great Britain. How could an imitator match the original?

Back when the United States was merely a colonial frontier, England had been setting standards for the emerging Thoroughbred breed. Although exported Thoroughbreds eventually took root around the world, Great Britain held what wine producers call *terroir*: the flavor absorbed from the landscape. Even Kentucky's famous Bluegrass region couldn't claim the same genetic blend, geography, and training conditions that produced such dominant racehorses in the first place.

Plus, there were problems with pedigree. In America, you could be forgiven for having several poorly documented ancestors. The proof wasn't on paper but in the pudding: did a horse win races or produce winning offspring? Pedigree didn't seem like a problem until nearly 1900, when American horses began winning lots of English races and American breeders infiltrated English bloodstock sales. Protecting their domain, British horsemen winched their eligibility rules tighter and tighter. Finally, in 1913, British officials decreed that *every* line of a Thoroughbred pedigree must trace "without flaw" only to horses found in the first volume of Britain's *General Stud Book,* published in 1791. More than 90 percent of Thoroughbreds foaled in the United States suddenly were considered "half-bred." These included the supreme champion and world record holder, Man o' War.

The arithmetic was ridiculous. According to English rules, Man o' War was half-bred because one of his thirty-two great-great-great-grandparents—a phenomenally successful American stallion named Lexington—had two ineligible lines far back in his pedigree. Whether those ancestors harmed or enhanced his racing ability was impossible to say. The stigma placed on American horses, however, was severe. If Man o' War himself were offered at stud in England, his offspring would be considered mongrels. Perhaps the greatest racehorse that America had produced would be officially invisible in the country where his breed began.

There were loopholes. Not wanting to punish its own horsemen who were stuck with outdated inventory, Britain allowed so-called half-breds to continue racing within its borders. Many found success in steeplechasing— that is, long-distance racing over jumps. But only one horse bred in the United States had won the Grand National—and even then, America couldn't take much credit. California-born Rubio had been exported to

England as a yearling, sold to a British owner, and trained as one of England's own. When Rubio won the 1908 Grand National, Americans didn't feel much connection. Other home-grown athletes would become popular heroes: Philadelphia's Bill Tilden uncorking "the soundest and brainiest tennis ever seen on English courts" to win Wimbledon; "American-bred" golfer Walter Hagen capturing the British Open by a single stroke. The *New York Times* predicted that "some day an American-bred and American-owned horse may carry off the Grand National." If that happened, it would be like an American sparkling wine surpassing French champagne.

But so far, American owners had done best with British runners. In 1923, Stephen "Laddie" Sanford had broken through with Sergeant Murphy, a thoroughly British gelding who had performed well several times at Aintree before Sanford bought and won with him. In 1926, the Wall Street financier Charles Schwartz paid $20,000 for a well-primed British horse, Jack Horner, only two weeks before winning the big race.

Could money buy merit? For some observers, Sergeant Murphy's success under American colors raised a deeper issue: it isn't only what you do, it's *how* you do it. "Now the shift of economic power to the United States brings to America the problem of aristocracy," newly created *Time* magazine declared. The writer saw two possibilities: the shortsighted-ness that had made King Louis XV of France not care if ruin followed his reign, as long as he lived in luxury; or the more demanding choice, where people who enjoyed the greatest privileges also were expected to serve the best interests of their country for the long run.

"Which tradition," *Time* wondered, "is being accepted by rich Americans?" Its writer supposed that "the answer will come from the sons of Rockefellers, Vanderbilts, Stotesburys, Armours, Mellons, Bakers, Biddles, Fords, who can, if they like, win Grand Nationals."

The magazine writer overlooked a couple of things. He left out one of America's most vigorous dynasties. And he failed to mention the daughters.

2

MARION DU PONT POSSESSED A BRILLIANT smile, when she chose to show it. Her deep-set blue-gray eyes could shine. When she saw a camera pointed her way, however, tensed eyebrows and narrowed eyelids often guarded her inner self. And even when cameras weren't present, Marion's behavior could seem abrupt or gruff. Some onlookers decided that she was rude. One friend formed a different opinion: "She was one of the shyest people that ever walked."

Marion's father knew that, despite their wealth, the world might not go easy on his daughter. Some people would damn the name DuPont for its destructive power, the killing force of gunpowder and dynamite, the fuel of war. Some people might seek her love or friendship simply because she would be very, very rich. And then there were the fault lines cracking within her strong, yet fractured, family.

William du Pont could not protect his daughter from every hard reality, but he could try to fortify her spirit. The year was about 1900; the place, near London, England. The little American girl was no more than six years old; her brother, no more than four. Their father, nearing fifty, brought his only offspring on a mission. He wanted them to be supremely brave. He took them to a cockfight.

Marion was used to riding in horse-drawn coaches with her father, or sitting beside him while he wrote letters to a friend in the United States and adding her own message: her love, a kiss, her latest discovery: "A.B.C." If her father thought she also belonged in a noisy, smelly room where men threw chickens together and cheered the bloody fight, she would pay attention to his wishes.

These weren't just any chickens, he would explain—they were game fowl, bred to be *game*. In this case, game didn't mean prey, to be hunted down. "Game" meant willing to keep trying, even when conditions got very hard, even when you seemed completely beaten. And that is what the father wanted his children to understand.

Many people would have felt that the cockpit was no fit place for children, or indeed for anyone. Some hated the brutal struggle of the feathered "stags" pecking and spurring each other. Some couldn't stomach the bloody stench. Others, who might be perfectly willing to wring a chicken's neck or cut off its head and cook it for supper, disapproved of the gambling that permeated every match. William du Pont, however, had something else in mind. The Greek general Themistocles, the story goes, once stopped his troops to watch two chickens fighting by the roadside. He wanted to show his soldiers that if those birds never gave up, no matter what damage they took, a human warrior should do no less. His army, outnumbered ten to one, then won the battle of Marathon. Chickens could teach a person an awful lot about courage.

Marion had experienced something that would fascinate her for life. She would come to love the warrior birds with their iridescent plumage and aggressive movements, eager to be released from their handlers' arms, flying up to meet each other in the center of the ring, creating in midair a few moments of what one spectator called "excruciating beauty." Eventually, she also might understand why courage shadowed her father, making demands that wouldn't let him alone. She might understand, and wonder at, the reasons why she existed at all.

William du Pont's family owed their fantastic wealth to a duet with danger, a dance that began shortly after his grandfather moved to America. Éleuthère-Irénée du Pont first glimpsed the United States on January 1, 1800, from the deck of a shabby ship proudly named the *American Eagle*. With his parents and extended family, he had left France a few weeks before Napoleon Bonaparte executed a coup d'état. The du Ponts took refuge in an experimental nation that had not yet moved its second president into its unfinished capital city.

While his family pursued various business ventures, Irénée at first seemed unsure of his own course. That changed during a recreational hunting trip, when his gun kept misfiring. Intrigued by scientific processes, Irénée had studied gunpowder manufacturing in France. He knew that the Americans, avoiding expensive imports but lacking their own proper powder-making facilities, were putting up with a poor product. He knew how to do better.

Securing the latest equipment, an effective formula, quality materials, abundant waterpower, and a workforce of French émigrés, Irénée du Pont opened a gunpowder factory beside the Brandywine River at Wilmington, Delaware. Whenever profits accrued, he folded them back into improving and expanding the business. His enterprise boomed in 1812, when Great Britain and the United States went back to war with each other and DuPont's reliable black powder powered much of the American military.

Irénée's descendants would build his company into America's largest explosives manufacturer while sharing the deadly risks taken by their employees. As Irénée's youngest son, Alexis, observed, "Sir, the man who follows my business should be ready to meet his God." Alexis made good on his belief in 1857, when an explosion killed four men who were working near him and set his clothes on fire. Plunging into the river, Alexis saved himself from the flames. Then he noticed more trouble: the explosion had flung a burning piece of wood onto the roof of a building full of gunpowder.

Workmen on the scene would remember Alexis, in the river, yelling at them to *run*. They remembered him racing back onto land and charging up onto the rooftop. They said he was about to grab the burning spar when the building blew up.

Alexis survived his terrible injuries for about a day. At his request, the men who had worked beside him in the mills passed through his room to say good-bye. His family thought of a teaching from Jesus, praising those who responded immediately, under any conditions, when their master knocked at the door. They chose that example for his epitaph: "Blessed are those servants whom the lord when he cometh shall find watching."

William du Pont was only two years old when Alexis died, far too young to know his gallant uncle. He would not be able to describe their interactions to his own daughter and son. But William would grow up with his family's adjustments to the empty space where his uncle Alexis should have been. Eventually, he would hear the story and see the monument in the du Pont family's private graveyard. What's more, he literally could feel the threat that had killed Alexis but also sustained the family wealth and social prominence. The du Ponts still lived so close to Irénée's original factory that when an accident happened, they felt the earth shake. And when that happened, you didn't run away—you ran toward the trouble, to see what you could do.

That alone was a daunting responsibility. Born as his parents entered middle age, William also came to realize that he was joining an epic in progress: the French heritage that lived on every time he and his siblings called their parents "Papa" and "Maman"; the pecking order within his immediate family; his father's control over other branches of their tight-knit clan. As he grew, William discovered that it wasn't easy to meet the standards of his father, Henry, a retired U.S. Army general now known as "Boss Henry" because he reigned as president of the DuPont company. Furthermore, William had to applaud the exploits of his brother Henry Algernon, seventeen years older, who had graduated first in his class at West Point, commanded Union artillery forces in the Civil War, and often recalled his triumphs. On the other hand, William's five surviving sisters* gave their baby brother an affectionate buffer zone. Although they were expected to become literate ladies and marry well, the girls did not have to compete with the Henrys.

William did share an interest with his father: experimental farming. Raising crops and animals wasn't supposed to be his career, however. In 1872, the year William turned seventeen, Boss Henry made his two sons his partners in the DuPont company. Colonel Henry, as Henry Algernon

---

*Evelina du Pont (1840–1938), Ellen Eugenia du Pont Irving (1843–1907), Sara du Pont Duer (1847–1876), Victorine Elizabeth du Pont Foster (1849–1934), and Sophie Madeleine du Pont Chandler (1851–1931) all survived until William reached adulthood. Louisa Gerhard du Pont (1845–1863), named for their mother, died when William was nearly eight years old. Mary Constance du Pont (born February 10, 1854) died at age seven months, nearly a year before William was born.

preferred to be called, felt entitled to the rank but wasn't much interested in the business details. William was willing to try. Later that year, he became the first du Pont to enter the rigorous Massachusetts Institute of Technology; he was going to be a scientist. Halfway through his freshman year, however, it became clear that William wasn't keeping up with his class. Intensive studying strained his eyes. He came under a doctor's care. Early in 1873, he did not pass required exams. William pleaded with MIT's president but soon had to tell his father that the president and faculty "could not make me an exception, although they would [have] liked to have done so." William had flunked out.

Distraught, he clung to the MIT president's parting message: "Tell your father that your failure here is no disgrace and that you have nothing to be ashamed of; for we know that you have tried to do your work and that if your eyes had not failed, you would have done it." Then William's deeper fears came tumbling out. He was eighteen years old, unable to meet his family's goal, unable to picture what he would do if his father didn't believe that he truly was blocked by an impassable physical hurdle, that he was giving his all and telling the truth. He would find a tutor, William told Boss Henry; maybe he could get back on track at the institute. "I also think that it is best," William added, "that I should remain in Boston and not return home." Despite his longing for acceptance, he was shying away, imagining explosions.

William practically begged his father to accept the medical verdict. The doctor said he should drop his textbooks and spend a lot of time either outdoors in the countryside or traveling. The doctor said this had to happen right away or else, William told his father, "I might strain the nerves of my eyes, so that they would never recover and . . . I might have this trouble all my life."

Boss Henry soon put his son at ease. Fulfilling his doctor's prescription, William spent several months touring Europe, chaperoned by his aunt Eleuthera. Eventually, he accepted a job for his father: farm manager. But he couldn't avoid his family's more ambitious plans for long.

At age twenty-two, William married a twenty-three-year-old cousin, May Lammot du Pont. Their merger was supposed to protect their wealth, ground William in his family and corporate responsibilities, and give May the social honor that a wife enjoyed, but they were not especially happy.

Years passed; they produced no children. Meanwhile, William left his father's farm and headed across the Delaware River to a DuPont subsidiary: the Repauno Chemical Company, a dynamite-manufacturing plant in southwestern New Jersey. Serving as secretary and treasurer, William reported to Repauno's president, his cousin Lammot. He was twenty-nine years old when another explosion altered his world.

A talented chemist, Lammot du Pont didn't rest behind a desk. He hoped to personally discover a way to recycle the sulfuric acid used in making nitroglycerine. If his theory worked, the process would become more efficient and Repauno would save money. But when he reached the mixing house on the crucial day, his experimental mixture was fuming like a witch's brew. Lammot knew this was an Alexis-in-the-river moment, a burning spar on a powder house rooftop, a time to act instantly. Like Alexis, he yelled to everyone within hearing: *Run!* Lammot and his lab assistant tried to quench the runaway reaction in the mixing vat, but it only became more violent. They dived behind a thick barrier. They might have survived—if someone hadn't recently stored three charges of nitroglycerine nearby.

People miles away heard the explosion. William du Pont felt it keenly. Another hole in his family, another opening in his life. Inheriting Lammot's job as Repauno president, he gained stature in the business world and also permission to live closer to his work, away from Wilmington and his familial gravity well. But his true liberation would begin five years later, after his father died.

Boss Henry, despite his assertive ways, had not named any one person as his successor at DuPont. Colonel Henry assumed that, as the eldest son of the late president, he should take over. William argued that, having successfully run Repauno for several years, he actually knew what to do.

Friction had been building between the brothers throughout their lives. William did not admire Colonel Henry's self-satisfied manner, sometimes calling him "Stuffed Shirt" or "Tin Soldier." By the time Boss Henry died, his sons' relationship resembled a gunpowder-dusted workroom, needing only a spark to blow it apart.

They tried to be practical. Recognizing that three of their cousins performed vital management roles, the brothers sold them enough shares to create five equal partners. Colonel Henry received the title of president but was supposed to stand aside while his cousins handled the daily operations. William stayed on in New Jersey at Repauno, while also making his presence felt at the DuPont headquarters in Wilmington. Visits were carefully orchestrated so that he and Colonel Henry would not meet.

When it came to family conflict, William typically chose one of two modes: forbearance or flight. Colonel Henry preferred attack. About two years after their father's death, Henry thought he had found a way, at last, to chase William out of his life. It involved a family friend, someone close to William's wife.

Annie Rogers had become a woman more quickly than William du Pont had become a man. At age eighteen, he had been a failed college student, uncertain of his adult role; she had married George Zinn, an older go-getter who had risen from lieutenant to brigadier general in the Union army during the Civil War. At nineteen, an age that found William touring Europe and holding no particular responsibility, Annie became the mother of a baby girl. Later, she bore a son. She was not, however, a typical housewife. She enjoyed a fashionable home at New Castle, Delaware, and a prominent role in society. Heads might turn toward the statuesque brunette with generous curves and a tiny waist. People would be drawn to her luscious appearance, then held by her personality.

As General Zinn's wife, Annie enjoyed many social events hosted by the du Pont family and bonded with William's wife, May. Three years older than Annie, May might seem big-sisterly. Meanwhile, Annie's marriage was becoming so untenable that, in 1890, she took the drastic step of seeking a divorce.

Society didn't blame Annie for wanting rid of General Zinn, who reportedly lived beyond his means and dallied with other women. Her du Pont friends felt sorry for her. Yet at the same time, Annie Rogers Zinn now fell below their standard. Divorce meant that someone admitted to terrible moral failings: adultery, cruelty, desertion. And even the wronged party, by seeking divorce, would be breaking a sacred vow. When Annie took legal action to end her marriage, she triggered a scandal. When two sympathetic du Pont ladies invited her to a party late in 1890, most of their family pretended that Annie was not there.

William, however, was reaching the point where he could no longer pretend. He was thirty-six years old and childless, and he dearly wanted children. He also sought more genuine companionship than was forthcoming with his wife. Now, Colonel Henry saw his opportunity. Gathering the family elders, he announced that William had taken a mistress. When that news failed to upset anyone, Henry told them her name.

Not Mrs. Zinn! William could have a mistress; many prominent men did. But he could not have *this* mistress. Never a divorcée. And Colonel Henry had even more dreadful news to deliver: not only was William carrying on with the unacceptable Mrs. Zinn, he intended to marry her.

That poisoned everything. During the ninety years that the Irénée du Pont family had been living in America, not one of them had resorted to divorce. But this time, when it came to his personal life, William would not give in to family pressure. Even his mother could not change his mind. Louisa Gerhard du Pont could not stop her youngest child from moving to the young state of South Dakota—the latest place where Americans could unhitch from their spouses with very few questions asked.

Spending the winter in Elk Point, William bought some land and established residency. In late January 1892, Louisa thanked him for sending his photograph "in your pretty little sleigh—It is a great pleasure to me to have it," she wrote, "though it gave me a great heart ache, when I first looked at it, for it brought before me so vividly your separation from us all, & your loneliness in that far off region of snow." Then the seventy-five-year-old mother implored her nearly middle-aged son: "If you come on to the East soon again—I hope you will take possession of your room here, which is always ready for you."

There was no way that William would take possession of his old room in his mother's house. His mind and spirit no longer fit within it. Colonel Henry may have meant to be cruel, but he had set his rival free. William's brother had provoked him into being true to himself.

May du Pont, who did not contest her separation from William, received most of the family sympathy. She would lose Colonel Henry's goodwill, however, after marrying her divorce lawyer. Eventually she would land in Washington, DC, with her new husband serving as a U.S. senator.

·   ·   ·

June 1, 1892, became thirty-seven-year-old William du Pont's second wedding day. He had wanted to do it sooner, but the government clerks of Wilmington seemed unable to process a marriage license for him and Annie Zinn. Crossing the Atlantic Ocean and getting married in London turned out to be less troublesome.

It wasn't a large family celebration, but William ensured that it wouldn't be second rate. He and Annie—called "Nannie" by her loved ones—made their vows at St. George's Church in the fashionable district of Mayfair. Nannie gave her home address as Wilmington, Delaware; William claimed Elk Point, South Dakota.

The groom was willing to sail back to the United States and settle at Wilmington while his family grew to accept his new wife, but the bride wanted tranquility. And so they stayed near London, bringing over Nannie's fifteen-year-old daughter, Mary, and nine-year-old son, George, and leasing an ivy-shrouded Tudor mansion in Berkshire. At Arborfield Hall, the family could enjoy gardens rich with roses in June or select a watercraft from their private boathouse in any reasonable weather and go floating along the serenely beautiful River Loddon.

Their tranquility didn't last long. In late January 1893, Mary Rogers Zinn suddenly died. The coroner noted that the girl, not yet sixteen, had fallen victim to "Heart Disease." Nannie and William brought her body home to Wilmington for burial. They gave up England and lived in a state of limbo, sometimes retreating to William's yacht, *Au Revoir*. Their first year of marriage had been far from what they envisioned when they broke from pretended respectability to live openly together. There had been little acceptance, much distress, little rest. Their bereavement struck a chord with William's past—he had lost his sister Louisa, a decade older than himself, when she was only in her eighteenth year. Nannie suffered the anguish of losing her firstborn child.

Something had to set them on a happier course. The day after their first anniversary, William bought them a house. Or, truth be told, a castle. It sat northeast of Wilmington, with a view to the Delaware River from its turret—yes, turret—and upper floors. Its builder, a wool merchant, had dubbed it Woolton Hall. William and Nannie rechristened it Bellevue Hall.

Between their travels, they began laying down roots, finding pleasure in planting flowers at their castle home. They imported many crates of fine home furnishings. And, from La Grande Maison de Blanc in Paris, Nannie ordered a layette.

That winter they nestled quietly at Bellevue Hall, a few miles from William's birthplace. William's family had made it clear, throughout Wilmington society, that the former Mrs. Zinn would not be "received." And yet William also felt their love. He maintained a friendship with his sister Sophie and a warm correspondence with his sister Ellen, who had settled with her husband and children at Staten Island, more than a hundred miles away. He rarely sought out his mother, about ninety miles distant at Lakewood, New Jersey. Louisa du Pont heard nothing from her younger son about the latest major development in his life until Ellen caught a hint in one of his letters that he and Nannie were expecting a blessed event.

"Do go to see dear Maman at Lakewood, and tell her!" Ellen urged her reluctant brother. "She grieves after you so, all the time, because she does not see you. She goes over and over, all you did for her and says—'Nothing could ever equal dear Willie's love and devotion to me!'—'I never could have lived or endured all my sorrows, without it!'—and she cries, and it is so pitiful to see her! Do go, and tell her yourself . . . she will be so pleased to know it from you."

William did. Thanking him, Louisa wrote, "I take this occasion to repeat to you that my love for you is always the same, & will remain unchanged as long as I live. I earnestly hope my dear son, that you will receive it, as I offer it, & give me yours in return. Let each be set aside as some thing apart from our everyday life—but always true & unalterable."

Some thing apart from our everyday life. There it was: no matter how they cared about each other, mother and son could not agree about William's wife. Nothing, it seemed, could reconcile them, not even the new life that greeted them in the spring.

The natural world ran riot at Bellevue Hall in early May: violets blooming, bumblebees cruising, robins hunting in the grass. The baby arrived on May 3, 1894, the day before Annie du Pont's thirty-sixth birthday.

A baby girl. Nannie had to be thinking of her first daughter, who should have been greeting the newcomer, should have been sixteen years old. There could not be another Mary, but her influence lingered. Nannie and William gave their baby girl one simple name, with one extra syllable setting her apart from Nannie's first child: Marion.

Three weeks later, baby Marion was at sea. Rather than hold the fort near Wilmington, her parents had decided to go cruising on their yacht. Although there were flashes of support from William's sisters—Sophie went to see her new niece and came away praising her—being home hadn't healed the hard feelings, after all. Ellen tried to lure them to her summer place at Marblehead, Massachusetts, hoping, she told William, for "the pleasure of knowing your wife, and seeing the dear little baby! Sophie says she is so pretty, with dear little soft brown hair!" But baby Marion did not sail to Marblehead. Her parents were touring as their moods guided them, then moving back to England.

And so Marion du Pont began her life in motion. Long before she had words, she became accustomed to the feeling of the ocean rolling beneath her body. This unconventional beginning eventually caused Marion's aunt Ellen—who had borne several children and knew how uncomfortable the recovery could be—to politely and doubtfully ask William, "I hope your wife feels strong and well after your summer afloat?"

Nannie was, in fact, rebounding. That autumn, she and William leased Arborfield Hall again but also were searching for a different country home within reach of London. During their house hunting, infant Marion learned the feel of the earth rumbling beneath her as she lay on a seat of her father's four-in-hand coach, attended by her nurse.

The du Ponts briefly rented an estate called Yewhurst, then found a treasure about thirty miles southwest of London. Little Marion couldn't understand the concept yet, but Loseley Park truly was a place fit for a princess. Made of stone from a ruined monastery, the manor house featured an authentic Tudor great hall and wood panels from Henry VIII's banqueting tents. The surrounding gardens, fields, and woods stretched out like a private kingdom.

On February 11, 1896, Marion's blue-eyed, brown-haired baby brother was born at Loseley Park. "He looks just as Marion did at his age," William wrote to a friend, "& both he & his mother are doing well. We are both very glad that it is a boy." William's joy carried across the Atlantic but not to his mother's home. Soon Ellen was imploring him, "won't you write dear to Maman and tell her about the boy! The heir makes me feel like forgiving my worst enemy!" But Louisa heard, instead, from her daughter Sophie.

"I rejoice with you over this new found happiness," Louisa wrote to William. She also praised the photographs she had seen of "dear little Marion," the granddaughter who was growing up an ocean away. But Louisa may have realized that her words had little effect. William could not warm up to anyone who slighted his wife. Nannie's hurts were his own. When William's sister Victorine tried to visit him in England while ignoring Annie, she found herself shut out. Unable to accept his spouse, she also lost fellowship with the brother she adored.

Staying in England year after year, William embraced his comfort zone. The ocean dampened explosions. Now, in William's world, the ground shook because his coach was rumbling down the road. The ground shook because horses were racing. In June 1896 he had the satisfaction of watching the race that had inspired the Kentucky Derby, the Derby (pronounced DAR-by) at Epsom Downs, and having his son christened William du Pont Jr. the following day.

At last, as William sailed into his forties, the upheavals that had blasted his world in Wilmington softened into a mature landscape. During Christmas 1896, he relished the cozy scene at gigantic Loseley Park with his young children, his wife, and her son George Zinn, whom William had taken under his wing. "We have a huge Xmas tree 14 ft high, & the children were delighted," William told a friend. After the holidays, he enjoyed reporting that whenever her older brother's name came up in conversation, two-and-a-half-year-old Marion chimed in, "George is at school, learning A.B.C." He proudly noted that his daughter—who had begun stringing "pretty little words together" the previous autumn—"is commencing to talk like a little steam engine, & Willie is getting four more teeth." His down-to-earth interest in their well-being balanced the fairy-tale setting of their home life. Later, William would hear through the family grapevine that a visitor had thought his children were "so bright and sweet"—and also "very unusual because they are so unspoiled."

Unspoiled did not mean without privileges. Before Marion turned three years old, William moved his family to an estate, Binfield Park, not far from prestigious Ascot Racecourse. Every summer, Ascot hosted a royal meet attended by the king. William du Pont joined the festivities, proudly driving his four-in-hand coach through an especially tricky gate. But more important, horses anchored William's daily routine. "I don't think my father had any real job to do in England," Marion would recall, "except drive his coach." She remembered him lifting her up beside stall doors to pet the coach horses' noses. From the start, Marion and her baby brother saw horses bringing purpose to life.

This continued as Marion turned four, five, six years old. At the same time, her father reconsidered his reasons for living abroad. Watching his stepson George Zinn's progress through public school, William realized that, as he told a friend, "English boys are only taught the history & geography of English possessions, so the United States is practically omitted." The same could hold true for Marion and Willie, if they stayed here. They wouldn't know their roots.

Another factor decided William's course. Marion and Willie were not thriving in the damp English climate. Doctors said that the children were "delicate." Marion and Willie may have been too young to understand that an older sister they never met had died while residing in a drafty, stately English home, but they lived with her quiet ghost, manifested through their mother's fear. Nearly smothered with scarves and thick sweaters, the children endured hothouse treatment. Marion would remember that one time an American doctor visited and, as she put it, "told the governess to get us out of those heavy things and into some V-necks so we could breathe. He also said the house was to be kept at sixty-five, not seventy-five." But however they dressed, the problem remained: the children were at odds with their surroundings. Surely there was a healthier place for them to grow up.

William began searching for the perfect environment. Bellevue Hall was not the answer; Delaware's humidity could aggravate breathing problems. The foothills of America's Blue Ridge Mountains, however, should have the air quality his children needed. And so, early in 1899, William launched what he called the "Virginia Farms Campaign," exploring properties for sale. A year passed without success. But one day in

February 1900, William found the perfect place while on the way to somewhere else. All it took was a shortcut, his driver saying, "We can cut through the back of Montpelier."

That name was familiar. Situated about thirty miles north of Thomas Jefferson's Monticello, Montpelier plantation had been the place where James Madison, fourth president of the United States, retreated to bolster his health and work out his deepest thoughts. Actually seeing it was a revelation. The land offered everything from rolling pastures to unspoiled forest. Stepping out from the old house's front door, a person saw the Blue Ridge Mountains spanning the horizon like a giant hedge, insulating and provoking, hinting at enormous possibilities.

Montpelier's current owner thought he had something extra special but wasn't sure how to fulfill its promise. Polo ponies occupied some of the barns and fields. There might be a deal to turn the place into a hunt club. When William du Pont showed unexpected interest, the owner demanded $100 per acre, about five times what an average Virginia farm would cost.

William returned to England with no deal made but his target in sight.

Meanwhile, another opportunity faded. William's mother suffered a small stroke; her health declined, blurring her lines between past and present, her mind slipping into timelessness.

Early on March 1, 1900, Louisa du Pont said her morning prayers and told her maid, "Now, Olive, I am going home." She began speaking to her late husband, then dozed off and never awoke. William's sister Ellen wrote to him that their emotional mother had passed away "so peacefully that she did not even unfold her hands, she was lying with them folded one within the other, the way she always rested." Reckoning that their mother had let the old hard feelings fall away, Ellen told William, "In the light of a clearer world than ours, she knows you were never to blame—I suppose she knew it already, with the prescience that comes when one nears the border."

Ellen also carried a message from their sister Victorine, whom William had turned away when she slighted his wife. "Victorine charges me to give you her dear love," Ellen reported, "and to tell you that she thought Maman's feeling about your marriage must have changed, because she noticed many times during the past year, that whenever they were alone together Maman began to talk of you—if she could only have lived until you brought your wife and little ones back to America I cannot help believing that we might all [have] been so happy, for when I saw your wife's face in her miniature [portrait] I felt sure she was noble-minded enough to forgive much for your sake, and the childrens'."

William paid his respects from afar. While staying in Europe, however, he kept pursuing Montpelier. Seven days after his mother died, he sent a telegram from Paris to his business agent in the United States: "Offer $50.00 per acre."

The year 1900 ticked by while William du Pont from Delaware, the first state to ratify the U.S. Constitution, negotiated for the estate where the Father of the Constitution had considered how to shape that nation-defining document. In November, William reached a deal. In January 1901, he received the deed.

For $74,000, Montpelier was his.

The old house had been waiting for someone to love its past as well as its potential. James and Dolley Madison had made it spacious and fashionable for their times, but times had changed quite a bit since 1794. By 1900, the Montpelier mansion was much too small for anybody who lived and entertained on a grand scale. Many of America's richest families—Vanderbilts, Rockefellers, Whitneys, and others—didn't want to rehabilitate residential relics. Inspired by European castles and chateaux, they were building fantasy estates from scratch. George Vanderbilt reached a summit of sorts in 1895 with Biltmore, a 250-room French-styled palace that truly lived up to its name. William Collins Whitney responded by commissioning a Tudor extravaganza out on Long Island that would have boggled Henry VIII. But William du Pont had a different dream. He could dress up an old house and make it work; most of all, he wanted a thriving farm.

While his wife and children traded damp, chilly England for humid Delaware, William spent more than a year overseeing Montpelier's renovation. Adapting the old-fashioned property for luxurious modern living, he had workers install an electrical power plant and nearly doubled the manor house's size. At the same time, he respected its history. As much as possible, vintage architectural features were either reused or concealed beneath new structures, rather than scrapped. Underneath the du Pont additions, Montpelier kept much of its original character.

In August 1902, Nannie, Marion, and Willie left Bellevue Hall and saw what William had done. The children picked up on their parents' cheerful mood—Marion said simply, "They were happy they had found a sunnier place with a higher elevation for us"—and soaked up the scenes as a long lane led them into their new property. They drove through woodlands, then across a field. They would learn that the physical remains of James and Dolley Madison rested under tall monuments in a little cemetery off to their right; closer to the manor house, slaves' bodies lay under small, unlettered stones. And up ahead, on a gentle hilltop, a tall house coated with mustard yellow stucco awaited them. Its face wasn't fancy, but its form was beautiful. A child might think its shape looked a lot like pictures of the White House, where the man who ran the United States lived. An adult would see that Montpelier, with dozens of rooms added by William du Pont, was even larger.

Entering the front yard, they passed through a gate set under an immense weeping willow tree. They climbed up onto the high front porch, maybe turned around to enjoy the Blue Ridge view. They entered the front hall, discovered their rooms, and let a new sensation take hold. Not a rental. Not a castle. *Home.*

Their personalities flourished. William filled the farm with animals for work, food, and recreation: hefty Percheron draft horses and high-stepping Hackney driving ponies; pedigreed cattle, hogs, and sheep; fighting chickens imported from England. Flowers, fruits, and vegetables filled Montpelier's new world-class greenhouse. Annie raised huge, willowy deerhounds and revived the Madisons' terraced garden beside the backyard, creating a formal outdoor space accentuated with European statuary, urns, and bowers. The children—to their parents' delight and occasional consternation—let their own true natures emerge. On the expansive property, eight-year-old Marion and six-year-old Willie discovered an adventure land limited by little more than their own curiosity. Meanwhile, governesses came and went. "We were bad kids," Marion claimed, before adding, "Well, not really. We liked to do what we wanted to do."

First of all, they wanted ponies. And Marion had to withstand her mother's objections.

Growing up in the outwardly strict Victorian era, Marion's mother had learned that a lady out in public not only kept her legs and ankles covered but also always kept her knees together. Doing otherwise could ruin a woman's health and good name. Some adventurous females flouted these conventions, but even during less rigid times they had seemed irresponsible. Back in the 1770s, Queen Marie Antoinette of France often went foxhunting wearing breeches rather than a skirt and sitting astride her horse, prompting her empress mother to write, "If you are riding like a man, dressed as a man, as I suspect you are, I have to tell you that I find it dangerous as well as bad for bearing children—and that is what you have been called upon to do; that will be the measure of your success."

Society agreed with the empress. For more than a century, sidesaddle continued to be the only acceptable riding style for genteel women in Europe and the United States. By the 1890s, however, a new wave of sportswomen challenged the status quo. When William and Annie du Pont were newlyweds, the bicycle-riding craze raised questions of women's health and morals all over again. When maidens, wives, and mothers dared to balance atop a bicycle seat, the old guard dug in. One critic harrumphed, "Straddling a saddle I regard as an abomination." A large tricycle, on the other hand, would let a lady sit as politely as if she were in a chair and pedal along in public without disgrace or physical harm. "I know many gentlemen in England," this critic asserted, "whose daughters ride on tricycles constructed on this system with entirely satisfactory results."

Physical fitness strained the limits of a world where women wore corsets and fainting couches were standard equipment in a gracious home. And even when women sat sidesaddle, horseback riding pushed the boundaries of what females were supposed to be able to do. A tricycle, after all, was far more predictable than a horse. Furthermore, anything that a grown woman could barely accomplish should be impossible for a female child. Two years before Marion du Pont was born, a respected riding instructor wrote that "a girl under sixteen has not the physique to endure without injury to her health such violent exercise as riding." A decade later, Annie du Pont knew that aristocratic families now were letting their prepubescent girls start equestrian training by riding astride ponies. But she didn't have to believe in it.

And so, when eight-year-old Marion wanted a pony, she observed her mother being "a little fussy, talking about how impractical it was—bowed legs, and everything." Nannie also may have worried for her small daughter's safety, and the same teacher who had written that girls younger than sixteen weren't fit for horseback riding's "violent exercise" would have praised her caution. "Surely parents do not appreciate what the results may be," he had warned, "or they would never trust a girl of eight years or thereabouts to the mercy of a horse, and at his mercy she is bound to be. No child of that age, or several years older, has strength sufficient to manage even an unruly pony, which, having once discovered his power, is pretty sure to take advantage of it at every opportunity; and no woman is worthy [of] the responsibilities of motherhood who will permit her child to make the experiment."

Nannie rose to her Victorian motherly responsibilities, but William prevailed. By the time the du Ponts moved to Montpelier, women from America's so-called Wild West had proved that riding astride did not harm their fertility. An American doctor went so far as to say, "If the horse was as recent an invention as the bicycle, no woman would think of riding any other way than astride." With science taking William's side, soon Marion and Willie were down at the train station greeting two registered Shetland ponies from an Indiana farm. The small, fuzzy fillies had friendly names: Barbra and Bonnie Bell. Riding lessons began.

An Englishman named Mr. Day trained Marion and Willie together. The children learned how to sit with one leg on each side of a moving animal and use their bodies to signal their intentions. Being older and taller, Marion received the taller pony, Barbra, while six-year-old Willie rode tiny Bonnie Bell. Unfortunately, Barbra turned out to be poorly schooled. Before long, William found another pony for his daughter "because," Marion said, "I got thrown off Barbra so much."

Grisette, whose gray coat was turning white, looked angelic. Her graceful face and body made her resemble an Arabian horse. Discovering true companionship with Grisette, Marion would call her "the first pony

I really liked" and—rather than giving her away to another child after outgrowing her—kept her for life. Grisette tested Marion, however, in one wickedly simple way. Streams were common in the Montpelier landscape; bridges were not. When fording a stream, Grisette would stop in the middle and paw at the water, splashing the little girl sitting astride her back. Then Grisette would slowly bend her front and hind legs, sinking into the streambed with her passenger, while Marion's white skirt floated immodestly above her britches. Each time, her riding companions shouted, "Keep on hitting her! Don't let her do that!" Marion—short and slightly built, and perhaps reluctant to punish her pony friend—couldn't seem to muster the will or strength. When she failed and Grisette sank into the stream, the adults yelled, "Turn your skirts loose and come out of there!" Marion would follow orders and watch her skirt float downstream.

The dunking threatened to become a ritual. Then, at last, Marion achieved a different result. Horses respond to a decisive leader. Urging Grisette across the water, Marion unlocked her own authority.

3

"HOLD THIS BOARD UP, MARION."

At Montpelier, she often heard her brother say those words. Willie duPont was only six years old, but when he wanted to build something he quickly learned how the parts should fit together. Given leftover boards and nails from the Montpelier renovations, carpenter Willie and his assistant Marion were transforming their new playground. Behind the house, next to the formal garden and the pony barn, sat an acre or so surrounded by a picket fence. This area would be their domain, a place to pursue their own visions. As Marion said, "You never knew what you'd find in there on a particular day." She and Willie first built a simple horse show ring, then pens for bantam chickens. Marion sowed her own garden with, as she put it, "anything that would come up quick." The children's whirl of activities reminded their father of America's foremost home of roller coasters and sideshows. With a twinkle, he nicknamed their playground "Coney Island."

Coney Island gave Marion the satisfaction and thrill of planting something herself and watching it grow. She and Willie also tried out their father's hobbies on their own smaller scale. The bantam chickens they raised were feisty, like their father's gamecocks. Some of the Shetland ponies they rode also pulled carts, a low-speed, low-stepping substitute for their father's Hackneys. They began learning how to match an animal with a particular task. You would look for the right individual, provide the right equipment. You would imagine, then learn by doing, adjusting, doing again.

Marion and Willie were less enamored with book learning. One by one, governesses ventured from New York City to the Virginia country-side. "And we gave them all a hard time," Marion later admitted. "I can't even name them; most didn't last long enough." One by one, the carefully chosen teachers decided that the cachet of working for du Ponts wasn't worth the trouble of this particular job—or, just as likely, they were fired. Marion noticed that when she and Willie failed to meet their parents' expectations, the governesses "would be blamed for everything we did wrong."

Even so, William and Annie wanted their children to do better in the classroom. Someday, as a leader of a DuPont business, Willie would need to hold his own with men who graduated from top universities. After several governesses didn't work out, Willie received a special tutor to coach him for prep school.

Marion faced a different standard. Although elite academies for females did exist, she could attend a finishing school that emphasized social graces, or simply continue being tutored at home, and not lose any prestige. After all, a young lady wouldn't be competing with men when she grew up; she would be aiming to attract them and secure the best possible husband.

And would Marion thrive if she went away to school? Exams made her anxious. Perhaps, remembering his own agonies at MIT, William didn't see any point in making his daughter suffer academic worries and separation from her family as well.

While educating their children at home, William and Annie also made sure that they weren't isolated or cut off from their Delaware roots. Later, some folks would assume that tension between William's family and his Delaware relatives had caused them to spell their last name differently, but that wasn't so. When William's children later spelled their last name "duPont," without a space between "du" and "Pont," it was only a convenience—a way to be listed under *D* instead of *P* in the telephone book. Marion and Willie traded visits between Montpelier and Wilmington with Delaware cousins, as well as making friends among well-to-do

Virginia families. Before long, one of Annie's relatives, Dr. John Sedg-wick Andrews, purchased an Orange County farm and began raising his own children there. Marion and Willie would grow up comparing agri-cultural tips with "Cousin Sedgwick."

At the same time, sister and brother maintained a special rapport. Be-ing only twenty months apart in age kept them close developmentally. Exploring Montpelier together tightened their bond in a way that their older half brother George Zinn, usually away at school and also nearing adulthood, couldn't fully share. "Willie and I used to love to go out on the place when they had sheep-shearing and things like that," Marion later said. "We'd run all over the fields to get the sheep for the men who would do the shearing." In fact, they loved it all. "We were hot stuff," Marion remarked with her typical dry humor, "helping supervise the dairy and nearly everything else on the farm."

Life at Montpelier proved that Marion and Willie, supposedly deli-cate, actually were athletic daredevils. At one point, a physical education tutor even trained them and two friends in gymnastics. Marion, small and lithe, often took top positions—climbing onto another's back, stand-ing on another's hands. One day, older generations gathered in Montpe-lier's spacious dining room to watch their progeny perform a tumbling routine. It started with a somersault but quickly escalated into dives and lifts. The grown-ups probably were prepared to see their sons doing handsprings and headstands. Maybe they were less prepared to see Mar-ion diving over her companions, standing on a boy's hands, riding on his shoulders, and placing her hands on a boy's feet while Willie lifted her feet into the air.

The performance ended with a long dive called the lion's leap, with Marion and the boys landing on their hands and rolling into a somer-sault, then springing to their feet and taking a bow. There should have been rousing applause. Instead, their tumbling tutor lost his job. "We didn't want him," said Marion, looking back. More likely, the children did but their parents did not. Marion stayed interested in gymnastics, always. Remembering the push from her own body, the lift of helping hands. Re-membering how it felt to complete a lion's leap.

· · ·

On November 6, 1915, something startling was about to happen in the National Horse Show at Madison Square Garden in New York. Donning her riding breeches and checking the girth on her flat saddle, twenty-one-year-old Marion duPont knew that she could cause a stir. Maybe she looked forward to the sensation; maybe she didn't care. As usual, she dressed as modestly as possible, with tall boots rising far up her calves and a long jacket falling below her boot tops. In the saddle, with jacket fabric draping over her knees, she would look almost legless. Inside the ring, her entire focus would be with her horse, while the audience stared at her. This year, the National Horse Show committee had announced a revolutionary move: women could choose to ride astride instead of sidesaddle. But would they? This would be a far cry from little girls jogging along astride ponies, something allowed here since 1907. This would be a grown woman daring to present herself riding like a man.

Decades later, Marion would confide that "in the show ring, if you wanted to put on a real good show against the men—the top riders from Kentucky—you had a much better chance riding like they did, astride. In top-class, nobody was giving anybody anything." If riding her high-stepping American Saddlebred sidesaddle meant looking ladylike but also being less brilliant, Marion was not interested in that.

"I could ride better astride a show horse because you had to take hold [of the mouth] and make their heads arch a little bit," she explained. "You had to have a feel of the bit in your hands. Riding sidesaddle, you couldn't do that as well. At least I never could." With her body facing straight forward, Marion felt her horse evenly balanced between her hands. She felt exactly how much to hold and release as each stride pressed up from her horse's ankles through his torso, through his neck, to his mouth. With her hands, her seat, her legs, she fine-tuned her horse's tempo like a symphony conductor guiding an orchestra.

And what a horse she had! Twenty-four Karat could have been named for his golden coat or the quality promised by his regal physique and attitude. Furthermore, he belonged in classes for the tallest Saddlebreds. When Marion centered on his back, her outstretched feet didn't even reach his belly. Her toes aligned with the point of his shoulder, halfway down his powerful chest.

The ringmaster summoned Class 80. Marion aimed her golden horse for the in gate. Twenty other riders did the same. A crowded class, of both women and men, including less experienced "novice" horses such as Twenty-four Karat and veteran "open" horses who had been champions against all comers. From their first moment in the ring to their final pose, Marion and Twenty-four Karat needed to shine. They needed everything to go right.

Entering the flower-decked arena, trotting past huge murals representing the English countryside, Marion got the judges' attention all right. She was the only woman using a flat saddle, like the men. Many eyes followed Marion as if she were the ball in a tennis match.

And they were impressed. Twenty-four Karat, the novice horse who had been very green when he appeared at the Garden a year ago, now moved and acted flawlessly. Marion drew praise for handling him "with ease and grace." She left the ring with a ribbon waving from Twenty-four Karat's bridle—the first blue ribbon won by a woman riding astride in New York.

She wasn't done. Having won in mixed company, Marion quickly changed clothing and rode Twenty-four Karat sidesaddle in a Ladies' class. This time, the horse's manners would count for half the score. And this time their main competition would be a mare named Gossip, defending champion from last year's National Horse Show.

Remarkably, Twenty-four Karat rose to Gossip's level. Walking, trotting, cantering—it seemed impossible to separate his beautiful manners and motion from those of the many-times champion. Deadlocked, the judges spent ten minutes comparing the conformation—angles, proportions, musculature—of their top two. Ten minutes! Nearly long enough for a horse to gallop four and a half miles, leap thirty fences, and win the Grand National. Finally, suddenly, Twenty-four Karat wore another blue ribbon while the die-hard horsemen standing ringside sanctified the result with their applause. A reporter noted that, by defeating Gossip, "Twenty-four Karat put himself in line for the championship of the show."

Championship day proved how far Marion duPont had come in the fourteen years since two Shetland ponies arrived at Montpelier. Along the way, a reporter at another show had praised her for "an exhibition of serene, competent and dignified horsemanship that has rarely ever been remotely resembled on this track." Now, at the show ring summit of her life, spectators saw her guiding Twenty-four Karat with "rare finish and skill." They saw Twenty-four Karat delivering "a perfect performance." Watching Gossip try to repeat as champion, they noticed that "the mare's hind action was noticeably faulty at times, and her manners were not the best." They were dumbfounded when Gossip won.

As one New York paper pointed out, this result "astonished nearly every expert horseman who witnessed the judging." What had happened? Did the judges feel unable to place a so-called novice horse above a previous National champion? Or was there another problem? Wanting to show Twenty-four Karat in his most brilliant form, Marion again rode astride. The woman riding Gossip used a sidesaddle. Did the judges refuse to give a grand championship to a woman using her legs like a man?

Though she would continue competing for several years, Marion began feeling, as she put it, "fed up" with show world biases. More and more, she took on challenges where performance mattered most of all and you learned not to be fooled by mere appearances.

Returning to Virginia, Marion carried on with a passion she had discovered as a teenager at Montpelier. Back then, she and her brother heard that their neighbor Dallas Watson, who appeared to be too fat for vigorous cross-country riding, actually enjoyed chasing foxes with his pack of hounds. Mr. Watson owed his success to a talented mule. According to witnesses, "He would ride this remarkable animal up to a fence, climb on top of it, cluck to the mule who would jump it from a standstill, remount, and gallop on." This was something that Marion and Willie had to see for themselves. Mr. Watson welcomed and encouraged them. Soon, foxhunting had become part of their selves. It gave the young duPonts an unpredictable quarry, a cross-country gallop with hounds in full cry, various obstacles to leap, sometimes wild comedy, sometimes a death—and also an unbiased result. Foxhunting wasn't like the show ring, where the judges' feelings could influence the awards. If you could handle everything well enough to be up near the hounds at the end of a run, no one could take that away from you.

Those cross-country gallops also might be a safety vent for a young lady near the edge of rebellion—a self-expression like piercing a ring through her nose or getting a tattoo. Foxhunting had become a fashionable pursuit, but not so long ago women who did it had seemed risqué. A female rider jumping seemed like a woman losing control. When Marion's parents were newlyweds, a prominent riding master had acknowledged that he could not stop females from leaping over things on horseback but seemed to wish they would not try. Picturing an ideal student, he wrote, "A secure seat, light hands, a cool head, quick perception, judgment, and courage form a combination which will enable her in a short time to acquire skill in jumping. Few women possess all these qualities," he proclaimed, "but an effort should be made to obtain as many of them as possible before trying to jump."

What would such a harsh observer make of Marion duPont? With people she didn't know well, Marion might chatter nervously or flinch away. She might not seem to have a cool head, quick perception, or courage. And yet the same man who would call her "one of the shyest people that ever walked" also noted that while interacting with horses she radiated "absolute confidence." The fascination that began while her father lifted her up to pet coach horses' noses, the understanding that formed while learning to communicate with Grisette, had formed a place where her mother's doubts did not penetrate. On horseback, Marion would face a fence and know that she could fly over it, because her horse accepted her almost as a part of himself.

Gradually, unofficially, Marion and Willie formed their own hunt and their own separate packs of hounds. Marion also continued raising, training, and showing Dalmatians—one more sign that shyness did not make her timid or submissive. Instead, her spirit rose to lead exuberant and nearly tireless dogs. Marion never had known her father's father, the DuPont president who had died several years before she was born, but, like Boss Henry, with utmost comfort she became leader of the pack. Like her grandfather, she heard groups of dogs eagerly greet her footsteps, clamoring to work and romp with her. Like him, she rewarded and scolded them, rejoiced in them, told them what to do.

If only real life could be trained like a puppy. If only true love, in human form, would come whenever you called.

· · ·

Launching into adulthood, Willie appeared to quickly surpass Marion. By the time he finished at St. Luke's School, the United States was involved with the European war and his father had a job for him with a DuPont firm. Twenty-one-year-old William duPont Jr. became a plant manager for the Ball Grain Explosives Company near Wilmington, helping to produce millions of timed fuses for rifle grenades. He also sped toward starting his own family. Foxhunting near Philadelphia had drawn him to Jean Liseter Austin, an expert horsewoman who would become his wife. After their honeymoon, Will and Jean would settle in southeastern Pennsylvania while gradually developing their own farm.

On New Year's Day 1918, Will and Jean made their wedding vows at her family home in Newtown Square, Pennsylvania. Wearing a dress of pink charmeuse and silver lace, with a picture hat of brown tulle trimmed with silver and pink roses crowning her costume, twenty-three-year-old Marion served as a duck-out-of-water bridesmaid. The wedding party's formal portrait with the attendants demurely seated in a row caught Marion sitting up straight but twisting her satin-shod feet like a squirming child and staring at something off to the side. From a distance, she looked slightly brooding. Close up, there was something captivating about her face: absorbed, intense, completely free of empty posing. Awkward Marion looked more alive than anyone else in the wedding portrait, including the bride and groom.

She also looked like a wild creature stranded far outside its natural habitat. In fact, marriage was posing a troublesome equation to Marion duPont, a tricky reconciling of financial status, social expectations, and personal appeal. In time, some outsiders would assume that she couldn't meet expectations and lacked appeal. It was true that Marion was not a conventional beauty. With adulthood, her once full-cheeked face had become a bit long and pointed. In a society where the ideal female face resembled a teaspoon, Marion looked like a knife.

But close friends knew her beauty. You would see it when she was in her element, unconcerned about anyone watching. You might see it behind the scenes at a horse show, where a candid photo of Marion lounging in a meadow with a female friend, and utterly relaxed with whoever held the camera, vibrated with charm. Wearing show ring clothing—tailored coat, breeches, high boots—but forsaking a hat and letting her dark hair rumple around the edges of her face, Marion met the lens full on with a direct, mischievous, blazing smile. Half a century later, she would have looked like a rock star.

You might meet that Marion on the tennis court, or motoring around Virginia horse country with a chauffeur and a good friend or two. She emerged at the giant game preserve known as Altama that her father had bought down in coastal Georgia, exploring the woods and swamps with a gun, a supply of DuPont Sporting Powder, and a bird dog she had raised from a pup. This passionate, private Marion fueled the outwardly reserved young woman who began appearing at field dog competitions and made history by handling all of her own dogs, rather than having a man do it, at the English Setter Club of America's Field Trial in 1919. Eventually, she would hire experts to show setters and pointers on her behalf, with much success. She did so well as a breeder and seller of sporting dogs that one November day at Montpelier in 1920 she wrote to her father in Delaware, "I had a terrible time last night straightening out the telegrams about the dogs etc—I almost sold the same dog to three people, that would have been disastrous!"

Privately, she saved a sentimental essay she found, written partly from a dog's point of view. "My love, old pal, is everlasting," the dog promised. "I can share your sorrow and your play. Only let me stay and the world may wag on and all may call, but my world holds only you."

Only you. Marion would go through her twenties, when her younger brother and so many of her peers were marrying and starting families, without celebrating such devotion with a young man.

But however she felt about raising her own family, Marion was a farmer at heart. She helped her father, now serving as president of the Delaware Trust Company and spending many days in Wilmington, run Montpelier. She evaluated draft and sport horses. She sorted through the registration paperwork for Jersey cattle and studied the milk and butterfat production of each individual in their dairy herd, aiming to maximize efficiency. At one point she discovered four *"very old* cows" which were, she reported, "nothing but pensioners as they haven't given any milk for the last two years—don't you think they had better go—even if only to Manley Carter for beef—he would probably give around $30.00 or $35.00 a piece—there are any amount of very nice heifers to come in [to the barn] this winter and there is no room for them." Marion understood animals as commodities, consuming some resources while producing others, sometimes shifting from one purpose to another, and always connected to a financial bottom line. Still, at times her feelings showed through alongside her business sense. When one mare suffered a bad injury, Marion told her father, "I don't know how much use she will have in the left leg—but I am fond of her & she will make a nice brood mare, if she isn't able to jump again."

Farming could not produce a carefree life. Animals often tested the traditional human vows "in sickness and in health, till death do us part." Crops lived at the mercy of the weather. Farming meant investing yourself in constant uncertainties, open to every kind of natural wonder or calamity. Marion grew up into this understanding. Still, she placed Elizabeth Barrett Browning's poem "Out in the Fields" in one of her scrapbooks. Except for mentioning a nearby ocean, it could have been written about Montpelier:

> The little cares that fretted me,
>   I lost them yesterday
> Among the fields above the sea,
>   Among the winds at play,
> Among the lowing of the herds,
>   The rustling of the trees,
> Among the singing of the birds,
>   The humming of the bees;
> The foolish fears of what might happen,
>   I cast them all away
> Among the clover-scented grass,
>   Among the new-mown hay,
> Among the hushing of the corn
>   Where drowsy poppies nod,
> Where ill thoughts die & good are born,
>   Out in the fields with God.

Many of Marion's good thoughts may have been born out in the fields or among the lowing of the herds, the rustling of the trees. But something powerful took hold in her out among thousands of people, when she was about twenty-six years old. Several times, Marion saw the Thoroughbred champion Man o' War race. "He just ran off from those other horses," she would recall, "like they weren't there."

Man o' War could seem almost like a magic spell for dreams come true. Except for one upside-down day, he *always* won. And he seemed to do it with some reserve untouched.

Gradually, the search to own that kind of horse would lead Marion far beyond her childhood garden of plants that would "come up quick." Man o' War planted dreams that could not spring fully formed into waking life but would need ample time to bud and blossom. He sowed ambitions that might need many years to reach fruition, if they bore fruit at all.

4

FIVE YEARS AFTER SEEING MAN O' War run away from his opponents like they weren't there, Marion arrived at the source. On a perfect mid-May morning in 1925, she and her father joined a special gathering at the farm where "Big Red" had been born. Many times they had visited Lexington, Kentucky, to buy Saddlebred horses or show them for championships. This time was different. Major August Belmont, the man who had bred and raised Man o' War, had died the previous winter. Today, at his farm called the Nursery, Belmont's Thoroughbred stallions and brood-mares were being auctioned and Man o' War's parents were for sale.

That alone could draw a crowd. But today, sixty-eight horses would pass through the auction ring, embodying a masterful breeder's choices over more than thirty years. For Marion duPont, this could be an experience almost like mind reading. Studying their pedigrees in the sales catalog, Marion had seen what matches Major Belmont had favored. Watching each horse parade in front of her, she would see the full range of his theories made flesh.

Marion and her father climbed a small hill and stepped into the pasture, surrounded by a band of trees, where the sale would take place. They entered an atmosphere that was part church, part country fair. Barbecue pits and iron kettles of savory stew known as burgoo smoldered and simmered near an enormous luncheon tent, spreading a sweet and smoky incense. VIPs lined the rail of a temporary ring, as if coming forward for communion. The empty ring waited like a chalice to be filled.

William and Marion du Pont took their seats among a who's who of the racing world. Spectators came from as far as England and from all of the most important Thoroughbred farms in the United States. Everyone recognized Samuel Doyle Riddle and his wife, the owners of Man o' War. Harry Payne Whitney, who had bred and raced Upset, the only horse that ever beat Man o' War, had traveled by private railroad car to take his place in this crowd. Brose Clark, who still employed Reg Hobbs as a horse master, also had taken the trouble to be here himself.

And then there were up-and-comers, folks who hadn't been in the game all that long but yearned for the top. Among them was Walter J. Salmon, a New York real estate developer who had won the Preakness and other major races within the past half dozen years with horses bred by other people. Now he raised his own racers at Mereworth Stud, a few miles from these fields where August Belmont had raised so many champions.

Tomorrow, many of these people—including Marion and William du Pont—would be down the road in Louisville, celebrating the Kentucky Derby at Churchill Downs. But for once, the Derby did not dominate their conversation. Today, August Belmont's entire private collection of Thoroughbreds would be open to them. This springtime, they had been entranced by Fair Play, a perennial leading stallion who had outdone himself and all other active studs by siring Man o' War. What price could be put on such a horse? As the auction day approached, *Daily Racing Form* had noted that people were asking "What will Fair Play bring?" as frequently as they wondered who would win the Kentucky Derby.

"What will Fair Play bring?" The answer would have little to do with commercial returns. Although Fair Play remained an active stud, he was twenty years old. His fertility might decline at any time; his life might not continue many more years. On the other hand, people who had viewed him shortly before the sale could hardly believe he was an equine senior citizen. John E. Madden, by some measures Kentucky's most successful racehorse breeder, said that Fair Play looked "like a five-year-old." In other words, like a horse entering the prime of life.

As the ceremonies began, hundreds of the most privileged visitors filled two rows of chairs encircling the tanbark ring. As many as two thousand people, mostly men, stood behind the seated circles, their close-packed hats forming a dimpled surface rising toward the horizon. An Episcopalian cleric welcomed the travelers from afar to the lovely Kentucky countryside. "We believe it is the greatest garden next to Heaven," Dr. Thomas Settle declared, "and we want you to help us enjoy what God has given us to enjoy. But we are sad today, some of us, to see this great stud of wonderful thoroughbred horses dispersed."

The rector noted how August Belmont had developed the Nursery "to a high state of perfection," building upon "the foundation assembled by his father on this beautiful place." When the sale began, that perfection would pass away. Dr. Settle requested "a moment in silent tribute to the memory of Major Belmont." Twenty-five hundred people stood and bowed their heads. The men removed their hats. For about a minute, there were no words, only the sounds of a farm breathing in and out.

"Thanks," said Dr. Settle. And the dispersal began.

Marion watched thirty-two mares, fillies, and colts pass through the ring, bringing more than $300,000. Then lunchtime arrived, with everyone moving from the dazzling sunshine into the tent where ladies from the Church of the Good Shepherd distributed sandwiches and ladled stew. The crowd had swollen to at least three thousand people, hungry for outstanding barbecue and burgoo, equally hungry for the moment awaiting them directly after lunch.

Around 1:30, the auctioneer introduced the horse who needed no description. There was no mistaking him, his head held high as a Saddlebred champion, his neck curved as if an archer with the surest, lightest touch were drawing the bow. His ears, straight up and focused forward, signaled complete confidence despite the strangers packed all around him and the huge white luncheon tent lolling against the sky. His coat reflected gold back to the sun. His eyes held a universe.

Fair Play.

William du Pont did not bid. Fair Play would not become his responsibility. He would not try to continue Major Belmont's dynasty. William's ideal horses wore harness, pulling wagons, plows, coaches, or fancy gigs. But Marion, intently watching, was forming her own ideal. Not a harness horse, but a runner. She sat at horse belly level as Fair Play strode by, able to see each foot and leg moving, every joint flexing. Also able to take a wider view and consider the whole animal, his remarkable balance, his sparkling attitude. If Man o' War had tantalized her with his mystery, his unfathomable speed, Fair Play sold her with his extraordinary substance and vitality.

The auctioneer invited the crowd to name a price. William du Pont did not bid, but someone else made a bold start in a quiet yet decisive voice. The words came from Walter J. Salmon, a dynamic man who built New York City skyscrapers, a man used to dealing in colossal possibilities.

"Seventy-five thousand."

This might have been the final price for a fine stallion, not the opening serve. Tomorrow, the Kentucky Derby winner would collect about $23,000 less. But someone volleyed the shot. It was Adolphe Pons, who had grown up in August Belmont's stable and had brokered many horse sales for him. Today, of course, Pons represented someone else. "Eighty thousand," said the auctioneer. Salmon answered, "Eighty-five." Pons said ninety. Salmon paused to think.

He may have known, or guessed, whose bankroll Pons was doling out. Regardless, it had to be someone with very deep pockets and passionate to win this one exchange. His chances were waning, but Salmon didn't want to give in. He said, "Ninety-five."

Without a blink, Pons offered one hundred grand.

The auctioneer caught Walter Salmon's eye. Salmon smiled, a triumph of politeness over emotion, and said, "I'm through."

An auctioneer rarely gives up right away. "Won't you make it $101,000," he urged. This time, Salmon only shook his head. The auctioneer tried to tease out a few more dollars: "Oh, come, make just one more bid. What do you care for expenses, you have plenty of them." The crowd chuckled, knowing full well how the bills poured in when you ran a large racing stable and also maintained your own breeding farm, keeping more than thirty mares and their offspring in the best possible health. Salmon smiled again and simply said, "I'm through." No one else stirred.

"Well, if you are through, and if I do not hear elsewhere an advance on $100,000, I shall sell him. Once, twice, last call. All done? Sold. Who gets him?"

It was the man who had helped Major Belmont's cash-strapped widow by buying all of the horses at the Nursery farm, then arranged this auction so that others might share in the Belmont bloodstock legacy . . . the man who had succeeded Major Belmont as chairman of the Jockey Club in New York, Thoroughbred racing's most powerful administrative body . . . a man whose fortune rolled as powerfully as his family's railway lines.

"Joseph E. Widener," Pons told the crowd. The three thousand spectators had been warned not to clap or cheer, not to startle Fair Play with a loud burst of sound, but some hands applauded anyway. Some people wiped tears from their eyes.

Walter Salmon would not own Fair Play, but he would not lose hope of breeding his own horse like that. In fact, he still might hold an advantage. Everyone who raised Thoroughbreds knew the adage, "Breed the best to the best, and hope for the best." But what if the selection process could be less of a gamble? Genetics had become a hot topic in recent decades, as scientists pursued clues from Gregor Mendel's experiments with bean plants. What if horse pedigrees could be decoded and the results of new matings became more predictable? What if a "speed miracle" such as Man o' War could be explained by a mathematical formula?

Walter Salmon was cultivating a partner that might find that explanation. At Cold Spring Harbor, Long Island, the Carnegie Institute's Department of Genetics generated groundbreaking studies of heredity, physiology, and how the laws of physics affect living creatures. Wasn't that exactly what racehorse breeders needed to understand? In 1923, Salmon had created a Cold Spring Harbor fund specifically for studying the Thoroughbred horse. Late in 1924, the scientist managing that money had assured him, "I believe that, with the present plan of organization, we shall be able to make a better analysis of the breeding of Thoroughbred Horses than anyone has yet succeeded in developing."

Anyone. Someone who cracked the code might leap past all that August Belmont had learned over a lifetime.

While waiting for answers, Walter Salmon respected the master. He came away from the Belmont dispersal with one Fair Play daughter, another mare carrying a foal by Fair Play, and a third mare in foal to Fair Play with a Fair Play filly by her side. Salmon also was blessed with an even more select opportunity. During the spring of 1925, he had been allowed to breed one of his mares to Man o' War.

Marion duPont left Kentucky with a new concept weighing on her mind, tipping between status quo and transformation. She continued her familiar duties and pastimes: always on the lookout for a good show horse or hunter she might buy, acting as her father's extra eyes for running Montpelier while he stayed at Bellevue Hall to be near his Wilmington business responsibilities, spending many hours on the tennis court and sometimes hosting tennis or billiard parties. At the same time, her familiar life could not quite stay in place. At the Nursery sale, Marion had seen uncommon dimensions of possibility. Of course she had known that the marvelous racehorse Man o' War hadn't sprung from nowhere, but now it was as if she had stepped inside the engine room of a mighty vessel and seen the working parts that had produced the phenomenon: the sire Fair Play, the mare Mahubah, the Nursery farm with its unsurpassed staff, all of the horses on display like diagrams of Major Belmont's genius. They illuminated a path of what had been and what still might be. And once you recognized a pathway—once you knew where and what it was—you could choose to explore that direction for yourself.

And yet despite her family's mighty wealth, Marion duPont had more freedom to imagine than freedom to act. Despite the many privileges embedded in her lifestyle, despite the boundaries she had pressed with show horses and field trial dogs, Marion's choices ultimately depended on her father's goodwill. She didn't have that much of her own money yet. Taking a company job to earn an executive's salary was out of the question—only males did that. Her homes were her parents' homes. With her father's blessing, she might travel the world, but she did not have a big enough allowance to buy the one and only Fair Play. She could only watch him appear, then go to someone else.

But now Marion pictured herself going somewhere that her father did not feel drawn to go.

When he traveled away from Montpelier, William du Pont often received messages from his daughter. Her Western Union telegram on Friday, July 3, 1925, hinted how much things had changed in recent months and yet remained unchanged: "Want to school my race horse early Monday morning will come up [to Willie's farm] Monday July Sixth."

Marion had found a horse to race in her name at casual Virginia competitions—that was fairly new. She was sharing resources with her brother—that was never ending, although the setting would be new. Willie and Jean's six-hundred-acre farm near Rosemont, Pennsylvania, held a half-mile training track and a racehorse barn, along with many other facilities for show horses and hunters. Keeping her racehorse at her brother's place and using his track, Marion could freely give training orders or even gallop her horse herself.

She had become a modern woman. Her mother had married and raised children without being able to vote in any public election, but now women voted for anything from dogcatcher to president. Her mother had first married at age eighteen, but modern girls relished being single for several years before settling down to married life. Hemlines jumped from ankle to just below the knee, and popular dances celebrated a wider range of leg motions. Though she wasn't a freewheeling flapper, Marion postponed marriage. For several years, she might sidestep the stigma of being an old maid and simply blend with her era.

But freedom became less carefree once a woman reached her thirtieth birthday. Several days before watching Fair Play light up the sales ring, Marion had turned thirty-one. Her most marriageable decade gone. Her chances of bearing her own children diminishing.

Reminders nudged her while visiting her brother's place in July 1925. Marion would see Willie's daughter Jean Ellen, now two and a half years old. She would see Will's pregnant wife Jean, now her own good friend as well, only a couple of weeks away from delivering a second child. She would notice how Will and Jean's new mansion was coming along and perhaps perceive it as her brother's antidote for nostalgia or homesickness—or simply an extension of a treasured place and times. The wedding-gift house could have been built in any style. Will and Jean had agreed that it would look just like Montpelier, with only the main hallway staircase placed differently. If Will couldn't live at his childhood home, in this way it would come to him.

Marion, meanwhile, didn't need a replica. Between travels, she always came home to Montpelier. She didn't even look far for her racehorse's first contest: a two-mile cross-country race at the nearby Orange County Horse Show. All she needed was a jockey. She found a young man, one of the better hunt club riders, to take the mount. She watched Jack Skinner guide her mare Safety Catch over the makeshift racecourse, later calling it "the worst ground you'd ever want to see." And her first runner became her first winner.

The race wasn't recognized by the Jockey Club in New York, but the thrill didn't need anyone's approval. Maybe this was as good as a blue ribbon. Maybe it was better. Marion began looking for other horses who might win other unofficial races at local hunt meets and shows. "Safety Catch probably had given me a swelled head," Marion later mused. Or maybe Safety Catch simply gave her confidence.

An extra dose of confidence couldn't hurt right now. So much else was shifting. During 1925, Marion mourned the death of her favorite servant, the nurse who had kept baby Marion safe on a bouncing seat while William's coach rumbled down English roads. And that summer, William du Pont turned seventy years old. With increasing urgency, Marion's father pictured the world beyond his own life span. Despite the inroads made by suffragettes and flappers, it still seemed like a man's world in many ways. Without him, what would happen to his brave, shy, single daughter?

William may have wanted to know that a younger man would escort Marion through life. He may have hoped that something would develop with Randy Scott, a charming and athletic kinsman of his bird-hunting buddy from Richmond, George Cole Scott. And then there was an Orange County family that Marion liked especially well, the Somervilles, with five brothers close to her age.

No one else would know why Marion had doodled hearts on a telephone pad one day in 1921, while taking down a mundane message for someone else. Around that time, she had visited the Scotts. But in 1925, she decided to marry one of the Somerville boys.

He fit into her life. Thomas Hugh Somerville shared Marion's enthusiasm for foxhunting and horse racing. He shared her pleasure in hiking through fields and woodlands with eager bird dogs, hoping for a clutch of perfect shots. As her wedding drew near, Marion told her father that she would like to give Tom a duplicate of "your big Parker gun which suits [him] so well." With her father's approval, one of his staff would order it for her.

Sixteen months younger than Marion, Tom Somerville stood several inches taller than she, but his slender body claimed only minimal space. Like her, he presented the striking contrast of dark hair and blue eyes. He was solidly Southern: Mississippi born, Virginia raised. But when the U.S. draft board came knocking in the spring of 1917, twenty-one-year-old Tom held a vital job above the Mason-Dixon Line, serving as a powder worker for the DuPont factory at Carney's Point, New Jersey. Later, he came home to Virginia, his father's farm at Cedar Mountain, about twenty miles north of Montpelier.

During the autumn of 1925, Marion's engagement triggered something that could gladden her mother's heart: a girlish shopping spree. The Marion who felt so at home tromping the countryside with her father in field boots, overcoats, and plain, practical hats soon would transform into a bride. Sumptuous bouquets and accessories came to Montpelier from Philadelphia and Manhattan. Packages from Fifth Avenue brought a white satin gown from Hollander's, with a beaded cap fit for a queen and a veil that would swirl far past her feet like foam along a seashore; a pair of white satin pumps; and additional gowns of blue, pink, and peach. And then there was the lingerie, purchased from the same posh company that had provided the layette for baby Marion. Instead of elegant but practical infant supplies came pink chiffon and crepe de chine negligees, irresistibly soft and delicate to the touch.

Quickly and quietly, Marion and her parents planned to hold her wedding at home. A noontime ceremony and a catered wedding breakfast for one hundred people. A bride's cake for display. One hundred monogrammed boxes, filled with cake, to be given each guest as a souvenir. Three attendants to stand up front while the bride and groom made their vows—maid of honor Jean Austin duPont, bridesmaid Alice Cole, and best man Randy Scott.

Marion thought of a personal touch, something to be handled at nearly the last minute. It would come from the greenhouse at the place where she had been born. "Could you send some carnations down from Bellevue for my table?" she wrote to her father in mid-December. "The white & pale pink ones I think would be nice."

The next day—only eleven days before the ceremony—her engagement announcement went out to newspapers, saying, "The date of the wedding has not yet been announced." But the invited guests already knew. They were respecting Marion's privacy. In keeping with her desire not to put herself on display, there would be no newspaper photos of newly engaged Marion duPont's luminous face—and her face would be luminous indeed on her wedding day, soft and full and centered, accepting her place at the center of it all. The public would not see that face, nor pictures of the new Mrs. Thomas H. Somerville looking like royalty in her wedding dress. On the other hand, the bride and groom weren't taking a completely private honeymoon. They would vacation at spacious Altama with family and friends.

On December 27, 1925, the day before their wedding, Marion duPont and Thomas Hugh Somerville visited the Orange County Courthouse and registered their marriage license. An ocean away, a small boy received his own pony for his birthday. In their separate lives, the same day held a lifetime of expectations: the hopes entwined with partnership, the expectations clinging to a father's gift.

Bruce Robertson Hobbs was an English child born in America, connected with both continents. His roots ran deep in Leicestershire, where Reginald Clonsilla Edward Hobbs had courted and married Margery Robertson shortly after the Great War ceased. Bruce existed when and where he did because of the international conflict and because of his father's superb horsemanship.

A month before turning nineteen, Reggie Hobbs had left his privileged job at Ambrose Clark's Long Island estate and sailed back to England. Landing at Liverpool on January 7, 1917, he gave his occupation as "Rough Rider," someone who can ride horses that never have been ridden before. Soon he was working for the British Army's Remount Service, training horses that others would use in battle.

Because of the horses, he served his country and stayed somewhat safe at the same time. Because of the horses, he had an enviable job with Ambrose Clark waiting for him in America. After the war ended, Reg stopped with his father in Leicestershire, trying out sport horses that the Clarks might want. He also checked out the local young ladies. In 1920, he had returned to Long Island with a wife.

With her comfortable status as a police superintendent's daughter and her considerable personal appeal, Margery Robertson probably had her pick of the local lads. Reggie Hobbs won her with "his sophisticated charm." Good-looking enough, he was—regular features, broad shoulders, athletic fitness—but style and personality set him apart. A worldly fellow whose riding outfits were always remarkably neat and fitted, showing off what the horsey set called "a good leg for a boot"; a confident man who wasn't afraid to show a woman how she fascinated him, how thoroughly she could be adored. Tall, shapely, blond Margery—"softly spoken, tremendously kind and well-liked, with a keen sense of humour"—captivated Reg. The horse dealer's son swept the police superintendent's daughter away to a fairy-tale estate where fortunate people kept horses for fun.

Their son entered the world at Mineola, Long Island, on December 27, 1920, not far from Ambrose Clark's Broad Hollow farm. But the home that Bruce Hobbs truly came to know and love was Leicestershire. Mr. and Mrs. Clark decided that their winters would revolve around the foremost foxhunts in the world. They leased an estate called Warwick Lodge, at the famous hunting town of Melton Mowbray, and put Reg Hobbs in charge of the stables. Reggie and his young family sailed back to England in mid-October 1922: Rough Rider, Housewife, and Child.

As soon as possible, Bruce began riding. Reg already had decided that his boy must become a famous horseman. When Bruce could guide a pony on his own, his lessons became rigorous.

"Keep your elbows in, Bruce. Sit up, boy. Sit up!"

That was how Bruce's day began, ever since he was four years old. There was Reg coaching him, demanding flawless form. No settling for mediocrity. As Bruce grew stronger, Reg also demanded stamina: every day, his boy spent three hours in the saddle. Bruce loved animals and enjoyed riding, but sometimes his father's unrelenting discipline was more than he could take. If he asked for any respite, his father only got tougher. Bruce learned that he couldn't negotiate with Reg and later would recall, "When he was extra firm—he used to bloody well frighten me—I would turn to Mummy."

Marge Hobbs saw no need for Reg to drive Bruce this way. Why couldn't their son grow up like her father—a notably kindly person, a well-regarded police superintendent? Why did it have to be horses and fame? At night, alone in his room, Bruce often heard his parents arguing "like hell" after they put him to bed.

Marge wouldn't back down, but neither did Reg. Instead of constant coaching, he sometimes handed the boy an especially stubborn pony and told him to ride out in a field for an hour, alone, performing training exercises. "I couldn't do it," Bruce admitted. "I used to stand in the gateway and blub my eyes out. I couldn't move the stupid pony and there was nobody there to help me. Then, when father came back again, he would say 'What have you done?' and I would say 'I can't move,' knowing very well that he would be furious."

Bruce learned that with his father, there was no such thing as good enough for now. As soon as the boy succeeded at one daunting challenge, Reg revealed another. "At one stage," Bruce recalled, "he frightened me to such an extent that for three months I wouldn't go near a pony." Marge must have hoped that this rebellion would change everything.

In the end, Bruce's own nature won out. He *missed* riding. Maybe some of that had to do with family pride—a young boy wanting to measure up with both his father and his grandfather, two of the best and most popular horsemen in Bruce's horse-centered world. Another part answered to nobody except Bruce—an affinity that simply was, a belonging beyond words.

By early 1926, while Bruce Hobbs tried to fulfill his father's expectations with Bombo the birthday pony, William du Pont's grown children had long since divvied up their own responsibilities to their dad. While William savored his customary winter vacation in Georgia, Willie dutifully reported from Wilmington that "the meeting of the Del[aware] Trust Co[mpany] on Monday passed off . . . without anything new." After William returned to Wilmington, Marion weighed in from Montpelier: "I went down to the garden and went all through the green houses, the grapes and peach trees look healthy and are fairly well set in fruit. . . . When I went down [the new gardener] ran around & cut flowers for me and tried to make a good impression—but I think where he fails is in vegetables. . . . I think if you were here he would be all together alright."

Marion probably was right. Her father had a knack for bringing out the best in his employees. He had been popular with the workmen who renovated Montpelier, discussing practical issues without putting on airs. Perhaps, despite his extraordinary wealth, William didn't take things for granted. He had been through the wringer with the DuPont Company: promoted early by his father, pummeled by his brother, resigning when he and Annie moved overseas, brought back onto the board of directors after returning to America, ousted from the board in 1915 when a cousin engineered a takeover. On the other hand, William still owned plenty of stock in the empire that his great-grandfather had ignited, and a leadership attitude emanated from him. A newspaper cartoon from 1925 emphasized the derby hat upon his head, round spectacles upon his nose, his mustache proudly blooming, and his confident stance: burrowing his hands in the jacket pockets of his fine suit while sticking his chest out. William du Pont had an unbreakable connection with his heritage, and it showed. But perhaps he didn't have a blind sense of entitlement. Perhaps his employees felt that.

Perhaps the relationship was more challenging for his son. William Jr. had missed all of his father's young, uncertain years; he had grown up with the father who served as president, then chairman of the board, of the Delaware Trust Company in Wilmington and expected his boy to successfully do the same. Marion didn't need to bridge those gaps. Will lived closer to Bellevue Hall and the Delaware Trust Company, where William spent many days; but Marion communicated with him less formally. Will sent his letters to "Dear Father" and ended them, as if it needed explaining, "your loving son." Marion sent hers to "Dear Papa" and ended them "Much love." And yet their devotion to horses and dogs and each other transcended any sibling friction. Beneath the changes it was still Marion and Willie, who always had gotten together to do what they wanted to do. As 1926 unfolded, William du Pont Sr. watched his grown children begin replacing their long-gone Coney Island with farther-reaching endeavors.

True to form, they reimagined landscapes. Developing his own foxhunting territory, William Jr. leased a farm in Cecil County, Maryland, convenient to his Pennsylvania home. He soon stitched together a swath of farms that he called Fair Hill, a vast preserve overlapping the Maryland-Pennsylvania border. He and his sister and father also began planning to hold hunt club races at Montpelier, where the big field leading up to the front lawn offered a lovely spot for steeplechasing on the grass and perhaps room for a dirt track as well. Will, whose early aptitude with hammer and nails had matured into a genius for design, helped to lay out the jump course. Marion also had her say, reporting in late October 1926 that one of their workmen "has the [steeplechase] race course looking fine—and I went around with him and picked out a place for the flat track." Will would tweak it; Marion decided where to proceed.

If her father had hoped she would be producing a grandchild by now, he was disappointed. Instead, Mrs. T. H. Somerville had been showing her new favorite foxhunter, a small, fast red-chestnut son of Fair Play who had been named, before she bought him, after a popular rosy-colored pill. Legions of Americans seeking relief from constipation depended on Phenolax. Perhaps too amused by his name to change it, Marion duPont Somerville won champion hunter at the Devon Horse Show during the summer of 1926 with Phenolax the horse, whose name was a joke about get up and go.

She also continued training a horse or two for racing at informal meets. "My bay mare is schooling so well with me," she told her father at one point, "I have decided not to have her schooled . . . [by someone else while I am away at] Bryn Mawr as I am afraid it might mix up my system on her."

But when it came to official Thoroughbred racing, her brother led the way. While Marion schooled hunters and cross-country racers, Will du-Pont began racing Thoroughbreds at major Maryland racetracks: Havre de Grace, Laurel, Pimlico. He paid $100,000 for the fastest two-year-old in England, a colt named The Satrap, and pointed him toward next year's Kentucky Derby. Meanwhile, his two-year-old filly Fair Star jumped up and won the important Selima Stakes in Maryland. A week later, she faced several of the year's best juveniles in the Pimlico Futurity, worth more than $55,000 to the victor. Marion and Tom Somerville watched from Pimlico's clubhouse that afternoon, delighted when Fair Star shot home first at odds of thirteen to one.

Should Marion venture into big-time racing? In eight days, Fair Star had earned more than $70,000 for Will duPont. In fact, she had become the top two-year-old money earner of the year. Suddenly, Will's future in the sport of kings felt limitless. Soon the Kentucky Derby, Saratoga, American racing's highest peaks.

There was someone missing from this excitement. After summering at Montpelier, Annie du Pont had sailed to England. This was a cordial time apart from her family, feeding different needs. Perhaps, as her husband reached age seventy and she turned sixty-eight, it had become mentally and physically harder for them to relax in the same ways. One wanted several close friends and the great outdoors; the other, the capital city of the world's greatest empire. And so, while William paused at his Virginia farm, then retreated to his secluded Georgia woodlands, Annie settled at an elegant hotel and took pleasure in London's peak social season. Every so often, she would write a long letter home.

And sometimes, thinking of loved ones and wanting them to think of her at a particular time, she sent cablegrams they would receive without delay. One arrived for William du Pont at Montpelier on Christmas Eve:

```
MERRY  XMAS  TO  YOU  MARION  TOM
HAPPY  NEW  YEAR  MUCH  LOVE  AS  WELL
NANNIE
```

With her mother across the ocean, Marion took charge in certain domestic ways. "Everything seems to be in order to go South," she notified her father as 1926 drew to a close, "but your short green coat is not in the small closet downstairs perhaps you have it at Bellevue or you left it South." Concluding her instructions about their upcoming visit to Altama, she underlined, "Don't forget the other gun."

William, Marion, and Tom began 1927 much the same as they had started 1926. But they had enjoyed their Georgia sanctuary for less than three weeks when an urgent message arrived from London. In her suite at the Jules Hotel, Annie du Pont had suffered a cerebral hemorrhage. She had lingered briefly, but nothing could be done. She had died that same night with her maid and a doctor present, her family four thousand miles away.

Saturday, January 22, became a strange, sad, feverish day for William,

Marion, and Tom. They were packing to leave Altama the next morning. They were heading up to Wilmington to receive Annie's body, which had to sail once more across the sea.

During the afternoon of February 3, William and his children joined fellow mourners at Old Swedes Church in downtown Wilmington for Nannie's memorial service. Then they followed her a few miles up the road. Annie Rogers du Pont was laid to rest in the du Pont family cemetery, well away from those who had shunned her—but with her husband's stout support, she had passed a test. Now she was included for all time.

In the world of Reginald Hobbs, being included often involved passing through some kind of trial. At age six, Bruce Hobbs began to see where his father's demands for attentiveness, obedience, and bravery came together and paid off. Reg's livelihood depended upon the six wintertime weeks when Brose and Florence Clark occupied Warwick Lodge. The Clarks kept a stable of fifty Thoroughbreds in Leicestershire, making sure that they and their friends always had fit and flawless hunters to ride during that hectic high season. Reg spent most of each year priming this troop of horses for those few supernatural weeks, choosing and developing new hunters each spring and summer while also keeping the veterans fit. Bruce was used to being behind the scenes in the stables and yard, but now his father drew open the curtain and urged him onto the stage. Reg prepared his boy with a good jumping pony named Tom Thumb, then brought him foxhunting with the Quorn.

A Quorn meet was a massive production, drawing hundreds of people costumed almost like a royal procession and sometimes actually including the prince of Wales. To reach the meet, the party from Warwick Lodge would jog a dozen miles or more, with Bruce and Tom Thumb typically bringing up the rear. Bruce would remember a dozen so-called second horsemen, assistants to the Clarks and their friends, wearing top hats and silver-buttoned livery and leading spare horses so that their employers could change to a fresh mount midway through the day.

When they arrived at that morning's chosen covert, a natural hiding place where foxes might be found, Bruce's real challenge began. Needing bold and knowledgeable leaders to assist him, the master of foxhounds would send Reg to the area where a fox might be most likely to get away. And Bruce's job ("whether I wanted to or not," he said, "and often I didn't") was to follow his father when a fox spurted off and Reg shouted, *"Come on!"*

Reg didn't care that Bruce's pony was about eight inches shorter than his own Thoroughbred. A shout, and he was gone. Whatever Reg jumped, whether wall, stream, ditch, or massive hedge, Bruce would be jumping, too. "If I fell off," Bruce would recall, "he never waited for me, just gave me a bloody good rousting when I caught up again."

And yet, at age six, Bruce soon rode well enough to be present when the hounds caught and killed a fox. The first time this happened, he endured the initiation of being "blooded" by a huntsman, having the fox's warm blood dabbed on his face while other hunt members smiled their approval. As Bruce rode home that day, everyone who saw him knew his achievement: tradition demanded that he couldn't wash off the evidence until that evening. Some children would become too upset to wear the blood all the way home; a few would be so proud that they didn't want to wash their faces the next day. Bruce tolerated the rite of passage. In his home, there was no room for squeamishness. In his home, he might have to pass through unpleasantness, discomfort, painful questions about why things had to be a certain way—but when he succeeded, he had earned something.

Perhaps problems could be useful. Perhaps it was good to learn how to handle difficulties and know that you could survive the bumps. Perhaps it was good to understand, when you looked across the big sky, that you were fortunate to have come this far and also might need to be ready for something worse.

5

WHEN ANNIE DU PONT DIED, THE world of her husband and children startled apart, then sighed back toward familiar shapes. Maybe the familiar shapes helped Marion get along. After the funeral, she returned to Altama as usual for February and March. She also looked ahead: that spring, a Thoroughbred stallion named Berrilldon would stand stud at Montpelier. Marion was eager to get flyers advertising his services printed up and distributed. "Sires heavy boned colts hunter types," she scrawled above a diagram of his pedigree. He looked like a good fit for the Virginia market, where folks wanted sturdy Thoroughbreds for hunt-racing meets, but Marion didn't expect him to sire world-beaters. Patrons could breed a mare to Berrilldon for only $30.

While Marion made modest plans, her brother monitored his $100,000 gamble. Willie sent The Satrap to Max Hirsch, one of America's best trainers, and hoped for the best. The brilliant colt had a touchy leg. He might not stay sound enough to make the Kentucky Derby.

In any case, Will's expensive horse was only a shiny detail in a much larger design. First thing on the morning of April 1, 1927, William duPont Jr. filed a certificate of incorporation for Foxcatcher Farms. The terms covered every aspect of raising and racing Thoroughbred horses. The date may have raised an ironic smile. Thirty-one years old, well known along the Eastern seaboard as an expert horseman, Will duPont was no

April fool. His affiliations included the Rose Tree Hunt near Philadelphia, where Sam Riddle and Walter Jeffords of Man o' War fame played leading roles and sometimes requested his help. Observing the champion racing stables that Riddle and Jeffords had built beyond Rose Tree, Will easily could think, *I can do that*. He had ample knowledge and resources—surely everything needed to make the leap. Of course he could not know whether the greatest success would come through himself, his sister, or someone else. He could only reach out for his true place in a world that seemed to be shrinking and expanding at the same time.

Late in 1926, a young American pilot contemplating an international aviation contest had decided that flying solo across the Atlantic Ocean couldn't be any worse than delivering airmail during stormy and poorly lit Midwestern winter nights. And if that was true, the transatlantic challenge that had killed several pilots more distinguished than himself wasn't any more fearsome than his regular job. Of course he would need the right tools and the best possible plan. He thought plenty about that plan. And then, since he didn't have anywhere near enough money to build the plane he envisioned, he sought sponsorship. The young man wasn't a natural salesman, but his logical passion for what an airplane might do convinced several businessmen from his home base in St. Louis, Missouri, to endorse his risky plan.

While Charles Lindbergh worked strenuously with engineers and mechanics to design, build, and test a plane that could fly nonstop from Long Island to Paris, more traditional experiments were taking their sweet time at Kentucky's bluegrass horse farms. Lindbergh needed an engine that was the least likely to misfire, plus a huge fuel tank. Racehorse breeders with similar needs sought another precious commodity: Man o' War blood.

With two crops now racing, Man o' War already had sired three champions for Sam and Elizabeth Riddle and two more for their niece and her husband, Sarah and Walter M. Jeffords. Few other breeders got the chance, for Man o' War never consorted with more than twenty-five mares a year and the Riddle-Jeffords family owned many of them. In 1925, the lucky outsiders had included Walter J. Salmon, who had tried to buy Fair Play. In 1926, Big Red had a date with another Salmon matron—a French mare named Quarantaine. Under normal circumstances, she never should have been there.

Quarantaine was bred to be a treasure, the genetic equivalent of an Impressionist painting or a Fabergé egg. Her sire—despite his off-putting name, Sea Sick—was a French classic winner and highly successful stallion. Her dam had a plow horse name, Queenie, but came from a gifted family. Queenie's mother had won the classic Prix de Diane or French Oaks, the French fillies' equivalent of the Kentucky Derby. Quarantaine was born in Normandy, not far from the Deauville resort where fashionable ladies and gentlemen enjoyed sea bathing, polo, horse racing, and casino gambling—a location worthy of the fabulously rich Rothschild family.

And in fact, she and Queenie belonged to a Rothschild son-in-law named Maurice Éphrussi, a Russian expatriate who had been raising fine Thoroughbreds at his own farms for more than forty years. Although he ran an important bank in Paris, Éphrussi defied the ugly stereotypes that haunted Jewish merchants and moneylenders and called himself a "landowner." At the same time, being married to Béatrice de Rothschild, Éphrussi embraced the world's most renowned Jewish banking family. Béatrice made a joke from the sound of his last name and called him "Frousse," French for "fright." Perhaps her sense of humor also prompted the name for Queenie's filly by Sea Sick. In French, "quarantaine" literally means "about forty days"—the length of time that a ship at sea would be banned from entering port if there were any outbreak of disease on board.

But during the spring of 1915, when the filly who would be named Quarantaine was born, France had no use for racehorses. All of Europe was at war. The splendid Deauville casino had been converted into a military hospital and troops of Thoroughbred horses were commandeered for the French cavalry. However, the French government did not want to wipe out their nation's best racehorse stock. Queenie and Quarantaine were fortunate: they were too valuable for battle duty, and the Western Front would remain at least 140 miles from their farm.

While the war burned on, Maurice Éphrussi died. His widow and her brother kept the stable together but their horses had nowhere to race. Normally, Quarantaine would have been aimed for the Prix de Diane at age three, but in 1918 there was no French Oaks. Instead, Quarantaine visited France's National Stud for a rendezvous. Rather than prove herself in competition, she would be the horse equivalent of a human girl who has a baby before finishing high school.

As winter drew near, the war finally ended. The next spring, Quarantaine nursed her new filly while her younger sister Quenouille won the revived Prix de Diane. Quenouille instantly became Queenie's most valuable daughter, while Quarantaine remained a question mark—unproved at the racetrack and with no offspring old enough to show whether or not they could win races. The Rothschild family kept Quenouille, who eventually would become one of their prized broodmares. Quarantaine they put up for sale.

In France's weak postwar market, she brought only 4,000 francs, about $500. She already held the potential for much more: the filly who would win the 1923 French Oaks with a stirring stretch drive. That filly made her mother notable throughout France and beyond. In 1924, once-again-pregnant Quarantaine boarded an ocean liner to America. She delivered her French colt the next spring at Mereworth Farm, then commenced what Walter J. Salmon had bought her to do: producing a Fair Play baby first, then mating with Man o' War.

On March 19, 1927, as the frame of Charles Lindbergh's experimental plane took shape in a San Diego hangar, Mereworth Farm welcomed its third foal from Quarantaine. Small and red and assertive, he slid onto the straw in one of Mereworth's famously hygienic foaling stalls.

He had inherited his sire's bold chestnut coat, plus a white star on his forehead and a white spot on the bridge of his nose a few inches above his nostrils. His little face also promised a more rugged version of Man o' War's slightly Roman nose. His high-set neck, like Man o' War's and Fair Play's, could crank up like a periscope. His legs had something that could not be added if a horse wasn't born with it: good thick bone. The one thing he clearly lacked was height. This colt would not become a Big Red. At best, he might be a spirited miniature. And yet he would be given a powerful name: Battleship.

It was an even more ambitious name than the one his sire had made legendary. A man-o'-war is simply a ship with some kind of cannon aboard. Battleship refers to a line-of-battle ship—heavily armored and armed with large-caliber guns, able to withstand and deal out a barrage. Maybe this extrastrong meaning was accidental; Man o' War progeny were receiving all kinds of navy names. Already, less fortunate sons and daughters were registered as Crow's Nest, Gobs, Purple Pirate, and Port-Hole.

But there was something about Quarantaine's colt that probably would have saved him from being named Port-Hole if that name had been available, despite being a grandson of Sea Sick. He wasn't the kind of horse who would hang back and peer through a window. He wasn't afraid to give back as good as he got. He might be up for an adventure that would make others turn back, challenging limitations that many took for granted.

Two months and one day after Battleship's birth, Charles Lindbergh squished out onto Roosevelt Field, Long Island, and pictured his takeoff for Paris. Conditions were not ideal. The muddy runway could bog down his overloaded plane, damp air made the engine rev too slowly, a slight tailwind meant more time needed to become airborne. If *The Spirit of St. Louis* could not leave the ground and climb quickly enough, she would snag the telephone wires just beyond the runway's end or simply smash into the trees.

While the propellor spun, the young pilot reconsidered everything. He trusted the mechanical integrity of his strong, fragile plane and the instincts he had honed as a barnstormer, taking off from cow pastures. He knew the math, which said that his little plane should be able to heave five thousand pounds into the sky. He knew that he could change his mind today and everyone, the whole crowd mistrusting the wet runway and wrong wind, would feel relieved. They would not blame him. They did not want him to die, as other pilots trying for Paris had done at this same place.

He considered everything, then told the crew to remove the chocks from *Spirit*'s wheels. He was going to go. "It's less a decision of logic than of feeling," Lindbergh later explained, "the kind of feeling that comes when you gauge the distance to be jumped between two stones across a brook. Something within you disengages itself from your body and travels ahead with your vision to make the test. You can feel it try the jump as you stand looking. Then uncertainty gives way to the conviction that it *can* or can't be done. Sitting in the cockpit, in seconds, [seeming] minutes long, the conviction surges through me that the wheels *will* leave the ground, that the wings *will* rise above the wires, that it *is* time to start the flight."

It is a near thing, but his feeling is right. *The Spirit of St. Louis* clears the telephone wires by twenty feet and is on her way. It is a moment grown from many moments managing lesser planes and equally poor conditions. It is made possible by the pilot's understanding of this particular plane. It will come to seem as unlikely yet inevitable as any one colt out of many thousands growing up to be *the* one . . . no less strange and wonderful than a mare growing up in wartime France and ending up at the court of Man o' War.

Two months and two days after Battleship's birth, Charles Lindbergh landed at Paris after a thirty-three-and-a-half-hour flight and won the transatlantic contest. He had done it with no copilot, no crew. The reticent young man, dazed by instant, overwhelming fame, had satisfied his conviction about how much airplanes could do. He also couldn't separate himself from the winged creation that made his triumph possible. While the world nicknamed him "the Lone Eagle" and celebrated his solo achievement, Lindbergh marveled at the stellar performance of his flying partner, *The Spirit of St. Louis*. Instead of promoting himself, he talked about "we."

When Marion duPont Somerville said "we" these days, she often meant herself and Tom. Eighteen months into their marriage, they had indeed formed a team—though their differences peeked out in 1927, when Will duPont moved his Foxcatcher Hounds from Montpelier to his new estate at Fair Hill, Maryland, and Marion registered her own Montpelier Hunt. Serving as Master of Foxhounds—an uncommon role for a woman—she took the lead in deciding when and where to meet. She studied the wind and weather, consulted with her huntsman about the hounds, compensated farmers for any damage done their farmyards or fields during a chase. She also appointed her husband as hunt secretary. Tom Somerville would handle inquiries from anyone who wanted to join their private pack for a run and would generally smooth through social chores that might stress his wife.

Chances are, he also needed to match her preferred ways of doing things. Of course Marion couldn't tend everything herself, but she wanted it to seem as if she had. "I found my horses + colts pretty well," she informed her father after returning to Montpelier from a summer trip, "but I usually find I have to rearrange things— Have been all over the place and gardens. . . . I have several suggestions to make when you come down this week." More than ever, when it came to Montpelier, she was talking with her father as her peer.

And the more responsibility Marion shouldered, the more she seemed to enjoy sharing the results. When Randy Scott and his kinswoman by marriage Hildreth Scott dropped by for a few days in June, Marion noted early on that "I think Hildreth + I went all over the place this morning and saw all the colts and the horses down at the barn as well." These included Safety Catch and Drogheda, being trained by Marion for hunt races. She also took pride in a promising young gray hunter she had found for her husband, noting, "He has a lovely conformation + manners + has quite some quality so [Tom] could show him next year."

Finding the right horse to give someone was one way to show affection and prove that you were paying attention to his needs. And that summer of 1927, Marion and Tom appeared to be nesting: building their own house at Greenville, Delaware, near other du Pont mansions of Wilmington. Or, rather, her father's money was building it. Tom Somerville could only cheer them on. He felt a flash of wanting to create something on his own but couldn't quite seem to manage it independently of his wife. That August, he wrote a careful letter to his father-in-law: "Dear Mr. duPont. I've wanted to thank you and tell you many times how much I appreciate your kindness toward me in every way," Tom began, "so am writing you my appreciation of the fact. Aside from my wants and other expenses, I've put aside some money and after talking it over with Marion she advised me looking it over with you, and getting your idea or advice as to investment." Then Tom named the amount he had saved, an amount that would be more than a year's salary for many Americans, an amount that might buy a couple of nice though not top-notch horses for his wife. "I've

$2,000.00 in bank that is not bringing in anything," Tom confided, "and certainly would appreciate your judgment as to investing it."

Despite his intimate place within Marion's life, Tom Somerville remained something of an outsider. He could not find equal footing with her family. Will duPont, on the other hand, had the opposite problem as he entered big-time Thoroughbred racing: administrators didn't instantly place him where he knew he belonged.

It wasn't about appearances. Willie put no stock in empty honors. He did know horses from the ground up and expected respect accordingly. He sometimes rode a winning race at a hunt meet and sometimes taught his own Thoroughbred yearlings to accept a rider. He looked like a weight-conscious jockey but didn't need crash diets to stay thin—constant activity kept him whittled slim. Although he stood only medium height, his daughter Jean would remember becoming old enough to walk a cross-country jumping course with him, "and I would have to run every inch of the way because he had a mile-eating stride."

Will duPont wanted to span Thoroughbred racing with that mile-eating stride. Confidence marched forth from his memos when he contacted top racetracks to reserve precious space in their barns. He made his requests with the polite but empowered tone of someone who of course would uphold the highest standards and bring credit to their racing meet. If there was any delay—and there usually was some extra wrinkle—he followed up with the detailed prompting of someone who suspects that other people might not manage their responsibilities as thoroughly as he managed his. He seemed surprised whenever racing's protocols failed to follow his steady logic.

Will hit several bumps when he requested much-coveted stalls and clubhouse box seats for Saratoga's August 1927 meet. Saratoga was a familiar luxury that his father had enjoyed and had introduced to Willie and Marion. Now Will thought he would get a jump on things, wrapping up his applications a couple of months in advance. But it didn't work that way. Saratoga's racing secretary, the gracious yet meticulous Victor E. Schaumburg, patiently explained the gulf between Will's specifications and Saratoga's well-tried system. In return, Will urged Schaumburg, "As soon as your allotment is made, I wish that you would notify me whereabouts my stalls will be located, as I am very familiar with your stables at Saratoga and want to get located back somewhere where it will be quiet."

This was like telling the maître d' of an exclusive restaurant that your large party of course needed their best table on their busiest night. Crickets chirped while Schaumburg let early July arrive and the usual chaotic process take its course. Then he delivered the verdict for Foxcatcher Farms—not sixteen stalls, but ten—and soaked Will duPont with a fire hose of reality: "The fact of the matter is that there are at least 40 horse owners racing around here that have asked for stalls, many of whom are nominators to our stakes, and whom we have not been able to place as yet."

Nor would there be a permanent clubhouse box for Will and Jean du-Pont that August, but the Saratoga Association president did find them a spot "in the last row for this year only." Schaumburg advised Will that the president thought "it would be best for you to take this box and have your name on [the] list of subscribers, and [he] will do his best to get a better one for you next season. If you desire above box kindly send us check for $110."

Will quickly sent the check. He and his wife would be seated in the last row, but Foxcatcher Farms had made the cut.

Will duPont returned from Saratoga with a passel of yearlings from the Spa's famous sales. He also reached out to his sister. Would Marion like a chance to win some of the big races that Will already had won? Like buying a raffle ticket, she could purchase one or two prospects from him.

Marion chose two fillies and kept them at her brother's farm. Meanwhile, her grown racehorses faltered. Safety Catch took a fall and hurt her shoulder, prompting Marion to have her shoes pulled off and turn her out. That left one racer for the hunt meets. But Marion was finding Drogheda "so unsatisfactory" that she considered selling him.

She also was feeling subverted within her household. Marion depended upon servants to keep her large homes running smoothly, and her personal maid was supposed to be a discreet, efficient ally. No such luck. "I can't stand Miss Lee any longer," Marion wrote her father that

October, with fury splintering her handwriting. Not only did this servant fail as a laundress, she was disrespectful. The last straw had been calling Marion and Tom Somerville by their first names, not to their faces but while talking with a family friend. The maid had quickly backtracked—*Miss Marion*, she had meant to say. But Marion heard the story, and that tore it: one more proof of her employee's careless disregard. "If it is OK with you I will give her notice . . . ," Marion urged her father. "I know we can do better than her—just wire Yes or No + I will know what it means."

It was a lingering wisp of a fading era: Marion needing her father's permission to fire the woman who laundered her unmentionables. William du Pont's remarkable energy was fading, though he oversaw the building of Marion and Tom's new Wilmington home and shared her pleasure with its progress. "I think we will call the place Manton Manor," Marion told him. "So you can break people onto saying that! I think that is the name that you liked too—"

He was seventy-two, she was thirty-three, but one thing hadn't changed: Marion needed her father's approval for many business transactions and wanted his praise on the home front. That autumn, she presented her handiwork at Montpelier for his admiration: "I have the billiard room completed covered the chairs + sofa myself and I am anxious to show you what a nice job I think I made."

In the sporting world, his blessing still mattered, but Marion seemed more assured. She still didn't have a baby, but she had helped birth a racecourse. During October 1927, she had been supervising the finishing touches, preparing everything for Montpelier's first racing meet. Looking out from Montpelier's front door, walking down into the front fields and surveying the transformation, Marion took stock and informed her father, "I want to make it permanent." Here and now, she was standing up for herself. Next year, her brother would be holding his own Foxcatcher race meeting in Maryland. Marion wanted *this* place. She wanted "a nice schooling course for steeplechase horses," her own horses. And she wanted it maintained year-round—"that way there wouldn't be half so much work to be done each fall."

Everything was ready, freshly painted, even blooming with late flowers. Marion looked forward to the unveiling and prayed, "Hope we don't have a frost before the races as it really looks very well for this time of year." She looked forward to her father's company and wrote him, "Just a reminder to you to bring some pajamas down as there are none here in your drawers unless they are put away in your bags."

Less than three weeks after the Montpelier races, William du Pont was hospitalized. He was suffering from myocarditis, an inflammation of the heart.

For William and his children, Thanksgiving this year meant doctors, nurses, uncertainty. In early December, William still was mostly bedridden but had rallied enough for Marion to leave Wilmington and head down to Montpelier. Day after day, she sent him long, newsy letters, painting pictures of country pleasures in her plain, direct way. She tried to give him senses of the coming holiday season: "I am having Joseph make the usual number of plum pudding and mince for pies as usual— We are going to have sausage and scrapple tomorrow for the first time." She shared news of the farm community: "Every one is pig killing around here today— The mornings are so cold it is good for that." She tried to bring him the sporting outdoors: "Started hunting at 9 a.m. jumped a fox behind Watson's + ran until lunch time—rejumped him + they are still running at 6.30— I came in and changed horses + got something to eat." She tried to save him a place at dinner: "There are lovely blue lace flowers and sweet peas on the dining table. I know you would admire the colors." She gently urged him, "Will you get the nurse or [secretary Earl Edinger] to write me how you are every day—how did you walk on Monday. . . . I will be up the end of the week."

She tried to live as usual but frayed here and there. At Montpelier, she enjoyed lunch one day with their old friend Hildreth Scott from Richmond but somehow kept failing to give Hildreth her father's convalescent address. Hildreth eventually procured it from Randy Scott, who already had wished William, in beautiful handwriting, "my sincere wishes for an early recovery," and added, "In case I do not see you before the holidays, I will take this opportunity to wish you a very Merry Xmas. and a happy New Year."

Five days before Christmas, Hildreth Scott poured out a letter of thanks and sadness and hope to William du Pont. She was "so grateful" for "the wonderful walnuts" he had sent to her family, so sad that her son was quarantined at VMI this Christmas because of a polio outbreak there, though grateful that he was fine. She noted that "Randolph Scott has just been with us for the week end and he is such a sweet boy I am devoted to him—we all are." She hoped that she, her husband George Cole Scott, and their whole family might join William and his party in January at Altama. She closed with "our warmest Christmas greetings and best wishes for the New Year."

William responded thoughtfully, though without wasting words, to her every concern. Regarding Altama, he leveled with her:

> I have been a very sick man + am still far from being recovered, and I am going to Georgia taking both a nurse + a medical attendant with me and it would be impossible for me to take any more than you and Mr. Scott in the car with me, or to have a house full of young people until I have very considerably improved.
>
> I still hope that you + Mr S will be able to go with us.
>
> Kindly advise Marion on this point. With the best of wishes for the N[ew] Y[ear] to Cole [and] all your family, I remain very sincerely yours.

In late January 1928, Charles Lindbergh and *The Spirit of St. Louis* made a flying tour of Latin America, boosting aviation in general while also blazing a trail for American industry. The New York Stock Exchange traded at all-time record levels. Billy Barton trained in England, preparing for his made-in-America Grand National attempt. In Kentucky, Battleship roughhoused with other new yearlings at Mereworth Farm. Farther south, William du Pont tried to conserve his life but prepared to leave it. On January 3, he updated his last will and testament.

Then it seemed that he might not need it for a good while. William couldn't tramp through the woods anymore, but he could be bundled into an automobile at Altama and tour his extensive property. He could hear birds, feel and smell the salt air, watch the Altamaha River feed into the sea. He felt better than he had felt for many weeks.

He was alert and apparently comfortable on Friday, January 20, settled in his plantation house drawing room at just past one o'clock in the afternoon. He had been talking with Marion and Tom and his personal secretary "with usual lively interest" while attended by his doctor and a nurse. Then someone summoned Dr. Ryan to another part of the house, and William started reading a newspaper as the doctor left the room.

And that is where William du Pont took his leave: settled in his chair, newspaper in hand, his daughter nearby. There were no dramatics from William, though Dr. Ryan rushed back and tried to revive him, having barely reached the hallway when he heard the nurse crying out. One moment, the gold-rimmed bifocals perched upon William's nose had a purpose—then they did not. One moment, Marion saw her father engaged with life—then an empty shell casing, crumpled on the chair.

He would be buried at Wilmington only two days later, beside Nannie, on the first anniversary of her death. His visions transferred to the next generation. William duPont Jr. received 60 percent of his father's considerable assets, including Bellevue Hall. Marion's 40 percent included Montpelier.

6

MONTPELIER SEEMED READY FOR WILLIAM DU Pont to return. Maybe you would find him in the billiard room, chalking his cue, glancing at the scenes of horse-drawn coaches decorating the walls. Perhaps he would be perusing farm records in his office, surrounded by sculpture, paintings, and many engravings of cattle: a bronze bull, *Landscape and Cows, Portrait of a Remarkably Fine Steer.* Or he could be outside, checking on his herds: two Jersey bulls, ten heifers, thirty cows; fifty-three sheep; thirty-three gray Percheron draft horses; thirty-two show-quality Hackneys. Not to mention the seventeen geese and four Berkshire pigs. Or his thirty-five chickens, bred to be game.

But it all was up to Marion, now. The two ice cream freezers awaiting their call to action; the laundry with its Whirlpool electric washing machine; the blacksmith shop and bunkhouse, smokehouse and schoolhouse, hothouses and toolhouse, sawmill, powerhouse; the gardener's cottage and overseer's house, the garage, the pay office, the dairy. The cockpit in the carriage house. The bowling alley. A village within a farm, all hers to maintain, all hers to possibly rearrange.

Of course Marion would not do it entirely alone. Her brother would oversee her investments and other business concerns from his office in Delaware. At the same time, Marion knew how to keep Montpelier well staffed and fully functioning. She felt the farm's everyday flow in a way that Will had left behind. He might advise; she would decide.

Appraisers said that Montpelier's livestock and furnishings were worth more than $102,000—less than half the value of the jewelry that Annie Rogers Zinn du Pont had left behind. In that sense, William's passions seemed more modest than his wife's. But Annie's legacy could exist behind lock and key, with only occasional polishing. His needed continual attention.

American history boosters hoped that Mrs. Thomas H. Somerville would let them take over that responsibility. Not for the livestock, which could go elsewhere, but for Founding Father James Madison's house and land. After William du Pont died, their agitation spilled out into newspaper articles. Montpelier should become a public destination like George Washington's Mount Vernon and Thomas Jefferson's Monticello. One journalist noted that Mr. du Pont had preserved many original features of Montpelier and had left the place "in splendid condition" but, unfortunately, "he was of a retiring nature and resented public inspection of his property so that the ever-inquisitive and eager patriots were barred from seeing the estate." Then a broadside blast hit Marion and Will:

Du Pont's heirs have not cared for the estate. Mrs. Somerville prefers to live in her fine house near Brunswick, Ga., and her brother William du Pont, prefers to live on his Delaware estate. Mrs. Somerville owns the Madison estate, but rarely visits it.

A place neglected by [its] owner is apt to suffer even though it is kept up. There are patriotic societies that would like to treasure what Montpelier stands for, conserving its sacred spots and it is the hope that the owner may care to dispose of the property at a reasonable rate if not by actual gift to persons who would care for it and hand it on as a shrine. Students of the constitution all over the country will be asked to contribute funds to help acquire the estate.

The public did have a right to care about Montpelier, but they didn't understand the duPont heirs at all. They didn't realize how far Will had gone to make his Pennsylvania house feel like his beloved childhood home and how attentive he still was to Montpelier's needs. They didn't realize that however many houses Marion might own and however many months she might spend away from Orange County, she had one heart of hearts. There was no way to buy her out.

Inside the house, she chose not to change much. Montpelier's rooms would keep speaking of William and Nannie du Pont. Past and present scenes would layer like onion skin, translucent, melding one with another. No matter how many times Marion migrated among Virginia, Delaware, and Southern resorts, Montpelier would hold the whole of her life.

Reg Hobbs didn't own the cottage where he and his family resided, but Leicestershire held many dimensions of his being. Sustaining his father's reputation for first-class horsemanship, satisfying his own desire to ride cross-country races, and transmitting these legacies to his own son, Reg could feel the rightness of his life. His wife, however, was the glass half empty as well as half full. The problem was, Reg's plans for Bruce were working. Their boy rode courageously, with beautiful form. Then Tom Thumb the pony stepped in a rabbit hole, and everything went dark.

Margery Hobbs must have been exceedingly grateful when she could begin letting light back into her son's room. Bruce had awoken from his concussion, from five days unconscious, from his long blackout. He was alive, he was whole, he was a normal young boy. But a specter settled beside Margery: as long as Bruce kept riding, the same thing, or worse, might happen all over again. And no matter how she challenged Reg after Bruce was tucked into bed at night, she was powerless to stop it.

Venturing back to life, the boy quickly knew that his father's conviction hadn't wavered. "Once he got me going," Bruce realized, "he was not going to allow me to stop until I was champion young rider." And although Bruce didn't want to do everything that his father required, he also was becoming his father's ally. He didn't want to quit.

Finding the right partner helped. After his accident, an extraordinary pony came to Bruce Hobbs. She arrived as champion ponies often do, a hand-me-down outgrown by a young partner but also treasured, needing a worthy home. She had been plucked away from a fishmonger's cart, once upon a time, and developed into a star of the show ring and the hunting field. Her show name was Lady Marvel; around the stable, they called her Kiss Me.

Here, in the form of a beautiful white pony, was the springboard to fame that Reg Hobbs craved. Winning at England's top horse shows would advertise Bruce's skill far and wide. Reg exerted every effort to make Bruce and Lady Marvel a flawless team, drilling them for show ring competition, pushing their "in hand" gallop to the edge of control. "They used to say that my grandfather [Tom Hobbs] won his championships by the speed and power of his gallops," Bruce would recollect. "I was made to do the same."

Training sessions were rarely fun. But then came the shows with Lady Marvel, and Bruce realized that, "funnily enough," he "adored" the performance experience. For those several minutes, Reg and Bruce were not at odds with each other. Their painful, painstaking preparations clicked. Lady Marvel strutted. Bruce watched for Reg's ringside cues and followed them diligently. He succeeded so well that in late June 1928 he and Lady Marvel were champions of the children's hunter class at Olympia, the spectacular annual International Horse Show in London. He was only seven years old.

Marion duPont had been horseless at age seven, waiting for her father to finish renovating Montpelier. Now, as her first year without him drew to a close, she was finishing Manton Manor and keeping horses there and everywhere she called home. She also was making a bet with the future: sending her brother several yearling Thoroughbreds she had bred, to be trained along with his Foxcatcher racing stable. She pictured them sharing Will's Saratoga barn next summer. She wouldn't have to make her own way. Like a gentleman, her brother would hold open the door.

Raising her own Thoroughbreds, rather than buying ready-made runners, would test her patience thoroughly enough. Racehorses needed a lot more time to develop than gamecocks or dogs, which could start competing when less than a year old. Once, when asked why she kept on fighting chickens, Marion replied with a humorous gleam, "I like the quick return." With that answer she was skimming the surface, gliding over the

courage that moved her so. But also, she was being honest about the pleasure of investing in something that paid you back fast.

In fact, some of her Thoroughbred yearlings came from early maturing bloodlines that might do just that. While she mourned her father, that
hope might feel especially fortunate. There was nothing like your own
young horses coming along to make the future seem sunny. Until they
proved otherwise, they all might be winners.

Early in the New Year of 1929, with her brother as usual tethered to
his Wilmington office, Marion returned to Altama. It must have been
strange, stepping back into the drawing room where she had last seen her
father alive. She arrived during torrents of rain, trusting her chauffeur,
hazarding their lives on slippery country roads. But when the weather
cleared, everything looked fine.

Back in Delaware, Will considered how to seamlessly bring Marion in
with him at Saratoga, sparing her the typical newcomer's delays. He told
the racing secretary that because Foxcatcher Farms also was managing
his sister's Montpelier Farms racers, they would need at least twenty-four
stalls—"about like Mr. Jeffords and Mr. Riddle's string," Will noted, em-
phasizing his friendship with leaders of the sport and his aim to stand
beside them. He and Marion would happily pay to double the size of the
Horse Haven barn that Will had liked last August. But Mr. Schaumburg
had another idea.

In his third year of targeting Saratoga, Will the builder hit his mark:
he bought some land along Union Avenue, not far from Sam Riddle's
barn. That summer of 1929, Marion's horses would share this private
perch at the Spa, made to Will's design. The Saratoga Association still
seemed unprepared, however, for women playing more than a cosmetic
role with racehorses. While paying stakes race eligibility fees—in other
words, aiming for elite events—Marion received more than one form
letter with "Dear Sir" printed at the top. Someone in the racing office
would strike a line through "Sir" and handwrite, "Madam."

Marion might frown at that, or she might give a wry smile. After venturing into sports alongside men so many times, being unexpected
could seem weirdly normal. In any case, Marion saw herself sticking
around. Registering her racing silks with the Jockey Club, she bought

the equivalent of a life membership. Her colors could be a pastel salute to the red, white, and blue flags of America, England, and France—and also foxhunting mornings with pink light warming snow-streaked mountains near Montpelier. You could see it all in the blouse and cap of gentle French blue, with two hoops of old rose and two of silver crisscrossed around the jockey's body like bandoleers. Ladylike, but subtly strong. And soon, as Safety Catch had done in a neighborhood race, a horse told her that she did belong.

At Maryland racing meets every April, the most precocious two-year-olds burst out like crocuses. Marion found herself with a bright early bloomer at Havre de Grace when Lost Agnes, a filly she had bred and raised, "sprang right to the front" first time out and won by four lengths. A racer whose name meant "lost lamb" launched Marion into the sport of kings.

She still belonged on horseback, as well. During the afternoon of June 1, 1929, the petite woman competing under the name Mrs. T. H. Somerville guided Phenolax, her Fair Play son, once more onto a jumping course at Devon, Pennsylvania. If they performed the best of fifty-five contestants in this class, she would win a sort of triple crown. Twice before, Marion duPont Somerville had won the hunter championship of the entire Devon show. If she and Phenolax succeeded today, she would bring the challenge trophy home for keeps.

Two riders attempting the same course suffered what the *New York Times* called "spectacular spills," but not Marion. Wearing her husband's name but using her own inner compass, she met each obstacle with skill and understanding and retired a trophy that said she had been best of the very best, not once, not twice, but three times.

Later that month, eight-year-old Bruce Hobbs enjoyed a last hurrah in the show ring with his lovely white pony. During two years together they had lost only two classes, both when Lady Marvel was distracted by being in heat. Now, nature imposed another limit on their partnership. Before long, Bruce's legs would start hanging below Lady Marvel's sides. Already, his spotlessly booted extralarge feet, like a puppy's outsized paws, hinted what a tall man he would become.

Although it couldn't be helped, Bruce's outgrowing his nearly surefire winner jeopardized the goodwill that Reg Hobbs radiated after each victory. "Father loved the glory of it," Bruce realized, "and every time we won, there he was in the forefront when the photographs were being taken for the press." The pageantry continued even when they reached their hometown railroad station after a show. Before walking through the village, Reg made certain that the victory ribbons were fixed just right onto Lady Marvel's bridle. Even their homecomings advertised their success.

And now, one more time. Bruce trotted Lady Marvel into the splendid arena at London's International Horse Show with a special goal in mind. Topping the adult hunters, Tom Hobbs already had earned a place in the Olympia parade of champions. If Bruce won the children's division again this year, he would join his grandfather on parade.

One more time, catching his father's signals. One more walk, trot, canter, and glorious hand gallop, both ways of the ring. One final triumph for Lady Marvel. But it wasn't his own performance that Bruce treasured. Following his grandfather around the arena in the parade of champions became one of his proudest memories.

Bruce also caught glimpses of life beyond the horse business. He loved visiting his mother's good-natured parents and especially enjoyed it when his grandfather Robertson, the policeman, sometimes drove his powerful car alongside the railroad tracks and raced a train. He saw his mother playing bridge, applying herself to the card game with a devotion that nearly matched Reg's horse mania. And for a brief time each summer, his family traveled to the town of Skegness, beside the North Sea, for Reg's golfing holiday. "We had a house along by Seacroft golf course there," Bruce would recall, "and the Whitton boys, who were my chums, were very keen golfers. I wasn't very keen. By now all I wanted to do was ride, despite the discipline and the falls." But as much as he loved horses, Bruce did not imagine growing up to be a professional horseman. "I had my heart set," he confessed, "on being a veterinarian."

Veterinary medicine didn't often offer glory. Then again, one could help animals and perhaps earn a good living. The same held true, Marion duPont Somerville had discovered, for those who trimmed and shod racehorses' feet. Her brother had found a superior farrier, Joseph E. Bell, who did an admirable job with Marion's yearlings that summer but also left her with a case of sticker shock. Worth it, Will insisted. "Make whatever arrangements you can with Bell to come every month or so to look after your horses," he urged his sister. "I know that he charges high, but it is money well spent." Because Mr. Bell had more than enough work near his northern Virginia home, Will warned her, "You will have to deal with him as best you can in order to get him to go over to Montpelier."

Marion actually was turning Montpelier into a destination, although not what patriotic and historical societies had envisioned after her father died. Montpelier's Thoroughbred broodmare band was growing and Marion was buying a son of Man o' War to stand at stud. It seemed like a perfect time to be expansive. That summer, Lost Agnes had won several thousand dollars racing at Chicago. That autumn, the DuPont company reported that its earnings from January through September had risen nearly $1 million per month, compared with the same span of 1928. Marion received extra dividends.

Meanwhile, racing fans heard nothing of the Man o' War son named Battleship. Too small and immature, he only exercised while other two-year-olds shone. And while he awaited his first race, the world for which he had been bred convulsed.

Horse racing wasn't traded on the New York Stock Exchange, but it had been surging along with America's economic boom. Man o' War yearlings sold at auction for as much as $65,000, a ridiculous price—yet leaving room for a sweet profit by winning one race, the Futurity, the richest in the world. So why not? On Wall Street and in racing, investors made increasingly far-fetched promises while optimal returns kept rising, seeming to justify their gambles. People borrowed and spent as if revenues always would go up. But during September 1929, the foundation beneath their fantasies started quivering. Small speculators without deep roots began sliding out of the market. Then came October 24 and 29, Black Thursday and Black Tuesday. Reality shook everyone.

Even DuPont stockholders couldn't be complacent. Black Tuesday—a sudden, violent "hurricane of liquidation," said the *New York Times*—swamped the blue-chip and gilt-edged stocks. DuPont dropped from 150 points to 70, losing more than half its price in one day.

On the other hand, the company founded on gunpowder no longer depended on any one thing for its survival and success. Nearly a month after the crash, a reporter noted that DuPont "[has] carried its diversification further probably than any other organization in the country." The DuPont arsenal included "paint, lacquer, rayon, coated textiles, industrial alcohol, fire extinguishers, motion picture film, chemicals of various kinds and other products that it manufactures directly or through subsidiaries." Along with being "the most influential group in the General Motors Corporation," DuPont had become "one of the largest investors in the country." Such heavy investment might sound like overexposure in a harsh business climate, and yet the robust root system delivered considerable strength. People who depended upon DuPont enterprises for their living would be better prepared than many others to ride out the hurricane.

Looking toward 1930, Marion duPont Somerville didn't back away from Thoroughbred racing but did keep a practical eye on expenses. When a filly that she had early nominated for a stakes race went off form, Marion decided to stop paying the periodic eligibility fees. Because her brother and his office handled her racing stable's paperwork, she contacted him—but this time, instead of requesting services, she wanted a recipe. This time she told Will to have one of his employees send her the racing secretary's name and address and also asked her brother "how you should word the letter when you want to take a horse out of a stakes." She was going to do it herself.

Signing her letter, "Affectionately as ever," Marion was starting to make her own way.

Finding your way. That was part of what foxhunting taught Bruce Hobbs: not only following the crowd, but also recognizing your own most effective path. You had to understand your own strengths and trouble areas. You had to be considerate of your mount and your companions. You always opened a gate for others, if they needed help, then left it how you had found it. You could gallop near the front, if you and your steed were up to it, but you couldn't be careless. You never, ever, trampled a hound.

Bruce adapted so well, the Quorn awarded him its full membership buttons for his hunting jacket while he was only eight years old. Adult riders did not always earn this honor.

The happiest parts of his Leicestershire life were a golden dream, held as fondly by Bruce Hobbs as Marion and Will duPont held Montpelier. The special enclosure he would remember, however, was nothing like their Coney Island. One of Reg's strategies to help Bruce handle everything and anything involved his jumping school at the Warwick Lodge stables: a small, high-walled, oblong outdoor space where the Clarks' hunters developed ideal form over fences. Several poles, which could be raised up to three and a half feet high, formed jumps along one side of the enclosure; the other side featured an open ditch in front of a pole fence. Reg would stand in the middle of the little arena, holding a whip, and turn a horse loose. The riderless horse, wearing only a halter, would canter the perimeter, leaping the poles. Bruce saw that "if they hit those jumps they went straight onto their noses, and they never did that twice." He also saw that when the horses learned they could stretch their necks in midair without a rider pulling at their mouths, "they really reveled in it." When Reg eventually brought his jumpers out of the school and into the countryside with a rider up, they were well-balanced, fit, and confident. Wanting the same for Bruce, Reg sometimes made him ride a horse while it was training inside the school.

Bruce was terrified. The horse couldn't wear a bridle with a bit and reins or a saddle with stirrups, because the jumping school's whole purpose was to keep equipment out of the horse's way. And so, with nothing in his hands or around his feet, the boy had to keep his seat. He couldn't control the horse's head. He worried about falling against the wall or under the horse's feet, with practically no room for escape. He understood why the loose school helped the horses, but for himself Bruce never stopped thinking that it was "quite unnecessary." Looking back, he called his father "a fanatic."

Yet, in his extreme way, Reg was fair. Bruce noticed that his father "applied the same rules to me as he did to his horses." Those rules boiled down to "perfection, perfection and still more perfection," but that was a form of equality. *No one* got away with less.

Bruce also noticed how the stable lads—teenage boys and grown men who served as both grooms and exercise riders—admired his father's ability, style, and daring. Preparing for the hunting season, Reg would lead these assistants and his young son on cross-country gallops. Calling, "Come on, follow me," he would choose what Bruce called "the trickiest little places" to jump or navigate. Reg didn't stop to explain. He simply went for it, and following his example the lads found themselves doing more than they would have dreamed.

Another transformation occurred the winter that Bruce turned nine years old. Mrs. Clark's nephew George "Pete" Bostwick, one of America's foremost amateur steeplechase riders and a frequent guest at Warwick Lodge, thought that Reg's talented boy needed a proper hunter of his own. He gave Bruce a horse named Fisherman, no giant at 15.2 hands yet big enough for many adults. "I was very small for one of that size," Bruce reflected, "but he had a perfect mouth and manners and could really gallop and jump." Chasing his father, out with the Quorn, now gave Bruce less frustration and more exhilaration. "There were a lot of people then who went out to hunt just to gallop across country," Bruce explained. "Once you got going, there was nothing greater. You would look round and there were hundreds of people behind you. . . . Even a grown-up had to have a good horse if he was going to be up there, let alone a child."

It was Bruce's first taste of what it might be like to race in the first flight of a crowded field at Aintree.

7

IT WASN'T SUPPOSED TO BE COLD during late April in eastern Maryland, but Marion duPont Somerville could handle that. When record low temperatures and morning snow flurries appeared as far south as Washington, DC, her wardrobe offered several stylish combinations of tweeds, woolens, furs, and accessories. Marion might not be the belle that her mother had envisioned, but she did know chic. And even though she had grown up seeming more like a pragmatic tomboy than a girly girl, she liked sportswear with touches of feminine allure: a trendy hat or smartly patterned fabric, a modish clutch purse or pair of sassy shoes. Never flamboyant, she still let her clothing flirt a little. With formal dress, she favored sapphires that accentuated her blue-gray eyes.

Now she stood inside the paddock at Havre de Grace, probably without sapphires but glinting with anticipation despite the drizzle of cold rain. Even when she didn't have a horse running, Marion looked out for ones she might buy. Today, Havre de Grace hosted an auction before the races, including several lots from Glen Riddle Farm. Marion would be keenly considering any with Fair Play or Man o' War blood. And something else made her mission all the more pleasant. Looking back at this particular day, she would remember enjoying the company of two attractive young men.

The younger one—tall, blond, with thoughtful eyes—was twenty-three-year-old Noel Laing, jump racing's latest sensation and Marion's new employee. The older—not as tall or broad shouldered, dark haired, with mischievous eyes—was twenty-four-year-old Carroll Kinney Bassett, an avid foxhunter and polo player who was becoming known for his graceful bronze sculptures. Laing and Bassett both dressed with the casual poise of prep school graduates but also looked like opposites, a yin-yang of strong and slight, light and dark. And yet people who came to know them would see that they shared a not-quite-tame quality that could cause a friend to smile and say, "hell-raisers."

Many years later, Marion would remember herself in the Havre de Grace paddock with Noel and Carroll, all three of them "drooling" over a certain horse. This may have been a rare time when she recalled not what *was* but what *should have* been. Noel Laing had no hunt races to ride that week and could have joined his new patron on a talent-scouting mission. But was Carroll Bassett really part of her life yet? Carroll had made few tracks in the racing world, none visible in Marion's life. Maybe she only came to feel that he had been there from the start. Maybe, toward the end of her own life, she couldn't picture that pivotal day without him—a person who would become so closely connected with what she wanted to do, who she wanted to be. Or maybe Carroll actually was there, not to work for Marion but as Noel's close friend.

They would make an interesting trio, the boys bending near to catch her occasional soft words. Beyond their skill with horses, the young sportsmen might not seem to have much in common with a thirty-five-year-old matron. And yet their affinity with her held more than loving horses and dogs and hunting and coming out on top. Like Marion, they would give their all in competition but also appreciated quietude. Like Marion, they were at home with friendly silences and could make a few words count.

Noel Laing had something else in common with his new boss, though she might not know it yet. Like Marion, Noel existed because his respectable parents had broken the rules.

Noel's father and mother had not been able to live together in their hometown of Ballina (pronounced bali-NAH) County Mayo, Ireland. William Armstrong Laing had served honorably as a cavalry lieutenant in the Boer War, but a relative had offended the most powerful man in

Ballina. Sir John Garvey would not let his eldest daughter marry a Laing, any Laing. Eileen Rose Garvey eloped. George Noel Armstrong Laing was born in Doncaster, England, while William Laing reported to the local British Army base and considered where to raise his family.

Ireland was out. America might do. And so Noel Laing took root in pastoral Dutchess County, New York, where his father served as riding master at the Bennett School, a private academy for girls. Noel learned the language of horses, how to read their intentions and transmit his own. He also saw his father keeping the stables stocked with appropriate lesson and show mounts, stretching the school budget by finding rough gems and shaping them toward perfection.

Horse dealing eventually brought William Laing to places that a military man might call target-rich environments: the foxhunting hub of northern Virginia and the sporting resort town of Southern Pines, North Carolina. And William decided, why should the Bennett School own his expertise? Some horses he found might become valuable hunters or show animals. What if he could resell horses he improved and his family could have their own farm? They could join the winter colony at Southern Pines and also establish a base near Warrenton, Virginia, where the rolling hills reminded him of Ireland.

Ireland came to his aid, in a way. Eileen Laing had an inheritance she hadn't collected, coming down from her deceased mother but controlled by her estranged father. When Noel was eleven years old, Eileen brought him overseas to meet his grandfather Garvey at Ballina. At home, seraphic-looking Noel was no saint—tussling with his brother Douglas, "stealing peas from the garden, running riot on the bowling lawn." But his presence at Ballina filled a need. Marion duPont had not been able to know her father's mother, who had longed to know her; Noel Laing may have helped melt away the distance between his mother and her father. Grandfather Garvey gave up his grudge. Eileen Laing went back to America with an emotional burden lifted and also financial support that would have been hers all along if her father had blessed her marriage in the first place. Eventually she was able to help her husband follow his heart to Southern Pines and also purchase a Virginia farm.

Staying in Dutchess County, Noel attended the prestigious Pawling

School. His schoolmates nicknamed him "Mouse." They were being ironic; well muscled and growing to be six feet tall, Noel played year after year on the football team and didn't shrink away from rowdy fun. Yet the name Mouse also told a truth: Noel wasn't noisy, he didn't create static, didn't broadcast himself. Instead, his charisma drew people near.

In 1927, Noel entered the University of Virginia. But he already had been infected by his winter holidays at Southern Pines, where riding and foxhunting formed his all-engrossing curriculum. Leaving school during his first semester, he told his brother Doug that college was "a waste of time." Noel wanted to spend his life with horses, polishing up the hunters and show prospects that his father brought home. Then his father brought him a racehorse.

In truth, when Ballast II came to the Laing family, he couldn't race. He was too scared and angry to do anything but shy away or fight. Up in New York, he had been a winner, then gone sour. Not long after Noel quit college, Ballast stopped cold about halfway through a steeplechase at Belmont Park. William Laing had bought a proven racer with fine bloodlines, but after arriving at Southern Pines, Ballast wouldn't even come out of his stall. And so that was where Noel's essential self went to meet him.

Noel couldn't bluff. Horses usually see through a lie. Horses also are quick to see a threat in any situation where they ever have been threatened. When Noel came to the barn, he knew that he didn't intend any harm, but Ballast did not see that. It did not take hours or days for Noel's gentle sincerity to reach Ballast—it took weeks. Finally, Ballast agreed to step outside of his stall.

Accepting the routines that lead up to being ridden, Ballast let Noel saddle and bridle him and climb onto his back. Then he would not budge. Days, weeks, months passed while Ballast gained confidence in Noel and finally agreed to walk, trot, canter again. When they had built their rapport in motion, Noel pointed Ballast toward a log on the ground and asked him to walk over it—the first step toward jumping. Days and weeks passed before Ballast would take that step.

And yet whenever Ballast did dare to step beyond his fear, with Noel he found a person who guided him without being in the way. Despite his football player height and breadth, Laing centered flawlessly on horseback. He didn't fidget in the saddle or fuss with the reins. Those who watched him ride said that he had "very quiet hands."

A year after stopping cold at a pliable Belmont Park hedge, Ballast carried Noel Laing over rigid timber fences in the Warrenton Hunt Cup. They finished five lengths in front, then were disqualified for a rookie mistake: going outside one of the flags outlining the course.

Ballast lay low during 1929, though Noel kept himself certified as a "gentleman rider"—qualified to ride races sanctioned by the National Steeplechase and Hunt Association but not a professional jockey. Noel's social standing placed him among the gentlemen; eventually, needing to earn a living, he would discreetly accept compensation. But before finding patrons, he needed to become good enough to earn their support.

In time, Ballast would bring him there. Meanwhile, the world he entered on horseback kindled friendships that would last a lifetime.

A hundred miles down the road from Southern Pines, another sporting family wintered at Camden, South Carolina, and leased a "cottage" called Goody Castle. Their castle actually was a clapboard 1820s mansion, with tall, square columns anchoring its proud piazzas. Its façade fit with languid scenes of the Old South, but a Northern man of means had made it his family's winter retreat. And so Camden was where Carroll Kinney Bassett practiced polo, foxhunting, and horse showing during the years that Noel Laing spent his own school breaks at Southern Pines.

During those winters, Carroll and Noel traveled in overlapping circles of horse people who shared many social and sporting events. They became friends within an atmosphere like Marion and Willie duPont's Coney Island, upsized for adults. A description of winter haven Aiken, South Carolina, at this time fit Noel and Carroll's world as well: "One may begin the day in the frosty dark with fox-hunting, watch the sun rise like a stage spectacle behind the boles of mysterious pines, thrill with a gallop and the cry of Southern hounds, return for a second breakfast and a morning of polo or lawn-tennis; after luncheon shoot or play golf or court tennis; then tea and bridge, then dinner and more bridge or puzzles. If only the thirsts of life could be assuaged with games, this would be the fountainhead where all could repair and be satisfied."

Games. There lay a key difference between two young men who would brighten Marion duPont Somerville's life. For Noel, his favorite games also meant business. For Carroll, they all were pleasant distractions; he was supposed to end up doing something serious with his life. Noel's father saw the worth in becoming an elite professional horseman, similar to Reg Hobbs. But Carroll Phillips Bassett was a different kind of seeker: a civil and mining engineer who belonged to several honor societies, a professor at Pennsylvania's Lafayette College who also built utilities plants from South Carolina to Connecticut, a "quiet philanthropist" who also took great interest in genealogy and proved that he was entitled to display a coat of arms. He hailed from Brooklyn but settled at Summit, New Jersey, where Carroll Kinney Bassett was born in 1905. Before long, the elder Carroll secured a building site on a hilltop where George Washington's Continental Army had kept a signal light burning and began developing a home worthy of his pride. The Bassetts moved into Beacon Hill, a twenty-seven-room custom-built mansion, when their eldest son was about six years old.

Growing up at Beacon Hill, a boy might get the feeling that anything less than knighthood would disappoint his family. Every time he passed the main stairway landing, young Carroll could see two coats of arms shining at him from the stained-glass window: his mother's Kinney crest with its three canaries, his father's Bassett shield with a chevron and three hunting horns. The canaries probably were a pun on the name Kinney, and perhaps they appealed to Carroll; he always liked birds. The ancient Bassett symbols, however, spoke of weighty responsibilities. The chevron represented the rafters of a house—someone who had been a mainstay, an essential support, while helping something momentous get done. The hunting horns signified, as one heraldry expert wrote, "an ardent and valiant sportsman, sometimes the keeper of the park of a king or of a nobleman, a position of great honor in olden times."

As a three-year-old, Carroll Bassett already sat beautifully straight in a rocking-horse saddle and beamed a winning smile. As a nineteen-year-old, graduating from the Westminster School in Simsbury, Connecticut, he appeared in his senior yearbook profile as someone itching for an old-fashioned sporting life rather than an Ivy League college degree:

> When Carroll isn't writing poetry or drawing, he may be found pruning the feathers of fighting cocks or instilling some of his own savage temper into pit bulls or wagering his weekly pay envelope on the sport of kings. As horse-racing cannot be found among the sports of the school, he had to take the next best thing and become manager of the track team. On pleasant days he may be seen bestriding his prancing steed and tearing up the turf of the football field, which he claims ought to be converted to use for polo. If he doesn't spoil his chances by accidentally studying and getting admitted to Princeton, he will soon appear as the Sportsman in the Art and Literature of America.

Carroll didn't go to Princeton. He tried the academic route not far from Saratoga, at Williams College in western Massachusetts. Then he jumped over to the Art Students League in New York City. Noel Laing's quiet hands were meant for encouraging a horse; Carroll Bassett's had a gift for modeling life into clay.

Cast in bronze, his sculptures didn't look like heavy metal. His horses seemed as if they might take a breath. Here was a career for Carroll within his world of games, a world in which rich people paid well for true portraits of the animals they loved. And yet he didn't seem hungry to do business. He sculpted what and when he pleased. He also competed as a rider, for fun. During the winter of 1930, while Marion and Tom Somerville sojourned at Altama, Carroll Bassett won a quarter-mile dash at the Camden Hunt races and ribbons at the Camden horse show. But he wasn't ready for the challenge that appeared at Camden in late March: a new steeplechase called the Carolina Cup.

This was a big deal and looked it. Set inside a six-thousand-acre private estate, Springdale Race Course was so spacious that the Carolina Cup contestants would race three miles without taking any jump more than once. Springdale also was so flat and clear that even though there was no grandstand, spectators could see every fence. On Carolina Cup day, their automobiles, saddle horses, buggies, and carriages surrounded the field where Noel Laing was going to make his name.

Most of the crowd weren't looking for Ballast II. But suddenly no one could miss him, blazing down the homestretch and seizing the lead from a well-fancied runner, winning by daylight. Soon word got around that the young man who put up a perfect ride not only owned and trained Ballast, he had taken a ruined horse and breathed the spirit of competition back into him. If Carroll Bassett didn't already know Noel Laing, he sure wanted to meet him now.

And if Mrs. Thomas H. Somerville attended the inaugural Carolina Cup, the newspapers didn't notice her. But she felt the ripples that Noel made and sensed the rightness of him when he and Ballast reappeared. On back-to-back weekends Noel and Ballast won the Middleburg Hunt Cup in northern Virginia and the Deep Run Hunt Cup near Richmond. They were vaulting toward the top rank of hunt racing when Marion du-Pont Somerville hired the quietly compelling young man to handle 'chasers for her and invited him to scout horses with her at Havre de Grace.

And Marion would remember another magnetic young man joining them, one who could match his family's Goody Castle with the Gothic revival castle where she had been born. A slender fellow with an unexpectedly deep voice and a roguish, gap-toothed grin. A person near the brink of an arresting future, whatever that might be.

Havre de Grace, Maryland, was a saltwater village built around taking a shot. Hunters had discovered it in the early 1800s, back when ducks and geese on the wing could blacken the sky above the Susquehanna Flats. Gamblers discovered it in 1912, when Maryland remained one of the few states that wouldn't outlaw betting on horse racing and New York sportsmen opened a fancy new track at this safe haven.

A devil-may-care flavor spiked its natural charm. From the racetrack's backstretch, folks who didn't mind skirting the law could step down to the Susquehanna River and enjoy bootleg whiskey from the houseboat *Bugaboo*. From the clubhouse, spectators could see beyond the finish line to the nearby Chesapeake Bay. In the paddock, watching young horses, they might see tomorrow. The vision might come any day, a random day, such as Wednesday, April 23, 1930.

The prerace auction had been disappointing; Marion bought nothing.

But later that afternoon, a high-headed red colt with a familiar swagger entered the Havre de Grace paddock. Seeing that Man o' War attitude, racegoers who didn't study past performances might wonder why this little powerhouse was the longest shot in the field. A small, lithe woman wondered something else. Earlier that week, she had admired Walter Salmon's strikingly handsome four-year-old Man o' War colt, Annapolis. Now, a current of understanding zipped between her and her companions. Within moments, Marion duPont Somerville set her sights on Battleship.

She saw beyond his face. Later, someone would remark that Battleship "wouldn't have won the head-over-the-stall-door contest, that's for sure." From some angles, his Roman nose and thick muzzle seemed to belong on a draft mule. From his intelligent eyes to his hind heels, however, Battleship looked like a flying machine. His lengthy, supple neck said balance and reach. His well-sloped shoulders let his front legs bend well up and reach far out. All four legs, perfectly proportioned, advertised strength and efficiency. His short back suggested the ability to carry weight easily, while the long underside of his body—setting his front and hind legs well apart when viewed from the side—indicated extra inches for each galloping stride. His neat hindquarters formed a motor with plenty of push and no unnecessary bulk. His face was rough-hewn; his body deserved a design award.

Watching Battleship circle the paddock, Marion could see him flying over fences. She was going to make that happen. She would tell Walter Salmon that she wanted to buy both Battleship and Annapolis, though perhaps not how *much* she wanted them. She knew how to drive a bargain. All her years as her father's shadow, then learning on her own, came into play; all her scouting trips as a twenty-something-year-old, motoring from Orange up to Warrenton and Middleburg, or over to Richmond, or down to Charlottesville to look at horses, horses, and more horses. She had to buy Battleship. Then she had to help him make the transition from someone else's demands to his own utmost abilities.

8

I F MARION'S FILLY LOST AGNES WAS a crocus, Battleship had started out like something that might not come up until autumn or maybe even a biennial that wouldn't bloom during its first year at all. He was too small at age two, actually small enough for Bruce Hobbs to ride if a child could handle a young Thoroughbred. Eventually, the little colt might justify the expense of importing Quarantaine from France and sending her to Man o' War. Successful racehorses weren't always large. On the other hand, Man o' War's best sons yet, champions American Flag and Crusader, were bigger than Battleship.

Battleship couldn't be rushed, but that was okay. During springtime, Walter Salmon focused on his three-year-olds, hoping to win his third Preakness Stakes in seven years. He would be delighted when his colt Dr. Freeland captured the 1929 Preakness in front of a crowd sparkling with celebrities, including the comedian Will Rogers.

A week later, something more surprising happened: a ponylike gelding named Clyde van Dusen became the first Kentucky Derby winner sired by Man o' War. Standing several inches shorter than his sire, Clyde looked so puny that his trainer warned his new jockey not to be disheartened when he entered the paddock for the big race and saw his Derby mount for the first time.

Clyde van Dusen's light body weight, however, may have helped him float over a deep, muddy track on Derby day. His smallness also recalled his legitimate heritage. Although the average Thoroughbred had become a taller, more imposing animal, old influences lingered in the genes: desert Arabians, hot-blooded Barbary and Turkish chargers, spry Irish Hobby horses, and tough, fleet Scottish ponies called Galloways. An ideal racehorse really wasn't any one size or type. What mattered most was fitting the task, and moment, at hand. The same held true for riders, champions as different as tiny Marion duPont Somerville and gangly young Bruce Hobbs.

Battleship made it to the races on the day before Thanksgiving 1929. He caught the tail end of Eastern racing, at Bowie, Maryland, a track that expected its patrons to be uncomfortable. Bowie's racing dates huddled within the chilly first days of April or final weeks of November. Its grandstand stared directly into the slanting late afternoon sun.

Spectators did not need to squint, yet, when Battleship appeared for the first race on Wednesday, November 27. It was nearly one o'clock; the sun was just beginning its downward slide, barely casting any shade. And still a shadow preceded the alert little horse who carried his rugged head on a periscope neck, the unmistakable mark of his sire. Whether they read his pedigree in the *Daily Racing Form* or read his ancestry in his physical form, people looked at Battleship and quickly saw Man o' War. And then they were partly blinded, no matter which way the sun was facing. They would see the father, no matter what the son revealed.

Many spectators watching Battleship today had seen Man o' War race in Maryland or New York. Some may have been at Belmont Park when the tall, lanky red colt won his debut by six lengths with his rider telling him to slow down. Man o' War simply was that much faster than his so-called peers, right from the start. But today, this colt, resembling Big Red and representing a leading stable, obviously had been delayed. By November of his two-year-old season, Man o' War already had won nine of ten starts and retired for the winter. Experts already had compared him with all-time greats. Battleship could not come anywhere near his sire's status at age two. Spectators might guess why he lagged so far behind.

They saw an immature colt, slow in physical development. They also might see an attitude problem. Man o' War had gone racing as naked as possible. Battleship needed blinkers. Leather crescents sewn onto a cloth hood shielded his eyes from distractions off to the side or behind him. The blinker hood added to his air of inexperience, not really knowing what he would be up against. Then again, most of his opponents today wore blinkers, too. Battleship seemed to fit in with this gang of borderline misfits, two-year-olds who had reached late November without winning a race—except he was the only one who never had raced before. Did he have more potential, because no one had beaten him yet? Or was he so far behind everyone that he could not catch up today?

Somewhere among the crowd, the vice president of the United States weighed his wagering options. Like many politicians, Charles Curtis found Bowie—only fourteen miles from Washington, D.C.—a convenient place to go racing. He also had an insider's view of the sport, having ridden many winners at his grandfather's bush league track in Kansas during the 1870s. Curtis had stopped race riding around age sixteen but fondly remembered how gamblers and fancy women who won bets on his horses had showered him with presents. One bawdy house madam had given him a new set of jockey clothes.

Vice President Curtis might be too savvy to bet on Battleship, the well-bred question mark. The little colt did draw his stable's top jockey, Lou Schaefer, who had won the Preakness six months earlier wearing Salmon pink with a diagonal blue sash and white sleeves. But one of many unknowns about first-timers was how they would handle the start. Each horse had to walk into "the machine," a line of partitions stretching across the track. Battleship had practiced standing in a stall, then galloping out—but now he stood smack in the middle of thirteen other babies who were supposed to behave until James Milton, who had triggered the barrier for Man o' War's Preakness, sent them away.

Milton hit the switch and for a moment Battleship echoed his sire, jumping out faster than all six horses to his inside. For a moment, he joined three others in the first flight.

Then the field swallowed him. While four other runners juggled first place, Battleship settled into midpack. His rider knew that they had a long way to run: seven furlongs, each furlong marking one-eighth of a mile. He didn't want to start out too fast. But when they hit five furlongs, where Man o' War's first race had ended, Battleship was well beaten and still had a quarter mile to go. Overwhelmed, he finished seventh of fourteen runners, one of whom had been left at the start.

Shortly afterward, Eastern racing closed for the year. Top horses took a winter vacation, staying in light training but out of competition. Battleship, just getting rolling, was sent after more experience. An assistant trainer took him far south, where mild weather offered slow bloomers a second summertime.

Florida. The name evoked a fantasy land where millionaires pretended Palm Beach was Monte Carlo and someone might sell you a swamp if you weren't careful. It conjured up a tropical frontier, a hiding place for the Seminoles, the only native tribe that never had surrendered to the U.S. government. It offered a gateway to Cuba, where playful Americans enjoyed winter racing at Havana. Florida also offered a track near Miami, another off-season option for barns that needed earnings all year in order to survive and rich stables schooling their second- and third-stringers.

In early December 1929, Battleship rode a train into Florida but stopped short of Miami. He disembarked near Bayard, a railroad rest stop halfway between Jacksonville and St. Augustine. Bayard contained no houses and only two businesses: a three-story post office/general store/ hotel and a hinterland racetrack called Keeney Park.

Clearly, horsemen didn't come here for the nightlife. They came for cash money at a slow time of year. Former silent movie producer Frank A. Keeney had sold his three Brooklyn vaudeville theaters to create this racetrack. Now he was being generous with horsemen who supported his dream. Keeney Park had given out $100,000 in purses during its previous meet and was promising $175,000 during the financially unsettled winter of 1929–1930. Hundreds of horses joined Battleship in the wilderness beyond Bayard. And yet everyone coming here knew they were making a leap of faith. Keeney Park's previous meet had shut down early, for a simple reason: betting on horse races was illegal in Florida.

This time, Frank Keeney thought he had the problem licked. Keeney Park would use an old dodge called the envelope system. For each bet, two people sealed their money into an envelope and a third person held it for them. After the race, the neutral third person gave the envelope to whichever bettor came out ahead. In theory, this was private wagering. In practice, maybe not—especially if professional bookmakers helped fill and hold the envelopes.

During opening day there was plenty of gambling at Keeney Park, where the county sheriff and a deputy patrolled the betting ring not to arrest wrongdoers but to provide security. But a showdown was brewing. Shortly before the second day of racing began, a legal team hired by Tallahassee newspaper publisher Fred Eberhardt told Keeney that an injunction to stop the meet would be coming his way. But outwardly, nothing changed. On day three, Battleship raced.

His second start would be stripped of prestige. No Preakness-winning jockey in the saddle. An assistant trainer, not Walter Salmon's expensive head trainer, strapping the saddle to his back. An $800 purse, the lowest amount offered by Keeney Park.

On the other hand, Battleship seemed to outclass the field he faced on December 17. Maybe a shorter race than his debut, six furlongs instead of seven, also would help him. And maybe, mentally, the little horse was growing up. You might not guess it from the way he fretted in the starting stall and streaked out of the machine, quickly taking the lead, but when a rival tried to start speed dueling with him, Battleship listened to his rider and relaxed. After a flying start, many young horses would be too excited to take back and wait. But Battleship waited until the homestretch, saving energy. Then his jockey said *Go,* and Battleship surged, easily holding first place. Coming to Keeney Park had paid off, and without much time to spare.

Three days later, Frank Keeney caved in. A spokesman announced that the track would close "until such time as the fair-minded citizens of the State of Florida shall insist that their legislators pass laws legalizing the pari-mutuel system of betting." Frank Keeney slunk away to parts unknown. Reporters eventually found him at Daytona Beach.

And the Keeney Park horsemen were stuck up a rotten tree. They were supposed to have three more weeks of racing here to make ends meet. They wouldn't abandon their Thoroughbreds, but where could they take them? The Miami track wouldn't open until January; Keeney Park had shut down on December 21. Trainers, grooms, and exercise boys camped out with their horses and depended on the track dining hall, the only eating place for miles around. Then, like an unreformed Scrooge, Frank Keeney reached out from his hideaway. Why should he pay to keep the track kitchen open? The stranded horsemen found their only eating place shut down and locked on Christmas Eve.

Battleship and his fellow horses had sufficient food, but for most of the humans, Christmas at Keeney Park involved hunger and hitchhiking and a pitiful lack of coffee and sending distress calls out beyond Bayard, which couldn't feed two or three hundred people. Provisions arrived late on Christmas Day, sent from distant cities at the horsemen's expense. As the story spread, one reporter noted that "Frank A. Keeney is about as popular with citizens of St. Augustine and Jacksonville as the Mediterranean fruit fly, which has cost the State of Florida untold millions."

Keeney may have loved racing, but it no longer trusted him. Soon he would sell Keeney Park. Fred Eberhardt, the antigambling crusader who had pressured Keeney into quitting, also found himself unpopular and tried to persuade his neighbors that he actually supported the sport of kings. "I believe that Florida should be the playground of the nation," Eberhardt insisted, "but not through violation of the law." Meanwhile, the state legislature considered the problem with all the speed of a banana slug.

This might have seemed like a good time to rescue Battleship from Florida, but his owner wasn't worried. Whatever the law said, Miami racing would open as usual in mid-January at Hialeah Park. The Miami Jockey Club reported to Joseph E. Widener, the Philadelphia sportsman who had bought Man o' War's sire for a hundred grand. Widener was investing mightily to improve Hialeah from a functional container for gambling to a resortlike destination. A few legal delays would not get in his way.

As 1930 began, the Wall Street crash seemed like an October nightmare that might dissolve in January daylight. Up in Manhattan, Walter Salmon pressed forward with his plan to build a Fifth Avenue skyscraper across from the New York Public Library. Construction would cost more than $2 million, but office space rentals should bring enormous profit. Down in Georgia, Marion and Tom Somerville roamed Altama with their guns and bird dogs. She found good hunting but also noticed several projects needed this year to keep the place in shape. Up in Delaware, Altama coowner Will duPont received her notes of all that needed to be done.

Down in Florida, racetrack and racehorse owners were hoping to transform Hialeah Park's plain concrete grandstand and drab brown infield into something special. When Battleship arrived, it looked like a place where mediocre horses would meet. Joseph Widener's crew prepared for upscale runners and visitors, however, putting the track surface in top condition, increasing the number of private boxes for posh spectators, and refreshing the clubhouse and grandstand decor with warm orange and tropical blue. Friendly reporters expected that Hialeah eventually would draw "the highest class of animals racing on our summer courses," the kind of horse that would win stakes races at Saratoga.

And Battleship, the Man o' War colt from a classic French family— where did he belong? Did he fit today's modest reality or tomorrow's visions? He had won his Keeney Park race with great authority, as if he might become one of that highest class. Would he outshine the "fair class of horses" that Hialeah attracted right now? Or would he prove no better than fair?

The betting public made Battleship a heavy favorite to win his Miami debut, a six-furlong sprint against other winners. The little colt jumped off to another quick start, but this time another horse sped past him. Rain had made the footing wet and heavy. The leader, Rain or Shine, loved it. Battleship didn't trust it and ran with a floundering stride. The *New York Times* praised his "game effort" in finishing second, but the finish wasn't even close.

About three weeks later, Battleship entered a one-mile event and finished next to last. He had gotten tired about halfway home. His pedigree said he should like longer races, so why did he stop? Two other issues— temperament and physical fitness—interfered. Battleship often slacked off during his morning gallops; he needed competition to get his blood up. But being eager to outrun the competition in the afternoon couldn't overcome not being fit enough. He also kept his bad habit of wasting energy at the starting line.

In late February, Battleship started in the one-mile Thoroughbred Record Purse, his first race that actually had a name. This time, he could not
dominate. Whatever Battleship did, a horse named Sand Fiddler did a
little bit faster. Every time Battleship tried for the lead, Sand Fiddler de-
flected him. But Battleship never quit. When a third horse came flying in
the homestretch, the little colt held him off to save second place. The slow
bloomer was almost ready for stakes company.

As always, springtime meant explosive growth in the natural world. Back
at Montpelier, Marion duPont Somerville welcomed new foals and approved a new season of matings. At the racetrack, a wave of maturity
rippled through the three-year-olds. Some already looked like men among
boys; others were just beginning to fill into their adult forms. Battleship
remained one of the shorter boys, but grown-up muscle was starting to
propel his bones. He had been born with a race car body, angled for
speed; now he was getting an engine to match. Maybe he would qualify
for the best race Miami had to offer. On March 4, he would show whether
he was good enough to enter the $10,000 Florida Derby.

Good enough? He was brilliant! This was how racing fans and reporters remembered Man o' War himself, but it was little Battleship jumping
away from the start of the Trial Purse "with the speed of a jackrabbit" and
leading all the way. He won by three lengths without being pushed, his
time only four-fifths of a second behind the track record. One reporter
actually began his story, "Shades of the immortal Man o' War flashed
around Hialeah Park yesterday . . ."—a comparison rarely made, because
it usually seemed ridiculous.

That was Tuesday. Saturday afternoon, Battleship went back out for
the Florida Derby. Four days could be enough time between races for a
healthy horse in good form. Then again, a longer race and faster pace
would make it tougher this time. Battleship grabbed the lead right away,
but Sand Fiddler, who had beaten him in late February, stuck by his side.
Battleship hit the first half mile a full second faster than his Trial Purse
pace, several lengths quicker than he'd gone four days ago. He cooked
Sand Fiddler, who fell back—but wasted his own fuel, too. Halfway
around the far turn, a colt named Titus stuck his head in front. Play-

fellow's Dream and Politen swept after the new leader. Down the home-stretch, Battleship ran on fumes while three horses he recently had beaten took over the race. He would finish more than six lengths behind the victorious Titus. Battleship's result looked bad, yet he performed honor-ably. Sand Fiddler, his speed duel partner, sputtered home ten lengths be-hind him. "Battleship was dead," one journalist bluntly observed, "but managed to save fourth money."

Another, more famous, reporter dismissed the whole race. Once upon a time, Neil Newman had covered Man o' War's career. Now he declared that Titus winning the Florida Derby "merely proves what inferior cattle his opponents were."

That wasn't how Battleship's barn saw it. Once again, Walter Salmon had his eye on Thoroughbred racing's most valuable trophy: the Wood-lawn Vase (pronounced vahz), a fabulous silver Tiffany creation presented each year to the Preakness Stakes winner. Three times, Mr. Salmon had laid hands upon this treasure during a victory celebration, before Pimlico officials took it away for safekeeping. This year, he might earn his own. In 1930, for the first time, the Maryland Jockey Club would present a smaller replica of the Woodlawn Vase to the Preakness winner. Battleship had about six weeks to show whether he could be the one to bring that trophy home.

He was back. Bowie, Maryland, the scene of his first race. A forest of pine and red oak hugging miles of curvy country road and the sudden, surreal sight of a modern concrete grandstand deep in the woods. The same rail-road stop behind the grandstand, convenient for racehorses and specta-tors. The same Battleship, yet different. Last November, he had been in over his head, a little kid pushed off the campground dock and not sure how to swim. Four months later he returned with skills, just in time to represent his sire in a unique way.

James Rowe, the masterful trainer who had handed Man o' War his only defeat with a colt named Upset, had died the previous summer. On April 5, Bowie saluted him with a stakes race, the James Rowe Memorial Handicap. The seven-furlong sprint for three-year-olds looked like a good fit for Battleship, but his presence could seem like an insult to the honoree.

To the last, Jimmy Rowe had been known for *hating* Man o' War, the superhorse he had beaten only once, the juggernaut who kept his own best colts from being champions. When Rowe talked, the glorious Big Red became "that clown," "that big bum," "that lobster."

As it turned out, Bowie couldn't have ordered up a better tribute day. An extralarge crowd, including Vice President Curtis, enjoyed a warm, sunny afternoon. James Rowe Jr. waited to present the trophy. Harry Payne Whitney, who had owned many of the best horses trained by Jimmy Rowe, entered two colts in the Memorial; the crowd favored Whitney's entry to win.

Restless and uncooperative while the seven runners lined up in the stall gates, Battleship didn't look like a good bet right before the start. And yet he timed it right, hitting the front in a flash. Then a long shot gunned for the lead and Battleship listened as his jockey said relax and let him go. Along the backstretch and into the far turn he sat by the leader's hip. Near the quarter pole he took control. Down the stretch, he made it look easy while Titus, the Florida Derby winner, toiled far behind and Harry Payne Whitney's best horse could do no better than third place. Another foe charged at Battleship, reached his flank, then seemed to be running in place. The little red horse didn't need to be hard ridden, didn't need the whip. Jimmy Rowe may have been flailing in his grave as Battleship, the Man o' War colt, won.

Battleship was ready for deep water. He would find it up the road at Havre de Grace, where leading three-year-olds entered a sort of brackets battle. If he did well in the Chesapeake Trial, he would advance to the Chesapeake Stakes. If he did well again—the Preakness.

As Battleship circled the paddock before the Chesapeake Trial Purse, three new friends watched intently from the crowd. A few days earlier, they had gravitated to his older stablemate Annapolis, another Man o' War son. Now they fell for Battleship—his pedigree, his athletic body, his plucky attitude. They began imagining a future with this colt, their interest fueled by three lifetimes of horsemanship, a fortune gained from high explosives, and the steely resolve of hundred-year dreams.

· · ·

Battleship slipped through the cold, misty rain, perhaps not taking any special notice of a small woman framed by a big fur collar, but for the first time having a full view around himself while heading to a race. Today, he did not wear a blinker hood. Instead of sharpening his focus, his handlers wanted him to relax and avoid a speed duel meltdown like the Florida Derby. Before the Preakness, he would have two races to perfect this longer-distance style. And if he won the Preakness he might never be for sale, even to a determined seeker like Marion duPont Somerville. But first, Battleship again would face something that his fiery sire never encountered: a starting gate.

In the decade since Man o' War had retired, American tracks were deciding that starting races from a webbed barrier was dangerous and unfair. Too often, keyed-up runners kicked each other or got turned sideways and left behind. Facing each horse forward in its own box did limit those problems, but new problems arose. Gates needed to be sturdy yet mobile, easy to pull off the course during races where the runners circled past their starting place. How could builders keep the stalls connected without blocking the exits?

When Battleship entered the gate for the Chesapeake Trial, two systems were being tested at various tracks. Many horsemen favored the Bahr gate, with a connecting metal beam secured so high above the stalls that a rearing horse's head couldn't hit it. Others thought this towering structure spooked too many horses and preferred the open-topped Waite gate, with its iron connecting bar sinking into the soil. Havre de Grace used the Waite gate and risked its worst fault. Every so often, a restless horse pawed through the dirt "cushion" and knocked a hoof into the heavy, grounded bar.

Today, entering a low-slung, rattling Waite gate, Battleship showed his restless side. When the stall doors popped open for the Chesapeake Trial, he broke last and finished last—though only about twenty feet behind a winner who was being boosted as a Derby horse. *Daily Racing Form* said simply, "Battleship was outrun." In fact, he was lame. He probably had jumped out of the gate with his right front foot stinging. Back at the barn, they found damage to the coronet band, the ring around the top of the foot from which the hoof grows.

For the time being, Battleship was done. There would be no Preakness. He would retreat to Kentucky and recuperate at Mereworth Farm. But even if he hadn't gone wrong, chances were that Battleship couldn't have done enough that spring. Shortly after the Chesapeake Trial, a long, sleek drink of water made his three-year-old debut up in New York. He hadn't always been the fastest two-year-old, but something about Gallant Fox was so tantalizing that legendary jockey Earl Sande (pronounced SAN-dy) had come out of retirement to ride him this season. It was true that Sande needed money, having lost heavily in the Wall Street crash, and Gallant Fox's owner promised him 10 percent of the colt's winnings. There also might be a matter of pride. Gallant Fox could be lazy once he made the lead; Sande, with his knack for gaining a horse's trust and not overusing the whip, might be the rare rider who could keep this colt's attention all the way to the finish line.

There also was history calling. If Gallant Fox captured the Kentucky Derby, Earl Sande would become only the second jockey to win that classic three times. Finally, there was the lure of pure sensation: galloping an exceptional animal with several gears to spare. Maybe there even would be a flash of extreme power like Sande had felt as a youngster in 1920, when for one Saratoga race he had the mount on Man o' War.

Marion duPont Somerville didn't get a Man o' War colt for her birthday, when May 3 came around and she turned thirty-six years old. Walter Salmon wasn't ready to part with Annapolis or Battleship. Marion had, however, heard his willingness to sell her "one in one season, the other on the next." She also had a runner chasing a big prize on her birthday: a race over post-and-rail fences, or "timber race," up at Warrenton called the Virginia Gold Cup. She had reason to believe he could be, as the saying goes, any kind of horse.

The Jockey Club registered his name as two words. Marion and her assistants rolled the syllables together like galloping hooves tapping the ground: Troublemaker. After seeing him in action, Marion was, she confessed, "absolutely fascinated by the horse." Trouble Maker had been sired by Berrilldon, who once stood at Montpelier. His body, with shoulders strong as pile drivers and a neck flexible as a ribbon, combined extreme power with extraordinary grace. He had utterly failed as an early two-year-old at Havre de Grace but shimmered in his new incarnation as a hunter and 'chaser. Marion saw him win the 1929 Deep Run Hunt Cup and other tough timber races. She decided he must be hers and finally offered a price that Randolph Ortman, who greatly enjoyed riding Trouble Maker out hunting as well as racing him, decided he would be foolish to refuse.

Now Trouble Maker carried Marion's colors into the Virginia Gold Cup, where he would be galloping three miles across natural country and jumping timber fences four feet high. His reputation was so strong that he would go off as the favorite, even though this was his first race of the year. Nearby, Noel Laing and Ballast lined up to go after their fourth cup victory of the year.

Moving steadily without ever reaching the leading group, Trouble Maker seemed out of his league. He would finish last of all. Ballast, on the other hand, raced the whole way near the front, showing his class while awaiting Noel's cue.

Ballast did nothing wrong, but the race suddenly seemed snakebitten as the leaders sprinted downhill toward the finish. Two fences from home, Fore Lark broke down. His injury would prove fatal.

Ballast soared across the final fence with one horse beside him. That horse, Marhill Boy, landed wrong and fell. Marhill Boy would be all right; his rider broke a hand.

Ballast was going to win. He was within fifty yards of the finish line, the best horse over a very challenging course, when Noel felt his hopes give way.

The rushing air that was massaging Noel's face fell still. Ballast wasn't racing, he was stopping. How strange. Noel jumped out of the saddle, his feet smacking earth baked hard from lack of rain. He looked down and saw two breaks where a supple limb should have been. Ballast had stepped in a hole—maybe a wild animal's burrow caving in under his weight, maybe a dent made by a wagon wheel—grabbing the hoof unevenly, wrenching the leg. The natural country had been too natural. Noel would have to say good-bye to his friend, his wary companion who had come to have faith in him and carried the young man into a life he wanted so much.

While three remaining runners trailed past the finish line, Noel made Ballast lie down. A gunshot was coming. He did not want his friend to go with a hard fall.

It was a terrible way to thank the horse who had shared all his courage and trust. Noel refused any attempted consolation from his family and friends. Alone, he walked the dozen miles back to Bunree.

No matter how disheartened he felt, Noel Laing was not leaving the horse business. Unlike all too many young men during the spring of 1930, he was lucky enough to be moving forward in his chosen field. If Noel let grief drive him away from work that he loved, he would hurt himself even worse.

That summer, drought hit the mid-Atlantic horse country. Kentucky became so dry that tourists weren't allowed to visit Man o' War at Faraway Farm—a stray cigarette dropped in the parched brown grass could set the whole place ablaze. Throughout the Bluegrass and across Virginia, horses who usually summered on fresh grass subsisted on hay, as if it were wintertime. With water hard to come by, beef cattle shipped to market early and sold at a loss. People who could afford a vacation from overstressed farmlands might as well take it. In midsummer, Marion and Tom Somerville, along with his sister Jennie and brother Hamilton, set sail for a month in England. They chose a ship from another age, the sister of the ill-fated *Lusitania*. *Mauretania* once had set many speed records crossing the Atlantic but lately couldn't keep up with the newest models from Germany. Entering middle age, she mostly went cruising rather than ocean crossing and, like the other Cunard cruisers, had been painted all white. The crew called her the "Wedding Cake."

Were Tom and Marion feeding each other cake, or smashing it for a laugh? There was dissonance in their answers to a routine customs form question, when Tom Somerville and his siblings each gave their occupation as "none." Marion, whether joking, being pranked, or being underestimated, had hers listed as "housewife."

Some housewife. It was a good joke but also a loaded word. As Eleanor Roosevelt, the New York governor's wife, told *Good Housekeeping* that August, "I think we must all agree that in the wife's job there are three fundamentals—being a partner, being a mother, and being a housekeeper and homemaker." Even without reading Mrs. Roosevelt's words, Tom and Marion were well aware of those common expectations. But how could Marion fulfill them? There still were no children to mother. And while Marion was capable of thoughtful domestic touches—telling her cook, for example, to include a friend's favorite dishes on a dinner menu— her housekeeping and homemaking often went no further than keeping servants who did what they were supposed to do. A managerial burden, but also a far cry from the typical housewife who maintained a home from top to bottom with little or no help.

So that left the third element of Mrs. Roosevelt's formula: partnership. And the way New York's first lady saw it, Mrs. Thomas H. Somerville could have a strong basis for her marriage despite the lack of children and home-making chores. Mrs. Roosevelt noted that, traditionally, "I think we would have put being a mother first and next being a housekeeper and home-maker, and then being a partner. But today, we understand that everything else depends upon the success of the wife and husband in their personal partnership relation. So from the modern point of view that comes first."

To the public, Marion and Tom's "personal partnership relation" would remain obscure. It might seem that they wanted a buffer between them, often traveling with one or more of his siblings. If Tom and Marion some-times slipped away together alone, it was not to cross oceans.

Marion did seem like a thrifty housewife compared with her brother, who made quite a splash during the summer of 1930 by spending more money for a select English yearling than anyone else in the world had paid for a young horse all year. As he had done with The Satrap, Will sent his prize to eminent trainer Max Hirsch. But within the colt's first month at Belmont Park, a headline told the sad result: "Leg Broken, $35,000 Gone."

"I just don't know what to say," Hirsch wrote to Will, "except, that it was one of those things that was unavoidable." Entering a schooling pad-dock, the colt had, Hirsch said, "made a kind of playing jump, half way reared and fell back in an awkward way." Any horse handler, no matter how expert, could experience such a moment. Will duPont would not be casting blame. But he might agree with Hirsch that they had been an unlucky team.

Marion would be saddened by the colt's death and sympathize with her brother. At the same time, compared with him, she seemed extraordinarily cautious. No large sums for an untried yearling, no matter how good-looking and well-bred. Rather than gambling much on untried babies, Marion negotiated fair prices for runners who had proved that they could win.

Of course it never hurt to buy when the market was low. In late September, Annapolis lost badly for the fourth time in a row. It was time for Marion to call in her promise from Walter Salmon and bring Annapolis to her barn.

That October, in the front yard at Montpelier, Annapolis won a hunt race on the flat for Marion. Noel Laing, making progress with a fussy new equine partner, won a steeplechase for her with Trouble Maker. Then Noel shipped a string of Marion's racers down to Southern Pines for hunting and training, stoking up high hopes for the New Year.

The year 1930 had earned a rare place in racing history. With Earl Sande in the saddle, Gallant Fox became the first horse since Sir Barton in 1919 to sweep the Preakness, Kentucky Derby, and Belmont Stakes. Although these rich classics weren't officially connected, a *New York Times* headline borrowed a phrase from England and praised Gallant Fox for winning a "triple crown." That autumn Gallant Fox retired to stud as the first horse to earn $300,000 in one year, bringing Earl Sande's 10 percent higher than anyone could expect.

Meanwhile, Battleship had become a puzzlement. Nine months after hurting his right front foot at Havre de Grace, he still was lame. Some days he might seem to be getting better; others, worse. The experts at Mereworth Farm weren't sure exactly what was plaguing him. They were stuck, unless . . . there might be one almost magical way to see the truth. In late January of 1931, they trucked Battleship a few miles from Mereworth to a University of Kentucky experimental farm. He was going to be the demonstration subject for a veterinary conference clinic on a cutting-edge technique: diagnosing horse ailments using X-rays.

For more than thirty years, X-ray technology had been changing what seemed possible. Physicists reconsidered the nature of matter. Quacks claimed all sorts of magical cures, while reputable doctors pioneered radiology for diagnosing internal problems and even fighting cancer. X-ray imaging seemed promising for examining racehorse injuries but had been slow to make its way from laboratories to fieldwork. When Battleship arrived at the Experiment Station, Dr. D. L. Proctor was popularizing the technique with Thoroughbreds, but most of his colleagues never had seen it done.

For Battleship, much of his Experiment Station visit echoed his recent experiences at Mereworth Farm. Men studied his motion as he walked and jogged back and forth. They flexed his joints, felt his tendons, examined his hoof. But then Battleship had to hold still while a man protected by a thick rubber shield aimed invisible particles at his lower leg and made his inner structure visible, a fortune teller summoning his future.

The X-ray delivered. The veterinarians could see a small spot interfering with the coronet band, a pressure point threatening to become arthritic, ready to form a growth called ringbone. Concussion would make it worse. Reducing stress on the area, however, could make Battleship well. Trimming his toe shorter while letting the heel stay relatively high could make all the difference.

With time and luck, Battleship would race again. Encouraged, Walter Salmon waited to see what the little horse might do for him in 1931.

9

IN MARCH 1931, WALTER J. SALMON completed his crowning glory as a real estate developer: a sixty-story office building at the prime location of 500 Fifth Avenue in New York. Piecing the lot together over many years, he had laid the foundation for a masterpiece. Now an elegant art deco skyscraper waited to be populated. Salmon sounded optimistic. Leases would be in demand, he said, despite the economic depression gripping the world like a boa constrictor and proving more tenacious than President Herbert Hoover wanted to admit.

Could optimism prevail? American factories and industries were cutting back more every month. About 25 percent of union workers were unemployed. Farmers were reeling from drought and price drops. But office workers, on the whole, were hurting less. Maybe Walter Salmon had built for the right niche at this terrible time. Maybe he could muster a survivor's smile when the *New York Times* lampooned America's recent progress as "government appropriations ten times as big, the national debt more than ten times as big, skyscrapers ten times as high . . . unemployment ten times as impressive, legal processes ten times as long . . ."

Maybe success would follow Salmon's faith that empty spaces could and would be filled in a positive way. Maybe people in worse circumstances would think he sounded naïve. Futility filled the news from Germany, where payments required by the Treaty of Versailles were expected to shackle its citizens for two lifetimes. Huge numbers of young people were flocking to the Nazi party, which rejected the punishing debt and promised a powerful identity. Chancellor Heinrich Brüning was trying to win them back but could feel his efforts failing. "Worse than the present world-wide depression," Brüning lamented, "is the shattering of a nation's morale. This nation, as a result of the experiences of the past decade, is beginning to lose faith in an intelligent and well-ordered world."

Thanks to the DuPont Company's deep resources and inventiveness, faith was something that Marion duPont Somerville did not have to lose. As 1931 began, she could feel her racing stable maturing, building her own version of 500 Fifth Avenue. At Camden in late March, she joined the throng pulling cars, carriages, and saddle horses up to the edge of Springdale Race Course and watched her colors parade to the post for the second annual Carolina Cup. Many people seeing her name in the program would know little about her—who exactly was Mrs. Thomas H. Somerville?—but they would admire the young man riding for her. They would respect the fact that Noel Laing, winner of the first Carolina Cup, presented her horse Drummer Boy in this particular race.

Win or lose, Laing was delivering the excellence that Marion had expected when she hired him. She wanted her horses to belong on days like this, in races like this. Today she might seem like a sudden arrival to the folks unfamiliar with her modest success at Virginia hunt meets. But to Marion, today would feel like a long-awaited graduation from Safety Catch's maiden race at the Orange County Horse Show to one of the most acclaimed steeplechases in America.

Today, Marion did not win. But she received encouragement when Annapolis, still new over jumps, ran third in the Springdale Steeplechase. She also was being seduced by Camden itself. Marion was starting to feel how this place harmonized with her self. An unpretentious town, laced with sandy lanes that felt easy under a horse's feet. A welcoming winter climate, with fragrant plants coming into bloom well ahead of her gardens at Montpelier.

Then it was April and Virginia racing. Noel finished second in the Deep Run Hunt Cup with her horse Racketeer, whom Marion said was "amusing to look at" because "he had a back long enough for three people to sit on." A week later she did not place in the Middleburg Hunt Cup, but

suddenly the racing world was admiring her entry for a lesser race—
Annapolis, a stallion so attractive that he was, one magazine told its readers, "worth going miles just to look at." And a winner that day, too.

Then it was early May, and Marion was about to turn thirty-seven
years old. Statistics estimated that despite all of her advantages, her life
was more than half over. And yet she was only now approaching her
prime. When she and Noel Laing teamed up for the Warrenton Hunt
Cup, strong threads were weaving together to mend torn fabric and create a striking new design. A year ago, Noel had lost his best partner when
Ballast stepped in a rut. Now he flew through the same race with one of
Marion's horses, bringing Grenadier Guard home first by twenty lengths.

But their triumph coincided with someone else's tragedy. Noel and
Grenadier Guard had set a fast early pace, alongside a horse named Bluemont. Six fences into the race, Bluemont took a bad fall and broke his
neck. Instead of admiring a lopsided victory, steeplechasing supporters
were asking, *why?* Maybe timber racing was heading in the wrong direction. At only two and a half miles, did the Warrenton Hunt Cup encourage reckless speed? Was it fair to send Thoroughbred racehorses rather
than slower halfbred hunters at such a pace over "practically unbreakable
fences"? That kind of sensational risk never had been the point of this
sport. Timber racing always had been about field-hunting skills, finding
the best route across several miles of countryside at a sustainable pace.
Could it not stay that way? "After all," one horseman observed, "there are
plenty of brush courses around the country for the speedsters to have a go
at, and there is not much fun in having a horse killed."

That was a sensible view. Brush races, using living hedges or wooden
frames padded with evergreen trimmings, gave jumpers a wider margin
of error. And yet only a few days after Bluemont died, many of the same
people who questioned his fate celebrated a horse who had ramped up the
speed craze, the anomaly who had shown "that it is possible to fly timber
jumps as if they were hurdles." Ever since then, others had been trying to
match his daredevil style. But there was only one Billy Barton.

At Pimlico Race Course on May 7, Marion duPont Somerville came to see
the real thing. Three years after leaping the last fence at Aintree along-

side Tipperary Tim, Billy Barton himself led a big field of jumpers to the post for a steeplechase named in his honor. The course also paid tribute to Billy's greatest effort: not post-and-rails like his timber victories, but fences covered with evergreen "brush" like the National course at Aintree.

Surpassing expectations, thirteen-year-old Billy projected such a robust aura that many spectators guessed he would give "a better ride than most of the entrants." At the same time, this race was supposed to honor horses who had something in common with him: only those who had been out foxhunting could participate. This year, Mrs. Thomas H. Somerville's Annapolis followed Billy Barton onto the course.

His presence was a credit to Marion's insight and Noel's fine handling. In only seven months with Marion's stable, Annapolis had gone from never carrying a rider over jumps to entering one of the better brush races in America. He easily could have been overwhelmed among seventeen other horses, "far too many," one commentator said, "for that small infield at Pimlico." But Noel placed him perfectly, saving energy until the final bend. Marion saw Annapolis finish as she had dreamed, blazing over the final jump and denying all challengers all the way to the finish line. He had earned her first major "big track" victory.

And once again, someone else's grievous loss offset her success. Two horses in the Billy Barton Steeplechase suffered fatal injuries. How could Marion risk her horses in such races? one might wonder. To understand, one would need to grow up with the farmer's daughter who believed in testing your livestock thoroughly to find the best lines and not overinvesting in weaklings. If Annapolis could not only survive but thrive racing three miles around Pimlico's cramped course, he proved his good preparation and worthiness. If another horse broke his leg at the fifth fence, maybe it was bad luck or maybe that horse had an inherent problem that blew up under pressure. If another horse fell hard at the nineteenth and injured himself too badly to be saved, maybe human error was involved, maybe he was unlucky, or maybe he lacked conditioning, endurance, soundness. Those situations were sad. But did that mean that no one should try?

To Marion, who rode the Montpelier Hunt's "rough and hilly country," the Thoroughbred horse was not a fragile sports car but a high-powered all-terrain vehicle. You wouldn't save that vehicle for smooth roads or hide it in the garage. Marion believed in seeking out questions and answers rather than backing away.

And beneath her tough-minded demeanor was a woman who knew all too well how it felt to work with a horse, to care about a horse, and to feel a situation jolt beyond control. She might remember when she was twenty-one years old and had to begin a letter, "Dear Papa—I am very sorry to tell you that 'Veronique' is dead,—I am so awfully sorry but it was an accident."

At Montpelier, Marion had been driving a pair of her father's horses from a light carriage. Finishing the session, she signaled them to back up. They would not. She had a stable hand try them with another vehicle, "and Veronique would not back a step," Marion explained. They decided that this particular mare needed a refresher in basic schooling, so the helper unhitched Veronique and asked her to back up using the lengthy reins known as long lines—"and she backed about a step," Marion told her father, "then she suddenly jumped up, reared, and fell over backwards on the back of her head—and she never became conscious again, I telegraphed help right away and they had ice packs on her head, and they thought she would come around, but she died last night at 11 o'clock."

And so young Marion had found herself balanced on the line between responsibility and . . . what? Bad luck? Fate? A horse's perception that knowledgeable humans had failed to understand? They had not been asking Veronique to do anything new, nothing that she had not done well in the past. Marion tried to analyze the fatal moment and seemed unable to name the problem: "The lines were loose on her when she reared up, she reared of her own accord I mean. I felt terribly about it," she had told her father, "but I suppose it could not be *helped*."

The mature Marion tended to act on things that *could* be helped. In June, she informed a sporting magazine that she, not Mrs. T. H. Symington, owned the horse who ran second in the Deep Run Hunt Cup. That had been how Marion started the 1931 season—unremembered, interchangeable. Now, thanks to Annapolis, she would not have to write such a letter again. Few among the racing public knew her true self, but Mrs. T. H. Somerville had their attention.

With Annapolis, Marion also drew extra interest from that charismatic young artist who was riding more and more often at hunt meets, the adventurer with twinkling eyes who sculpted what and when it pleased him. Before long, Carroll Bassett was shaping wire and clay into a beautifully natural likeness. His finished bronze of of Annapolis somehow held more than the outer shape of a horse; it spoke of a relationship. It was perhaps the best piece he had ever done.

The portrait strengthened the bridge between Carroll's world and Marion's, though he remained his own boss. Carroll had his own designs, including racing 'chasers in partnership with his friend J. Spencer Weed, under the name Ram's Head Stable, and the silks he wore while riding them: white with red cap and cuffs, plus a bold red emblem like curled horns on his chest. That summer, he and Marion were friendly rivals during the exclusive hunt meets at Brookline and Framingham, Massachusetts.

Despite Noel Laing's best efforts on her behalf, Marion did not win up north. But with every race in each new place, she gained a more specific idea of what it took to succeed further and further afield. Her horses were preparing her for the uncertain road to a mountaintop, for realities she might imagine but did not actually know. They were schooling her to leap forward or step back with equal willingness, depending on their needs. They were intimating that sometimes the best gift you received was one you couldn't open too soon.

Nearly a thousand miles southwest of Brookline, one of Marion's dreams was slipping out of dry dock and back into circulation. Battleship was leaving Kentucky. The little horse found his situation familiar yet completely new when he stepped out of a railroad car on a Saturday night at Homewood, Illinois. A groom led him to his latest home, the backstretch of Washington Park Race Track. If his foot held up, Battleship would spend his summer racing near Chicago.

Sunday morning, Battleship ventured out onto the biggest course he ever had encountered, a full mile and an eighth around, and logged a slow five furlongs. Wednesday morning, he practically crawled three-quarters of a mile. Before racing, he needed a serious tune-up—and he needed to get his mind back in the game.

A dozen mornings after moving to Washington Park, Battleship headed out with a workout partner: Walter Salmon's champion filly Snowflake, who had run third to Gallant Fox in the 1930 Preakness. Snowflake held Battleship's interest. The pair zipped a mile side by side, finishing only one-fifth of a second behind the fastest work of the day. It was time to choose a race. But which one? The last time Battleship competed, he had been like a college freshman trying out for the varsity. Seventeen months later, it was as if his entire class had become sophomores, juniors, seniors, and graduated without him. Where did he fit now?

His barn had covered the best-case scenario, nominating the little horse for several stakes races on the Chicago circuit. First time out he wasn't ready, however, for the Stars and Stripes Handicap at Arlington Park, worth more than $20,000. He would enter the Nashville Purse, worth $1,800.

On a holiday Monday, two days after the Fourth of July, Battleship stepped into a familiar dream. Someone buckled a blinker hood over his bridle—a reminder not to goof off—and boosted his original jockey, Lou Schaefer, onto his back. For the first time in nearly a year and a half, Battleship paraded past a clubhouse and grandstand, then approached a starting machine. Changing details the way dreams will, instead of a low-slung Waite gate, a skyscraping Bahr gate greeted him. But one of his opponents made the scene weirdly familiar. The last time that Battleship had finished a race, Ned O. had been galloping beside him. Seventeen months later they reunited more than seven hundred miles away, carrying the same weight as they had in the Chesapeake Trial. When Ned O. rejoined Battleship on the track, the perfect measuring stick for ground gained or lost appeared.

Battleship ran as if he were on a mission. When the stall gate sprang, he was the first one out. He agreed to let another horse take over the early lead but easily regained control when that rival tired. At the end of the mile, there was no horse as good as Snowflake, none who could keep pace with Battleship. He galloped home first by several yards. Ned O. never fired and finished ten lengths behind him.

There would be no resting on this success. Only two days later, trainer Jack Pryce sent Battleship out in the seven-furlong Missouri Purse. But maybe the little horse was tired or felt less motivated. Believing that the blinkers were unnecessary, Pryce had gotten permission to race him this time with "blinkers off." Battleship broke well but finished third, five lengths behind the winner.

He would spend the rest of July proving himself, showing that he really could handle basic racing pressures and might be capable of much more. With blinkers back on, he weathered a jockey change and went hard to work. Battleship may have been tired when he ran next to last in his third race in ten days. But then he rebounded, outgaming a former Louisiana Derby winner to take the Racine Purse by a nose and five days later scoring a "handy win" in the Lake Geneva Handicap with yet another rider. During the month of July, Battleship ran *five* races—and won three of them. He was becoming king of Chicago's $1,800 milers. Now he would get a chance to redefine himself. That summer, a champion had set up camp in Chicago. His name was Sun Beau, and on August 1, winning the Arlington Handicap, he became the richest racehorse in the world. On August 8, Sun Beau would enter the Hawthorne Handicap and Battleship would take him on.

This would be Battleship's biggest moment since the 1930 Florida Derby, and actually much greater: facing a proven champion, chasing far more money. He was a minor leaguer finally starting in the majors, a vaudevillian opening in a legit show on Broadway. He might earn a second prize worth nearly as much as he had gathered from five races this July. Or maybe—with luck—he could win. Sun Beau would carry 131 pounds; Battleship, 104.

The weight difference in a handicap race gave owners of lesser horses incentive to take on a champion like Sun Beau. And the longer the race, the more difference each pound could make. Carrying 27 pounds less than Sun Beau while running more than a mile was like Sun Beau spotting Battleship about 20 lengths.

The Hawthorne Handicap might have made up for his Florida Derby failure. Instead, Battleship's do-over turned into déjà vu. Instead of biding his time, he streaked into a speed duel with Dark Sea and Silverdale. Perhaps his featherweight rider had trouble holding him or lacked experience in big races and forgot his strategy. Battleship was going too fast, too soon, to last a mile and an eighth with America's reigning champion older horse. Around the far turn, Sun Beau passed him easily. Battleship faded, beating only Silverdale. Sun Beau looked like a sure winner. But near the finish, one horse blew past him: long shot Plucky Play, carrying only 106 pounds.

With the right rider, helping him save energy for the homestretch, could that have been Battleship surging late?

But what-if had evaporated. Battleship resurfaced in an $1,800 race. This time he carried extra weight but also his best rider; this time he waited, then accelerated around the far turn. With Schaefer urging but not resorting to the whip, he held a one-length lead at the finish line.

Only three days later, Battleship stepped out in a better race, the Great Lakes Handicap. Everything clicked. The favorite held steady down the homestretch but Battleship did more than that. With Schaefer driving hard, he willed himself across empty space, up beside the favorite, then beyond, finishing first by the length of his body. His time for the mile and a sixteenth was only one-fifth of a second slower than the track record. The victory paid $5,025. It was the richest race he ever had won.

The Great Lakes Handicap might have been a springboard to greater things, or at least set Battleship upon a higher plateau. Instead, when the Chicago circuit moved to Lincoln Fields, he dropped into a race where he outclassed the field and didn't draw a first-string jockey. He won with a rally the *New York Times* called "a great stretch run." Then his handlers messed with success. Sprinting next time out, and carrying his heaviest weight assignment of the year, Battleship wilted and finished third. Was it overwork, or something worse? Other Thoroughbreds raced every few days, but horsemen knew it wasn't a pace you could keep up indefinitely. It was a hot iron you kept striking until something went wrong. Battleship now had raced ten times in seventy-one days; champion older male Sun Beau would race fourteen times during the entire year.

Overall, Battleship's return had been a success. So far, at age four, he had won six of ten starts and collected more than twice the money he had earned at age three. One turf reporter hailed him as a fine example of Man o' War progeny improving with age. And yet he had not secured his future. In mid-September, the Salmon stable sent Battleship to New York—where, for the first time, he would enter a race that offered him for sale.

With wintertime only three months away, Walter Salmon was formulating next year's business plan. Battleship already might be past his peak as a racehorse. His right front foot wasn't reliable; he might not stand training in 1932. With his top wins being the James Rowe Memorial and the Great Lakes Handicap, he also had an underwhelming résumé for stud. And that summer at Saratoga, Walter Salmon had seen how badly even the best auction market for young Thoroughbreds was floundering. Yearling colts had averaged a little over $1,700; fillies, less than $700.

All of this meant no cushy retirement plan for Battleship. In September, he traveled to Aqueduct and entered the Bayview Claiming Handicap. The race did provide one protection: only the winner would be offered for sale. But that horse could be bought for $15,000. If Battleship won, licensed owners and trainers would decide whether he was worth that much—a good sight more than he was likely to earn in racetrack purses or a season of stud fees.

Despite getting bumped and sent wide, Battleship *tried*. But he collected only third place. His barn hoped for better luck in the October 3 Edgemere Handicap. *Daily Racing Form* would note that Battleship "raced well in spots and came again at the end." Respectably close, he missed by just over four lengths. But he finished last, bringing no money home.

After twelve races in just under thirteen weeks, the hot iron had gone cold.

Battleship left New York without winning there. He trundled down to Bowie with his stablemates but lived on the sidelines. His foot was ouchy again. It was time for Walter Salmon to give Marion duPont Somerville her chance.

Would she still want the horse? For the second time in his racing career, he was lame. On the other hand, since Marion had last seen him, Battleship had gone from work in progress to professional. A veteran of eight different racetracks, victorious at most. Partner of seven different jockeys and a winner with most of them. Battleship had a problem with one foot, but not with his soul.

"I told Mr. Salmon I would like to take the horse," Marion would recall, "and if he got over this problem entirely, and if he'd let me pay part of the money down, I'd still take him." Because he had been willing to lose Battleship for $15,000 in the Bayview Claiming Handicap, Salmon couldn't ask more than that. They settled on $12,000, $4,000 less than

Marion had paid for Annapolis, who had not been lame. She made a down payment, leaving herself a way out. "The contingency," Marion explained, "was that if he got sound enough to win at the big tracks, in stakes class or near it, I would buy the rest of him."

Once again, Battleship laid up at Mereworth Farm. Marion, meanwhile, headed northeast of Nashville. She had a date with Trouble Maker at Gallatin, Tennessee.

Grasslands racecourse was supposed to be America's answer to Aintree—perhaps even tougher. It turned out to be a fantasy. Most of the horses who ran the Grasslands International Steeplechase in early December of 1930 and 1931, before the Depression killed it, were not really prepared for Aintree afterward. You could build a two-mile circuit in the Tennessee countryside and send a horse four miles, over twenty-six fearsome jumps, and the course might look like Aintree's younger brother—yet it wasn't the same. You could wrestle with Grasslands and not have any promise that Aintree wouldn't throw you. But it was an experiment that Marion was willing to try, on the way to the real thing. Trouble Maker finally was coming to hand.

After buying him, she had discovered that the horse actually could be a troublemaker, though not deliberately. A fretful soul, he needed lots of reassurance around the barn. Sometimes he got so keyed up that for several days he would barely eat. But Noel was willing to give him quiet, constant encouragement and not ask too much too soon. More than a year after Trouble Maker had become hers, Marion had begun seeing what this team might be: her big anxious horse flying his fences like an improbably graceful waterbird, while Laing's improbably strong body centered lightly over his heart. After Trouble Maker ran second in Long Island's famous Meadow Brook Cup, Marion decided that he was ready for Grasslands.

She was right, although he did not win. Far in front came Glangesia, the only Aintree veteran in the field. Fifteen lengths behind him, flying late to grab second place, came Trouble Maker. He had qualified for the 1932 Grand National, but Marion would not send him. An ocean voyage, then only three months to acclimate for the world's toughest steeplechase—no, she would not do that to her high-strung horse. On the other hand, she could feel good about the Grasslands experience. Although only five of thirteen starters finished the course, none of the horses had been hurt.

That weekend, steeplechasing wouldn't come under fire for being too dangerous. That weekend, newspapers took aim at something else. During the autumn of 1931, forty American men and boys had died from football injuries. Forty dead. A very small percentage of all who played the game but more than double the fatalities of the year before. That horrible difference was forcing people to decide how much risk they could tolerate in the name of fun. The St. Edward, Nebraska, school board banned high school football after two players there died. Others argued that football couldn't be separated from physical violence, so if you loved the game you accepted every possibility.

Where should society draw the line? People who didn't ride steeplechasers or play football might be thrilled to watch others do it or might find someone else's risky passion as baffling as Albert Einstein's calculations. When someone got hurt taking a chance he loved but others feared, the fearful ones might find it easy to condemn instead of sympathize.

Could safety be insured, somehow? The question shadowed more than sports and recreation. As 1931 waned, economic depression hit the world with a stark, contrasting light. Could communism turn financial weakness into strength? Could fascism rebuild a badly fractured national character? Could people who believed in less radical systems ride out these rough times without being crushed by the extremes?

Soon after Marion duPont Somerville came home from Grasslands, Chancellor Brüning of Germany delivered an impassioned radio address. Knowing that the further cutbacks could infuriate the German people but desperate to turn back inflation, the government had issued yet another set of emergency decrees. Brüning pleaded with other nations to be generous while Germany made drastic efforts to repay its grievous war reparations. He also warned the swaggering Nazi party that the sitting government would use every power available to prevent an unconstitutional coup. But what if deprivation and desperation pushed even more people to Adolf Hitler's side? Trying to defuse outrage, the latest decrees prohibited political demonstrations until after New Year's Day. Germany's elected leaders were trying to enforce peace. But would their people accept the same risk? Could they, while feeling so much hurt and fear? Where would they decide that safety lies?

Nearly as long as he could remember, Bruce Hobbs had felt how agreement could be a tricky thing. An older person might have pondered how entire nations and worlds could agree when sometimes a man and woman who had vowed to love each other forever could not. A child might not try to analyze the situation but would experience the results. At some point, if a union wasn't going to rupture, someone would not get what he or she wanted.

Bruce's world came apart in 1931, though his parents stuck together. It all stemmed from his father's work. Their American patron, Ambrose Clark, scaled down his horse activities and gave up Warwick Lodge. Reg Hobbs lost his amazing job preparing hunters to perform with the Quorn. Margery lost control of the spacious cottage that a few servants helped her maintain. Bruce would no longer push the Quorn emblem through the buttonholes of a tailored wool coat and send Fisherman along with the first flight.

Marge might have been happy enough if Reg had teamed up with his father, dealing horses in Leicestershire. But losing Warwick Lodge gave Reg an opening, like a racehorse stuck in traffic shooting through a sudden seam with a full head of steam. Brose Clark wasn't leaving Britain altogether. He promised to support Reg in another district and career.

And so, one morning in 1931, ten-year-old Bruce Hobbs left his beloved Leicestershire. His parents drove him away from dreams of growing up to be a veterinarian and toward his father's evolving identity. Margery, unhappy to leave her relatives and friends and worried about her husband's choice, drank too much during their lunch stop and fell into a sulky mood. Reg became a bit tipsy, too, but grew exhilarated as their destination neared. Bruce, feeling sick, thought his new surroundings looked ugly. He never would love West Berkshire the way he had loved Leicestershire. And yet, as his father enthusiastically pointed out the special features of their Upper Lambourn training grounds—home to the famous Grand National veteran Easter Hero—Bruce began feeling excited about his daddy's new profession. From now on, Reg would train racehorses. Steeplechasers.

10

THREE DAYS AFTER CHRISTMAS, MARION AND Tom Somerville spent part of their sixth anniversary quail hunting with her brother. On New Year's Day, Will and Jean duPont marked fourteen years of marriage, a celebration dampened by illness: their three children were "still pretty sick with colds," as Will wrote to Marion, though his ailing wife was feeling "a little better." Will assured his sister how much he had enjoyed their shooting expedition and encouraged her, "Be sure and write me if there is anything you want me to do before you go away."

"Away" meant Altama but also may have meant a side trip to Kentucky. Marion stopped in to check on Battleship, "and you could see," she would recall, "he was going to be sound." She completed the sale with one final condition from the man who had brought Quarantaine over from France and matched her with Man o' War: whenever Battleship retired to stud, Walter Salmon could breed five mares to him. While cashing in most of his investment in the horse, Battleship's breeder still considered the future.

But now Marion would call the shots. She sent Battleship to Montpelier. Then the man who would help him get right came down from Middleburg. He was the farrier that Marion's brother had urged her to keep using, despite the extra expense, back in 1929.

Joseph E. Bell understood how a fault that might seem minuscule, like a human runner flinching from a blistered pinky toe, could throw an entire foot and leg out of alignment and cause chronic damage. Watching Battleship jog away from him and back, Bell studied an engineering problem that could be solved with properly angled hoof trimming, custom-fitted leather pads, and carefully shaped metal. Then he fired up Montpelier's forge and hammered out a solution.

Like the world at large, Battleship needed both stability and flexibility. His foot, his most basic support, was supposed to let him easily move sideways as well as back and forth. Right now, pain was in the way. Mr. Bell trimmed the little stallion's toes short, so he wouldn't need extra flexion to keep from tripping over them. He placed shock-absorbing leather pads between sole and shoe. And for Battleship's problematic right front foot, Bell made a bar shoe—not open-heeled but connected underneath, to keep weakened areas from spreading. At the right side of the heel he added extrawide support, additional metal that, as Marion put it, "kinda went out and around, under the place where he wanted Battleship to grow his hoof back."

For an even foundation, thick shoes and padding went on the other three feet as well. For a few months, Battleship's footwear would resemble a recent movie sensation: Boris Karloff clomping around in Frankenstein's monster boots. The correction would happen slowly. But six months—maybe two inches of hoof growth—should solve the problem.

Marion, meanwhile, did not find it hard to wait for Battleship. She had other worries on her mind.

That winter, hard realities of being caretakers beset the sister and brother who used to have fun pretending they were in charge of sheepshearing at Montpelier. Life, more than ever, demanded stamina.

In mid-January, Will duPont's four-year-old son William Henry had needed two blood transfusions. Then Marion, reaching Altama after stopping at Southern Pines, received a note from her brother's assistant at the Delaware Trust Company: "Will was just in the office for a few moments and was in a hurry to get back home and asked if I would write to you about the children. The girls are getting along all right but William

Henry is very critical. The pneumonia has spread to both lungs and they have him in an oxygen tent." There was hope, but no guarantee, that the little boy would survive.

Marion also worried about a member of her Montpelier family. Essie Seavey Lucas, the farm manager's wife, had become a leading portrait artist in the sporting world. One of Marion's treasures came from Essie's skill: a painting of Marion with her hunter Phenolax and several foxhounds in the front yard at Montpelier. But as Essie reached her sixtieth year, success was overwhelming her. More commissions than ever! It should have been a blessing, but it was too much. Essie couldn't fulfill every request—and yet she couldn't seem to let herself stop or even slow down. The result was what newspapers delicately called "a nervous breakdown."

When one of Marion's trusted employees was in trouble, she was likely to give assistance. In fact, as one remembered, she would offer "more than what you asked for, most of the time." Chances are, she helped send Essie to the Oconomowoc Health Resort in southern Wisconsin, which strove "to give a homelike atmosphere and eliminate as far as possible every suggestion of institutional life." The northern climate should appeal to Essie, a native Vermonter. The extensive gardens and wide range of both indoor and outdoor activities should feed her artistic soul. But in mid-January, while Marion fulfilled familiar rituals at Altama, came the news that Essie suddenly had died.

Maybe distance blunted the impact. More than a thousand miles from Essie's presence, Marion did not see constant reminders of Essie's pain. And perhaps that was a relief, even a relief that a more callous person would have needed less. Marion could appear to be not easily moved, yet in all likelihood she poured energy into keeping her shields up, coating tender emotions with an impressive layer of reserve. "She was," confided one longtime servant who received Marion's unconditional support through a family tragedy, "a very compassionate person."

Marion did not rush to her brother's side while her nephew struggled for breath. Her feelings flew to him through telephone, telegram, and letters written by her own hand. And in a way, her continuing as usual at Altama may have made Will duPont feel a little less like the world was collapsing. He was holding the fort as best he could, at home and at work; she did the same.

Still, as the fourth anniversary of their father's death approached, both Marion and Will reevaluated what they needed from life and what they could give back. Thank goodness, William Henry, though fighting ear infections after turning back the pneumonia, was rallying. At least Will was emerging from his own exhausting siege. But Marion and Will were increasingly feeling that their connection with Altama had run its course. It belonged to a time when they both had borne far less responsibility. While demanding ever more attention, Altama drifted further and further from the main channels of their lives. Even the sense of reward that Marion usually felt from abundant hunting there started waning during her stay. The weather turned unusually dry; the game birds retreated into the swamps.

Then Marion learned that local men had been poaching deer from Altama's vast woodlands. Will's secretary, Earl Edinger, investigated their legal options and reported that "an absentee landholder never does have much influence in the local courts." By mid-February, Will was telling Marion that they could inform the Federal Game Commission that "we are trying to preserve game that is being devastated and that the local officials will not cooperate. That might bring a political influence, which is what you would have to have to meet the situation." At the same time, Will didn't think they should invest in fighting that fight. "Before you come up," he urged Marion, "why not have Blanchett & Calhoun, the Real Estate men run down and look at Altama and have them put it on the market for us."

Perhaps that was easier for Will to say, anchored at a farther distance from the Georgia coast, unable to spend many days at Altama anyway. But Marion agreed.

They would not resolve the poacher problem. It rattled on after Marion returned to Montpelier and Manton Manor. When their resident manager complained in late August, Will responded, "We are planning to sell 'Altama' and, of course, if any prospective purchasers come around and find that we are having trouble with these hunters, it might interfere with the sale, so do the best you can under the circumstances as it is more important to us to sell the place than to arrest the outlaw hunters."

They would release Altama to the past and bring other things to maturity.

Fruition. The idea resonated with a gardener like Marion. You evaluated a landscape and identified what plants should thrive there. You went after the best specimens and gave them whatever nourishment they required. You knew that no plant could bloom constantly but each should come to a peak. You arranged them not to compete with each other but to ripen in wave after wave. Sometimes you waited on one that should be glorious whenever its time came. And one such wait ended for Marion in late March of 1932. Noel said he was ready: Trouble Maker was going to run in the Carolina Cup.

Only three years old, Camden's big 'chase was fast becoming an institution. The Carolina Cup even had an official emblem now, a bas-relief sculpture by Carroll Bassett with a Latin motto that looked important though its message seemed rather obvious: "He has done better than those he left behind."

On Carolina Cup day, Marion's horses seemed ready to fulfill that motto. She watched Noel Laing and Tereus, a fast flat racer she had found in France, battle Carroll Bassett and his good 'chaser Peacock, in the Springdale Steeplechase. Only two miles long, the Springdale was a sprint as jump races go—and Noel and Carroll turned it into a front-running duel. Noel had the faster horse on the flat, but Carroll rode the more polished and proven jumper. Tereus barreled over the brush, then could barely manage his landings. "Two or three times his speed nearly sent him to the ground after taking the jumps at full tilt," one reporter observed. The only saving grace for reckless Tereus was his rider's finesse: somehow, as a journalist noted, "Noel Laing cleverly kept him on his feet."

Tereus nearly tumbled at fence number eight, fueling Carroll Bassett's reckless side. Maybe hustling Peacock along would keep Tereus off balance. But Carroll miscalculated. Peacock took off too far from fence nine, muffed the landing, and hurled Carroll over his head. Peacock got up, unhurt. Carroll brushed himself off and commented, "It's all in the game." Tereus sauntered home first by more than fifty yards.

Last year, a win like that would have been about all that Marion could ask. But this year, Trouble Maker emerged like a revelation from his winter training grounds at Southern Pines. From the start of the Carolina Cup, he and Noel did not hold back. Heading into the final turn far in front, they ran strong while challengers melted from their pace. Then spectators saw an unlikely quick movement among the trailers: rider Ray Woolfe kicking Primero into high gear.

Galloping alone through another zone, Noel thought that he and Trouble Maker were home free. One more jump, then a procession to the finish line. But as they collected for that one last leap, Noel heard an astonishing hoofbeat crescendo—Primero nearly upon them, making Noel "the most surprised man in the world."

Surprised, but not immobilized. As Trouble Maker's front feet landed and his hind legs swung down to push forward, Noel threw his own momentum forward with his horse. Trouble Maker felt his urgency and sprinted as well as he could, the crowd shouting for him and yelling for Primero, he and Primero closing into "one of the hardest and fastest three miles ever run by steeplechase horses." They ended with about four feet separating nose from nose, four feet that Trouble Maker would not give away.

Walking back to the paddock, horses and riders were engulfed by the cheering crowd. Then someone extracted Marion from the mob, bringing her forward for the formal ceremony, standing close by the winning post while a Fox Movietone newsreel camera whirred and the governor of South Carolina speechified and handed her the cup. She stood before the exuberant crowd with the founders who had made this day and other men who led the sport, while her husband and her brother watched. Soon her image would flash before the eyes of strangers, aimed at movie screens.

That evening, hundreds of people attended a ball at Camden's Kirkwood Hotel, "an occasion of unusual brilliance," the local paper bragged. Noel and Carroll and other riders who had thrown themselves into the afternoon's sport galvanized the atmosphere, dressing like elegant gentlemen but also bringing a form of nakedness to the party, because everyone had seen their characters laid bare on the course. They would seek out Marion and Tom Somerville, Tom's brother Wilson, and Marion's brother Will, the newcomers savoring a breakthrough success. And Marion could be thinking, *Maybe this is it.* Maybe Camden is the place where we should meet up in midwinter, our new Altama. Our Southern Saratoga. This place where people live and breathe *horse*.

That night, they celebrated what had just been and probably imagined what could be next. Tereus, the tearaway brush racer, would aim for big track purses at Pimlico. Trouble Maker would not chase purse money but rather a bigger challenge: the toughest steeplechase in America.

Four miles, twenty-two timber fences. A loving cup for the winning owner, a large silver tankard for the rider who could brave those obstacles and get home first. Not a public racecourse but the confluence of two farms in the Worthington Valley northwest of Baltimore, where cross-country riding remained a way of life. Only one race for the entire day and not a penny paid for any placing in it—but a nation's top timber horses gathering for that one race and a small city's worth of people coming to see it. This was where Marion duPont Somerville, Noel Laing, and Trouble Maker landed on the last day of April 1932: the Maryland Hunt Cup.

"To look up at the broad, steep hill from the paddock that nestles at the bottom, and see those thousands of faces," gentleman rider Bill Streett reflected, "and then to glance around at a handful of horses, only eight this year, and know that anyone of those spectators would give his eye tooth to own the winner, or even a horse capable of starting, brings home forcibly the greatness of the event. There is a feeling that one gets in the paddock of the Maryland absent from any other race."

Marion had come to watch it several times. Never had she dared to enter a horse. Owners could take a casual long shot to some races, but this one demanded the right horse at the right time. Now she brought Trouble Maker, nine years old, a talent several years in the perfecting. She entrusted him once again to Noel Laing, who had walked the daunting course and talked strategy with other horsemen but was riding it for the first time.

They would be facing seven select opponents. As one commentator wrote, "There have been larger fields starting in the Maryland; but none better." They would be facing last year's winner and another who had set the course record two years ago: Brose Hover, with the redoubtable

Downey Bonsal up. One thing heaped extra uncertainty onto an already chancy event: Bonsal was riding "heavily bandaged" underneath his silks. Two days earlier, he had dislocated a shoulder. Now he was going to gallop four miles with an eager horse, jumping unforgiving fences up to five feet high.

Setting out from the start near the spectators' hillside, Trouble Maker led the field back past the paddock but angling leftward and crossing Tufton Avenue, entering the fields that held most of the course. He safely leaped the towering third fence, nicknamed "Union Memorial" because it had sent so many riders to the nearest hospital. He led the field over pasture fences with flags marking which panels to jump, turning left and uphill, then left again and into the tree-lined backstretch that paralleled the spectators' hillside across the road. For a while, Trouble Maker traded the lead with Comea, the least distinguished horse in the field. Then Brose Hover shot forward like a car with a stuck accelerator. It was too early for such speed, but his rider couldn't help it. Downey Bonsal's bad shoulder had slipped out of its socket. For the next two miles, he would be hurting like hell and trying to guide his headstrong horse with one arm.

The others let Brose Hover go. No sense chasing a runaway—though to the crowd it looked as if Trouble Maker kept trying to close the gap and Brose Hover kept stretching it out. No one else threatened.

Then they were inside the final mile, Trouble Maker just a length behind Brose Hover now, recrossing the road and aiming for a brook overlooked by a fence only three boards high. Scanning the hill beyond it, wanting the quickest way to the final fence, Noel tried to slide to the left of Brose Hover and seize the inside path. But Brose veered left, nearly causing a foul. Instead of gaining a shortcut, Trouble Maker lost ground. A fellow rider watching from the hillside realized what was happening and would write, "Then Noel, with the race slipping from his grasp, sat down to ride for his life."

Noel and Trouble neared the final fence with about two lengths to make up on a formidable leader. Brose Hover jumped it like a prudent timber horse, not hurtling forward but collecting his weight through his hips, setting back on his hocks, safe but ever so slightly slow. Noel gave Trouble a different message: go at it with an unbroken gallop, taking the fence not with a pause but in full stride.

Noel said *fly*.

He unlocked the horse who for two years had been a hint, a problem, a promise. Over the final fence, Trouble Maker took off at the instant Brose Hover landed. Brose Hover took one stride, and suddenly there was Trouble Maker at his right side.

The moment was here: an all-out drive to the winning post, down an alley of twenty-eight thousand hollering people, the riders holding back nothing except the whip. Noel knew Trouble didn't need hitting; Downey needed his one working arm to manage Brose Hover's reins.

They drove with body weight and willpower, the willpower of riders and horses rising together, neither greater than the other. Trouble Maker edged up from Brose Hover's hip to his girth, his girth to his shoulder. Downey flicked a look to the right and sent all he could to Brose Hover. Brose gamely rallied one more time.

But Trouble Maker answered, amplifying the perfect power and rhythm from Noel's quiet hands. A dead heat, thirty feet from the line. The hooves said *troublemaker, troublemaker,* and there was Trouble Maker's head in front at the winning post. Pressed by Brose Hover, he had bested the course record by roughly eleven lengths.

Marion met them in the paddock, her brilliant horse being stripped of his wet saddlecloth and sheepskin breastplate, her brilliant rider shrugging a tailored jacket over his sweat-soaked silks and tying a jaunty scarf around his throat, turning from jockey to gentleman for the trophy presentation. An eavesdropping journalist heard Noel saying something unexpected: the whole way, Noel had felt he could get by Brose Hover anytime he wanted. He hadn't started trying until the next-to-last fence. Earlier, it had only looked as if Trouble Maker kept challenging and failing because Trouble ran steadily while Brose sped and slowed unpredictably.

Then it was time for Marion and Noel to stand above the crowd, receiving the most coveted honor in American steeplechasing. Beaming the brilliant smile that she rarely shared in public, Marion held the loving cup that most everyone here would give an eyetooth to earn. Noel juggled two trophies that could be more than ornamental, gripping the tall tankard's handle with his left hand and balancing the silver cigar box on his right forearm. There was no romance between them, yet they had carried each other over a threshold—joined forever in the slim chance of actually winning America's toughest race. On this side of the Atlantic Ocean, there wasn't any bigger dream they could dream.

Marion wanted to hold this afternoon forever. Soon Carroll Bassett began sculpting three panels that she would display over her trophy room fireplace at Montpelier, where each day's changing light would stroke new life across its graceful highlights and shadows. Carroll told the story from left to right—before, during, after. His "after" image was the least inventive: an elegant portrait in profile of Trouble Maker the winner jogging back toward the paddock, nostrils flaring wide for maximum breath, Noel sitting deep and tall like a diagram of perfect form. The extralarge middle panel portrayed the race, but not exactly as it happened. Instead, harkening back to the photographs made in 1878 that revealed how galloping and jumping horses actually move, Carroll showed five Hunt Cup racers in different phases of approaching, leaping, and landing a timber fence. And rather than placing Trouble Maker first in line, Carroll made him the center of everything: the only one above the fence, in flight.

But Carroll's most inspired vision for this piece was its beginning, a three-dimensional sketch catching his friends as they truly were. "Saddling Troublemaker," said letters carved above the scene: the eager horse, supple neck arched, front foot pawing; the neat groom calmly facing him, soothing, while Trouble nervously lipped at his sleeve; and muscular Noel bending forward to fix the horse's girth, giving the lucky viewer endless hours to admire his physique.

Cast in bronze, the day that Noel unlocked Trouble Maker celebrated years of Marion duPont unlocking herself. Integrating the Maryland Hunt Cup victory with all the layers of her life at Montpelier, she realized that her mature, modern self didn't belong with her mother's lavish Edwardian designs or her father's coach horses. It deserved the place of honor in a new room, the one out of dozens at Montpelier where Marion stripped away her parents' choices. With delicious irony, the girl who had joined her brother in resolutely doing "what we wanted to do," who had performed gymnastics with alarming freedom in Montpelier's dining room, created her own space with Trouble Maker as the focal point.

Marion's need for fresh expression found an answer in Carroll Bassett, who helped her harness the streamlined power of art moderne. Friends invited into Marion's new sitting room would find only clean lines, accented by chrome and glass. Instead of modest pastels, they would see three bold colors: carmine red couches, black and white tiles checkerboarding the floor. Looking down, they would see her playful variation on the trophy room cliché of displaying stuffed animal heads: an authentic zebra-skin rug. Looking up, they would see a wind direction indicator mounted in the ceiling, helping Marion to decide where the Montpelier Hunt should cast its hounds on any given day. And surrounding it all, racehorse photos trellising the walls.

She made a space that her parents couldn't have imagined, while marking boundaries she had passed. Last year, winning the Billy Barton Steeplechase at a big track had seemed momentous. But this year, limits had exploded—the Carolina Cup and the Maryland Hunt Cup, both hers, barely more than a month apart! And so much remained.

On a rainy day at Pimlico in mid-May, Marion sought her second consecutive Billy Barton Steeplechase. Noel would ride Annapolis, her defending champion, saddled with top weight of 170 pounds. Someone lighter needed to handle Tereus, at only 153. And so Carroll Bassett exercised another of his talents on Marion's behalf.

Sinking under his heavy burden, Annapolis hated the waterlogged footing and finished far back. Tereus capered over it. And so it was a mud-soaked Carroll Bassett posing for a victory photo that would decorate Marion's "Red Room."

Carroll fit Marion's bold, elemental side, yet he seemed to belong sparingly, like the color red. Noel complemented the Marion who had chosen soft blue, rose, and silver for her racing silks. When they all competed near Boston that June, it seemed fitting when a reporter noticed that Marion, "dressed in her racing colors . . . made a pretty picture standing with her jockey, Noel Laing, while her Annapolis was being saddled in the paddock."

Marion, Carroll, and Noel drifted through summer alternately far from and close to each other, as if connected by elastic bands. Back in New Jersey, Carroll consulted Will duPont about adapting a local hunt course's old-fashioned fences to Will's thoughtful new design. Marion enjoyed traveling to Saratoga with one of her Richmond friends, Alice Cole. Noel came up to ride Annapolis in a Saratoga steeplechase, but his stretch rally went overboard: Annapolis fell down. That might have been the moment when Marion, looking ahead, decided that Carroll Bassett would ride Annapolis next time out. Or the change might have been inevitable, because Noel soon would be going away. And that was all because of Trouble Maker.

Winning the Maryland Hunt Cup that spring, Trouble had qualified for the Grand National. And Marion decided to go for it. In mid-August, her beautiful big hunter set sail for England. Now she had to negotiate for her big beautiful trainer to join him. Trouble Maker never handled change easily. If he were going to have any chance at Aintree, Noel needed to comfort him through this winter in a foreign land.

But a trainer spending nearly half a year far away from his business, concentrating on *one* horse? That was a lot to ask. Of course Marion could make it financially worth Noel's trouble. But Marion wasn't his only client, although she owned many of his trainees. Noel needed to charm his other owners, assuring them that he still valued their patronage. While he was away, they all would be placing a great deal of trust in his home team.

Of course Marion did the same. And she had a special interest among the horses engaging Noel at Bunree Farm. Not a veteran jumper gearing up for competition nor a veteran hunter legging up for autumn. One that still thought a fence was something to stay inside. But not for long. That April, Battleship had moved from Montpelier up to Bunree. That summer, he started learning his new job.

11

H E HAD BEEN LIVING IN A good old-fashioned barn set into a hillside, a red barn with a silvery gambrel roof, a dairy underneath, and dovecotes above. They had given him the biggest stall, the box where he would feel the least like a prisoner. His window looked out toward the mountains.

Each day of feeding, grooming, turnout, and gradually increasing exercise had given Noel Laing and his stable hands many chances to understand what made Battleship tick. Much like Man o' War, the young stallion could be feisty with strangers but pleasant with familiars. Once Battleship settled in, they found him remarkably even-tempered. He didn't need soothing like Trouble Maker. He didn't want or give lovey-dovey treatment. He *would* do what you asked, without wasted motion. Perhaps he had learned that cooperation was the best way to fulfill his contract with his caretakers and then be released to his own time.

Outside at Bunree Farm, Battleship found surroundings where a cross-country horse could learn to handle just about anything. Using the landscape as he found it, Noel would jump his horses over pasture fences and work them across fields and hills stretching toward the Blue Ridge. But with a horse who had never jumped, Noel started small. A step. A hop. Finally, a leap.

Battleship had been working toward that moment with basic gymnastics. At the racetrack, he had jogged clockwise to warm up and galloped counterclockwise during serious exercise. Now he developed both sides of his body equally at a walk, trot, canter, bending to the left, bending to the right. Before starting over jumps, he needed to be limber all over. He also needed a flexible state of mind before he started foxhunting.

In the universe that Battleship had left behind—a world where you ran straight toward what you wanted—sending a racehorse out following hounds might seem like a strange detour. If you were aiming for racecourses, why bother with idiosyncratic farmyards and crotchety gates, with hectic runs and blank days where no quarry appeared? Why take the long way around? Teach your horse to breeze on a level course over identical obstacles and cash in with relatively short, uncomplicated hurdle races. Or choose steeplechases on terrain manicured like a park. Some stables preferred those options. But that wasn't the way to Aintree.

And the reason was *integrity*. The Grand National had been born from real conditions, racing across brooks and roadways, a solid stone wall, even a plowed field. It wasn't supposed to be artificially easy. If anything, it had been too real. Eventually, they dismantled the stone wall. Eventually, the plowed land dwindled to a ceremonial strip, then disappeared altogether. But the Aintree course kept its haphazard drops, its brooks with uneven banks, its sharp left turn to avoid plunging into the canal. It wasn't a place for park racers. It was the ultimate test for real hunters, horses you would trust with your life in any kind of country.

For Marion duPont Somerville and Noel Laing, the Grand National reflected their own experiences out hunting—communion with the natural world, surprising chases, and sometimes ending up somewhere you never had been before. Bringing Battleship into that world served more than one purpose: he would become that much more competent, and he also could enter races for "qualified hunters." To become eligible, he would need to earn a certificate signed by a Master of Foxhounds.

Some people took the qualifying process more seriously than others. A bogus "hunter," a horse named Trillion, had won the first American Grand National chase in 1899. Trillion hunted like a wrecking ball: careening wildly, busting fences, interfering with anything that got in his way. When the moment of reckoning arrived, Trillion's rider—thoroughly embarrassed but determined not to waste all that effort—approached the Master of Foxhounds and asked him to qualify the horse. "I will give you a certificate," the Master decreed, "on one condition—that you never let me see him out with the hounds again in my Mastership."

More recently, owners of excitable racehorses had found another option. Instead of chasing an unpredictable wild animal, they could follow hounds chasing a scent that had been dragged over a predetermined course. This had become a popular strategy at Southern Pines and also at Aiken, South Carolina, where many steeplechasers wintered and Mrs. Thomas Hitchcock served as Master for "the world's fastest drag." Whenever Thoroughbreds sporting racing riders appeared at the Aiken Drag, pragmatic Mrs. Hitchcock would say, "When the hunt starts, keep behind a hundred yards or so and stay there. If at the end of the Drag you have been able to keep your place behind and jump the fences, I will give you a certificate."

That option certainly was open to Noel Laing. But would Noel make a hunter less authentic than himself? Especially when he started a horse up in Rappahannock County, where the countryside had hardly been tamed. Especially when they ran with a pack led by a man who didn't want to be tamed, either, following Sterling Larrabee and the Old Dominion Hounds.

The Old Dominion Hounds had begun with two army officers hashing out a problem over drinks. Major Louis Beard commanded the cavalry Remount Depot at mountainous Front Royal, Virginia. Captain Sterling Loop Larrabee—an intense outdoorsman whose service ranged from the Philippines to Gallipoli and who let good friends call him "Loopy"—had been foxhunting at Warrenton but was feeling fed up with bumptious crowds and organizational politics. "If you want to hunt in the bushes," Major Beard declared, "with nobody bothering you, in a bold country, with plenty of big obstacles and plenty of foxes, you ought to go around Flint Hill." Or maybe Beard talked more like Larrabee remembered: "Why in hell don't you go up in Rappahannock—that's the best country in America today, and Joe Thomas has left it and gone to Millbrook, New York." In other words, hunting rights to the territory were up for grabs.

Captain Larrabee went exploring in his Model T Ford and discovered that even where roads existed, they were so rough that he had to travel many of them on horseback. Larrabee liked that. He located his kennels several miles west of the spot where the Laings were establishing Bunree Farm and experimented with chasing stags and wild boar as well as foxes. When Battleship arrived in Rappahannock County, its wildness remained much the same. A fashionable sportsman who visited Larrabee's kennels a few years later would recall, "After about seven miles of state road we branched off on a road of most uncertain character—being one hundred per cent red Virginia clay . . . Never again will we venture off a hard road in Virginia, unless we are well mounted on a Ford station wagon." Describing his own rash attempt at driving there in luxury, the man joked, "I don't know what they do with the Rolls-Royces. I guess they must melt them down and turn the precious metal in to the government."

Battleship had arrived where a good horse was the Rolls-Royce. That autumn he discovered a world outside the railings that had confined his life, far beyond paddocks and pastures, far beyond any oval of dirt. Noel took him where blue giants with names like Fogg Mountain lounged across the horizon, but Battleship didn't see them as a limit. The wild land fed his enthusiasm. Barriers employed by northern Virginia farmers— post and rails, zigzagging "snake" fences, stone walls—demanded his caution and engaged his entire body. As Sterling Larrabee warned people who wanted to hunt with him, "For the most part, these obstacles are stiff and solid and the rider who tries to fly them will soon come to grief. He should make his horse approach them collectedly and jump from the hocks."

A step. A hop. Finally, a leap. Noel Laing had got Battleship going. But now it was time for Noel to be on his way.

Trouble Maker had done nothing much for several weeks, simply getting used to different food, water, weather. Then, leaving his bustling racing stable in other men's care, Noel joined him. It was only the first week of October. Noel would stay with Trouble Maker all the way to the Grand National next March. Back home, much would depend upon Noel's father, overseeing the stables at Bunree, then Southern Pines. Much also would depend upon Noel's main assistant, a young man whose image in bronze stood over Marion duPont Somerville's fireplace with Trouble

Maker nibbling his sleeve: a light-skinned black man named Shirley Banks.

Compared with many African Americans of his place and time, Shirley had grown up with advantages. Both of his parents could read and write. His father, a farmer, owned his own house. Yet they couldn't avoid being categorized by their skin color. Drawing time-worn distinctions, the U.S. census listed the Banks family as "Mulatto."

In Virginia or the Carolinas, Shirley Banks would not be allowed to sit in a restaurant beside Noel Laing. But he had been Noel's emissary to Camden early in 1932, where the official taking entries of Tereus and Trouble Maker for Carolina Cup day wrote, "Trainer—S. Banks." Noel would come down from Southern Pines to ride their races; in the meantime, he counted on Banks to take care of business.

When Battleship came to Bunree Farm, Shirley Banks became one of his teachers. When Noel joined Trouble Maker in England, Shirley looked after Battleship's daily progress. Because of segregation, he might not be allowed to ride Battleship out with the Old Dominion Hounds for "cubbing" season in early autumn or when their formal hunting season began in November. *Maybe,* as a personal favor from Sterling Larrabee to his good friends the Laings, Banks could have ridden behind the hunt as a groom. Or maybe Noel's father, or another friend, took Battleship out with the pack. In any case, the little horse began earning his certificate.

Meanwhile, Noel's absence from the American hunt-racing scene elevated Carroll Bassett. Carroll rode Noel's own horse, Fairy Lore, and also brought in multiple winners for Marion. His strong finish for her stable, after Noel's strong beginning, helped Marion earn more victories than any other hunt-racing owner in America that year. But Carroll's most important campaign took hold two days after Thanksgiving, at a lovely young lady's social debut.

She emerged during a dinner dance at the River Club in Manhattan, an exclusive new venue with a private dock where members could park their yachts. Her guests included twenty-year-old Alfred Gwynne Vanderbilt, who would inherit an enormous fortune at age twenty-one. But she was going to be drawn to an older man, twenty-seven years to her eighteen, an artist on horseback as well as in a studio.

Jane Bartholomew Fowler offered much to please an artist's eye. That evening at the River Club she might seem like a river nymph gliding through the blue and silver ballroom, shimmering in her gown of light green crepe de chine. But in everyday life, you were more likely to find her near horses. She had graduated from the Foxcroft School for young ladies at Middleburg, Virginia, where foxhunting was practically a required subject. Her sporting side would appeal to Carroll Bassett. So would her looks—a sunny blonde with a teaspoon face, just the right height to rest her head on his shoulder.

It was too soon for promises, but that winter offered new prospects for Noel Laing, Carroll Bassett, and Battleship. The young men stepped into new dimensions of work and personal life. The little stallion literally saw new horizons in December, when William Laing reopened his stables at Southern Pines and Noel's horses followed.

Back in Virginia, a fresh way to take chances appeared about fifteen miles due west of Amissville, where adventurous motorists were driving up into the Blue Ridge and sampling the first section of the new Skyline Drive. "Guard rails have not been erected as yet," the *New York Times* warned people eager to try it. "When the highway becomes slippery with sleet, snow or ice, motorists will not be permitted to pass over it. Those who have visited it to date have been given printed slips stating that they are doing so at their own risk, and intimating that if they are picked up at the bottom of a 3,000-foot precipice they will have only themselves to blame. As yet there have been no serious accidents."

On December 28, 1932, Marion and Tom Somerville marked their seventh wedding anniversary by submitting paperwork to the Orange County Courthouse. He paid her $5 cash. She gave him the deed to nearly 450 acres adjoining Montpelier, a farm called Mt. Athos that she had bought in 1929 for $25,000 cash.

The timing seemed sentimental. The gift itself seemed like a sign of increasing distance. Tom wouldn't have to go far afield to have his own house. He would be nearby much of the time when Marion wanted or needed him. He would continue as secretary for the Montpelier Hunt. But as Tom well knew, his wife was on the move.

In late January 1933, a letter went out to Marion while she was heading somewhere else. "I am now settled on Altama and enjoying the place," Georgia businessman and philanthropist Cator Woolford wrote. "I want to extend an invitation to you and your good husband to come and visit me whenever it suits you." Mr. Woolford extended the same invitation to her brother and assured Marion, "If I do not happen to be there I will turn the place over to you."

But now that Marion had turned the place over to another owner, she was not looking back. Instead of lingering at Altama she was steaming across the Atlantic aboard the *Berengaria,* a luxury liner that had been created as the *Imperator,* Germany's supersized answer to the *Titanic,* and had come to England as a war prize. You never knew how time and circumstance might affect your identity, *Berengaria* might whisper to Marion; though, outwardly, her circumstances showed minimal change. Marion sailed with her husband and his brother Wilson, this time along with their sister Jennie. The Somerville siblings all gave their occupation as "none." Marion remained "housewife."

Which was, of course, as laughable as ever. Considering her vast investments through the Delaware Trust Company, her income from real estate, railroad equipment, municipal bonds, and the DuPont company, she should have declared her real function: capitalist. Though that would have been unusually bold. Americans talked about the "modern woman," who claimed the same freedoms as a man, but still extolled the traditional woman who had no career outside the home. This example often appeared in movies, notably when Norma Shearer portrayed *The Divorcee.* The husband had been unfaithful and expected forgiveness, saying, "It didn't mean a thing," then wouldn't forgive his wife for doing and saying the same thing. After divorcing, he became a drunk and it became her job to patch everything up, ultimately reconciling with him. The Loretta Young vehicle *Week-end Marriage* promoted a similar theme: a rising executive wife eventually tells her less successful husband that she has been fired—when actually she has quit her lofty job so that her man will stop feeling embarrassed and take her back.

Week-end Marriage reached theaters at a time when the United States suffered more than 20 percent unemployment and men were expected to be head of household. Tom Somerville occupied a contrary reality where unemployment brought privileges and his wife would not follow his lead.

Instead, Marion had the *Berengaria* take them to France for a little vacation and then went exploring British studs, where Thoroughbred stallions she and her brother had studied from afar held court. She went to watch 'chasers race at various English park courses and wrote her brother to explain how those fences compared with the ones he designed. And of course she checked in at Newmarket to see how Trouble Maker was adjusting—or not—to the land of his ancestors. Officially he was being trained by an Englishman named Mr. Digby, because Noel had no license to train racehorses in England, but Noel was the one who knew how much, or how little, exercise Trouble Maker could take. Many racehorses would pack away several quarts of oats daily, but Noel had to balance Trouble Maker's exercise with his poor appetite. "You had to kind of nurse him along and take a chance on whether he was fit enough," Marion observed. "He wasn't like a horse who would go out and work in such a way you could count on him to be ready."

Trouble Maker had needed nearly five months in England before entering a race. He and Noel had finished last. A witness noted that Trouble Maker "was still jumping the last fence when the winner passed the post," but that performance might not be as bad as it sounded. Trouble didn't like the soft ground sinking under his feet, and carrying top weight of 180 pounds made it worse. Even so, taking that last fence, Trouble Maker had been "racing with his ears pricked and apparently dead game." He had run willingly, giving many pounds to good opponents. There was room for hope.

Preparing for Aintree, Noel had to keep asking enough without demanding too much. He would bridge the space with one more race, about a month after Trouble Maker's English debut. And so on February 21, Marion found herself spending a wintry afternoon in the English Midlands. Trouble Maker might have fared better this time, carrying less weight over firmer turf, but no—the water jump tripped him up. Trouble Maker did not fall, but he lost all momentum. The winner beat him by an estimated one hundred yards. Trouble Maker beat only a horse who did not finish the race.

Aintree? There was just over a month left for deciding, and Marion wasn't liking what she saw. "Trouble Maker is not doing well and is not fit or really acclimated," she wrote to a friend. "I RATHER DOUBT START-

ING HIM AGAIN. He ran at Derby—a bad luck race throughout, but even so he did not show anywhere near his American form." Back in the States, as her comment made the newspapers, racing fans wondered whether she meant forgoing any more prep races or ditching Aintree altogether.

Meanwhile, choosing an English holiday inspired by one horse, Marion had sacrificed her chance to watch her others. The same day that Trouble Maker stumbled and plodded through the Derbyshire Handicap, Battleship performed a final tune-up at Camden. After more than a year invested in his care, he was about to run his first steeplechase. And Marion was missing it.

12

WHILE NOEL LAING STRUGGLED WITH TROUBLE Maker on a cold English afternoon, Carroll Bassett considered how he was going to navigate a balmy South Carolina course with Battleship. He knew that the six-year-old stallion was a green jumper, unseasoned. Before riding Battleship in Camden's Cherokee Steeplechase, Carroll wanted to see how the little horse performed for someone who knew him well. So he asked Shirley Banks to guide Battleship over three brush fences—and was amused by what he saw.

Out hunting with Noel and his deputies, Battleship had been a good student. Perhaps too good. When Banks aimed him at the pliable brush, Battleship treated it like unyielding post and rail: crouching carefully for takeoff, launching into an extrahigh, slow arc, achieving remarkable hang time that Bassett called "probably 16½ minutes over each fence." Carroll knew right there, they weren't going to win. Tomorrow, he would use what the green horse understood right now, not try to force new techniques on him during the excitement of a race. At least the horse was an athlete, all right. And sensible. Carroll got his buddy Raymond Woolfe to ride his own Ram's Head Stable entry and resigned himself to giving Battleship a gentle debut.

Fourteen months after Marion had bought him, Battleship finally did what she had chosen him to do. It could have been any jump race, but he was starting in style: Washington's Birthday at Springdale Race Course. Every February 22, America saluted the tall, compelling general who had accepted Great Britain's surrender and shored up the brand-new role of president with his personal integrity. In his spare time he also had fox-hunted, avidly. So it was fitting that Battleship made his leap from fox-hunting to steeplechasing on the day that George Washington, if he were literally immortal, would have been 201 years old.

Reaching the paddock, the red chestnut stallion impressed a reporter with his "noble-looking" attitude, the look of eagles that his sire had perfected and passed along. He only had to race two miles and beat two horses. The crowd favored him to win.

But once they were racing, Battleship made a startling display, carefully soaring his way to last place. "Carroll Bassett gave Battleship as classy a ride as a horse could wish," the Camden newspaper declared, "but Battleship proved just a battleship compared to the two torpedo destroyers as to speed." Marion soon heard the result. She did not hear the sound that floated around Springdale while Battleship vaulted over brush the same way he would have respected a stone wall. She did not have to hear the spectators laughing.

With his shakedown cruise out of the way, Battleship received a new training goal: learning to take his hedges with a flatter, faster arc. He would get the message galloping beside Tereus and other good ones from Marion's barn, eventually matching their style in order to keep up. Carroll recruited Ray Woolfe to ride the other horse.

Woolfe came away impressed. Riding "boot to boot" with Bassett, Woolfe glanced over in midair and saw not Carroll's face beside him but Battleship's belly. The Camden crowd had laughed because the little stallion looked so funny, jumping far higher than the course required. But Woolfe felt something else—a flash of awe for such uncommon power.

Noel had started Battleship the right way, strengthening the right muscles, not pushing too hard too soon. Now, Carroll encouraged him to be bold. Battleship's brush-jumping technique improved. His innate power remained.

. . .

They had not met, but heiress Marion duPont Somerville and horse master Reginald Hobbs were united in one thing this winter: sizing up their Aintree chance.

For Marion, the decisions became streamlined like her modern Red Room back at Montpelier. As long as Trouble Maker stood a reasonable chance of being fit for the challenge, Noel would ride him and she would pay the final acceptance fee. Reg's hope depended on one of Marion's American friends, a grandmotherly figure with silver hair and librarian spectacles who foxhunted enthusiastically and had been managing her own steeplechasing stable for twenty years. This winter, Mrs. Ambrose Clark faced a gentle dilemma: owning a very promising National horse with three worthy riders. Should she choose her nephew, Pete Bostwick? The loyal professional jockey, Dudley Williams? Or the man who had helped start it all, Reg Hobbs? Each had set his sights on her fine young prospect, seven-year-old Kellsboro' Jack.

Now, there was a steed to tempt any Aintree rider. Everyone seemed to want credit for plucking him as a yearling from a pasture in Ireland near the Seven Castles of Kells. Many credited Mr. Clark himself. Some said that Mr. B. M. Slocock, whose stallion Jackdaw had sired many fine jumpers, pointed out this particular Jackdaw colt. Bruce believed that his father, acting as Mr. Clark's agent, actually did the picking. In any case, the rangy gelding had a perfect pedigree, physique, and attitude for steeplechasing. Reg taught him jumping, and before the Hobbs family left Warwick Lodge, he and Kellsboro' Jack were leaping bullock fences—sturdy, sloping hedges—said to be seven feet high.

Reg Hobbs easily could imagine Kellsboro' Jack as his own Aintree ride. But he was unlikely to replace Dudley Williams, the professional rider who had nearly won the 1929 Grand National and had partnered Kellsboro' Jack to all of his wins so far. And then Mrs. Clark's nephew entered the picture.

Not only did Pete Bostwick look like a professional jockey—all 125 compact pounds of him—some called him "the world's best amateur rider." For several years, he had won more steeplechases than any other amateur jockey in the United States. He also had won notable hurdle races in England and of course had hunted many times in Leicestershire with his aunt Florence and uncle Brose. Pete thought, why not the Grand National?

That January, Pete had schooled Kellsboro' Jack over fences and figured this bright young promise was his Aintree match. Then Jack faltered in his races and Pete began looking elsewhere. Perhaps the trainer Ivor Anthony breathed a surreptitious sigh of relief. Ivor didn't know whether Kellsboro' Jack would make the National, but if he did, why burden him with a rider who had never even seen the treacherous course? Meanwhile, Dud Williams weathered 'chases over ground softer than Jack liked and made sure the trainer knew that he wouldn't trade places with anyone.

Even with Pete Bostwick backing away, Reg Hobbs knew his chances to get the mount on Kellsboro' Jack were slim. But the Clarks wanted Reg to fulfill his Aintree dream. So Brose Clark promised him a horse. When the final acceptance fees were paid, Hobbs was named as the jockey for Chadd's Ford. At age thirty-five, Reg would ride the Grand National at last.

He was fit for it, physically and mentally, the same dashing Reg who would call, "Follow me," and bounce over the tricky places. Except one day out hunting he failed, and failed badly. Less than a week before the National, there was Reg helpless on the ground. Here was another of his wife's "I told you so" nightmares come true: her roving husband immobilized with a fractured thigh.

Beyond feeling sad, scared, and angry, Margery Hobbs may have found some satisfaction with the situation. Because Reg was slowly recovering at the Melton War Memorial Hospital in Leicestershire, when she and Bruce weren't visiting with him, they might enjoy the company of old friends and family nearby. And maybe, after all the grief Reg had caused her, urging their son into dangerous work and not forcing himself to resist when attractive girls fancied him—maybe he deserved several weeks anchored alone in bed.

Looking back, Bruce Hobbs wouldn't dwell on those days when his twelve-year-old self and his conflicted mum sat beside his captured dad. Bruce wouldn't describe the emotional tensions but would recall a breaking point: a moment when the apparatus holding his father's leg in traction "snapped," Bruce said, "and the twenty-one-pound weight fell with a crash." Physical repairs were the easier ones, after all. Reg's raw pain from that crash could ease up that same day, tended by skillful attendants and good drugs. But day after day, Reg lay with the pain of being left behind while others took on Aintree.

While nursing his hurt, Reg would be sincerely cheering for Mrs. Clark's good young horse and wishing the best for Pete Bostwick, who so generously had given Bruce his first real hunter what seemed like a lifetime ago. Pete had come up with a mount named Dusty Foot, owned by American sportsman John Hay Whitney. Determined to send out a National winner, Jock Whitney entered one or two or three horses every year and had already had runners finish second and third. Now, *Daily Racing Form* commended Dusty Foot as "a safe jumper of the slow, but sure, type" who should give Bostwick a good introduction to Aintree—although Dusty Foot had not especially enjoyed his own introduction to Aintree in 1932, stopping at the Canal Turn. Still, Pete brimmed with enthusiasm, saying, "I anticipate a thrilling ride around the most difficult course in the world. This will be the first time I've ridden in the Grand National and indeed I've never yet even seen Aintree, but I feel confident that with Dusty Foot I've a tip top chance."

While reporters sought out Pete Bostwick, the other American gentleman taking his first crack at the National proceeded quietly. Many guessed that Noel Laing's six months in England would be wasted—Trouble Maker would not run. But just after American newspapers called Trouble Maker a "doubtful" starter, Noel Laing's parents arrived in London and headed north to root for their son.

Two days before the National, the *New York Times* marveled at Noel Laing's candor, declaring that he "broke some kind of a record as he admitted he didn't honestly know whether he could ride the American jumper to victory on Friday. Every other trainer and jockey seemed confident of the merits of his horse and its chances." Noel soft-pedaled Trouble Maker's conditioning issues, telling the *Times* that the horse had acclimatized all right, "considering the comparatively short time he has been in England." Was he good enough? Noel said only, "I am hopeful without being confident."

On Thursday, March 23, Aintree opened and Pete Bostwick got his first look at the giant triangular circuit he would be aiming to complete tomorrow, not once but twice. That morning, he breezed Dusty Foot. That afternoon, Pete raced one of his own horses over the hurdle track snugged inside part of the National course. That challenge fit with his proven excellence. He won. Then, of course, someone asked what he thought of the National fences.

"I anticipate a thrilling ride around the most difficult course in the world," Pete had said not long ago, when Becher's Brook and the Canal Turn and the Chair were merely words and photographs to him. Now there was no fantasy. Pete saw what a tall task he had set for himself, and there was no way to cram for the exam. He could only admit, "They're big—even bigger than I thought."

And yet he projected confidence, happy with Dusty Foot's condition, believing they would do well. The bookies said Pete was a long shot, offering Dusty Foot at sixty-six to one. But among the American hopes, that wasn't so bad. Trouble Maker and Noel Laing were being held as high as two hundred to one.

Still, when thirty-four horses galloped away from the National start, what would those manufactured odds have to do with reality? That night, one commentator wrote, "It is a fair guess only that not all will finish. At least," he accurately pointed out, "they never have."

Had there ever been a more perfect day at Aintree? Cool but remarkably cloud-free, "an all-sunshine National," someone called it. Only those whose horses preferred softer ground supporting the bright green grass would have changed it. From their box seats, Marion and her party beheld the phenomenon that happened here every year: people packed all around the immense racing space, becoming part of the landscape all the way to the horizon. Visiting the paddock, Marion became one of the many "French, German, Scandinavian, and American women [who] mingled shoulder to shoulder with a great host of English." Their easy coexistence flew against yesterday's news from Germany, where the Reichstag had given chancellor Adolf Hitler the power to make any laws he wanted. Meanwhile, putting politics aside, parliamentarian Winston Churchill showed up at Aintree with a mighty pair of binoculars that one wag said "looked more like a pair of astronomical telescopes."

Telescopes weren't needed to see that one of the very best-looking National entries was Kellsboro' Jack. He had redeemed himself ten days ago, racing well on firm turf. Now he looked ready to repay everyone's faith, every hop from an Irish farm to Ambrose Clark to the racing stable of "Mrs. Brose." "You are very unlucky," Ivor Anthony had told Mr. Clark along the way, during a losing streak. "I wish you would make a present of Kellsboro' Jack to your wife." Brose Clark had been startled but not selfish. Maybe an offering to lady luck was needed, after all. Out of the blue, he asked his wife to give him one British pound. When she handed over the money without question, he remarked, "Now you can have Kellsboro' Jack." Today, the horse would reveal the full measure of his gift.

Not far away, Marion realized the size of her own gamble. The Carolina Cup had been something special. The Maryland Hunt Cup, with nearly thirty thousand people blanketing the hillside and celebrating her gallant horse, had felt transcendent. Now her horse carried her colors over turf where the world's best had proved their courage for nearly one hundred years, before a crowd numbered in hundreds of thousands. Trouble Maker and Noel, tall and magnificent, took part of Marion's self with them out onto the course. Whatever happened, when they came back she would not be unchanged.

She became part of the hush, almost like church, as the horses paraded to the far end of the grandstand, then cantered back toward the start. Marion saw Trouble Maker line up with thirty-three other horses . . . regroup after a false start . . . then bound away into the roar of history. She could spot Kellsboro' Jack near the front, while Trouble Maker settled into midpack. One horse tumbled over the first fence, spilling his rider several feet to the right of Trouble Maker, causing Noel to glance over with a Buddha-calm expression. Another runner nearly came down at the first—17.2-hand giant Pelorus Jack, who had been such a gawky youngster that his handlers called him "the Circus Horse." Yet somehow his rider stayed on; Pelorus Jack got up off his knees and found his stride.

The field stayed intact over the second fence and then the third, five feet high with an open ditch gaping on its takeoff side. Here were the thrills that Pete Bostwick had expected, disconcerting at first but seeming to normalize with straightforward tall hedges fourth and fifth along the course. Then came Becher's Brook.

Here the ground sloped slightly upward, misrepresenting what lay on the other side. The horses took off over a now familiar-seeming hedge and suddenly found themselves hanging over a nearly seven-foot drop. Here, Aintree lost any resemblance to a park course steeplechase or an oversized hurdle race. Here it found out the true hunters, the horses and riders with the coordination and spirit of big-wave surfers.

Pete Bostwick didn't lack spirit or athleticism. He might have succeeded with a different horse, a different moment, or more time to adjust his mind from thrill seeking to proper but not overwhelmed respect. Afterward, he would say that Dusty Foot took off from "a slight depression" in the ground and did not jump far enough. Pete's initiation ended a few feet beyond Becher's Brook, with Dusty Foot sliding down onto his left side and Pete sailing face-first into the turf. Stunned but conscious, he lay still, hearing hoofbeats all around and knowing he couldn't dodge the flying hooves, waiting for them to pass. When the air grew quiet, he rose, unsteady, with scratches all over his face, luckily nothing worse, and his horse nowhere in sight. Pete Bostwick, the hurdle racer, was out of the National. Noel Laing, the hunter, kept going.

Noel had met Becher's beautifully, keeping Trouble Maker clear of runners clumping ahead and behind while aiming him over the middle of the fence. He sat down perfectly as Trouble Maker took off, lining his shoulders, elbows, knees over his horse's withers and reaching his shins forward with Trouble's shoulders, ready to stand up with him as they dropped. If Marion had stood just beyond Becher's she would have seen her big horse rising with extraordinary grace, arching his swan neck, then Laing leaning back over the saddle cantle, holding both reins in his left hand, swinging his right arm up and back to balance them down. That part he couldn't plan, only feel. And then move on.

The field cleared the smaller fence after Becher's, angling left to line up for the Canal Turn. Uphill, the last few strides. Then a regular leap and landing, but the instant after landing always confounded someone. Land, recover, turn nearly ninety degrees left. Thirty-one horses attacked the Canal Turn at, as one spectator said, "a burning pace." Here the betting favorite, the Irish mare Heartbreak Hill, proved why riders tried to jump either exactly beside or one stride behind an opponent but never a half length behind. When Forbras took off, half a length ahead of her,

Heartbreak Hill launched with him. With a mighty leap she cleared the extra distance, but her rough landing and quick left turn hurled her rider over her right side.

Disqualified from the race but galloping with the herd, Heartbreak Hill held her position as the field charged into the country. Her path put her in front of Trouble Maker. No rider enjoyed following a loose horse, which often veered unpredictably. But Noel Laing marveled at the surreal sight of riderless Heartbreak Hill jumping "straight and brilliantly" over Valentine's Brook and everything else between the Canal Turn and the grandstand. The vision continued as they neared the Chair—five feet two inches, the highest jump at Aintree—and Heartbreak Hill delivered, Noel said, one of the biggest jumps he ever had seen.

From her box, Marion had a good view of the horses rippling over the Chair and on toward the water. She could see the pacesetter, Remus, clearing the fifteen-foot-wide water jump with "a great raking leap," Kellsboro' Jack close behind. She saw Trouble Maker step awkwardly in the water, then scramble safely on his way.

Cornering back toward the starting place, Heartbreak Hill saw her chance to scoot back to her stable and exited the course. Twenty-five other horses with riders aboard headed past the start; never had so many National runners begun the second lap—so many that commentators called it "abnormal." Firm ground and unusually good visibility seemed to be helping them keep their feet. The conditions looked good for a brilliant young horse named Golden Miller, but Golden Miller wasn't happy. Recently he had won Britain's ultimate park course 'chase, the Cheltenham Gold Cup. Today, at each jump, he kept veering to the right.

The field homed in on Becher's Brook with Kellsboro' Jack in front. Jack led them over and onward, up and around the Canal Turn. "I have never seen a more polished and flawless performance," a spectator would declare. "He met every fence right, never disturbed a twig, and [upon landing] was straight away again into his stride." It was the perfection molded by Reg Hobbs in his loose school, carried out into the countryside.

At the Canal Turn, Golden Miller went down. He would go on to win a record total of five Cheltenham Gold Cups and also one Grand National, but today he was out of his depth at Aintree.

So was Trouble Maker, but not because the drops were too steep, the turns too sharp, or the fences too high. He was handling all that. But the pace! Halfway through the National, Noel could feel his horse already slowly losing ground. Heading back into the country, the young man began doing what he could to finish the race while sparing his horse as much as possible. Noel aimed for spots where the hedges had been broken, the lowest places for Trouble to jump.

Nearing the four-mile mark, the leaders were laughing at Trouble Maker's Maryland Hunt Cup record time. Rounding the final bend, Noel could feel his horse's engine thumping steady, but they were far behind and running low on fuel with nearly a half mile still to run.

And Kellsboro' Jack—in his element, doing exactly what Reg Hobbs and Ivor Anthony had prepared him to do—seemed to be winning easily. Three fences from home, only one runner began closing the gap. Two fences from home, here was ungainly Pelorus Jack the "Circus Horse" jumping beside Kellsboro' Jack!

One more fence, then the run home. Spectators would argue later about which horse had been going better. Kellsboro' Jack's rider kept still, not changing his horse's rhythm, waiting to clear that final hedge before urging the last great effort. Pelorus Jack's rider tried to seize an advantage, pressing the accelerator, lurching his horse past the perfect takeoff point.

Two Jacks rose together at the modest final hedge. Kellsboro' Jack, to the inside, rustled across and landed clean. Pelorus Jack knocked his front hooves into the brush, jolting his rider off balance. They had recovered from a worse mistake at fence one. More than four miles later, gravity won. As his feet touched down, his legs folded. Pelorus Jack sank to his stomach as if he were going to have a nap and rolled onto his right side. Kellsboro' Jack ran toward victory. He was not quite alone: a riderless horse, Apostasy, bounded past the winning post first by a few yards, his long ears straight up, bunny rabbit style. Then Kellsboro' Jack won the Grand National for Mrs. Ambrose Clark, finishing in record time.

Outwardly composed, Marion duPont Somerville had been handed a cocktail of disappointment, pride, and happiness. She had seen her weary, wonderful horse run the toughest course and never fall, never quit—even though, as a chart maker would comment, "Trouble Maker climbed over the last fence on his nerve." He finished fifteenth. In that moment, Noel

Laing—Irish blood, English born, American grown—became the first American rider to finish the Grand National. Noel had ridden a beautiful race. He simply didn't have a fast-enough horse.

Marion could mix her pride in Noel with happiness for her winning friend. Wrapped in a large fur coat and beaming with joy, Florence Clark looked out from the summit of all 'chasing and tried to take in its meaning. Swarmed by friends and well-wishers, then seeing a mounted police escort nearing the stands, she edged through the crowd to shake hands with the trainer and rider who had brought her this prize. Now was the moment when everyone expected her to take hold of a leather shank clipped to Kellsboro' Jack's bridle and walk him back to the paddock. Happy voices called to her, "Go and lead him in!" But Mrs. Clark only smiled; she could not make herself do it. Brose Clark did the honors and he also seemed overcome, unable to form a quote for reporters even after Kellsboro' Jack stopped in the winner's unsaddling stall with bystanders shouting, "Whoopee!"

Pete Bostwick was still somewhere out on the course, trudging his way toward iodine for his scratches and a change into clean civilian clothing, when the last National horse came back. It was Dusty Foot. He had been caught in the faraway backstretch by the unhorsed riders who had started the race aboard Apostasy and Heartbreak Hill. Now he jogged into the paddock safe and sound, with two jockeys glad to avoid a long hike riding tandem on his back.

In the aftermath, there were many words about a beautiful day and a beautiful ride. "We always expected to win," Mrs. Clark told the press. "At least Ivor Anthony, our trainer, has always predicted it." Then, even though seven-year-old Kellsboro' Jack was a couple of years younger than the average National winner and might pursue another victory or two, Mrs. Clark announced that her brilliant Aintree horse would keep racing but never would enter the Grand National again.

Meanwhile, Marion duPont Somerville realized her own misconception. Those extratall, big-boned English and Irish 'chasers weren't what she had believed, "the kind of horse you think a fat man would ride in the hunting field." They also had speed over a long run. As Marion put it,

"They could turn it on." Talented and game as Trouble Maker was, he wasn't an Aintree horse.

While Marion pondered her mistake, Florence Clark honored an old debt. A few days after his grand performance, Kellsboro' Jack stopped by the Melton War Memorial Hospital. A handler led the National winner to an open ground-floor window. The horse brightened as a well-known face came into view and a well-known voice floated out. For several minutes, he communed with the immobilized Reg Hobbs, his original partner over jumps.

13

THREE YEARS HAD PASSED, FROM AN idea to this day. Three years since an aerodynamic colt caught their attention at Havre de Grace. At Camden, he had been tested and adjusted. It felt natural that his transformation would accelerate here at the Deep Run Hunt Races on Saturday, April 8. Curles Neck Farm had, as Marion noted, "an ideal course for inexperienced or young jumpers." Now she and Noel and Carroll would see their idea in action.

The three of them hadn't thought they would be able to watch him together today. Noel had another horse to ride for Marion in the same race, and Carroll was honoring a commitment to ride for another owner. The boys had thought they would be competing against Battleship in the Malvern Hill Steeplechase, not standing here pulling for him to win.

But the Malvern Hill, on Deep Run's beginner-friendly course, drew so many entries that if they all showed up they'd overcrowd the track. When race day came and the field stayed too big, the officials split the Malvern Hill in two. Noel and Carroll both ended up in the first division, Noel winning with Marion's gelding Grenadier Guard. Now the young men were free to toss tailored jackets over their silks and perhaps join Marion, appraising Battleship all over again, eager to see what he would do.

For each of them, his progress would seem like a different sequence of time-lapse photography. Because of their travels, Noel and Marion had not seen the little horse for several months. Carroll, of course, had ridden Battleship only six weeks ago and practically still could hear the Camden crowd laughing. Now the three of them watched Battleship carry Marion's colors onto the course with professional jockey Dick Williams aboard and wondered how much he had improved.

Most of the crowd made a different kind of comparison. Battleship presented a brand-new picture to them, and his appearance among typical tall 'chasers didn't look promising. Steeplechasing worked much like professional basketball would operate someday: an extratall body needed less effort to step over fences or reach up to dunk the ball. When Battleship took up steeplechasing, he looked like a six-foot man playing in the twenty-first-century NBA.

It could be done, but there weren't many short stars. Marion's friend Dr. John M. Hughes, an official with the Deep Run races, had seen Battleship at Montpelier and thought he looked like "a pony, very powerful, with a short back, immensely strong loins and magnificently sloping shoulders, but still a pony." Like Dr. Hughes, the crowd today wondered what chance he had against his larger opponents. But also, in this neck of the woods, a so-called pony sent out by Mrs. Thomas H. Somerville might count for more than a horse from someone less astute.

For the first half of the two-mile race, Battleship settled in with the herd while Dornoch tore off into a twenty-length lead. Entering the second mile, Dornoch faded back and Battleship easily shared the lead. And waited, until his rider in effect shook the champagne bottle and popped the cork. Then Marion saw the horse she hadn't witnessed, only imagined. While everyone gave their best, Battleship widened—two, three, four lengths in front. Next thing she knew, Marion had won both sections of the Malvern Hill chase. But Battleship had beaten Grenadier Guard's time by five and one-fifth seconds, a Man o' War–like gap.

Just like that, Carroll Bassett wanted the mount back. And Marion promptly sent Battleship to a big track, to the well-seasoned trainer who had taken Annapolis while Noel was overseas and now was keeping a division of her stable. Noel Laing and Shirley Banks still would see the little horse sometimes at racing meets. On a daily basis, however, Battleship dealt with someone else.

Preston Morris Burch looked more like a professor than a racetracker. But his father had sustained a Hall of Fame career training Thoroughbreds, and someday his son Elliott would do the same. Although Preston Burch had trained in such rambunctious places as Tijuana, Mexico, he was a complete Georgia gentleman. Burley Parke, a trainer who was mentored by Burch, would recall, "He was a teacher who imparted the principles of fine and honest moral living along with education in how to train a race horse and how to race that horse with honor." Those qualities had led Will duPont to hire Burch, and Marion soon followed. Marion also would find Preston's brother Selby Burch to be a thoughtful and capable trainer for her jump racers.

Battleship soon became familiar with the Burch headquarters, the old Bennings racetrack, which had become a training center, near Washington, D.C. It was only a few hops from the active big track where he would hit his next learning curve.

Pimlico was a far cry from the grassy plain at Camden or the country gallop at Curles Neck Farm. Battleship found himself in a hybrid situation: crossing the kind of dirt track he knew so well to reach an infield turf course, then galloping much farther than any of his dirt track races but inside a smaller oval and making tighter turns. He got away last of fourteen in the Linstead Steeplechase and never gained much momentum. Bassett let him coast home near the back of the pack. His performance was so nearly invisible that people soon forgot Battleship ever raced at Pimlico on May 1, 1933. On the bright side, the shakedown cruise set him up for Marion's real target ten days later: the Billy Barton.

Several hours of rain had just stopped when Battleship carried Carroll Bassett onto squishy turf at Pimlico, following a legend. Billy Barton himself again led the post parade, looking as grand as a king. So far, he was a king without an heir, still the only all-American horse to give a great performance at Aintree. Watching him and remembering her Grand National failure, Marion might try to perceive what Billy Barton had that Trouble Maker had not. Then Billy Barton left the course, and it was Battleship's time to show whether Marion duPont Somerville could win the Billy Barton 'chase three years in a row.

He had adapted to Pimlico. Today, Battleship started well, and his cruising speed helped him avoid trouble in a crowded field. He probably wouldn't trip over a fallen comrade because only one horse went out ahead of him. Somewhere behind him, during the second circuit, two horses came to grief. People rushed out to take care of them; the field swept on.

After following a leader for two and a half miles, Battleship took over on the final turn. Behind him, three more jumping horses fell. Beside him, a horse named Kim flew up on the outside. They took the last fence together, Kim jumping better, Battleship not so polished. But when their feet hit the turf, Battleship knew very well how to gallop home. He won the final fifty-yard dash, opening daylight on his rivals, closing the distance between his old and new identities. As a three-year-old, Battleship never made it to Pimlico. Today, twice as old, he shone there like the classic horse his breeder had intended him to be.

It was funny how intentions could end up wrong and right at the same time. Marion showed a glimmer of the old-fashioned lady that her mother had taught her to be, a lady who wrote correspondence on beautiful stationery with her elegant monogram embossed at the top. But Marion also represented herself with her now renowned racing colors, her initials MdPS stamped in old rose and silver on pale blue paper. And along with managing her own routines, her responsibilities during these hard times included the unforeseen, such as helping her brother finance work relief projects in Delaware.

Throughout it all, she cultivated relationships that had deep roots in her life. She jaunted to Richmond for the June wedding of Harriet Hildreth Scott, a longtime friend whose parents had bonded with Marion's parents. Then Marion joined forces with another member of the George Cole Scott family, Alice Cole—a companion nearly her own age, who shared memories of Marion and Tom's wedding; a bride-to-be who might ask Marion for advice about marriage later in life (next month, Alice was going to marry Dr. John Hughes, a leader of the Deep Run Hunt); a friend who might help Marion evaluate her life then and now, or might simply enjoy a horsey getaway. Without husband or fiancé, the ladies ventured to

Boston. On June 15, at the first country club ever opened in the United States, Battleship would race for the National Hunt Cup.

Racing at The Country Club in Brookline, Massachusetts, had a certain zest for Carroll Bassett, who once upon a time had galloped his horse on the Westminster School's football field. Once a year here at Brookline, club members sacrificed part of their golf course to galloping Thoroughbreds. Bassett also had his sights set on a special prize: the Bryan Trophy, for the winningest amateur rider at The Country Club's meet plus a single day at Raceland, a private estate near Framingham. Last year, Carroll had tied for first place but lost the drawing to break the tie. To succeed this year, he of course had to ride his best—but he also was counting on his friend Mrs. Somerville. As the *Boston Herald* noticed, Marion was bringing "two great horses which stand out prominently in the more than 300 entries"—Annapolis and Battleship. Both were Carroll's mounts now. Marion had decided that Noel Laing would handle her timber horses; Battleship and Annapolis raced over brush, Carroll's specialty. Also, Annapolis often competed on the flat rather than over jumps. Carroll, weighing less than 140 pounds, was light enough to ride flat races at the hunt meets.

And so Carroll returned to The Country Club with designs upon the National Hunt Cup, the Bryan Trophy . . . and maybe, a girl. Jane Fowler, a shapely figure among the hunting folks who gathered to watch morning workouts, a sweet face among the gallery in the afternoons who wouldn't begrudge Carroll for doing his best to outrace her brother, Andy.

Despite her own horseback prowess, Jane wouldn't picture herself riding races here. Except maybe one. For several years now, The Country Club had been offering the provocative spectacle of a Ladies' Race. Young women revealing their forms in tall boots and flared breeches made one gentleman picture the club's original patrons, Victorian families who wouldn't even say the word "leg" in polite company and might blush at the suggestive shapes of furniture. "What would be the feelings of the women folk of our early members," he wondered, "ladies who, if history lies not, felt that propriety demanded that they drape the 'limbs' of their tables!"

Riding in the Ladies' Race made young women feel fantastically modern. Watching them, Marion duPont Somerville became a link between generations. Her twenty-one-year-old self had seemed so bold, daring to fork her legs around a horse at Madison Square Garden. But now she seemed a far cry from this younger set wearing light pants without covering jackets and hustling to the finish line like male jockeys with their bottoms in the air.

Though amusing to watch, doing that kind of thing wasn't for Marion. She wouldn't even lounge at home wearing loose-fitting slacks, as some fashionable young ladies did. But Marion had something in common with young matrons who dared to ride the Ladies' Race, sporting what looked like their husbands' clothes. Once upon a time, she had worn pants when they helped her perform a specific job. Marion wasn't going to dress more acceptably and perform worse. Neither would these women. Instead, they ran their race in the morning, clad as they pleased but leaving plenty of time to change into proper dresses for the afternoon. And then, with the ladies looking ladylike, the men got down to work.

The Country Club's opening day highlight would be Battleship's race. His top rival would be a team Carroll Bassett knew especially well: Anderson Fowler and the good horse Peacock, which Andy had bought from Carroll a few weeks back. Andy might feel especially good about his chances today. Battleship would be carrying 162 pounds, Peacock only 152.

They set out to cover three miles across lush fairways, dirt-covered strips of "automobile road," and part of a conventional track. Noel Laing showed the way with Mrs. Jock Whitney's Rosy Covert, who had run away during the post parade. Peacock hovered close. Carroll rated Battleship several lengths behind, relaxing, saving ground.

They were galloping uphill near the grandstand when Noel fell out of the race. Instead of rising above the Liverpool hedge, Rosy Covert busted through, stubbing his nose on the turf, Noel kneeling on his withers as they came to earth. Behind them, slightly to the right, Carroll had about one stride for keeping Battleship in the clear, taking off, and hoping they gave the falling horse and rider enough room. Everyone succeeded. No one, horse or human, got hurt. Peacock, Battleship, and the rest motored on for the final lap.

Conserving his high-weighted mount, Bassett let Battleship idle well back. With a half mile to go, he had plenty of horse but also the leaders blocking him, no way to slingshot up the rail unless—thinking fast—Bassett took a reckless chance. Near the transition from golf course to flat track, The Country Club's temporary steeplechase course didn't have a permanent inner rail. Instead, a man stood like a living fence post, holding up a long tape where a rail would have been. Stuck in traffic with time running out, Bassett charged Battleship at the tape man. The startled fellow jumped back, pulling the "rail" with him, creating an inner path.

It was a move only a rogue could imagine and only a bold horse would perform. Without technically going off course, Battleship bravely shot through the narrow opening. Up ahead, Peacock looked like the winner, but Battleship was in the race.

Battleship felt two whip slaps, Carroll's signal to go all out. Then he needed only the strength of Carroll's hands pushing, the spark of Carroll's wild energy, and the sight of their target ahead. Battleship knew: catch that horse. At the finish, there was Andy Fowler well streamlined with Peacock, a picture book ride, but Carroll finding something from beyond. As Battleship plunged his head past Peacock, squeezing his body beside the rail, Andy could not help glancing over at the force of nature that was beating him when he should have won: Carroll flinging all his force straight ahead, Battleship matching him. The *Boston Herald* called it "one of the most thrilling finishes" that The Country Club ever had seen. Battleship beat last year's winning time by more than thirty seconds.

No one doubted the little horse's quality. Some might question his rider's sportsmanship. Some laughed at Bassett's audacity, making the boundary man jump back. Others cringed. But Andy Fowler, who had the most to lose, did not claim foul. Quite possibly, he didn't perceive any foul to claim. Even the racing stewards considered the rules stretched but not broken. They let the result stand.

Everyone took a day off. Then Carroll did something during day two at The Country Club that really got people talking. This time, he couldn't do it without Marion's help.

Annapolis started the afternoon in sparkling style, easily winning a flat race at a mile and a sixteenth. The crowd didn't reckon they would see him again that day. But Annapolis also had been entered in the third race, a mile and a half on the flat. And when the field assembled, here was

Annapolis entering the paddock and Carroll Bassett stepping up to ride him again. The same horse, twice in one afternoon.

"This is something I had heard of but never before saw done at a big meeting," Bill Streett reported. Country Club displeasure showed through as he wrote, "It might be done somewhere in the sticks but not at a place like Brookline."

Experts weren't accusing Marion or Carroll of mistreating the horse. Streett, himself a prominent owner, trainer, and rider, noted that "Annapolis ran a corking good race both times" and took the second race "in just as easy a fashion as he did in the first." Somerville and Bassett had double-dipped with a fit horse who thoroughly outclassed his opponents. But their tactic made Marion seem greedy. And she had been, in a way, although perhaps not for herself. The key was Carroll: his unluckiness losing the Bryan Trophy in 1932, his chance to capture it in 1933, if he and Marion dared.

Carroll made the tie-breaker again, thanks to his rule-bending rally with Battleship and Marion's willingness to let people talk when Annapolis ran twice in one day. Carroll's 1932 performance, two winners, would not have been enough. This year, three wins put him in a three-way tie for top honors. Carroll won the draw and took the trophy home.

For Carroll Bassett, riding and racing horses had become something to do instead of going to Princeton and becoming an executive or an academic, something instead of marketing his fine art, something that didn't add up to anything world changing, compared with his father's teaching and engineering work, but validated the restless reaches of Carroll's soul.

Was it the same for Marion? Years later, a racing reporter would ask her which of her many horse activities she enjoyed the most. "Raising Thoroughbreds," Marion promptly replied. "The only reason I didn't have them at first was because I just did not know them, but they really are the finest of all." She had come to racing as a connoisseur and stuck with it as a true farmer, testing the full capabilities of the horses she bought and bred because that was how you improved your produce—not coddling, not denial, but realistically searching out weak spots. In a way it was funny that the girl who had worried when her governess

administered exams did not shrink from testing her horses thoroughly.
Or maybe it made perfect sense. Overseeing her racehorses so closely that
she even consulted with her brother about the best liniment mixture
to use on Racketeer's legs and how to apply it, Marion invested part of
her self in her horses' progress. When they faltered, she gave them various chances to do something well. When her horses overcame their
obstacles, Marion triumphed, too. Their successes became a way of vindi-
cating herself.

Racehorse ownership could be a superficial, self-promoting thing.
Collecting gold and silver trophies could proclaim the owner's importance, a version of the spectacular jewelry that later generations would
call "bling." And yet the racers also gave splashes of awe to people not
easily awed. A trophy room could be a bragging display—but also a scrapbook of moments when a soul was transported by a horse. Sometimes a
trophy was a reminder of a romance.

During August 1933, the search for pride and passion led people back
to the Saratoga yearling sales, where once upon a time Man o' War had
begun transforming Sam Riddle's life. This year, shoppers paid special
attention to the first offspring of Triple Crown champion Gallant Fox. A
Gallant Fox colt brought the summer's top price, a paltry $13,000. The
buyer was baking powder magnate Warren Wright, busy converting his
father's Calumet Farm from harness racers to Thoroughbreds.

Marion duPont Somerville joined the auction crowd without making
any headlines. It was almost as if she moved in a parallel universe, inhabiting
the same Saratoga as Warren Wright yet holding different ideals. She came
here not to buy Gallant Fox babies but to race a well-bred stallion the same
age as Gallant Fox, a runner peaking too late for things that most owners
thought mattered most. American racing invested heavily in early bloomers and big earners on the flat. A six-year-old steeplechaser? Most people
did not throw their hearts and fortunes into helping a horse become that.

Yet for Marion, the stallion racing for her here said something about
competence. Instead of giving up with a problem foot and shuffling off to
a minor chance at stud, here came Battleship parading past the famous
Saratoga clubhouse, favorite for the Eastern Horse Club Hunters' Steeplechase Handicap. He crossed a main track "very deep in mud" and didn't
seem to mind. He rated kindly for Carroll during their first lap of the slip-

pery turf, took the lead with a mile to go, and won with speed to spare despite carrying top weight of 165 pounds.

But Battleship had far to go to match the pride of Marion's barn. In the landscape of her racing operation, Trouble Maker was the cathedral built and perfected over many seasons, towering along the skyline. He proved it even when things went wrong for his American return at the end of September, stepping into the Meadow Brook Hunt Cup wearing number thirteen. He looked vibrant. But Noel Laing had fallen ill that afternoon, running a fever of 103 degrees. Trouble Maker went racing instead with Bobby Young, an outstanding Long Island amateur rider who was new to him, in the saddle.

Trouble Maker stood sideways as the flag fell, and for a moment Young did nothing. When the starter did not recall the field, Trouble Maker began his race about five lengths behind. Then misfortune melted away. Trouble Maker easily reached contention and performed beautifully. Down the homestretch he drove clear, winning America's oldest hunt club race with authority.

Battleship cruised into autumn with an excellent record of four wins from his first six races over jumps. Then his luck turned. In mid-October, despite beautiful weather at Joseph E. Widener's eastern Pennsylvania estate, Battleship and Bassett fell at the eighth fence of the Erdenheim Cup and did not go on. (Their mishap wasn't considered important enough for details to be published.) Reappearing eleven days later at Far Hills, New Jersey, they were thwarted by a loose girth. Maybe Battleship had acted like his daddy, but not in a good way. Man o' War had a habit of tensing his abdominal muscles while being saddled, inflating his middle just before his trainer, Lou Feustel, fastened the girth. Feustel had to make sure that Big Red had deflated, then cinch him tighter, before sending him out to race. Maybe someone let Battleship get away with the same trick. As the little horse rose to the first fence in the Bedminster Chase, his saddle slipped sideways and flung Bassett off. They had no chance to regroup before the field galloped far away.

From jumping laughably high to dumping his rider overboard, Battleship ended his first year of steeplechasing as it had begun: with unsophisticated comedy. Trouble Maker ended his season with noble drama, winning the Piedmont Gold Cup in northern Virginia and the Alligator Cup in

Maryland. Both shared in the honor of bringing a second consecutive title to Marion: America's leading hunt-racing owner, Mrs. T. H. Somerville.

That Christmas, Marion and Tom Somerville gave refuge to an old friend whose plans had fallen through. Around Thanksgiving, their friend had sailed to England with a buddy who would get married there. He was planning to serve as best man, a role he knew well. But the groom became ill and put off the wedding indefinitely. In mid-December, the best man returned alone to the United States. Instead of hunkering down at his parents' North Carolina home or catching up in California with the woman gossip reporters kept saying he might marry, he landed at Montpelier. And so Tom and Marion spent Christmas week with their best man, Randolph Scott.

He was the same genial, outdoorsy fellow they remembered, even though he now lived in Hollywood. How was that going to turn out? Marion might wonder. When Randy had managed a springtime visit with her family a couple of years ago in Augusta, Georgia, his career hardly seemed like much to write home about. Hollywood had quickly thought that Scott looked like a leading man, then just as quickly realized that his acting ability hadn't caught up with his looks and charm. When Marion saw Randy at Augusta, she might have been more impressed by his near-professional golf game than his upcoming feature film, *Women Men Marry*. "A Thrilling Drama!" newspaper ads would scream. "Vividly Portraying the Escapades of Wandering Wives and Loose Husbands." The lurid publicity seemed out of keeping with her friend who impressed everyone as a genuine gentleman.

This Christmas, Scott could describe the progress he had made since April 1931 and also joke, with typical modesty, about his struggles. He now had a contract with Paramount Pictures, but Paramount was not dazzled by his acting and was cashing in on his skills with horses and guns. While Randy labored to improve his range, his housemate Cary Grant vaulted toward the A-list. Grant recently had played the main love interest of the outrageous Mae West, a top-ten box office attraction, in *She Done Him Wrong* and *I'm No Angel*. Randy toiled away mostly in Westerns—*The Thundering Herd, To the Last Man, Broken Dreams*. Perhaps he discussed his dreams for something better as he sat in Marion's Red Room, admiring the Trouble Maker bronzes over the mantel and describing how his work in movie Westerns nearly got him trampled.

Hollywood gossips wouldn't care about Randy's conversations with Tom Somerville, which probably featured their shared passion for golf. They might easily overlook the reticent Mrs. Somerville, not recognizing that she saw connections between Randolph Scott the movie actor and Randy Scott the adolescent "social lion" from the Woodberry Forest School, only a few miles up the road from Montpelier. The movie colony knew that Scott came from a more elite background than the typical Hollywood vagabond but still couldn't picture how much he inhabited a different world from theirs. Marion knew that young man, the one who had written a gracious note to her father during his final illness. Hollywood might not guess that out-of-the-way Orange County, Virginia, could seem as much like home to George Randolph Scott as anywhere else on earth.

As 1933 waned, Scott returned to Hollywood. Marion motored down to Camden with her Somerville posse, renting a handsomely simple white clapboard house only a couple of blocks from the Bassetts' Goody Castle. In January, she might visit St. Augustine, Florida, when her husband played in a golf tournament there, but this winter, rather than go questing to England, she would stay near all of her racehorses. Some of them carried her out hunting. That winter you could see one of her best new racing prospects, Wild Son, acting anything but wild while Marion rode him sidesaddle. She also would deepen old and new friendships when Carroll Bassett's parents welcomed Noel Laing and Jane Fowler to Goody Castle as their houseguests.

Marion wouldn't know about a development across the sea, where hurdle races and steeplechases ruled the winter season. Two days after Christmas, Bruce Hobbs turned thirteen years old. Reg Hobbs, back on his feet and immersed in the busiest season for his training yard, promptly put his boy to work in the early mornings before school, employing him as an exercise rider and all-purpose stable lad while cutting expenses. As Bruce declared, "I was just the unpaid apprentice!" His rewards came in other forms, galloping and jumping actual racehorses alongside jockey Tim Hamey, the 1932 Grand National winner.

. . .

Although they lived in the same hemisphere, the spring equinox played a different rhythm for Battleship than for Bruce Hobbs. Over in England, Bruce felt the 'chasing season's energy peaking for the Grand National. Down at Camden, Battleship felt the nudge away from vacation. After a winter of relaxing and hunting, he was racing again.

Over at Aintree, the world's best steeplechasers climaxed their season by racing nearly five miles. Down at Springdale, Battleship began his season racing only two. Off to a slow start but jumping well, he rallied late to finish second in the short, quick Springdale Steeplechase. It looked as if Battleship would need longer races, where stamina overcame early speed. But Marion would see him sharper two weeks later, going about two miles at Deep Run. And she would see a duel that racegoers would remember, perhaps recalled "by more people than any single race ever run at any of the Deep Run Hunt Club meets." They would remember because heavy rain and many no-shows turned the Richmond Plate into a match race: Battleship and Carroll Bassett versus Fairy Lore and Noel Laing.

Usually, having only two starters is disappointing, but the spectators perked up as the contestants entered the paddock: *Bassett versus Laing*. As Dr. John Hughes of the Deep Run Hunt put it, "Carroll and Noel were bosom friends, but staunch rivals when riding against each other. So the setup was perfect: two top horses, two top gentleman riders, and each rider trying to outride his friend."

Someone asked Noel who he thought would win. Never one for false confidence, Noel figured that Battleship "was a little more fit." Marion, on the other hand, thought the race could go either way.

The race became Noel and Carroll's poker game. They galloped side by side for a bit, then Fairy Lore rolled out front and Battleship stalked, each rider aiming to keep his own horse comfortable while putting just enough pressure on the other. This time, two miles was not too short. Battleship pounced near the final fence and won by a measured half length, Bassett throttling down as much as possible to conserve his horse for a bigger event to come.

Later that soggy afternoon, Noel brought Trouble Maker home fourth in the Deep Run Hunt Cup. A huge disappointment from the heavy favorite, but when conditions weren't right, all you could do was try, then finish safe. They would hope for better going three weeks later in the Maryland Hunt Cup—the knightly challenge where, as one reporter wrote, "swashbuckling gentlemen jockeys, bravest of the brave, pull on their boots, as soft-bottomed as bedroom slippers, and ride for nothing where professional jockeys would not ride for a small fortune."

Maryland cooperated. "It was a perfect day, whether your fancy led you to golf, contemplation, amorous dalliance or horse racing," the sportsman Stuart Rose reported. "Some twelve to fifteen thousand of us chose horse racing." Many also chose Trouble Maker, cofavoring him with last year's winner, Captain Kettle. If Trouble Maker succeeded, he would give Marion two of the three wins needed to retire the challenge trophy that had gone unclaimed since the inaugural Maryland Hunt Cup in 1894.

A voice inside the paddock called, "Up, gentlemen, please." Twelve riders swinging up into saddles, twelve horses heading down to the start. Then a cheer of beginning, and a long shot named Fugitive spurting away to a big lead with Trouble Maker hovering in fourth place. Everyone cleared the first half dozen fences. Fugitive fell at the seventh, a relatively small obstacle beside the backstretch woods. Fortunately, he was okay and his rider bounced back up with the reins in his hands. Unfortunately, the reins had come over Fugitive's head during the fall and he had stuck his front legs through them. Instead of remounting and continuing the race, jockey Burley Cocks stood there untangling his horse.

Eleven others completed the first lap and cleared fence thirteen, a giant twin of the infamous fence three. Then the course began taking its toll. Brose Hover dropped his rider at fourteen and, scrambling away, kicked him on the forehead. Two more racers came down before the field galloped back across Tufton Road and Noel rallied Trouble Maker for the run home.

Trouble Maker flew the final fence like a fresh horse, closing the empty yards to Captain Kettle's hip. It looked like a replay of Trouble Maker's greatest hits, the final kick and relentless finish. And he *was* relentless but suddenly had no more kick. Three horses overlapped past the winning post, Trouble Maker staunchly third, the gray Menelaus driving his head into second place, Captain Kettle in the middle with the victory. A photo caught the winning rider's surprised backward glance—staring at Trouble Maker's bloody chest.

Noel hadn't known. His horse hadn't found any extra push in the final yards, but he never faltered. The blood trail led back to fence thirteen, where Trouble Maker had torn the lower right side of his chest on a stake, ripping open a triangular wound that a horseman on the scene called "as big as your two hands and deep." Pumped with adrenaline, Trouble Maker dug in and ran on, leaping the nine remaining fences as if nothing were wrong.

While the winners accepted their accolades, Trouble Maker's handlers hustled him to a nearby barn. With no veterinarian handy, Marion and Noel watched a plastic surgeon who happened to be in the crowd patiently clean and stitch the ragged wound. Meanwhile, at Union Memorial Hospital, the only rider who had been hurt that afternoon waited for a doctor's attention. Lex Wilson had survived Brose Hover's kick to the face and was getting off relatively easy, with one black eye and a cut above it. "Put a few stitches in this thing," Lex told his attendants, "and I'll be off."

But the hours meandered by, and Wilson was no closer to getting out and catching his train. He agitated: "Why doesn't a doctor sew me up?"

They assured him, "You'll be taken care of any moment, just as soon as Dr. Hallahan is finished."

"I've been waiting three hours," Wilson fumed. "What in the world is he doing?"

The answer could seem normal only near the Maryland Hunt Cup.

"What's he doing? He's sewing up Trouble Maker."

Forty years old. Forty years since little Marion du Pont was born at Bellevue Hall and spent a summer afloat with her unanchored parents. Dark haired as ever, still youthfully slim. A chiseled face with deepening weather lines accenting her blade-sharp eyes. A gentle mouth, easily lost among the harder landscape of her face because she kept it natural pink instead of dramatic red—a look that suited her, counterbalancing those penetrating eyes.

Marion the gardener might look at herself and see maturity, four decades from pollination to germination to full bloom. But did she see fulfillment? Or only more challenges to pursue?

While Trouble Maker healed—fortunate that his injury had been messy but not severe—Battleship followed Billy Barton to the post at Pimlico on a stormy May afternoon. The public bet that he would give Marion her fourth straight victory in Billy's namesake race. For the first mile, then two, Battleship waited far back, Bassett trusting his late rally. They needed to make up more than a hundred yards in the final mile—and Battleship did, flying through the rain. One more fence, then his speed should win out. One more fence . . . and Carroll's mistake, from holding nothing back. Battleship soared like a cowboy horse leaping a canyon, too long, too hard. Landing, he slipped on the rain-slick turf. Bassett popped out of the saddle and hit the ground. Battleship scampered away. Noel Laing won the Billy Barton with a twenty-to-one shot, Our Friend.

But Carroll won a chase even dearer to his heart: Jane Fowler agreed to marry him. Their announcement decorated mid-May newspapers: the nineteen-year-old bride with her teaspoon face on a flower-stem neck, the twenty-eight-year-old groom's credentials as a sculptor and a member of an elite patriotic society, the Order of the Cincinnati. Their wedding would take place in July.

Everything was aligning for Carroll Bassett, for the Somerville stable, for Battleship. They were going racing in New York. They were about to celebrate a time when everything rushes in on a full tide.

14

THEIR HIGH TIDE BEGAN WITH A parade of battleships: the U.S. fleet streaming into New York Harbor on Memorial Day 1934. And not only were there ten battleships to admire, but also carriers, cruisers, destroyers, mine sweepers, hospital ships, repair ships, store ships, submarine tenders, oil tankers, and ocean tugs—"the greatest assemblage of naval vessels in the history of the United States," the *New York Times* declared. Fresh from a record trip through the Panama Canal, resplendent with new gray paint, they filed past the *Ambrose* lightship while President Franklin D. Roosevelt reviewed their procession from a gun turret platform of the USS *Indianapolis*.

The president was supposed to sit down during the ninety-minute program. The public knew that he wore leg braces because polio had stricken him more than a dozen years ago. They knew that his legs had been weakened but only saw their leader overcoming that problem. Roosevelt did not reveal how much he also relied on his wheelchair. During public occasions he would walk to his assigned seat, beaming greetings, letting his high-wattage smile and sociability distract from his halting walk. For a long ceremony such as this, no one would have thought twice if he had claimed his seat and stuck there.

But as the battleship *Pennsylvania* emerged through distant mist, the president could not help himself. "The sight of the warships obviously moved the President," one witness wrote, "as he resolutely stood, bracing himself with his hands on the rail of his platform and refusing to accede to requests that he rest. He kept his eyes glued to the line of vessels, hat in hand, while others in the party attempted to see all that was going on and had about the same difficulty as a spectator at a five-ring circus." And no wonder. There were nearly a hundred navy ships slapping over the swells, and overhead two hundred navy airplanes carving dogfight patterns in the air. Aircraft engines whined and thrummed, each navy vessel honored the president with gunfire salutes, and the president's ship answered each one with a voice a reporter called "a deep bass roar." Among it all, about a hundred spectators' boats of all sizes gleefully sounded their whistles and horns.

That evening, thousands of civilians gathered near the Hudson River, waiting along the Palisades of New Jersey and Riverside Drive of New York for another show. And suddenly caught their breath. All at once, columns of pale blue light—navy signal lights—shot straight up from the water. From Manhattan to Yonkers, the lights began crisscrossing the sky. For an hour, battleship crews drew patterns on the heavens. If they wanted, Carroll Bassett and Jane Fowler could have watched from the River Club, where they had danced within heavenly platinum and blue.

That night, the fleet declared, *We are ready.* The next day, Long Island saw what the racehorse Battleship had to say.

That afternoon, a perfect afternoon, brought a host of navy officers on liberty to Long Island for the United Hunt races. And in the Roslyn Steeplechase, what could be a better bet than Battleship? One man who noticed the sailors "having a fairly enjoyable time, unhampered by discipline," reckoned that "it was up to the chestnut seven-year-old to do his bit."

In fact, Battleship was about to come into his own. He was about to prove how age is a flexible idea, measured differently depending on the challenge. When Kellsboro' Jack had won the Grand National at age seven, during his second season of steeplechasing, everyone called him young. Now, the *New York Times* would call Battleship an "old campaigner," although he was only seven years old and this was his second

year of jump racing. A world that thought Battleship old at age seven was
the same world that saw a woman—even one so vital as Marion duPont
Somerville—heading "over the hill" at age forty. Horse racing and the
world at large preferred a romance with youth. And yet some challenges
were made for maturity.

Today showed that Battleship and Carroll had perfected their style,
racing several lengths behind the pace, reeling them in along the backstretch of the last lap, surging on the final turn. This time they sailed the
water jump alongside What Have You, who was carrying 10 pounds less
than Battleship's 163. A photograph told everything: What Have You
dragging his hind feet through the brush, his neck flat, his rider sitting
almost upright like a foxhunter in an old print; Battleship in full flight, his
hind feet about six inches above the hedge, his neck slightly arched but
also reaching for every forward inch, Carroll crouching for speed like a
jockey on the flat. What Have You and his rider's body language showed
effort and uncertainty. Every line of Battleship and Bassett showed flu-
ency and said, *We're going for it.*

Battleship won easily. He was ready for Belmont Park, the biggest
"big track" in the United States. He was ready to prove he was first class.

The fact was, Battleship's detour from flat tracks to hunter races could
seem like a downgrade. The general public paid a lot less attention to
jumpers in general and hunters in particular. And until recently, hunt
race horses rarely had excelled when they entered professional steeplechases at the big tracks. As one expert noted, "It was generally thought
that only second- or third-raters ran at the amateur affairs." But that perception hadn't kept up with reality. Marion had bought Battleship knowing that the hunt meets were changing, that owners were upgrading their
stables, that more and more winners needed big track speed. This was
true even when Battleship's Belmont Park debut was called the Aiken
Hunters' Steeplechase.

Only seven days after navy officers cheered him to victory, Battleship
raced at the showplace where Man o' War had racked up four American
records. He went off as the favorite, but many insiders thought that Inception, who had beaten a good field at Pimlico that spring, was "ripe" to
win today.

And Inception looked sharp as he led for the first mile, but Battleship was always at his heels. By the second mile, he had sauntered up outside Inception and casually relieved him of the lead. Battleship let Inception come back beside him, and Ray Woolfe had another look at the little horse who had leaped ridiculously high at Camden—another look until the last half furlong, when Battleship pulled away to an easy win.

And oh! He had done it fast. Last year, the Aiken Hunters' Steeplechase winner completed the distance of about two and a half miles in record time of four minutes, fifty-seven seconds. Battleship clocked 4:46 $^3/_5$.

He wouldn't rest yet. Next week, Battleship would seek his third win in sixteen days. And his most momentous. At The Country Club in Brookline, the National Hunt Cup challenge trophy had gone unclaimed for nineteen years. All a horse owner had to do was win the race twice, with the same runner or different ones—but no one had. If Battleship could carry 170 pounds to victory this year, Marion would be the one.

Maybe it wasn't Carroll Bassett's fault, but audacity seemed to be spreading at The Country Club this year. It cropped up during the early morning workouts, where riders were supposed to tell a track official which horses they were exercising. Afterward, Eastern Horse Club president Bayard Tuckerman Jr. complained, "You ask them 'What horse is that?' and all they say is 'Mae West' or some fictitious name like that." It seemed as if too many stables wanted to keep their hopes for a betting coup to themselves. Carroll, whose commute had been delayed by thick morning fog, was not among the perpetrators. And anyway, The Country Club might recognize handsome Annapolis and rugged little Battleship.

Annapolis and Battleship both came racing on Saturday, June 16, a sunny but surprisingly cool afternoon, chilled by a wind blowing in from Boston Harbor. Marion looked summery in a light-colored hat and short-sleeved dress but warmed her hands with white gloves and her shoulders with a fur stole. Carroll Bassett drew attention from spectators wondering if he had "tucked the tips of his ears under his [jockey] cap" to keep them warm. Then he won the opening race with Annapolis, while his fiancée and her cousin who would be her maid of honor watched along with Marion.

Soon it was Battleship's turn for his third race in just over two weeks— but it was easy. He relaxed, then swooped past his opponents. He was much more than fifteen pounds better than Arundel, much more than eight pounds better than Our Friend. A sportsman stated that "he fenced beautiful and received a handsome ride." Again, Battleship made quick time with energy in reserve. The *Boston Herald* ran a photograph of Marion accepting the elusive challenge trophy for her permanent collection, printing it under the headline, "Succeeded Where Men Failed."

Marion got a scare a couple of races later, when her horse Billy Bozo fell at a fence in full view of the grandstand and threw Noel Laing. While Noel was down, a passing horse's hoof hit his head. It was the kind of moment that killed jockeys in the days of silken caps and no helmets. Noel was lucky: skullcaps made of dense fiber were now required. He came away with a concussion—"Laing was dazed for about an hour after the race," a journalist reported—but he was alive.

Except for Noel's accident, it had been a joyous day. Three wins in all for Marion and three for Carroll, two of these as a team. They looked forward to the meet's second day, even while reminders of a troubled world drifted into their sanctuary.

Jane Fowler was watching the races again on Monday, June 18, but not from her aunt and uncle's box. Mr. and Mrs. George S. West of Chestnut Hill, Massachusetts, were hosting a special guest from overseas, in town for his twenty-five-year reunion at Harvard. The Country Club crowd took his presence calmly, but his return to the United States had ignited controversy. To attend his reunion, Dr. Ernst Hanfstaengl had needed special permission to take leave from his job as chief foreign press officer for German Chancellor Adolf Hitler.

Slipping away from his ocean liner in a tugboat rather than landing openly at the New York docks, Dr. Hanfstaengl had dodged fifteen hundred protesters chanting, "Down with Hitler." Arriving in Cambridge, he had been spared the sight of posters that sprouted overnight all around Harvard Yard and were stripped away by university police:

GIVE HANFSTAENGL A DEGREE, "MASTER OF CONCENTRATION CAMPS"

MAKE HIM A MASTER OF TORTURE

MAKE HIM A MASTER OF STERILIZATION

A BACHELOR OF BOOK-BURNING

FREE THAELMANN AND ALL THE IMPRISONED ANTI-FASCISTS

Many Americans, unwilling to get tangled up in another European conflict so soon after the horrific world war, found it easy to dismiss the protesters as radicals and cranky minorities. The *New York Times* remarked that the demonstrators lying in wait for Hanfstaengl's boat were "mostly Communists," with "a few hundred Young Socialists and representatives of anti-Nazi organizations" for good measure. When a Boston reporter asked him, "What did you think of your welcome?" Hanfstaengl enthused, "The welcome was splendid! Splendid! All the *real* people were graciousness itself." He stressed the word "real" "almost imperceptibly," the reporter said, but the message was clear. Friends and dignitaries who welcomed Dr. Hanfstaengl, entertained him, and lodged him in their homes were real; anyone who questioned his work for the führer was not.

Hanfstaengl insisted that he was not here to discuss politics, though he realized that some Americans were outraged by the severe anti-Semitic policies being instituted by Hitler's government. At a Boston press conference, he said only that the situation "will be normal before long." Rabbi Joseph Shubow, editor of a Jewish newspaper, asked him to clarify that statement.

"Did you mean by extermination?" the rabbi inquired.

Dr. Hanfstaengl didn't blink. "Now, now," he replied soothingly. "That's a political question."

"Dr. Hanfstaengl stood smilingly waiting for further questions," a reporter observed, "but [the superintendent of the Harvard yard police] pushed through the group of reporters, shoved Rabbi Shubow aside, seized Dr. Hanfstaengl by the arm and propelled him out of the yard." That night, six Boston policemen guarded the house where Hanfstaengl slept. The next afternoon, four accompanied him at the races. The Country Club's policies, which kept Jewish people out, did not welcome detectives William Goldston and Benjamin Goodman onto their grounds.

Reporters noticed Dr. Hanfstaengl ensconced in the West family box, with a friend occasionally running wagers to the bookies for him. Word got around that Hanfstaengl picked one winner "because the rider wore a brown shirt like the Nazis." The public couldn't actually see, however, into his heart. Hanfstaengl let them guess, let them assume, because assumptions might keep him safe. He had helped promote Hitler as a supreme leader, perhaps relishing his own closeness to power, but he was losing influence over what he had helped create. He would feel unsettled less than two weeks after this day at the races when Hitler decapitated his own militia, having dozens of Brownshirt leaders arrested and killed during the Night of the Long Knives. Hanfstaengl would return to his job, but his doubts would start to show. In 1937 he would escape Germany. Eventually, he would share inside information about Hitler and the Third Reich with the White House. But right now, Dr. Hanfstaengl smiled and laughed away deadly serious questions, doing and saying what he figured he needed to get by.

His opposite stood near the paddock, a small, trim woman who said only what she meant. And maybe that freedom was her greatest luxury, beyond even her historic home or the racehorses sporting her colors.

And today, she triumphed. Today, Marion duPont Somerville won all four races that her horses entered. Carroll Bassett rode three of them, matching his previous record of three wins in one day. Marion had no entry in the final race, so Carroll picked up a ride on someone else's good horse, and when he won—the only rider with four wins in one day at Brookline—the crowd did not stream for the exits but "stayed to roar an ovation" as he returned for the victory ceremony.

Today, Carroll had come of age. Everything he had been studying for the past handful of years coalesced. These races were his Princeton final exams. These victories, his A-plus.

As the crowd thinned, a *Boston Herald* reporter noticed the two leading figures of The Country Club meet locked in conversation. Not quite daring to eavesdrop, or being discreet, he only wrote, "Mrs. Somerville and Bassett had a heart-to-heart talk after the final race, probably reviewing a very glorious week-end." Reviewing, perhaps, but they had so much to discuss: Marion's racing plans for the rest of the year; Carroll's wedding, about six weeks away; Marion's offer to build a cottage at Montpelier where he and Jane could live.

They had one more day of sport before leaving Massachusetts, hopping down the road to Framingham. Marion's only starter at the Raceland meet won, giving her eight victories in three days. This time, Carroll enjoyed being a spectator rather than riding. A newsman noticed him strolling around Raceland, "complacently smoking a huge cigar."

Mr. and Mrs. Carroll K. Bassett were exchanging their vows in Peapack, New Jersey, and sailing off on their Bermuda honeymoon while Mrs. Thomas H. Somerville supervised the Orange County Horse Show in late July. Eventually, Marion would hear details about the ceremony and reception, a small, family affair because one of Jane's grandmothers recently had died. She may have thought back to her own wedding, with its reception catered for a hundred guests. She could have thought on how it felt to be in Jane's shoes, so young and pretty, sharing a romantic island getaway. Or she may have been too busy with her visitors and show horses and the horse show ball. It may have been significant when a newspaper mentioned that Dr. John Hughes and his wife, Marion's old friend Alice Cole, were staying with Mrs. Somerville at Montpelier that weekend—and said nothing about Mr. Somerville's whereabouts. Or that may have been an oversight, though the same paper had reported that both Tom and Marion stayed with Dr. and Mrs. Hughes during the Deep Run meet back in the spring.

Whatever was happening privately, Marion kept up her routines. Saratoga as usual in August, though Battleship did not race. And she looked forward to a breakthrough for her brother. On August 25, Will duPont hosted a race meet on his Fair Hill estate in Maryland. Fellow horseman Bill Streett took it all in and wrote, "It is impossible to say too many good things about an establishment like this." Designing everything himself, Will had not launched his meet until everything was right. For several years he had been tending the racecourses at Fair Hill until the ground became, as Bill Streett proclaimed it, "as near perfect as possible." Then, only a few weeks before the racing, Will duPont added huge brush obstacles up to five feet eight inches in height, several inches taller than anything found at Aintree.

He had created a breathtaking spectacle. But Will wasn't aiming to hurt horses. He wanted to balance forgiveness with respect. The horse should respect the fence; the fence should forgive the horse. Extreme height got a horse's full attention, and yet the top several inches of brush were flexible, letting a horse ruffle safely across even if he didn't jump clear. Comparing Will's work with old-fashioned or status quo obstacles at other hunt meets, an expert commented, "Mr. du Pont put up what might fairly be described as the course of tomorrow."

Will's ideals now were on display at Fair Hill, open for others to try. Marion's were flourishing at Montpelier, mostly out of public view. That September, an ambassador arrived in the form of Humphrey Finney, a charming fellow about a decade younger than herself, his voice recalling his roots in Manchester, England, an up-and-comer in the racing world who for some time had been describing various Thoroughbred stud farms for readers of a leading racing publication, *The Blood-Horse* magazine. Whatever he found, Finney presented it tactfully. But Marion clearly astonished him. Instead of being handed over to a farm manager and shown a few highlights of the place, Finney found the owner herself serving as "my highly competent guide on one of the most thorough inspections I have ever made on any breeding farm."

Marion not only acted as if she had nothing to hide—she proved it. Amazed and amused, Finney reported that "if there was a horse we did not see, or a spot where one could have been 'hidden out' that we did not visit, I do not know where it could have been." Furthermore, Marion didn't wait to see whether Finney noticed, as he put it, "any hidden defect of conformation or soundness in the few instances they were present." She pointed out any flaws right away.

Montpelier's horse facilities were not magnificent—Finney called the mail-order barns and other equipment "adequate, practical and not at all elaborate"—but Finney was impressed. He admired the consistent quality of Marion's broodmares, "deep, roomy individuals about 15.2 or 15.3 with that indispensable motherly look about them." He saw an entire herd of Thoroughbreds "in excellent bloom . . . and in healthy, lean condition." He agreed when Marion said, "Fat can cover a multitude of ills."

Speaking to a bloodstock industry dominated by men, Finney applauded Marion's way of raising a hardy racehorse. He wrote that her yearlings were "in the barn only long enough for their feeding and training, which is directed by Mrs. Somerville." He confided that "it is Mrs. Somerville's opinion—and her trainers bear her out—that she is less likely to have trouble with bucked shins and other ailments of overworked immature bone if her horses spend most of their time outdoors." Admiring Montpelier's landscape, he recommended, "It is quite logical that these animals, having the run of these wide rolling fields, should develop a tougher bone than their more pampered brethren confined to their stalls most of the time."

Even the most thorough inspection finally had to end. His tour seemed to put Finney in a reflective mood, remembering the champion show horses raised by William du Pont on this very land back in the early 1920s, when Finney was a young horseman new to America. He poured his thoughts into a sentence long enough to reach from one era to another. "Having seen a few old 'chasers at the big training barn," Finney concluded, "I drove Mrs. Somerville back to the house preparatory to leaving, and remarking on the general good disposition and soundness of her horses I found her, too, to be a worshipper at the shrine of the triple godhead, conformation, constitution and disposition, and I left with the thought that, with such material at hand and with such common sense management, the Montpelier Stud would make as great a mark in Thoroughbred breeding as its predecessor had in the Hackney world of the past."

That certainly was Marion's goal. First, however, she would aim for the top with a horse she had not raised herself but had guided toward his highest potential.

For two years, Battleship had built his reputation in races for qualified hunters. He had maintained a special status, like an amateur athlete staying qualified for the Olympic Games. But now Battleship had won the National Hunt Cup twice. Within his division, he couldn't climb any higher. He could aim for more of the same next year, accepting everhigher weights—or he could graduate. Marion decided to risk not going back. She went ahead and entered Battleship in the Grand National at Belmont Park, open to the top brush horses in America.

And when September 15 arrived, it looked like a horrible day to try such a thing. Surly gray skies stopped raining only an hour or so before Battleship's race, leaving the main track deep in mud and turning the turf course into a bog. Battleship would carry Carroll Bassett three miles over that course. He would be getting fifteen pounds from the favorite, Canandaigua, but giving weight to his other foes, including the veteran Arc Light. Arc Light was ten years old now and didn't win as often but still was especially dangerous at Belmont Park. He had won this very race in 1929 and set a course record in 1930.

Battleship stepped up to the start as jaunty as Carroll's first rocking horse, a high-headed creation with eyes and ears pointed to a distant prize. As usual, he wore his forelock, mane, and tail neatly braided, a practice brought to racing from foxhunting, where a flowing mane and tail could catch on branches and hedges. For two and a half miles he tracked lightly weighted Wrackon, conceding the younger horse fourteen and a half pounds but Carroll expecting to pass at will.

And so it proved. A half mile out, Battleship darted to the front. Arc Light charged up at his right side and Battleship drifted out toward him, not bumping but taking his opponent a bit wide. Here was the personality that Marion had come to expect from her confident little stallion. "If he came up to a horse and didn't like the looks of him," she noticed, "he'd muscle in on him. He was a toughie all the way."

Unwavering, they opened half a dozen lengths on the third horse. Arc Light never quit but tired more quickly in the final yards. Battleship edged away by a length, then a bit more, even though he was carrying one pound more. Afterward, Arc Light's rider claimed foul for interference. The stewards not only disagreed, they fined him $25 for making a "frivolous" objection.

Riding back from his biggest victory, Carroll looked like the little boy he had been twenty-five years ago, delighted with the finest rocking horse money could buy, sitting up fluently straight and beaming to his audience. Battleship strode back to the grandstand with his neck lathered, the braided mane near his rider's hands rumpled undone, his ears brightly up, his face as fine and blunt as a prehistoric stone axe, his gaze as inscrutable as a dinosaur's.

He had become a full-fledged champion, the best horse over a brush course in America this year. He had nearly balanced his books, if you didn't count all his maintenance expenses—only $480 short, now, of earning back the $12,000 Marion had paid for him. And he had got Carroll anticipating what could lie ahead.

Yet his triumph seemed inconspicuous compared with what happened at Belmont Park later that afternoon. First, a pack of two-year-olds splashed out for the richest race in the world. In less than a minute and twenty seconds, the Futurity winner would earn nearly $78,000. For several moments it looked as if that lottery winner could be Will duPont's homebred colt Rosemont, who briefly took the lead. But Rosemont faded out of the money in the homestretch, while Joseph Widener's colt Chance Sun romped. Far back, a burly colt from the first crop of Gallant Fox regrouped from early traffic trouble and rallied fast for fourth place. Next year, in longer races, the world would hear a lot more from Omaha.

But the most powerful memory of this day came from the race right after the Futurity: a tremendous duel in the Jockey Club Gold Cup, with Dark Secret and Faireno running the whole two miles as a team. Dark Secret, last year's Gold Cup winner, bobbled in the final strides but kept his head in front at the wire. Then he nearly fell down. While the crowd gasped, he wobbled to a three-legged halt. While his jockey jumped off, Dark Secret held his right front foot above the muddy ground, useless, broken at the ankle. A great day deflated with a brave horse lurching into an ambulance, soon to meet his death back at his barn, and many spectators wiping tears from their eyes.

Dark Secret's sacrifice became legendary. He had fractured his leg near the end of the two-mile Jockey Club Gold Cup and somehow dug in to win. His spirit would touch Marion and Carroll—and then they would move on. They had their own horses to consider, and maybe even a brilliant future. Carroll was having a vision about Battleship. He could see the little horse who had started out wasting "sixteen and a half minutes over each fence" doing four and a half miles and thirty fences in ten minutes. "Marion!" he urged, "you've got to run this horse in England. He's the one horse in America that I think can win the Grand National at Aintree."

Marion would not decide right away. Already it was too late for a good shot at the 1935 National. Trouble Maker had gone over in August and still had difficulty acclimating for Aintree in late March. She wouldn't

ship Battleship that autumn, if he went at all. And while Marion and Carroll argued pros and cons, what seemed distant but within sight rico-
cheted even farther away.

No one could call Marion duPont a quitter. Or Noel Laing, or Trouble
Maker, either. They tried to get Trouble Maker a repeat victory in the
Meadow Brook Cup during weather that Bill Streett called "the worst day
one could possibly imagine . . . driving rain, wind and mud." Landing the
second jump, Trouble Maker slid down to the ground. Noel remounted
and tried to get back in the race, but they were too far behind.

That failure could be put down to bad weather and bad luck, but the
hunt-racing crowd started to wonder when Trouble Maker finished fourth
in the Piedmont Gold Cup, which he had won the previous year. He was
eleven years old now and had not won a race in several months. When
Trouble Maker appeared for the New Jersey Hunt Cup, a few days before
Halloween, word had started going around that he was over the hill, not
the kind of thing that any former champion's connections would like to
hear. But at the end of four cold, wet miles there was Trouble Maker leading home some of the best 'chasers brought together all year. Noel Laing
told reporters what he had believed all along: "Trouble Maker is no antique yet."

Marion could feel especially proud of her senior champion. And especially glad of his good news, because there was a problem with Battleship.

After winning the American Grand National, Battleship had gone
back to his training camp near Washington, D.C. Although he seemed all
right, his hard effort on a boggy course at Belmont Park may have started
something going wrong. Deep, wet footing puts extra stress on ligaments
and tendons, the stretchy tissue connecting muscle with bone. In early
October, three weeks after Battleship's championship win, a tendon in
his right front lower leg puffed up. Selby Burch saw that the middle of the
tendon was beginning to curve like an archer's bow—an injury known as
a bowed tendon. Right now it wasn't much, but hard exercise would
make it worse. Burch knew that Marion would want the best for Battleship. The little horse went home to Montpelier.

There he did nothing, while Trouble Maker disappointed in the Piedmont Gold Cup and succeeded in New Jersey. After a month of nothing, Battleship's leg felt cool and firm to the touch. He was ready for a treatment that was supposed to stop tendon trouble from returning. Marion had an expert come down from Baltimore, an old-school vet who had the right touch with a firing iron.

It may have been one of the roughest experiences of Battleship's life, when Dr. McCarthy gently drew lines across his injured lower leg with a thin blade of hot steel. The idea was to create inflammation all around the injury that would toughen the tissue. Done correctly, these lines did not break the skin. But the hot edge hurt, even an edge only a sixteenth of an inch wide. During the procedure, Battleship felt the pinch of a tightened rope or chain called a "twitch" squeezing his upper lip, a tactic that distracted him from other pain while releasing endorphins in his brain.

Afterward, for a while he might need to wear a wooden neck cradle—the horse version of the conelike collars that prevent dogs and cats from licking or biting surgery sites—to keep him from rubbing or biting his leg. Battleship would stay inside a large box stall for several days while the wounds healed without bandaging. Every so often, someone would apply salve over the weeping lines.

It was a painful interlude for the brave horse but a good prognosis. Dr. McCarthy said that Marion's team had caught the problem quickly, and their caution would pay off. Battleship could resume training in the spring.

But should he?

Marion debated the problem with her favorite experts, weighing what they could gain or lose. She decided, why rush? Battleship could have a winter and spring vacation. She could try him at stud, then consider what should be next.

The year 1934 ended with an honor that had become almost expected and also with a striking change. For the third year in a row, Mrs. Thomas H. Somerville topped hunt racing's winning owners' list. And on December 9, Tom Somerville's ailing father died. Tom had lost one of the anchors of his life, and Marion no longer had a father-in-law to disappoint, if she were having second and third thoughts about her marriage.

She wintered at Camden, joining Carroll and Jane, and stable lads in the mornings galloping steeplechasers at a private training track. Jane, with her boyish cap and breeches and jockey crouch, blended in with the men as they sped by. Her seamless presence hinted at a day when women riding racehorses could be commonplace instead of unthinkable. Marion stood out: the only one using a sidesaddle and boldly running near the front of the pack.

One morning when a photographer caught up with the group, Marion was working Billy Bozo. It might seem like a surprising picture: the small woman wearing a long skirt, planted sideways on a horse with white-rimmed eyes, the horse who had fallen dramatically with Noel Laing at The Country Club back in June. But Billy Bozo was an old friend, one of Marion's hunters, one of her long-running experiments. He had won only two races during a five-year career, and at one point Marion had taken advice from a cousin who raised champion cattle. "Well, Cousin Sedgwick kept telling me I'd move Billy Bozo way up, really improve him, if I'd feed him fish meal," she recalled. "I did. It made no difference. Except, when you sat on him, he smelled like it."

Now she had retired Billy Bozo from racing. This winter at Camden, they were at home together. She might be questioning what would be next for Trouble Maker, for Battleship, for herself. But during these mornings on horseback, Marion was in her element. Galloping Billy Bozo, Marion was not afraid.

15

EARLY IN 1935, AMERICA'S BOOK-OF-THE-MONTH CLUB featured a new "fantasy" novel by the British author Enid Bagnold. There was nothing supernatural about the story, but reviewers called it a fantasy because *"National Velvet"*—featuring a fourteen-year-old girl riding an unlikely horse to first place in the Grand National at Aintree—defied reality. And yet the book coincided with something true. That springtime, young women saw a real-life example of imagining what you might do and following through.

In April 1935, photographs of a wispy, dark-eyed girl standing with racehorses, exercising racehorses, or simply staring soulfully into the camera decorated newspapers all over America. Twenty-two-year-old Mary Hirsch had been working as her father's assistant trainer since age eighteen. At age twenty, she applied for her own Jockey Club license to train racehorses in New York. The club wouldn't hear of it. The spokesman, Algernon Daingerfield, told the *New York Times* that although "there was no express prohibition in the rules of racing stopping women from being jockeys or trainers, the use of the masculine pronoun 'he' in Rule 209 and in all other cases where a jockey or a trainer is discussed seemed to indicate that the rules excluded women." Instead of reconsidering the Rules of Racing grammar, the licensing committee quietly tabled Miss Hirsch's application. The following year they denied her again, and the polite young woman well known at Saratoga and Belmont Park as "Miss Mary" decided to bypass them. She traveled west, where traditions might not be as stuffy. During the summer of 1934, Mary Hirsch secured a trainer's license in Illinois. For the first time in American history, a woman officially prepared Thoroughbred horses to race.

When the world did not end, the Jockey Club could not hold out for long. They were not facing a nobody like the *"National Velvet"* heroine, a village butcher's daughter. Mary Hirsch had grown up absorbing horsemanship from her popular father, eventual Hall of Fame trainer Max Hirsch. His stable kitchen offered the best breakfast at Saratoga, and his powerful clients included New York Racing Commission chairman Herbert Bayard Swope. If ever a woman was going to break the timeless taboo and receive a Jockey Club license, there could be no one more acceptable than Miss Mary.

On April 2, 1935, young Mary Hirsch became the first female trainer sanctified by the Jockey Club of New York. Their approval let her train Thoroughbred racehorses anywhere in the United States and in Europe as well. Speaking for the New York Racing Commission, Herbert Bayard Swope congratulated Miss Hirsch and said, "Certainly, no opposition could be expressed because of sex. The Jockey Club, to take this view, showed itself, in my opinion, to be abreast of the time."

Miss Mary's breakthrough created a flurry of speculation. Who would be next? One reporter considering prominent, practical horsewomen who might follow her example named Marion duPont Somerville as a worthy candidate. Marion's ability had been well known for years, even remarked upon by the *Wall Street Journal* when her father was alive and able to appreciate the honor.

Like her forebears who built the DuPont explosives empire, Marion personally handled some situations that others left to servants. Once at a foxhunt, while she stood readjusting the bits in her horse's mouth, a male onlooker sniffed, "There she goes, always fixing her horses. Why doesn't she let a boy do it." Another man, watching the same scene, praised Marion for having "no pretense, no foolishness in her make-up" and being "a thorough sportswoman in taste, ability and execution."

Marion duPont Somerville would not become the next Mary Hirsch— she wanted more freedom than full-time racetrack duties allowed—but she would continue directing the early training of her yearlings and supervising her made jumpers. She didn't need the Jockey Club's permission to call the shots with her own employees.

Meanwhile, she and Noel Laing faced a turning point. In early April, Trouble Maker braved "the worst weather in the history of the annual races" at Richmond in the Deep Run Hunt Cup, staying close to the early leader but tiring and finishing last. He was twelve years old, still healthy, but with nothing to prove. Maybe one more distinction lay within his reach: becoming a rare two-time winner of the Maryland Hunt Cup.

Laing seemed wary of this test. A dozen days before the Hunt Cup, he told a reporter that he wouldn't hesitate to ride in the Grand National at Aintree again but didn't look forward to another go at America's toughest timber race. "At Aintree the fences are brush," Laing explained, "[so that] if a horse hits the top of one of the obstacles it does not always mean that he is going to come down. But down in Maryland those fences are just as high and are made of solid timber. A horse hitting one of them is cooked."

The day before the Maryland Hunt Cup, hundreds of people motored out to the Worthington Valley to walk the course and examine the fences that jockey Bill Streett said "looked like one mountain after another." As usual, Baltimore hotels flooded with visitors.

On Saturday, April 27, Baltimore County woke up to, as one visitor put it, "a superb day, more like June than an April afternoon." Today, a jumping race offering no purse money would attract as big a crowd as Man o' War had drawn to the rich Preakness once upon a time. Near four o'clock that afternoon, eight select racers made their way between close-packed spectators into the paddock for saddling.

Standing with Trouble Maker in that enclosure near the finish line, Marion duPont Somerville gave Noel Laing perhaps the best gift she could imagine. "Go ride him for me today," she told Noel, "and when this race is over he is yours; you deserve him."

Underneath Noel's calm surface, his heart might leap with gratitude and relief. Trouble Maker would retire. He would be Noel's companion, his pet hunter, spending the rest of his life with the man who cared for him so well.

Then Noel was up in the saddle and they were off, cantering down to the start. The turf felt perfect, neither too hard nor too deep. It would not jar the horses' legs, grab at their feet, or make them slide on landing.

Captain Kettle, gunning for his third consecutive Hunt Cup win, got away first. Trouble Maker did not hurry, but after clearing the first fence he moved up to press the pace. "We were all settled in our stride by the time the second fence was reached," Bill Streett reported, "and never before in the seven Maryland Hunt Cups I have ridden has the pace been more suited to the course." This year, there were no rash, runaway horses rushing the big third fence and falling down before they could understand their challenge. This year, they were sensible veterans. After the second fence, Trouble Maker led them, respecting his task, a reporter admiring how Marion's champion "sailed the famous big third fence with a great deal to spare." Then Trouble Maker showed the way up the hillside and along the tree line, over fences six, seven, eight. At the eighth, Mullah became the first runner to fall. Two horses moved past Trouble Maker as they reached the halfway point, but it was early yet. Trouble took a breather while staying close to the front.

The hunt-racing world had thought he might be past his best, but today the old man seemed to shake the years away. "Standing off" at each fence—taking off several feet away—Trouble Maker sailed far across each obstacle. He cleared fence thirteen, safely passing the place where he had been injured last year. He cleared fourteen and curved to the left, galloping uphill to fifteen. Riding in midpack, Bill Streett watched for any of the leaders to show signs of getting tired but was disappointed: "Charlie White still had a good hold of [Captain] Kettle, Hotspur was running very strong, Trouble Maker was going as easily as any horse." About two and a half miles into the race, everything seemed remarkably smooth as they entered perhaps the trickiest part of the course.

Making the left turn after fence fifteen, there was no such thing as level ground. The earth tilted uphill and leaned sideways at the same time. Every horse galloped with his right feet higher than his left feet. And they were racing toward one of the biggest obstacles on the course. Trouble Maker galloped uphill to fence sixteen and cleared the five-foot obstacle, the last supersized jump in the race. He landed on the slanted, roller-coaster earth and quickened his pace, as all the riders sought a good striking position for the final mile.

At first, you could barely tell that another fence lay ahead. The ground swelled like a cresting wave, rising toward the hillside horizon. To the left, a white spot fluttered like a buoy anchored behind the swell. In a moment, its red twin appeared several yards to the right. Two flags, marking the target. Then a dark line grew out of the ground. It could have been the deck of a badly loaded barge, its prow jutting up toward the tree line, its stern sinking toward the valley. Then one dark line became panels two, three, four wavy rails high. The ground ahead, the cresting wave, softened to a ripple; the sideways tilt remained.

Hotspur, in the lead, held his course to the right. Noel and Trouble Maker aimed for the left, where in a little while they would cut the corner turning for home. Midafternoon light warmed their backs, illuminating the relatively low rails up ahead—fence seventeen, described by Bill Streett as "the black sheep of the lot . . . a stinking little fence sitting down in a dip." And Trouble Maker did not meet it right.

Horsemen know that sometimes it's the stinking little fence, not the fearsome giant, that invites the worst fall. Obvious hazards generate respect; small ones encourage overconfidence. Trouble Maker's hind feet smacked the ground far in front of unremarkable fence seventeen, his body vaulted into the air, and suddenly everything wasn't all right. Trouble Maker had taken off too far away. His front legs sailed over the timber; his hind feet struck the top rail, hard, knocking his hindquarters high up and sideways like a foul ball off a baseball bat. While Trouble Maker's front feet reached for the ground, his other end pitched and twisted in midair. Noel stayed well centered, his body beautifully able to stay out of his horse's way. Airborne, even wrong, their partnership continued strong as ever. Then Trouble Maker's right front hoof hit the slightly uneven earth, triggering the moment where one soul stays in this life and another vanishes.

The astonished crowd saw Trouble Maker plow headfirst into the ground, hurling Laing off with a violent somersault, and lie still. Other horses whooshed by, continuing the race. Laing rose, looked for his partner, and knew. Marion's favorite had broken his neck. Before Noel had been able to stand, before the last racers had passed, he had gone.

Noel kneeled by Trouble's elegant head, refusing to leave his friend. He stayed, in tears, while men dug a large hole by the edge of the woods and buried Trouble Maker near his final obstacle.

Marion struggled to understand what had gone wrong. Reaching the scene, she would see Trouble Maker's vacant body, his shining unflinching eyes; behind him, timber panels as high as her shoulders, with one broken top rail. *Had Noel been completely blinded to this fence?* she would wonder in later years. *How could Trouble Maker have hit it?* "He was too good a jumper for that," she believed. Had a heart attack stricken Trouble Maker as he took off, making him smash through the rail?

But Bill Streett, riding several yards behind, had seen a horse named Gigolo come up after Trouble Maker and break that rail at fence seventeen. Remarkably, Gigolo had recovered himself and galloped on. "It does seem strange," Streett thought, "that two horses can hit the same fence, one break a rail and not fall, the other not break the fence but come down." Picturing Trouble Maker, he sadly wrote, "I have never seen a horse fall harder."

Soon after the race, someone developed a photograph showing Trouble Maker an instant before his crash, his body high above completely unbroken wood. Marion saved a copy of the photo, stamped "Proof"—ironically, because she couldn't prove to herself why such a thing should happen to such a brilliant horse and rider. "That finished me on timber," she would say many years later. "Never again." She did forsake the Maryland Hunt Cup. But in reality, Marion wasn't finished with timber racing when they buried Trouble Maker near fence seventeen because she wasn't done with Noel Laing. As long as he made his living training and jockeying timber horses, Marion would support him.

A person might wonder, how could she? When disaster struck down the horse closest to your heart, why keep sending horses out over fences? Why justify an entertainment that could end in death?

Perhaps it had to do with living all the days that go right: majestically beautiful animals in motion, adventures shared with friends, a saga rolling forward in who could know what thrilling ways. Anticipation, strategy, beauty, community—all these ingredients fed Marion's soul. Of course she could have sought them somewhere else. But she was, after all, a farmer's daughter, familiar with the ways that death and renewal travel hand in hand. And she was a general's granddaughter, not so distant from days where survival depended upon man and horse working together through a fight. Maybe she needed an outlet for a feeling that went far back with her family, to the dramatic actions of Alexis and Lammot du Pont trying to quench explosions. The feeling that you should be ready. You should be ready to risk it all. In its way, steeplechasing filled a hole between that noble expectation and sleepy reality.

In Marion's world, Trouble Maker's death caused great and lasting sadness but no outrage. Until fence seventeen he had been jumping superbly, demonstrating every strength he had developed through his life. He wasn't necessarily too old for the job—Hotspur, the eventual winner, was the same age. And this particular Maryland Hunt Cup had been sensibly run, more sensibly than usual. "I can't tell you how much more pleasant the race was to ride this year than it has ever been in my experience," Bill Streett remarked, "because of the difference in the pace. As far as the actual time of the race goes, I suppose it was slow, but I believe it was run at the proper speed."

Thinking of Trouble Maker, Marion did adjust her choices here and there. But she saw his death as an anomaly, not a reason to lose all faith. How could you separate the uncertainties of racing from the uncertainty of life itself? Marion remembered when Triple Crown champion Sir Barton's half brother, Sir Martin—a horse tough enough to run thirty-two races and win eleven stakes—had been safely retired for a dozen years and then suffered a fatal leg break while turning suddenly inside his roomy stall. Bill Streett would survive the toughest jump races in Maryland and England, safely retire from the saddle, then drop dead at a dinner party when he was only thirty-five years old. The biggest chance taken in a lifetime often wasn't the last.

Trouble Maker haunted his survivors, in friendly and poignant ways. There would be stories of people passing along Tufton Road at twilight seeing a loose horse happily grazing near fence seventeen—a loose horse belonging to no one in this world. His impact never would leave Marion. Even toward the end of her life, she rarely talked about Trouble Maker, although his large portrait presided over Montpelier's Red Room, because speaking of him made her cry. And yet throughout those years she still needed the jump races, still wanted their guidance in balancing between timidity and recklessness. Still needed their bridge between the-ory and reality. Still accepted their help in practicing for moments when everything is at stake.

Accepting a trophy won by her homebred filly Sable Muff only a month after Trouble Maker died, Marion looked vibrantly well. She met the camera's gaze with an almost flirtatious smile, lips barely parted—perhaps the Mona Lisa smile of a woman making life-changing choices, reaching for a hidden happiness.

Battleship was turned out to laze and graze at Montpelier during the summer of 1935, carrying nothing on his back except sunshine. Marion had decided not to push him to the races this year. His name fell away from news reports, while the reputation of his classmate Gallant Fox glowed as brightly as ever. Omaha, a strapping colt from Gallant Fox's first crop, had won the Kentucky Derby that spring and the Preakness, too. Marion had been pleased when her brother's colt Rosemont grabbed a moment of glory, beating Omaha fair and square with a fast mile in the Withers Stakes. But when Omaha and Rosemont met again for the mile-and-a-half Belmont Stakes, it was all Omaha in the homestretch, just like his daddy, becoming the third winner of America's emerging Triple Crown. Gallant Fox was the overnight success who could brag about his own achievements and his talented offspring at the class reunion. Battleship was the middle-aged bachelor who had done some pretty swell things that few people wanted to talk about.

Though, from a horse's viewpoint, Battleship had it pretty good right now. His injured leg felt fine again. Like Marion's tough yearlings, he was enjoying a lot of time outside. His handlers didn't want much from him. He could simply be.

His owner, meanwhile, was changing what she needed to be.

There were tinges of something new, along with continuing old hab-its, when Marion went up to Saratoga Springs. She had given Carroll Bas-sett a string of horses to train for her at the Spa, settled in at the barn that Will duPont had built there several years ago. Marion could be seen lunching with Jane Bassett and Battleship's former trainer, Selby Burch, at the resortlike Gideon Putnam hotel. A few days later, on August 12,

Marion and Tom Somerville signed a legal document that began, "Whereas unfortunate disagreements and differences have arisen between the said parties, adversely affecting the health and happiness of the parties, as a result of which they are now living separate and apart from each other . . ." It was a property settlement agreement. She was giving him Manton Manor in Delaware and planning to build herself a new house near Wilmington. In Virginia, he would keep Mt. Athos Farm and she would keep Montpelier. Without fanfare they were disengaging, officially claiming the right to live their own lives.

Their division was so low-key that when Saratoga hosted the Travers Stakes on Saturday, August 17, Mr. and Mrs. Thomas H. Somerville, along with his brother Hamilton, were together watching Gold Foam win the classic race. Then it was time for Marion to fly. By Tuesday she was twenty-seven hundred miles away, ensconced at Rancho del Sierra near Carson City, Nevada. She had taken a path shared by many socialites and movie stars—the path to Reno, where a confidential divorce could be granted after six weeks in residence.

When Marion du Pont was nineteen months old, her father had marveled at how many people thought his little girl looked like him. "Every one seems to see it," William wrote to a friend, "all though I do not my self."

The resemblance went far beyond the shape of a nose or an expression in the eyes. It flared out when something reached the point where they could not, or would not, take it anymore. At that point, for William, there had been South Dakota. For Marion, there was Reno.

And, frankly, Marion's choice was more acceptable. When William resorted to South Dakota in 1891, any divorce had seemed scandalous, even sinful. Forty years later, many people still found divorce unthinkable or offensive, but an increasing number found it practical. By the early 1930s, the gossip columnist and broadcaster Walter Winchell could joke about unhappy wives and husbands being "Reno-vated." There was no political calamity during the summer of 1934, when President Franklin D. Roosevelt's daughter Anna Roosevelt Dall obtained a divorce in the same town near Reno where actress Mary Pickford, "America's Sweetheart," had dissolved her first marriage in 1920.

Marion duPont Somerville would draw far less attention. The Associ-
ated Press reported her presence in Nevada, presumably for divorce, but
couldn't dislodge any juicy details. Back in Virginia, the *Richmond Times-
Dispatch* collared Tom Somerville at Montpelier but couldn't get him to
comment. Marion avoided the notoriety drawn by Barbara Hutton, heiress to a $20 million fortune, during a Reno divorce and rapid remarriage
earlier that year. And yet, whether she thought of it this way or not, Marion carried something from her father with her to Nevada: a sense of
shame.

Even late in life, Marion would skirt the issue of her father's first wife,
saying, "My father had been first married to a cousin. She died." Yes, William's first wife had died—when Marion was thirty-three years old.
Whatever details she knew or did not know, William du Pont's little girl
felt the effects of disgrace. And yet Marion existed because William du
Pont had defied conventions and embarrassed his family. So that was
worthwhile, wasn't it?

Tearing away from the domestic life that her father had pictured for
her, much like he had left the marriage blessed by his own parents, Marion settled into her six-week residence. She would not have to endure
public scrutiny at a hotel or a "divorce ranch" where soon-to-be ex-wives
flirted with cowboys. Instead, a grandmotherly woman welcomed her
into a private sanctuary, a large wooden home with a farmhouse veranda
encircling its first floor and a dramatic Gothic window rising for two stories above the front door. Marion could look out from that simply styled
veranda and feel like a pioneer, resting from hard labors. She could con-
template that window, with panes of red, yellow, and blue glass capping
its pointed arch, and feel as if she were in church. She could play billiards
upstairs or ride out into a silver and blue landscape, snow-sided mountains rising above shallow Washoe Lake. If she wished, she could talk
with her hostess, Neva Winters Sauer, about this ranch that Theodore
Winters had built, about pedigreed cattle and Thoroughbred horses that
Neva's father had bred, champions whose names—El Rio Rey, Emperor
of Norfolk, Yo Tambien—resonated from west to east. Neva understood
legacies; she was living one.

And, as always, Marion could count upon her brother looking out for
her: depositing investment income in her Special Account and advising

her, "The du Pont Company gave an extra 65¢, which will give you about double the amount you usually receive in September"; letting her know not to worry about the annual Montpelier foxhound show held in September, he would handle it; telling her, "I was talking to Carroll Bassett on the phone yesterday and he is shipping [your horses] down to Belmont Park early next week." Encouraging her, as always, "Be sure and let me know if there is anything I can do for you."

In some ways, Marion already had decided what she would transfer from her old life into the new. She was giving Tom Somerville the house that her father had built for them. The things she would retrieve from Manton Manor were relatively few—accent pieces such as three hooked rugs, a few nice but small pieces of furniture, and "all personal pictures." And a painting of Phenolax.

Tom, in return, had until late October to remove his personal property from Montpelier. His assets included twenty-four horses and seven bird dogs, trappings of a lifestyle that his own earnings couldn't support. To a degree, Marion had agreed to help him continue these expensive habits. But she would not tolerate endless bickering about moneys owed. Signing their settlement, she and Tom had relinquished "any and all claims for the payment of money that he or she may have, or might have, or claim to have, against the other . . . from the beginning of the world to the day of the date of this agreement."

And yet she would not try to keep Tom Somerville far away. Along with Manton Manor, she was giving him $10,000 toward building a new house at Mt. Athos, beside the Montpelier estate. Furthermore, she would let him keep using a skeet-shooting field at Montpelier, adjacent to Mt. Athos, only noting that she would no longer pay to maintain it. He could stay in her neighborhoods, as long as he fulfilled a requirement of their property settlement agreement: "Neither party shall molest the other, nor compel, nor attempt to compel, the other to cohabit with him, or her."

During her six weeks at Rancho del Sierra, Marion received news muffled by distance: Carroll winning a flat race at Fair Hill with her stallion Annapolis, who had served at stud that spring; Noel breaking his collarbone in a fall from her timber horse Wellbourne Jake.

At last the day she awaited arrived, Tuesday, October 1. Marion drove away from Rancho del Sierra to Reno, where neon letters arching over

Virginia Street proclaimed THE BIGGEST LITTLE CITY IN THE WORLD. Before the county clerk's office officially opened for business, Marion's
lawyer filed her complaint. At 9:30 A.M., in a hearing closed off from
the public, Marion testified. Although everything possible had been
done to protect her privacy, there was no escaping this brief but painful exposure—the personal confession to a judge. Her words then were
sealed, for her lifetime and beyond. Newspapers could learn only the bar-
est legal reason why she was granted her decree, two words: "extreme
cruelty."

The sealed details weren't necessarily shocking. Because divorce
courts in 1935 did not yet recognize the wide range of problems later covered by "irreconcilable differences," couples who didn't blame adultery
for ending their marriage often entered an extreme cruelty plea. Marion
duPont Somerville, still using her ex-husband's last name, went home to
Virginia and let the world wonder. Gossip would flare, then cool down. In
the eyes of history, Tom Somerville would become increasingly insub-
stantial, faceless and threadbare like a scrap of material left outside and
worn down by the elements. Only a summary of Marion's complaint
would be allowed to come to light:

> That for cause of divorce . . . extreme cruelty consisted entirely of mental
> cruelty.
>
> That since the marriage, the defendant has treated the plaintiff with
> extreme cruelty. That all of the acts of cruelty on the part of the defen-
> dant were without cause or provocation.

Perhaps not surprisingly, Tom Somerville denied all of the cruelty al-
legations. Perhaps there had been persistent squalls instead of a long, intense storm. Several years later, volunteering to meet with Tom to settle
a business matter, Marion instructed their representative at the Delaware
Trust Company to "warn him ahead of time that we want him" and to get
Tom's promise in writing if she did agree to help him, because "he is so
changeable." This did not sound like someone interested in humiliating
her ex-husband, only a good manager's practical, wistful words.

She was interested in problem solving, not punishment. Returning east, Marion quietly resumed her sporting life and her relationship with other temperamental creatures.

Paging through her October issue of *Polo* magazine, Marion would read about September races she had missed at her brother's Fair Hill meet and see one of her best horses through someone else's eyes. She might appreciate the reporter's honesty in writing, "Annapolis won [the longer flat race] as he pleased, which is exactly the phrase to use. This son of Man o' War is not an easy horse to ride, for he acts as though he were going to stop two or three times in a race, taking deep breaths when the spirit moves him; furthermore, if you hit him he sulks and tries to look around to make faces at you, disgusted."

Now that was funny. Even Carroll Bassett, on the receiving end of those disgusted looks while urging Annapolis toward the finish line, might laugh. And might think, Who could blame Annapolis? Maybe the stallion had thought he was done with being a racehorse, after spending springtime breeding mares at Marion's farm.

But in mid-October, when Annapolis competed in his first steeplechase of the year, Carroll ended up disgusted, too. They were at the Monmouth County Hunt meet in New Jersey on a beautiful afternoon. It should have been a pleasant return to normality for Marion. Annapolis finished first, well clear of everyone. But he had not won. Maybe he had been headstrong, or maybe Carroll had been too willing to ride recklessly. "Coming around the last turn," another horseman reported, "Annapolis barged into Drapeau and Drapeau was pushed into What Have You, knocking both horses off their stride." Drapeau's rider complained to the racing judges, and the judges upheld his complaint. Instead of winning, Annapolis was disqualified and placed last. Carroll was *furious*. He did not accept the stewards' decision. Instead, he swore that he was done. Done! No more riding races. No more hunt meets where the officials didn't know what they were doing. He wouldn't even ride Marion's fast filly Sable Muff in the final race of the day. Sable Muff, who might well have won, didn't run.

Marion either had to find another jockey, soon, or someone had to help Carroll give up his grudge. Apparently this took more than a couple of weeks, but he had cooled down in time to pilot Marion's horse Wild Son at Pimlico in early November. "We were all rather surprised to see Carroll Bassett back in silks after his many threats and determination never to ride again when Annapolis was disqualified at Monmouth County," rider Bill Streett remarked. "But because this race is run at one of the big tracks and not at a Hunt meeting Carroll condescended to ride, although the National Steeplechase and Hunt Association has full jurisdiction over this race as well as the Hunt meetings." Giving credit to an outstanding animal rather than acknowledging any pressure on Carroll from Marion, Streett added, "I should think it *would* be rather hard to turn down rides on such horses as Wild Son."

Whatever convinced him to put on the silks, Carroll expertly threaded Wild Son through traffic and then sat chilly while the classy black horse drew off by half a dozen lengths, giving Marion her third Master of Foxhounds Steeplechase victory in a row.

Coming back to the races after making vehement public declarations that you *never* would be back might not be something to do for fun. It might, however, be something to do for someone who had become almost like family. Carroll and Jane Bassett now had a home at Montpelier, a handsome cottage set within woodlands down the road from Marion's mansion. Consistent with her willingness to buy prefabricated Sears, Roebuck barns for Thoroughbred horses, Marion had installed a prefabricated Hodgson House for the Bassetts. But it was a charming residence, with elegant touches and outdoor space for Carroll and Jane to design a garden. And perhaps it felt especially good to Marion, right now, having two young friends of hers living nearby.

Marion had made it through October, securing her divorce decree and extracting Tom Somerville from Montpelier. She had postponed the Montpelier races until mid-November, a month later than usual. In late October, her situation might have been too raw. By the time the races came, Tom Somerville's possessions had been gone from her house for a month. Anything he had failed to take away had become absolutely hers.

So she hosted the races as usual, free and open to the public. Also as usual, she had served as president of the Montpelier Hunt Races committee, with her brother as vice president. Committee members included Carroll Bassett and Noel Laing.

Then winter was upon her. Marion would not spend Christmas at Montpelier alone, nor would she camp out with her brother and his family. Scouting the British Isles for new horses to hunt and steeplechase, she sailed to England in mid-December with Jane Fowler Bassett (occupation, none) and Carroll Bassett (occupation, sculptor). More ironically than ever, Marion still traveled as "housewife." Back in America, "Mrs. Thomas H. Somerville" led the hunt meet owners' list for the fourth year in a row.

Marion, Carroll, and Jane arrived in London five days before Christmas. The day after Christmas, they celebrated Jane's twenty-first birthday. Later that week, if they went to the races, they might see steeplechasing welcome a new name: Bruce Hobbs.

On the last day of 1935, about a hundred miles northwest of London, barely fifteen-year-old Bruce Hobbs rode a horse named Seaway onto the revered Cheltenham Racecourse. During the past year, Bruce had ridden jump races here and there at minor meets—and he loved it. Not only the riding but also the camaraderie with his fellow riders. "From the first moment that I went into the [jockeys'] changing room . . . ," Bruce would recall, "I knew I was among friends."

Some of the older riders who were friends with Reg Hobbs looked after Bruce, helping him get oriented to new surroundings and situations. And they liked the boy in his own right. Bruce was notably well mannered without being prim, and he had such an understanding way with a horse. He was green when it came to steeplechasing, but the other jockeys respected his attitude and ability. Bruce, in return, enjoyed their free-spirited company while not expecting any favors during competition. "There was a grand spirit in the changing-room in those days," he would reminisce. "All the jockeys were always fooling about and laughing but there was no quarter shown when you went out on the course."

Now, at age fifteen, he was facing the best in the sport. Bruce finished fourth with Seaway in his Cheltenham debut—but he did finish. As a child learning to ride and perfecting his jumping skills, he had complained of his father "always overfacing me," but now that Bruce was competing against professionals, Reg was developing him through careful steps. Unlike the fictional heroine of *"National Velvet,"* going directly from unofficial neighborhood competitions to Aintree, Bruce Hobbs improved his jockey skills in two-mile hurdle races at sanctioned tracks, known as park courses, that offered quick-paced racing over less extreme obstacles and terrain. Reg still wanted his boy to be famous—oh, yes—but first he would make sure that Bruce had an unshakable foundation.

Margery Hobbs tried to be there for her son. When he started out as a jockey, there she was at the course, supporting him—"but," Bruce noted, "she would stand with her back turned to the action when I was riding, so that she could not see if I had a fall. I suppose you couldn't really blame her," Bruce continued, "because there were one or two fairly hairy chance rides." And as Margery knew, her son didn't have much protection from injury or worse, only a fiber skullcap, like the one that had saved Noel Laing at The Country Club but left him concussed. And if a fall came at the wrong angle, no hat could save your neck. "I was riding at near-by Taunton on the day when poor Jack Baxter got killed, falling at the open ditch, which was the fence in front of the stands," said Bruce. "We had no proper crash-helmets in those days and when the following horse put his foot on his head, that was the end of him." It was no wonder that Margery turned her back. It was no wonder that, eventually, she gave up coming to Bruce's races altogether.

While Bruce Hobbs entered a profession that his mother couldn't stand to watch, Marion and the Bassetts left Britain several weeks before young Hobbs won his first race. They had found some English and Irish horses to take home, and they were looking ahead to a very full year. One of Marion's first engagements back in the States was a dinner at the Mayflower Hotel in Washington, D.C., where former New York governor Al Smith would give a speech, broadcast nationally on radio, on behalf of the American Liberty League.

The league had been incorporated in 1934, "to combat radicalism, preserve property rights, [and] uphold and preserve the Constitution." It was an outlet for anyone who believed that President Roosevelt's New Deal would put America on a path to communism. Marion and her brother were making loans to the league (though not nearly so large as loans made by some other du Ponts). Jane Fowler Bassett's stepmother served on the league's National Advisory Council, along with such diverse individuals as Army Remount station manager Maj. Louie Beard, racehorse owner Warren Wright of Calumet Farm, and Hollywood mogul Hal Roach (whose creations included the "Our Gang" franchise, later known as the "Little Rascals," and the Laurel and Hardy comedy team). But while Marion took an interest in business and politics, there was something more alluring on her mind.

Nine weeks after returning to the United States, Marion remarried. Her new husband seemed a surprising choice for such a publicity-shy woman. He was a Hollywood movie star, the dear friend of fellow star Cary Grant: handsome, charming, elusive Randolph Scott.

16

B ENEATH HIS EASYGOING EXTERIOR, GEORGE RANDOLPH Scott resembled a safe-deposit box. Some of that likeness came from his father, the most influential certified public accountant in North Carolina. Scott did care about money and managed his investments well. But in a pinch, you could trust him with more than dollars and cents. As he had proved in the battlefields of France and the minefields of Hollywood, you could trust him with your life.

And yet, from the start, his lifeline told more than one story. He said that he had been born in Orange County, Virginia, while his mother was visiting relatives, yet the Orange County Courthouse would hold no record of his birth, as if his family did not want his story to begin there. Applying for a U.S. passport as a young adult, he signed his name to the statement, "I solemnly swear that I was born at CHARLOTTE, in the state of NORTH CAROLINA, on or about the 23 day of JANUARY, 1898 . . ." Yet his actual age would seem to be a flexible thing, depending upon what he wanted at the time.

And that deception was a paradox, because those who knew him agreed that Randolph Scott had something rare. The director Michael Curtiz, whose film credits included *Casablanca,* would declare, "Randy Scott is a complete anachronism. He's a gentleman. And so far he's the only one I've met in this business full of self-promoting sons-of-bitches!"

Scott's gracious manners were real. Virginians would remember Randolph Scott the movie star being pestered for autographs at the Montpelier races and tipping his hat to each autograph seeker after signing each one. Yet from boyhood onward, he also seemed to need something not quite within his reach. Maybe he needed to define himself apart from his five older sisters and a brother seven years his junior. Maybe he needed to replace something that had faded when his brother Joseph was born and Randy was no longer the only son and the baby boy. Maybe he needed permission to live differently from his father, who found satisfaction in drafting North Carolina's first certified public accountant law and chairing the state board of accountancy.

The Woodberry Forest School at Orange, Virginia, widened his world. Randy threw himself into everything from football to glee club and made a host of friends. Between sessions, he often scooted away from his parents in Charlotte and "popped in unannounced" at his pal Andrew Harriss's home near the Carolina coast. "Sailing and swimming at Wrightsville Beach shared equal importance in our lives with campus activities and interschool athletics," Harriss would recall. "By then, Randy was adopted as the sixth Harriss child and maintained his permanent cot in my room." Maybe these visits were Randy's way of running away yet feeling safe at the same time.

Eventually, he wanted real adventure. During their spring break of 1916, eighteen-year-old Randy Scott and seventeen-year-old Andrew Harriss thought of something thrilling to do instead of returning to school: help the U.S. Army hunt down Mexican revolutionary leader Pancho Villa. The army, however, preferred to assign them to a National Guard unit, North Carolina's Coast Artillery Corps. Their parents expected them to finish school. They ended up back at Woodberry Forest, being chided for irresponsibility.

But in 1917, their wild ambitions met an undeniable need. Not long before Randy graduated, the United States joined the world war. Andrew Harriss, already licensed in the Artillery Corps as "corporal artillery-observer, 1st class," got permission to train Scott and team up with him. Not for the first time or the last, Randy proved willing to learn from someone younger but more advanced. It wasn't so different from Harriss teaching Scott how to manage a sailboat during their school holidays, even though Scott the upperclassman outranked and sometimes disciplined Harriss on campus.

From Fort Caswell, North Carolina, they whipped over to England for a blur of training with pistols, rifles, bayonets, and gas masks. Because they might have to travel on horseback in emergency conditions, Harriss ran a horsemanship class where Scott became certified "to mount and ride in a slow walk, gallop, or dead run *without saddle*." Then in mid-May 1918, they joined the wave of nearly a million American troops mobilizing into battle.

They had dreamed of fighting for General Pershing in Mexico. Now they followed him into France at a time of crisis, with German troops just thirty-seven miles from Paris. Scott and Harriss served as forward observers for the 2nd Trench Mortar Battalion, 19th Field Artillery, sharing a so-called bomb-proof shelter at the front lines. Every time a shell missed its target—too long, too short, too far right or left—they figured a correction using trigonometry and signaled their gun crew. They sweated through near misses from bombs and premonitions of hand-to-hand combat whenever a rat rustled near their hideout in the night.

Meanwhile, George Grant Scott lobbied to bring his son home. In late July, a North Carolina senator nominated Sergeant Randolph Scott for admission to West Point. A hometown newspaper declared that Randy would be "exempted" by General Pershing "and sent back home."

But he was not. During that summer and autumn, while Miss Marion du Pont served on a committee of Virginia ladies planning a massive garden party to fund-raise for Allied soldiers blinded in the war, Randolph Scott remained on duty with Andrew Harriss. Scott would never publicize this time. Whatever memories seared into his mind were not for the world to know. Harriss also did not describe the awful things they saw; he preferred to remember their mutual respect. "During our constant sojourn with death from snipers and the gory mess, we never spoke a harsh word toward each other," Harriss wrote. "After every close call—and there were many—we ended with a labored and thankful smile, the reading of our personal pocket Testaments, and the blessing of our dog-tags and the St. Christopher's crosses on our necklaces."

Writing after Randy had died, Harriss could have embellished his stories about his old friend. Instead, he did not make any sensational claims.

"As close as we were," Harriss reflected, "we always reserved a sort of privacy between us. . . . My realistic evaluation of him, based on the very hard and intimate conditions we jointly endured in the lines with infrequent rest periods from May to November 11, 1918, enabled me to observe the patriotic Christian realist he was."

They endured six months at war. Then came the almost unbelievable silence of the armistice. Harriss and Scott were swept off to artillery officers' school in the Loire Valley. Scott, nearly twenty-one years old, was allowed to enroll. Harriss, too young, went home with his platoon, eventually graduated with Woodberry Forest's class of 1919, and resumed his military career. Although he and Scott would remain friends, they lost the closeness of school days and sailing, of army training and their wartime ordeal.

And Randy Scott had to change from calculating shell trajectories to figuring his own life course. He returned to the United States in early June 1919 and during early September spent several days catching up with Virginia friends. His circle included twenty-five-year-old Marion du Pont, helping her father run the Montpelier farm, overdue to find a husband.

It wouldn't be twenty-one-year-old Randy Scott, the prep school athlete with an honorable army record. Scott was heading for college—a Southern school with a famous engineering program would please his parents—and hoping to join a powerhouse football team. The Georgia Tech Yellow Jackets had been national champions in 1917 and ranked second only to the Pittsburgh Panthers in 1918. Football fans called them "the Golden Tornado." Scott was aiming for the top when he showed up at Grant Field in 1919 to try out for legendary coach John Heisman.

His character fit with Heisman's way of doing things. Although Randy had succeeded in the army, surrounded by earthy language, he disliked profanity. So did Coach Heisman. In fact, during Heisman's tenure, the stadium rang with voices singing, "I'm a Ramblin' Wreck from Georgia Tech and a heckuva engineer!" instead of the traditional "helluva helluva helluva helluva, hell of an engineer!" Of course character alone could not make Scott one of the Georgia Tech eleven, playing both offense and defense. But his size, speed, and determination earned him a place as a second-string end. On defense, Scott could block wide runs; on offense, he might receive one of Heisman's innovations, the forward pass.

"It doesn't make any difference where you drop Randolph Scott, he makes good," an observer told a Charlotte, North Carolina, newspaper that autumn. "He has fine nerve, loves the game, knows how to go under interference, listens to coaching and is learning fast." Randy thought he was catching hold of a dream at Georgia Tech, but the dream had barely formed when it began dissolving. Scott suffered a back injury, and even if he could heal well enough to play again in 1920, Coach Heisman would no longer be there. Divorce was driving the coach away from Atlanta. "I have agreed that wherever Mrs. Heisman wishes to live, I will live in another place," the coach announced. "This will prevent any social embarrassment."

Scott was supposed to avoid social embarrassment, too. Losing his dream of making the All-American football team, he took up business studies at the University of North Carolina. He entered the School of Commerce as a "special student," a category reserved for adults who wanted to improve their skills without spending four years earning a degree. Randy stayed only a year.

During his early to midtwenties, George Randolph Scott became a study in frustration—not anger, but incompletion. Everywhere he went, he easily found acceptance but did not reach fulfillment. During those same years, Marion duPont had followed through time and again with her own goals, at least in the realms of horses and dogs. Randy Scott was steady like a hummingbird, hovering near a goal, then darting away. He didn't stick with college or a job with his father's auditing firm.

And perhaps George Grant Scott understood that he couldn't turn his son the adventurer into an accountant. Randy never seemed to be without time or money to try something new. He became a charter member of the Civitan Club of Charlotte, "Builders of Good Citizenship," then convinced his father to let him go touring Europe. Returning to North Carolina, he joined Charlotte's most prominent Freemason lodge, where he studied the "Ineffable Degrees" of the Scottish Rite, contemplating the nature of God that goes beyond words. He served as best man at several weddings, including that of Tom Somerville and Marion duPont in 1925, but did not make it to the altar himself. He went exploring Florida in 1926 and ran into a storm that the U.S. Weather Bureau called "probably the most destructive hurricane ever to strike the United States." He came home and continued his Masonic studies, leading toward the conclusion to "always look for the good in all and make allowances for others' short-comings . . . trust the Supreme Architect to lead us to friendship, moral-ity and brotherly love."

And then he took off to Southern California, with a young friend who had vacationed out there before. Francis Jackson Heath, "Smiling Jack," recently had placed second in the Southern Amateur Golf Championship, which many had expected him to win. He seemed to spring from the same mold as the great amateur champion Bobby Jones, another medium-sized Southerner. Jack Heath and Randolph Scott had golf in common, their Charlotte roots, their sunny personalities and blond hair. They even had a family connection: in 1921, one of Jack's older half brothers had eloped with Randy's fourth sister, Virginia.

Like Randolph Scott, Jack Heath had studied at Georgia Tech and at the University of North Carolina. But Jack was nearly five years younger. Randy soon would turn thirty years old—a notable threshold between carefree youth and grown-up responsibility—and still had not found his niche.

Maybe they weren't trying to break into motion pictures when they visited Hollywood in 1927. Randy always would describe their trip as a "vacation." They arrived like elite Southern boys seeking their own kind, with a letter of introduction to Ella Rice Hughes, a young lady from the leading family of Houston, whose rich young husband loved playing golf. He also was producing movies. Golfing with Howard Hughes led to Ran-dolph Scott and Jack Heath touring a movie studio, then dressing up as army officers to serve as extras in a silent feature film called *Sharp Shoot-ers*. Before long, Jack Heath went back to his job running a car dealership in Charlotte. But Randolph Scott had found that thing, that place, where he could stick. Except for holiday visits back east, Randy stayed.

Right away, Hollywood thought he looked like a movie star. In fact, he looked a lot like rising star Gary Cooper: strong but slim, standing about six foot three, with a manly face that also radiated a boyish gleam. But screen test after test showed that, unlike Cooper, Scott was not a natural in front of movie cameras. He guarded his inner self too well. As his bomb shelter partner Andrew Harriss said, "I always felt that Scotty was not comfortably designed to be an *actor*."

So why try? Why exhibit yourself? Why let a camera magnify you for the whole world to examine?

Randy's choice to appear on-screen was something that his longtime friend Marion duPont Somerville might struggle to understand. She might easily see, however, why Southern California had bewitched him: beautiful people, beautiful weather, golf anytime he pleased. And breathing room. Twenty-five hundred miles away from parental pressure, Randy could date whomever he pleased without raising talk of wedding bells and grandchildren. He also might earn his living without being tied to a desk.

Maybe at first Hollywood felt like an eternal vacation, but Randolph Scott could not sell it to his family that way. He might describe movie acting as a calculated risk, an investment that eventually could yield a much bigger payoff than his father's accounting firm. But for many months Randy subsisted as an uncredited extra or a bit player, often in conventional silent films rather than the experimental "talkies." In 1929, his authentic Southern accent earned him a speaking role, of sorts: dialogue coach for Gary Cooper, who was starring in *The Virginian*. Scott may have been impressed by Cooper's easy style. He surely was impressed that Coop, under contract to Paramount Pictures, was earning $3,400 a week. Working with Gary Cooper, Randolph Scott could try to measure the difference between himself and success. It wasn't looks or charm. Was it an inborn talent? Or was it something that a person could learn?

While Marion duPont Somerville studied horse racing and decided to master steeplechasing, Randolph Scott decided that he could learn acting—and found out that his father was not going to pay his way. He threw himself into low-paid performances at the Pasadena Playhouse and lived in a rented room with none of the cooking or cleaning services that his family took for granted. His prized possession was a present from Howard Hughes, who dropped by one day and discovered tall Randy struggling to sleep on a bed only six feet long. Hughes soon sent a replacement with a note declaring, "Here's one bed that you won't kick the foot off."

Randy carted his comfortable bed from rooming house to rooming house, picking up occasional minor movie roles and breaking through with good reviews in a couple of plays. Movie studio scouts began calling, but Randy held out for a long-term offer from a certain studio. It arrived in 1932, when he signed a seven-year contract with Paramount Pictures, becoming, he might hope, their successor to Gary Cooper. Studio publicity called him "young." At age thirty-four, Scott still looked youthful enough that the public could believe he had lied to enlist in the world war at age fourteen and was now only twenty-eight years old.

Early in 1932, Randolph Scott stepped into the role of a boy next door, an embattled young woman's "gentle, understanding sweetheart," in a drama called *Hot Saturday*. During filming he became fast friends with the actor playing his rival, a "nonchalant young libertine." And so, while making a movie about the destructive power of gossip, Randolph Scott formed the most talked-about relationship of his life. Soon he was sharing a West Hollywood house with Cary Grant.

Randy's new roommate could have been an advertisement for the power of imagination: both his own ability to seize possibilities and also the dreams he could inspire in a movie audience. As a young teen, he had seen his way from a broken home in Bristol, England, to a job with a traveling acrobatic troupe. Touring New York City at age sixteen, he pictured himself on Broadway. When Hollywood scouts noticed him on Broadway a decade later, he could picture himself working in motion pictures, too. Yet all along he understood his progress as a continual process, not an instant transformation. "His scripts were full of little notes to himself," the director Stanley Donen noticed long after Cary Grant had become a major star. "The tiniest details: That's what he was great at. He always seemed real. It wasn't a gift from God. It was the magic that came from enormous amounts of work."

There were gifts at his command, too. Impish dark eyes, an alluring face with a memorably dimpled chin, a unique voice that his audience would enjoy imitating. But more important, the essence of being an actor—not pretending, but taking action—fitted Archie Leach, who became Cary Grant. Even though he was several years younger than Randolph Scott, Cary was the one who had developed an acrobat's agility and a mime's clarity, the one who knew how to make the hard work of acting look effortless.

And whether it came from escaping a fragmented family or from some innate quality, Cary seemed to feel free to play with boundaries. "You never saw any fear in him when he was acting," Stanley Donen said. For Cary, performing might be a place to forget about fear. For Randy, it may have become a place to confront fear, because he seemed so deeply reluctant for anyone to catch him crossing a line. He was wary of what reporters might say about him and what his folks would think back home. Early in 1932, when newspapers started crowing that Scott was crazy in love with sexy actress Lupe Velez, Randy sent a letter to his mother explaining, "It's just publicity." And instead of staying private, that letter made its way from the Scott family into the news, as if his genteel parents were rising up to defend Randy's honor.

Randolph Scott had quickly discovered that presenting yourself honestly was an unwelcome challenge inside the Hollywood publicity machine. The average American expected Hollywood to be an extravagant, provocative place, but during the 1920s it had gone too far. Audiences started rejecting movie stars who appeared to be *too* wild. Romance could be good publicity, but eventually, there should be a wedding—a wedding of girl meets boy. If a glamorous, desirable star stayed single for too long, the public would start wondering why.

Randy and Cary lived within a hall of mirrors, their true selves surrounded by images multiplied to infinity. On the one hand, the entertainment world was an oasis for men who liked men, women who liked women, and those who might swing either way. Many a small-town boy or girl had fled to Greenwich Village in New York City or the Hollywood scene of Los Angeles knowing that they would play it straight for the general public but also could enjoy a social life where they didn't have to pretend. At the same time, actors weren't necessarily bisexual or gay, and same-sex roommates or housemates often were not lovers. In the 1930s, most Americans thought that a man and woman living together without being married was disgraceful. Respectable roommates had to be the same gender.

But by 1933, Hollywood needed more than that.

This was clear from the career of one of Cary and Randy's Hollywood friends. William Haines had grown up in Staunton, Virginia, a straitlaced little city not far from Marion duPont's Montpelier. In the late 1920s, Billy

Haines became a movie star. By 1930, he was a top box office draw. Billy would kid reporters that he was going to marry a middle-aged woman who was one of his favorite movie comedy costars, but all of Hollywood knew his boyfriend, Jimmie Shields. Billy and Jimmie also were frequent weekend guests at William Randolph Hearst's San Simeon, part of an in-crowd that included Randy Scott and Cary Grant.

In 1933, Billy Haines disappeared from the silver screen. His friends hadn't deserted him, but the movie industry had started censoring itself to ward off government regulation. That meant a moral code for movie content and pressure on nonconformist movie stars. When MGM leaned on Billy Haines to get married, Billy answered, "I'm already married." MGM let his contract expire, and no other studio picked him up.

Those were the stakes late in 1933, when Cary Grant decided to marry the lovely blond actress Virginia Cherrill, who had starred with Charlie Chaplin in *City Lights,* and Randolph Scott was supposed to be Cary's best man but ended up spending Christmas at Montpelier. Billy Haines was a rare success who defied the system: openly staying with Jimmie Shields for the rest of his life and also launching a satisfying career as Hollywood's leading interior designer.

But he had to leave movies to do that. Whether cynically or realistically, Hollywood easily could believe that Cary Grant married Virginia Cherrill to protect his leading man status. When Cherrill filed for divorce only ten months after marrying Grant, and then Cary and Randy reunited as housemates, it was easy to assume that the men preferred each other's company rather than consider all the reasons why heterosexual marriages can fail. The director Garson Kanin summed up Hollywood gossip by saying, "Facts don't interest people. Everyone likes to be in on the inside story. Whether it's true or not is a secondary consideration. If it's spicy, then it's interesting."

Randy and Cary certainly were spicy—two of the most attractive men in a city thick with attractive men. From a distance, their appearance could fit whatever the viewer wanted to see, from playboy bachelor buddies to lovers committed to each other. The rumored lovers made light of the situation, joking about it with friends. In March 1935, they rented a Santa Monica beach house that the Hollywood press soon nicknamed "Bachelor Hall." Their parade of girlfriends offered a mix of sincere personal interest and defense against public hints that the two actors were devoted to each other.

And somehow, in the midst of all this, Randolph Scott secretly courted Marion duPont. Was it business? Was it love? Was it a mixture of affection, security, and yearning to complete an ideal self that he had in mind?

He trusted her. She trusted him. But maybe their marriage could not have happened if it weren't for football and Fred Astaire.

In December 1934, Randolph Scott finally earned his first A movie role. Although he lacked Jimmy Cagney's electrifying dramatic power and hadn't developed Gary Cooper's ability to let deep emotions pierce a stoic persona, Randy's good looks and affable personality had considerable appeal. But he could have stayed stuck in Westerns indefinitely if RKO Radio Pictures hadn't needed someone who looked like a football star to play Fred Astaire's sidekick and Irene Dunne's love interest in the third Astaire and Ginger Rogers film, the musical comedy *Roberta*. Paramount loaned him out. Scott and Astaire became good friends, and their rapport came across on-screen.

Georgia Tech football hadn't made Randolph Scott an All-American, but now Hollywood did. Portraying an earnest athlete with the catchphrase "Gee, that's swell!" Scott excelled in awkward comic moments or simply standing hat in hand and beaming hopefully. His dramatic acting remained a work in progress. During love scenes with Irene Dunne, the director aimed his camera past the back of Scott's head, gathering the needed passion from Irene's expressive eyes. Still, Randy's winning performance gave him a chance to leave Westerns and help other leading ladies shine. After seeing how well this attractive man complemented his partner without stealing scenes from her, female stars began pestering Paramount to borrow him.

During the spring and summer of 1935, Randolph Scott reached his highest professional standing so far in his life. He was more than a dabbler, a well-bred drifter. He had found his own center of gravity. Perhaps this change in him convinced Marion that her old pal, as pleasant as any person you ever would meet but coming and going like a moonbeam, was ready to be true to her.

They were not seen together, and it is hard to imagine when they could have spent much time together. That summer, Marion stayed east until her six weeks near Reno, while Randy camped out in a beautiful California fishing lodge at Malibu Lake, filming a leading role in the Civil War romance *So Red the Rose*. That autumn, Marion went back to Virginia while Randy stayed in Hollywood working in another Astaire-Rogers film, *Follow the Fleet*. When that production wrapped, Marion was enjoying the winter holidays in Great Britain with Carroll and Jane Bassett.

But before she sailed, Marion may have known that movie critics were praising Randy's performance in *So Red the Rose*. His humor and sincerity rang true as a character who didn't believe in war but eventually joined the fight, with a vengeance. Randy's strength in the part may have blended his own experience as a soldier with memories of his grandfather Tarlton Woodson Scott, a Confederate veteran who had lived until 1919.

And that winter, Randolph Scott made his father proud. Randy hadn't followed a path that his father would have imagined, but George Scott realized, now, what a sensation his older son had become. He experienced it firsthand in late January 1936, when the women of his workplace heard that Randy was visiting his folks and prevailed upon George to bring his movie star son to Raleigh and walk him through the state Department of Revenue. Randy's presence caused a flurry of flirtatious excitement probably unprecedented in the Division of Accounts. The next day, North Carolinians read about the "chorus of nervous giggles, sometimes reaching a shrill crescendo" that accompanied Randolph Scott's progress from desk to desk. George Scott could bask in a reporter's praise: "The father enjoyed it, the girls were thrilled and the son proved that he either is very good natured or a very good actor."

To some extent, Randy was both. He greeted the Department of Revenue ladies as if he were sincerely pleased to meet them, and perhaps in those moments he truly was. Yet he knew that their lives had nothing to do with his dreams.

Not long after Randolph Scott returned to Hollywood, Marion duPont Somerville was briefly nearby. She and her brother took a train to Southern California, arriving shortly before Will duPont's horse Rosemont ran in the famously rich Santa Anita Handicap. If Marion saw

Randy during this quick trip, they completely avoided attention. Scott apparently was not at Santa Anita Park on February 22 when Rosemont emerged from a homestretch bumping match to finish third. Marion apparently was back east before the evening of Wednesday, March 4, when Randolph Scott received word that his father had suddenly died.

George Scott had collapsed out in the open, felled by a heart attack on a street corner in Raleigh about ten o'clock at night. Fellow citizens tried to help him, but before he could be treated at a hospital, he was gone. He was only sixty-four years old.

It was early evening, California time, when Randy heard the news. He retreated to his beach house in Santa Monica, saying nothing to the press. His housemate Cary Grant likewise made no public statements. The press knew only that Randy flew back east on Friday. On Saturday, home in Charlotte, he attended his father's funeral.

That same Saturday, March 7, Marion settled some personal business down in Camden. She was revising her divorce agreement: Marion would not give Tom Somerville an annuity from Delaware Trust Company preferred stock, after all. Carroll Bassett served as the witness while Marion and Tom each signed the amendment. Marion's reasons for making this change were not stated in the document—only her decision and Tom's compliance.

And while Tom Somerville lost even more status, Randolph Scott scored a professional coup. A role he had been chasing for several months would be his: starring as Hawkeye in a new adaptation of the classic American novel *The Last of the Mohicans*.

It was not the right time for celebrating too obviously. Randy's fans would be happy about his further success but also knew that he was in mourning. They might not understand what he did only nineteen days after his father died. Marion would understand Randy's situation and also might consider her own reputation—her divorce had been final for less than six months. A serious new romance might seem *hasty*. She and Randy talked. They agreed. On March 23, 1936, they set out on a secret mission.

· · ·

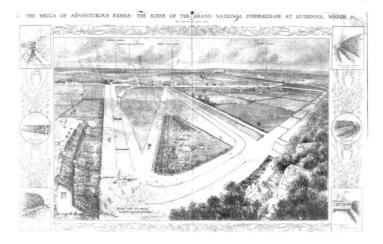

Aintree's vast Grand National course (outer loop) as it looked in 1928. The original caption said, "Not only must it be a good horse that can stay the course, but the jockey must have judgment, pluck, nerve, endurance, and last, but not least, good luck, if he is to be the first past the winning-post." *Photo courtesy of Melton Prior*

The final fence: more than four miles into the 1928 Grand National, Tipperary Tim (far left) will gallop to victory. Billy Barton (far right), weary from his troubled trip and crowded by the riderless horse, will fall when he lands. *Photo courtesy of Getty Images / Popperfoto*

Snow-covered Montpelier, after William du Pont's renovation, viewed from the front field where Marion and her brother would build a stee-plechase course. The magnificent "willow gate" tree, leafless during wintertime, appears toward the left. *Photo courtesy of Montpelier, A National Trust Historic Site; duPont Scrapbook 6*

Marion duPont communing with Grisette, "the first pony I really liked." *Photo courtesy of Montpelier, A National Trust Historic Site; duPont Scrapbook 2*

Three generations of superb horsemen: Reginald, Bruce, and Tom Hobbs with champion pony Lady Marvel. *Photo courtesy of Getty Images / Hulton Archive*

Relaxing at Montpelier with her brother, William duPont, Jr., and a patient, unidentified dog, Marion duPont shows her playful side and beautiful smile. *Photo courtesy of Montpelier, A National Trust Historic Site; duPont Scrapbook 5*

Two young horsemen who helped Marion duPont Somerville develop the best hunt-racing stable in America: Noel Laing (holding trophy) and Carroll Bassett (muddy). Shown here at The Country Club in Brookline on June 17, 1932, Bassett had won a flat race on a slippery course with a horse owned and trained by Laing, giving what the *Boston Herald* called "a brilliant exhibition of racing skill." *Photo courtesy of* The Sportsman *(August 1932)*

Trouble Maker (airborne) and Noel Laing launch their winning move in the 1932 Maryland Hunt Cup. *Photo courtesy of* Polo *(July 1932)*

Battleship (#2) and Bassett sail toward victory in the Roslyn Handicap. (Writing on print by Marion duPont Scott.) *Photo courtesy of Montpelier, A National Trust Historic Site; duPont Scrapbook 13*

Jane Fowler Bassett and Carroll K. Bassett in step. *Photo courtesy of Fine Arts Center of Kershaw County*

One of many mid-1930s publicity photos where housemates Cary Grant and Randolph Scott show their rapport. *Photo courtesy of Getty Images/John Kobal Foundation, Moviepix Collection*

Camera-shy Marion duPont Scott and camera-friendly Randolph Scott go racing together at Will duPont's Fair Hill meet, September 1936. *Photo courtesy of AP Photo/Morgan*

They aimed Battleship for Aintree: **Marion duPont (Somerville) Scott and Carroll K. Bassett** (wearing a **suit over jockey** attire). *Photo courtesy of Montpelier, A National Trust Historic Site; duPont Scrapbook 14*

He would ride Battleship in Aintree's famously dangerous Grand National: Bruce Hobbs with "Budge." *Photo courtesy of Montpelier, A National Trust Historic Site; duPont Scrapbook 14*

Battleship shows the long reach of his hind legs—a very big stride despite being a small horse—while tall Bruce Hobbs shows why, during this era, he won a dance prize for "biggest feet in the ballroom." *Photo courtesy of Tribune Photo Archives*

Nellie Pratt Hobbs rides Battleship for one of his last gallops before the Grand National. Her understanding manner helped him accept a foreign environment and settle down to work. *Photo courtesy of Mrs. Robert Leader*

"Battleship" at Becher's Brook 1938

Taking the most difficult inside path and refusing to let his underside touch the brush, Battleship leads Royal Danieli and Workman over Becher's Brook. (Writing on print by Marion duPont Scott.) *Photo courtesy of Montpelier, A National Trust Historic Site; NT1984.07.151*

Dressed up to meet his father's high standard and uncomfortable with the noisy welcome to New York Harbor, Bruce Hobbs looks after Battleship. *Photo courtesy of Getty Images/Popperfoto*

They didn't want to do it where anyone would talk. Not Charlotte, where Randy would be noticed like a prince. Not Camden, where Marion's whereabouts might be whispered through the grapevine. They settled on Chester, South Carolina, a small country town about halfway between their home bases. A convenient place where they could legally wed without any waiting period or publicity, quickly and quietly. A spiritually comfortable place where the probate judge who granted marriage licenses also was a minister.

Randy could make some excuse and set out from Charlotte alone. Marion, from Camden, would do the same. They would arrive separately and meet inside the courthouse. They needed a witness who would keep their secret, and Randy's web of friendly relationships provided one. Not his old buddy "Smiling Jack" Heath the automobile salesman, who had helped him discover Hollywood but might have trouble sitting on a story like this; instead, one of Jack's middle-aged half brothers, Gilbert Brown Heath, who ran a cotton mill near Chester.

The bride and groom told the truth on their paperwork, mostly. Marion said that she was thirty-eight years old, the same as Randy, though her soon-to-be-husband knew that she actually was forty-one. Their full names were taken down but mostly avoided—if reporters got nosy, who would care that "Marion D. Somerville" had married "George R. Scott"? Marion signed her last name correctly, but the clerk spelled it like the season "summer" and filed their marriage license under "Su." A natural mistake, or covering their tracks? They were so determined to keep the news from getting around, Randy would not tell his own mother.

Then came a simple ceremony. A kiss. Not much chance for a honeymoon—family and friends would notice if they disappeared for very long. Instead, only four days after marrying Marion, Randolph Scott arrived back in Hollywood to start work on *The Last of the Mohicans*. Everyone assumed that he still was a bachelor, though the columnist Inez Wallace would claim that his behavior had changed. Randy Scott seemed pleasant but guarded, and Inez didn't know why. Much later she would write, "Because you thought you were being loyal to a wife that none of us even knew you had married!"

Back east, Marion continued using the name Somerville, though her brother knew the truth. With utmost confidentiality, Will duPont had one of her automobile insurance policies, effective April 1, made out to Marion duPont Scott. Discreetly, he and Marion began the long process of erasing Mrs. Thomas H. Somerville.

Five days after Marion's remarriage, her horse Oliver C., with Noel Laing up, narrowly missed winning the Carolina Cup. They were unlucky to lose this one; Noel's saddle had slipped. But there would be no slip of the tongue during April and May, while Marion continued the hunt-racing circuit as usual. And she was not the only one keeping a secret.

Noel Laing always looked like a born rider when he settled into a saddle, but this spring, for the first time, he looked like a jockey. While his cheekbones held their wide stance, the fleshier planes of his face looked as if someone had been at them with a vacuum cleaner. Maybe there was something working on him, something beyond the rubber suit that he put on whenever he needed to sweat off a few pounds, beyond those days when he simply "wouldn't eat" because he needed to be extra trim for a race. Maybe the life he had been building for seven years, from a single racehorse to a string that overflowed his barn at Bunree Farm, from limited responsibilities to constant riding, training, serving on committees, and promoting horse sports at Southern Pines, had started wearing on him. Perhaps he was literally spreading himself too thin. Maybe he owed himself a real vacation.

He made it through springtime. Marion didn't have a horse in the Deep Run Hunt Cup, so Noel won it for someone else. Then he met the same horse, Ghost Dancer, up the road in Warrenton for the Virginia Gold Cup. It became one of his most brilliant days. For Marion, Noel won the featured brush race, the Virginia National. Then he and Ghost Dancer, who was not the favorite, triumphed on the timber course in the Gold Cup. It was not only a big win but also a moment where Noel revealed everything he could be. "It takes years of heady and courageous riding to reach the point he holds in the affection of the public," a reporter from New York wrote, "but seldom, if ever before, did he ride as he did today."

Noel savored his victories, smiled his enchanted smile, and didn't announce what really was going on. He wrapped up the month of May with a big easy win up in New York State. Then, back at Bunree, he told his parents that he needed a break. He and his brother Douglas were heading out to Minnesota for a few weeks on "a fishing trip." But not the kind of fishing that their family envisioned. Noel checked into the Mayo Clinic.

Three months had gone by, from March through May, while Noel increasingly knew that he wasn't well and figured out what to do. That June, while his friends thought he was relaxing, Carroll Bassett and Shirley Banks—Noel's assistant was a licensed hunt meet jockey now—raced horses at Long Island. And that June, while Noel hoped that radiation could solve the problems attacking his belly and his throat, Battleship began working under saddle again. The little horse was sound, he was handling light training, and Marion and Carroll were thinking about Aintree.

If Marion was going to try the Grand National again, she needed a horse with stamina plus *speed*. Annapolis was fast but also, Marion noted, "had to have things his own way. The grass should be nice. Nobody should bump him." Marion would keep Annapolis at stud and never send him overseas. Now, with Carroll's urging, she considered her other fastest jumper. She didn't care that he was three inches shorter than Billy Barton, who in turn had been smaller than most Aintree horses. She knew she had "a big little horse," in physique and attitude. Battleship, Marion realized, "would take a crack at anybody. He was always full of himself."

Aintree was on. She would send Battleship.

But who, in England, would help him prepare? Not Noel, this time. Not Carroll, who, despite his brilliance over American brush courses, never would try Aintree. Despite all of his boldness in competition, there seemed to be something in Carroll that didn't want to take the ultimate test. What if Aintree asked him a question he couldn't answer? It was another thing when Carroll felt he had the upper hand. When Battleship had come to him, at first he had been amused, but then perhaps he started wondering if he measured up. A journalist discussing Battleship later said, "At least one fine horseman close to him has always been conscious of trying to hide an inferiority from him, feeling deep down in his heart that Battleship knew much more about racing than he could ever learn." This description fit Carroll: privately, keenly aware of how he limited himself.

But the horse . . . the horse was another story.

Battleship carried such riches inside himself. He had come to Marion with twenty-two races under his belt, a veteran of Bowie and Keeney Park, Hialeah and Havre de Grace, Arlington Park and Hawthorne, Lincoln Fields and Aqueduct. He knew the webbed barrier, the Bahr gate, the Waite gate, palm trees and pine trees, Midwestern winds and saltwater breezes . . . the soothing and intrusive hands of grooms and veterinarians . . . the bounces, swatting, clucking, and shouts of a dozen or more riders who had balanced on his back. He knew morning gallops where he liked to hold back, staying well within himself, and afternoons where the shouting crowd and driving rider expected so much more. He could not guess that there was any such thing as an ocean to cross or a Becher's Brook to leap over. Battleship wouldn't imagine himself trying but failing. If the moment came, he would mix all that he knew with whatever his people wanted him to do.

Who would take Battleship to Aintree? In the end, Marion trusted the advice of Irish-born rider and trainer Jim Ryan, whom she had known for several years. Now flourishing as one of American hunt racing's leading horsemen, Jim was too well set in the States to move overseas with Battleship, but he made a strong recommendation. More than a decade back, someone in England had helped the struggling Ryan land his first American job. Marion could do no better, Jim testified, than hire that superb horseman. Battleship would be in the best possible hands with Reginald Hobbs.

Ryan knew that his old friend Reg also employed some of the best stable help anywhere. He perhaps could not realize what an exceptional "two-for-one" deal was developing in the Hobbs family. On June 1, 1936, with the British steeplechasing season nearly done, fifteen-year-old Bruce rode his second winner. This time, the winning trainer was Reg Hobbs. With childlike affection, Bruce still called him "Daddy."

17

Shipping out of New York Harbor, Battleship slipped quietly through a gateway from one world to another. Several days earlier, there had been quite a crowd here, cheering more than three hundred human athletes on their way to the Olympic Games at Berlin. Hundreds of African Americans showed up especially to greet track star Jesse Owens, whose success would puncture Hitler's doctrine of white supremacy. Before setting sail, the athletes watched the Olympic flag being raised on board their ship. Few people on ship or ashore paid attention to a single protester pacing the dock with a sign saying "Boycott Hitler Germany; fight for tolerance, freedom and liberty."

Even fewer people took notice on Friday, July 24, when two sons of Man o' War sailed away in the hold of a former U.S. Army transport ship renamed the *American Banker*. Marion sent Battleship with an unraced three-year-old gelding named War Vessel for company—though if horses could make small talk, Battleship and War Vessel might not find much in common. An old-timer traveling with a greenhorn.

But an ocean voyage was new to Battleship. Stepping out onto the pier, walking into a covered crate, being hoisted high into the air. Then landing, but not on solid land. Walking into a larger box, with padded walls. Confined there for several days, feeling a disconcerting rolling motion underfoot. If he felt sick to his stomach, there wasn't much he could do about it.

Unlike seasick humans, horses are unable to vomit. At least he would be closely watched, fed well but not overfed, given plenty of soothing hay.

While Battleship set out across the Atlantic, Marion celebrated another stallion's safe arrival from England. This year, marrying Randolph Scott hadn't been her only secret mission. At her brother's request, she had gone seeking a top-notch Thoroughbred sire they could bring to the United States. She had found one, all right: Blenheim, who had won the 1930 Epsom Derby and sired the 1935 Epsom Derby winner, Mahmoud. But his owner, the Aga Khan, wanted a tremendous price. Marion ended up recruiting several partners, including Warren Wright of Calumet Farm, to bear the cost. Importing Blenheim—known as Blenheim II in the United States, because there had been another Blenheim registered with the Jockey Club in New York—to Kentucky would be her last great contribution to horse racing under the name Mrs. T. H. Somerville. In his first American crop, Blenheim would sire Calumet Farm's 1941 Triple Crown champion, Whirlaway.

While Battleship began his ocean journey and Blenheim settled in at Claiborne Farm, Marion wrote a big check for a project especially dear to her brother's heart: $40,000 to the Delaware Steeplechasing and Race Association. The state of Delaware finally had approved pari-mutuel wagering on Thoroughbred racing. A handsome racecourse was being built—and Marion once again became the carpenter's assistant, contributing money instead of holding boards in place. Like their backyard Coney Island so long ago, Delaware Park would be Will duPont's design.

Marion had her own big design in mind, of course, but her materials had their own thoughts, patterns, and preferences. She couldn't position a trainer, a jockey, and a horse like wooden boards and make everything stay just right. Her design depended on understanding: Reg Hobbs on the ground and a jockey in the saddle comprehending the immense challenge of Aintree and also clicking with Battleship. She waited to see how this all would play out; she waited to hear what Reg would say.

On July 28, Reg Hobbs made his way to the London Docks to fetch Marion's horses. Meeting Battleship, Reg began comparing a faraway woman's ambitious plan with his own view of reality. He had been told about Battleship's tendon trouble. Had the last year without any riding done the trick? Could the nine-year-old stallion move from light training into the hard work that would be needed if he were going to race at Aintree, or even race at all? Reg let the ocean travelers relax into their new situation, taking several days watching Battleship loosen up. Then he wrote Marion, "The leg that was fired feels and handles real well and I see no reason why he shouldn't stand training and racing over here."

Meanwhile, the Saratoga racing season began, and Marion supported a big public project—an interesting contrast with the American Liberty League's conservative beliefs—when she checked into a resort hotel funded by the New York State government. But oh, the temptations! The Gideon Putnam hotel had been designed, as one reporter put it, "to produce restful reactions, to dispel gloom with bright colors, yet avoid jazzing things up so as to jangle the nerves." The spacious property included updated versions of the mineral baths that had helped make Saratoga a famous health resort in the first place, plus a temperature-controlled outdoor swimming pool, tennis courts, and a three-thousand-yard golf course. Marion sheltered here about a mile from the racetrack, accompanied by Carroll and Jane Bassett. Her secret husband remained in Hollywood, filming his role as a love interest for Mae West in *Go West Young Man*.

The time arrived, however, to admit the truth. On August 13, Saratoga Springs would host the movie premiere of a story set nearby: *The Last of the Mohicans*, starring Randolph Scott. The day before the premiere, Will duPont announced that his sister had been married to Randolph Scott for nearly five months. This revelation made August 13 headlines all over the United States.

Out in California, Scott corroborated the news and flabbergasted Hollywood. The movie world had figured that he was a "confirmed bachelor." And who was this woman? Marianna? Mariona? A socialite, an heiress, a du Pont. From Montpelier, Vermont? Not knowing her, they made many mistakes and fell back upon stereotypes. Not knowing Randy's true age, many also assumed that this mystery socialite had snared a handsome fellow a decade younger than herself, when in fact Randy was three years and not quite nine months younger.

Neither Randy nor Marion attended the movie premiere. Perhaps their sensational announcement generated enough publicity to spare them from that burden. Scott explained that they had delayed the news until his bride could wrap up various business matters and claimed that Marion soon would join him in California. But for the time being she stayed in Saratoga, enjoying the Travers Stakes with her brother and his wife and Carroll and Jane. Marion also hired a contractor to build her new Wilmington house, located within her brother's Bellevue Hall estate. She signed the paperwork "Mrs. George Randolph Scott," embracing the cozy, old-fashioned sound of it, wrapped in Randy's name.

She had to wait until mid-September for their honeymoon. Randy met her at Wilmington, where he could see the spot chosen for their house. Then down to Virginia, where Orange County friends celebrated them with dinner parties, and Marion had Montpelier's basement floor lowered so that tall, fitness-conscious Randy could set up a gym where the Madison kitchens had been and work out without bumping his head.

For the first time in nearly a decade, Marion's racing stable didn't seem to be the main focus of her energy. Its momentum carried onward while she nourished another part of herself. And she was reminded again, as her gardens and greenhouses and animals often reminded her, that you could not make assumptions, not even about younger people who should be especially durable and strong. There had been bad news for Noel Laing. The Mayo Clinic staff could not halt his disease.

That summer, Noel came home from his "fishing trip" and told his parents the truth. And his truth did not include giving up the horses that several owners had trusted him to train, even though Noel could not ride anymore. He could not jump the pasture fences and gallop out across the fields; he could not travel to racecourses; he could not take his green hunters out cubbing with the Old Dominion Hounds. But from a window at Bunree Farm, he might watch them go by. He could listen to what Shirley Banks and Andy Fowler, who exercised and jockeyed them, had to say. He could ask the right questions and make plans. Noel's family had a telephone installed beside his bed so that his deputies could keep in touch even when they were far away.

Noel relied upon Shirley, upon Andy, and upon his own father to keep going. And they relied on him for the same. Maybe they would continue this way for a good while. Perhaps the extrapowerful X-ray treatments available in Washington, D.C., could not completely cure Noel, but maybe science would buy him a healthier life.

Every day, Noel soaked up the news about the horses he had been handling only a few months ago. Their names might bring back a wealth of sensations—of movement, of outdoors. And every so often, Noel would hear a report from overseas. He might picture England and the little horse he had started over fences four years ago.

Battleship had encountered many a rolling field and racecourse but nothing quite like this. A few years ago, Bruce Hobbs had felt awestruck when he first rode a racehorse to this hilltop and saw the miles of beautiful turf that his father shared with other racing stables. Now this multitude of slopes and flats, loops and straight gallops, hurdles and steeplechase fences would shape Battleship's routine. Light work on Mondays and Thursdays. Tuesdays and Fridays, some schooling over jumps. Wednesdays and Saturdays, a strong gallop. Stall rest every Sunday. At some point, actual competition. In between, strings of emerald mornings branching off from the hill called Mann Down.

An ideal place for racehorses, but unlike his young companion, War Vessel, Battleship was not certain that he wanted to be here, doing this. Jogging around Montpelier had been simply relaxing; stepping back into serious training meant facing greater and greater demands. Reg Hobbs found himself on a diplomatic mission: winning a nine-year-old stallion over to his side.

Reg could see promise. "Battleship is a fine mover," he wrote to Marion in late August. "I like the old horse a great deal." In September, about six weeks after Battleship had joined his stable, Reg put the little stallion over fences and reported, "He went and jumped beautifully." In early October, Reg sent Marion another cheerful message: "I am pleased to say that both horses are going on very well in every way, particularly Battleship who I feel sure will be a useful horse here, but the ground is still hard with us so, I can't say a lot about the horses yet."

Reg told Marion the truth, up to a point. He didn't want to say that Battleship actually had given him a problem to solve. Not a physical problem—his attitude. Reg employed only stable lads who met his sky-high standards, and yet Battleship wasn't cooperating well when this lad or that lad rode him out to exercise. He was wasting energy, fussing with his riders instead of of settling down to work. But Reg wasn't going to complain about that to Marion, who had hired him because she expected him to be capable of meeting every challenge. He considered all options, and eventually Reg realized that the answer wasn't a lad. It was a woman.

Thirty-year-old Nellie Pratt belonged to a racing family who lived near the Hobbs home in Upper Lambourn. Her father, Fred, was a well-regarded trainer. Among her great-uncles was one of Great Britain's greatest jockeys, the late Fred Archer. And watching Nell on horseback, you knew that she practically had been born there. The perfect posture, the gentle hands, the knack for inviting a horse to do what the trainer wanted, without making it seem like a demand. The respect that Battle-ship required.

"A useful horse," Reg promised Marion. She would get that message later. She was vacationing with her husband. They appeared at her broth-er's Maryland estate for the Fair Hill Races, where a photographer caught them sitting together on the grass. Marion frowned with her eyes at the intrusion, though her mouth was not unfriendly. Randy smiled his bright, professional smile. If Marion had smiled with him, she could have been alluring. Even with her wary expression, she looked like a vivid art mo-derne creation, her nearly black hair making a sparkling contrast with her light skin. There was no diamond sparkler on her left hand, with its pret-tily manicured fingernails, just something resembling a miniature metal sculpture above a plain wedding band. A delicate charm bracelet dangled from her left wrist, featuring a tiny horse.

This moment at Fair Hill showed that when Marion teamed up with Randy, she could have been the Cary Grant in the picture, the one whose extra wattage draws the eye, even beside a damn handsome man. But she did not want to be conspicuous. So Marion dimmed her lights while Randy shone obligingly. A few days after Fair Hill, a reporter catching sight of them in North Carolina described the moment as if a male model had emerged from a magazine: "A tall, handsome collar-ad alighted from a taxi in front of the Hotel Charlotte late Tuesday night, stepped back po-litely to let us pass down the sidewalk, bade the driver a cheery goodnight and walked away. . . . And not until he had walked on into the lobby did we realize he was Randolph Scott, the movie actor." As an afterthought, the reporter noted, "With him was his wife, the former Marion DuPont."

Of course she still *was* Marion duPont, but augmented. Like a schoolgirl, Marion kept trying out different forms of their combined names: Mrs. George Randolph Scott, Mrs. G. Randolph Scott, Mrs. Randolph Scott, Marion duPont Scott. She pushed the Montpelier races off until November again, while she focused upon being with her husband and finishing their new house. Still, she could feel her historic home sidling up beside her, wanting her attention, tugging at her sleeve. While she and Randy woke up in the Charlotte Hotel on October 7, an eighteen-foot-tall pin oak that Marion had sent from Montpelier was about to be planted at Madison Square in New York City. She had provided this tree from James Madison's estate as a special gift celebrating the hundredth anniversary of Madison Avenue. But the Virginia man who had lobbied Marion to provide the tree told the *New York Times* about his greater goal: that James Madison's Montpelier should join George Washington's Mount Vernon and Thomas Jefferson's Monticello as a national shrine. It was the same refrain that Marion had been hearing ever since Montpelier came into her keeping—a connection that she honored and a wish that she ignored at the same time.

That autumn, Montpelier's future was not her urgent concern. It had dropped far behind her newlywed activities, her Aintree hopes, and her worry about Noel Laing. Noel had been seeing a doctor who seemed to be making progress in treating inoperable cancers with, as one article put it, "X-ray dosage five times as great as has been feasible before." But in Noel's case, there had been no improvement. He reached a point at which home life became unsustainable. On October 10, Noel said good-bye to Bunree Farm and entered Garfield Hospital in Washington, D.C.

His friends followed. Katharine Boyd, who with her husband had shared many winters foxhunting with Noel at Southern Pines, noticed an unusual aura in the hospital room. Instead of his friends trying to cheer up Noel, it seemed to work the other way around—"as if," said Katharine, "they gathered there for reassurance and to renew their courage at his never-weakening bedside." Everyone could see Noel's body getting weaker and weaker. The remarkable thing was, Noel still was choosing who he wanted to be.

It wasn't about career anymore, even though he kept looking forward and directing his racing stable. His friends saw Noel choosing to be as considerate with them as he always had been with his horses, sparing them as he had spared Trouble Maker through the second lap at Aintree.

Noel knew that he wouldn't see Aintree again. And yet, hearing the latest from England, he might have a feeling that what he had given was not lost. Noel had been hospitalized for two weeks when Battleship ran his first race in two years. Reg Hobbs didn't expect much, not first time out after such a long layoff and an ocean voyage, facing good competition, and carrying top weight of 168 pounds. This race was only the casual step that you take when you have to begin somewhere. Reg told jockey Tim Hamey to give the little horse "a real nice school" rather than push hard. Battleship fidgeted, expecting more than a workout, proving "a bit troublesome" while Reg secured the saddle.

Reviving old habits, Battleship also acted up at the start. "I feel sure he will get over all that," Reg told Marion. The main thing was what Reg saw when Battleship engaged in the two-mile race, finishing fifth of eight runners—but, Reg wrote, "jumping wonderfully." Those words may have made their way to Noel's bedside, carrying a sense of how Noel's gift still mattered, even if the giver could not be saved.

It would be only natural to wish that life could settle into a form where everything harmonized, but Bruce Hobbs could feel everything shifting out of key the day he rode a heedless horse named No Reckoning. No Reckoning was no secret: in training or in a race, he would run away. At home, Reg often exercised the horse using draw reins that kept his nose down and gave the rider greater leverage, but that equipment wasn't allowed in races, where No Reckoning seemed intent on placing his own picture in the dictionary beside the word "uncontrollable."

And so Bruce felt his fellow riders' disgust when they realized what Reg was trying next. Bruce saw professional jockey Gerry Wilson confront his father. "We all like you, Reg, and we think—or rather we thought—that you were a decent chap," Gerry began. "But if you put that young lad of yours on that sod of a horse, then we think you're a bastard! You've got no right to do it to any boy, let alone your own son, [despite the] fine horseman that he is." But Reg dug in his heels, and fifteen-year-old Bruce felt no need to complain. "What the others never realised," Bruce said, "was that I had total confidence in my father. I knew that he was the complete master of his craft."

And so Bruce did the only thing he thought he could do: let No Reckoning run away for the whole two-mile hurdle race. "I could steer all right," Bruce explained, "but I couldn't do anything about holding my horse. . . . I just sat and suffered." There was just enough left, at the end, for No Reckoning to win by half a length.

Reg was jubilant. He had triumphed, he was right. He invaded the jockeys' room and gave his detractors a piece of his mind. "They smiled wryly but said nothing," a journalist later wrote. "Reg had undoubtedly been wrong, but the boy was even better than they thought."

That scene was not the turning point for Bruce. His world began shifting after Reg left the jocks' room and had a drink with their friend, neighbor, and sometimes exercise "lad" Nellie Pratt. The next thing Bruce knew, Nell was joining him and his father for the drive home.

There was nothing wrong with celebrating a win or giving a neighbor a lift. There was something unusual in how many times they stopped at pubs, where Reg and Nellie could make merry while Bruce could take refreshment but not imbibe alcohol. They reached Upper Lambourn well after dark, with Bruce aware that they had taken much longer than they should. At least it was nearly over. The Pratt family lived only about five hundred yards away from the Hobbs residence. Reg should drop off Nell, then come home with Bruce. But he did the opposite.

"I am just going to take Nellie home," Reg told Margery as Bruce climbed out of the car. So the boy and his mother endured a fuming wait, like a long fuse burning, until they heard the car come back. Reg's casual returning words stayed with Bruce for a lifetime: "Old Fred asked me in for a drink."

Maybe he had. Nell's father was on good terms with Bruce's parents, and Bruce often played tennis with the family. But soon it would be too late for innocent explanations. Soon everyone saw the sparks between Reg and Nellie, and Fred Pratt felt mortified.

But Fred's disapproval couldn't quench their attraction. When Nellie eventually moved a dozen miles away, trying to give up her married beau, Reg began sending more horses to race meets in her new district. Nell did not resist. This was more than a fling. This was looking into someone's eyes and seeing yourself reflected as you were and as you wanted to be. Reg was not receiving such approval from his wife, who hated this racing business, the world where Nellie fit effortlessly. On the way back from those convenient racing meets, Bruce often waited in his father's parked car while Reg spent about an hour visiting inside Nellie's home.

The boy was in the path of a natural force as intractable as No Reckoning. This time, there was going to be a divorce. Soon, Bruce once again had to choose between his parents; Margery was moving back to Leicestershire. She urged Bruce to join her. Reg convinced him to stay. Or maybe Bruce didn't need convincing, when his father's voice only echoed what he heard within himself. "[I] was so heavily involved in my racing career," Bruce recalled, "that, much as I loved my mother, I knew that my future lay with him."

In early November 1936, Noel Laing was racing toward the point where the word "future" had no substance. Although holding on to consciousness, he accepted the relief of sedation. His doctor admitted that Noel was unlikely to recover.

Maybe Noel heard the disappointing news that Reg Hobbs wrote to Marion on November 9: "I have decided not to run Battleship at [the] Liverpool [autumn meeting], as I have only been able to give him one run up to the present and I didn't think it would be fair to the little horse." This meant that Battleship wouldn't get a practice lap around the National course in November, something that numerous National winners, including Kellsboro' Jack, had enjoyed.

Reg hadn't officially ruled out the 1937 Grand National, but he was exercising delicate diplomacy, encouraging Marion enough to keep Battleship in his stable while inching away from Aintree. Bad weather had interrupted his training and racing schedule; more crucially, Reg dreaded what might happen if Battleship faced those great National hedges with daunting drops on the landing side. There was a reason why not many stallions tried that course, and Battleship was living proof: whenever he sailed over a tall brush obstacle, the little stud tipped his hips up to protect, as the Hobbs family put it, "his marriage tackle." Lifting his hips so high made Battleship land at a steep angle, with his nose too low. Reg feared that this precarious style could be fatal at Aintree.

Reg did believe that Battleship could succeed over the less challenging park courses. Unfortunately, Marion's horse lost his rider in his next race and didn't finish. Soon afterward, "lost rider" meant something worse.

Noel Laing was reaching the point where stopping could feel not like robbery but relief. Still, he looked ahead when Andy Fowler dropped in on a Tuesday night, consulting about the Montpelier races coming up that Saturday. There must have been something in Noel's frailty that made Andy wonder, Should his horses run? If they didn't, everyone would understand. But here was Noel still picturing each horse and telling Andy his strategies. Here was Noel making Andy promise that they would race, no matter what.

Tuesday night became Wednesday midafternoon, with Noel's parents and his brother Doug keeping vigil in his room. Then came Noel's moment, tumbling like Trouble Maker in their final Hunt Cup, taking the fall that no one can stop but landing weightless this time, without impact. Except on those he left behind.

November 18 had been a transitional day at Montpelier, wrapping up Marion and Randy's time together for a while. Tomorrow, Scott would fly to Dallas, where the United Daughters of the Confederacy's national convention would honor him for his military service and his performance in *So Red the Rose*. Then he would return to Hollywood. Marion would stay at Montpelier, preparing for the Saturday races and dealing with other practical matters. The news about Noel floated in among these many details, sitting down beside questions of preparing the new house near Wilmington and the process of legally leaving the name Somerville behind. Collecting herself, Marion put the pressing concerns of this day into a few plain words to her brother's business manager in Wilmington:

> *Dear Mr. Edinger—*
>
> *I expect it would be a good thing to put some insurance on the house. You better go ahead with it.*
>
> *Please change name on stock as you suggest.*
>
> *Noel Laing died today—we are all very sorry, he was such a fine boy—*
>
> > *Sincerely,*
> > *Marion Scott*

She had not planned to be at church in Warrenton that Friday afternoon, fewer than twenty-four hours before the Montpelier races, but there she was with Noel's family and dozens of his friends, trying to comprehend why he was gone, why he could not live past twenty-eight years old. He was going away in his racing silks, the scarlet and white he had worn while making his name with Ballast. Marion would carry the memory of twelve pallbearers lifting the casket and bringing it into the tranquil graveyard—twelve horsemen, Noel's comrades from the races, among them Andy Fowler and Carroll Bassett. The next day, they met at Montpelier and carried out Noel's request.

His horses ran, and they ran well—a winner, along with a couple of other prizes. But with Noel's final breath, the air went out of Bunree Farm. After the season ended, the racehorses were sent away. Noel's father left the horse business, keeping only his personal hunters, and concentrated on raising cattle. The family would say that Noel's mother never really got over losing him.

On his headstone they engraved a line from the poet Lord Byron:

BRIGHT BE THE PLACE OF THY SOUL

And then two lines from the New Testament, Jesus telling his disciples:

WHAT I DO THOU KNOWEST NOT NOW

BUT THOU SHALL KNOW THEREAFTER

They left Noel with their own hopes. The hope that somewhere, he was well. The hope that someday, everything would make sense. The hope for understanding and a new start.

Since coming to England, Battleship had raced twice and failed to hit the board. If he was going to make the Grand National next year, it was time to get serious. In early December, Reg matched the nine-year-old stallion with the most promising jockey at hand: fifteen-year-old Bruce.

The boy looked like an outline for a future that he could not yet feel or fulfill. Already taller than his father but not yet needing to shave. A narrow body with oversized feet that made his fellow jockeys laugh. Bruce laughed along with them and would enjoy remembering some of their jokes—such as the time that Frenchy Nicholson saw Bruce lying on a jockeys' room massage table with his feet sticking up in front of the window. "Get off," Frenchy told him. "You're shutting out the light!"

At least those feet fit with the rest of him. Bruce already stood nearly six feet tall. He did not *look* like a good fit for little Battleship, whose shoulder blades stopped barely five feet two inches aboveground. When Bruce settled onto Battleship's back and folded his long legs for a jockey crouch, his toes still could nearly touch Battleship's elbows. (If Bruce let his legs hang straight down, his feet would reach Battleship's knees.) And after he folded himself into Battleship's saddle, Bruce balanced his long body over a smaller center of gravity than he enjoyed with larger horses. Jumping with Battleship, Bruce had practically no margin for error with his own position in the saddle. The little horse's agility came in handy, but when they went racing instead of merely training together, would he and Bruce together have enough stability?

Reg wasn't sure. But Bruce, in the saddle, felt Battleship's extraordinary cleverness. When Reg worried about the little horse tipping his hips up too far and falling end over end, Bruce responded, "He's got five legs, Daddy, not four." Battleship was a rare jumper with the invisible gift that horsemen call "an extra leg," the ability somehow to right himself when a fall seemed inevitable. Rather than doubting his own security, Bruce had faith in his horse.

On December 2, Battleship and Bruce made their debut together at Newbury racecourse, within twenty miles of Reg's training yard. They set out to race three miles over water-soaked ground rated "soft." They finished only fourth. But now Bruce understood, much better than he could from training gallops, Battleship's habits in competition, his rhythms, how much a rider could ask of him, and when.

They tried again ten days later at Sandown Park, not far southwest of London. Reporters thought that two and a half miles might be too short for Battleship's late rally to succeed. Their opinion seemed justified when Bruce let his horse settle well back of the leaders while about two-thirds of the race went by. But then, if they were paying attention, the critics saw Bruce gradually bringing his horse forward. With one fence left, Battleship had only one horse to beat.

And at that fence, past and present merged. All the times that Reg had called, "Follow me," and Bruce threw his whole self into the chase had become second nature to the boy. "The manner in which Mr. Hobbs charged the last fence . . . ," a London reporter declared, "was a delight to see. The horse flew the fence, and instead of being a length and a half behind he landed on the flat side by side with Borris Band."

In one jump, Bruce and Battleship swooped from second place to sharing the lead. That was Reg, that was Bruce—and that also was the power Battleship had discovered with Carroll Bassett: making up ground in the air.

A reporter marveled that Bruce seemed utterly calm when Borris Band's rider appeared to give Battleship "very little room," not knowing how many tricky situations the boy already had faced in a decade on horseback. Nor did he know how bold Battleship could be in a tight spot, even if it meant chasing a man out of the way and squeezing in between a rival and a wooden rail. The reporter simply saw Bruce "riding home with power and artistry" to win by three lengths. "It is no exaggeration," he told readers of the London Times, "to state that I have not seen a better piece of riding for a long time than this riding by Mr. Hobbs."

Bruce wouldn't be called "Mister" for long. That title went with apprentices and amateurs. On December 26, the day before turning sixteen, Bruce rode his ninth and tenth winners. That tenth win ended his apprenticeship. Suddenly, he had to stop and get either an amateur permit or a professional jockey license—which wasn't a hard choice, because Reg was not going to limit Bruce's earning potential by making him a "gentleman" rider. On his sixteenth birthday, the newly minted professional won with his first two mounts. "So my last two rides as an amateur and my first two as a pro," Bruce noted, "had all been winning ones."

And so, even while his parents' marriage was ending, Bruce Hobbs felt a great sense of belonging. The jockeys welcomed him. He was very good at his job. His father always had some critique of his work, never resting on success, but Bruce could sense the deep undercurrent of belief and pride. When he had to choose his home—with his mother or with his father—there was heartache but no serious doubt. In this way, young Bruce might have a lot in common with Marion duPont Scott.

For Christmastime, Marion left Virginia and traveled to her new husband's other world. She had visited California several times, but never had she stepped inside the movie star colony. And that experience was far stranger to Marion than her horse-racing world was to Randolph Scott, even though there was beauty in a climate where citrus trees didn't need greenhouses in December, even though she could appreciate the view from Randy and Cary's Santa Monica beach house "where," said one visitor, "the waves do everything but wash the breakfast dishes."

Entering Randy's Hollywood life, Marion came to a place famous for make-believe. Movie people could be quite sincere about their careers, but their business was pretending. Marion's was reality. Other farmer's daughters came to Hollywood dreaming of having their own mansions and living like princesses. But Marion had Montpelier. She already ran a kingdom and wouldn't trade anything for the real thing. She could only hope that her husband felt the same way.

They hadn't been together in California very long when stories began circulating. Four days after Christmas, a gossip column reported that Randolph Scott and his bride were "reaching a domestic compromise." They would have to compromise, if they wanted to stay married, because Marion rejected Hollywood and Randy wasn't willing to end his movie career and be a "gentleman farmer" back east. Not now, when *finally* he was becoming valuable in his own right. Randolph Scott was not going to give up his hard-won earning power or submerge his emerging identity. He was not going to let himself become another Tom Somerville.

When the New Year came along, Randy stayed in California to begin filming his starring role in *High, Wide and Handsome* with Irene Dunne and Dorothy Lamour. Marion went home, although there were signs that she and Randy shared friendly intentions. On January 11, she stopped at Charlotte, North Carolina, and bought a sporty Auburn 852 Sedan. The salesman was Jack Heath, Randy's young friend who once upon a time had ventured with him to Hollywood.

18

Bruce Hobbs greeted the New Year of 1937 by himself in a five-star hotel room. He was barely sixteen years old, and yet he never had misbehaved when his father sent him away to a racing meet supervised by an older jockey. This time it was Sandy Scratchley making certain that Bruce settled in for the night, then running out for his own fun. Bruce would remember how quickly his chaperone left him:

"You'll be all right now, won't you?"

"Yes, Sandy."

"Don't go out and I'll see you in the morning."

Bruce obeyed. Sixteen years old but not ready to defy his father. He was the boy who waited in the car while Reg dallied with Nellie, the boy who sometimes fell asleep on a couch while his father drank and gambled through poker night with a party of friends. The boy who felt that these things weren't for him, not yet. The boy who also wanted to ride races as well as he could, and accepted that getting a full night of sleep might help.

He raced on New Year's Day but lost by a neck. Then he had to catch a train alone to meet his father but took the wrong one. "Instead of arriving at Oxford at nine o'clock in the evening," Bruce said, "I got in at three o'clock the next morning. Father was still waiting for me. Having got beaten a neck and kept him up half the night, I was not the most popular boy in the world, I can tell you!"

But even though Bruce was six hours late, Reg *was* waiting, strengthening the boy's feeling that he could count on his father, even when he lost, even when he *got* lost and couldn't reach him to explain.

Reg and Bruce were near their old home, at Leicester, on January 5 when Battleship ran again. The bettors weren't sure what to make of the little horse nominated for the marathon Grand National but racing only two miles today. His American Grand National win seemed to say that Battleship liked three miles. After today's race, handicappers still were puzzled. Maybe Battleship was a sort of sprinter, after all?

What they actually had seen was that Bruce Hobbs understood his horse and the course. The Fosse Chase was only two miles, but the homestretch here at Leicester was unusually long. Two racers cleared the last fence well ahead of Battleship—but then Bruce sent him on. The spectators on that winter day saw what Chicago crowds had seen on summer afternoons. Battleship turned on the speed that had made him so effective going a flat mile in the American Midwest. He turned apparent defeat into victory by half a length. A reporter would think it over and write, "Whether Battleship will ever stay the distance of the Grand National remains to be seen, but his jumping yesterday left nothing to be desired."

February began poorly but ended well. Battleship trailed home seventh in the rich Troytown Handicap Chase, over turf so heavy that Bruce pulled up his horse in the only other race he rode that day. On the 24th, however, he won the two-and-a-half-mile Swindon Chase, also over heavy turf, carrying 168 pounds—a short but strong performance less than a month before the National, feeding Marion's hopes.

She was thinking, in a way, that she could have it all. Her own training track at Camden, a full mile around, already under construction. A trip to Southern California, watching her brother's horses compete in the world's new richest race and maybe also spending time with her husband. A trip to England in March to see Battleship take on Aintree.

She tried to get her brother on board, but he was such a busy man. In midwinter Marion opened a letter from Will that said, "I know I will be unable to arrange to get out to California in February, and I doubt very much if I could be absent from town for the trip to England though I know I would enjoy it very much." She was on her own.

Maybe she was feeling nostalgic. During early February, Marion visited the luxury resort at Sea Island Beach, Georgia, not many miles from Altama. Then back to Camden, where she could see Jane Fowler Bassett win a blue ribbon in the show ring, riding at the Camden hunter trials, and where her brother did show up, with his wife, in time to fine-tune the training track construction and also enjoy the Washington's Birthday races.

And then Marion took off across the United States to see her brother's horse Rosemont in the Santa Anita Handicap. He was favored to win it, even though his opponents included a rising champion: Seabiscuit.

That Saturday, February 27, Marion duPont Scott joined a record crowd of more than fifty thousand people at Santa Anita Park. In the clubhouse she could have rubbed elbows with the aviation mogul William E. Boeing, the boxer Gene Tunney, or the baseball star Joe DiMaggio; with movie producers including Jack Warner and Cecil B. DeMille; or with a parade of movie stars. Charlie Chaplin was here with his alleged wife, Paulette Goddard. Clark Gable and Carole Lombard probably steered clear of Gable's estranged wife, also present. Fred Astaire and Bing Crosby enhanced their reputations as die-hard racing fans. The list went on. But reporters did not mention Randolph Scott, hard at work on *High, Wide and Handsome,* which was proving to be a challenging shoot. Still, Marion may have been disappointed that Randy was not at Santa Anita enjoying the day with her.

But Rosemont came through. Literally. He had started from a flimsy temporary stall outside the regular starting gate, because there weren't enough permanent spaces for eighteen horses and he had drawn post seventeen. He put up with close quarters during the early running. In the homestretch, he was stuck in traffic while Seabiscuit firmly held the lead. Marion would have thought the race was lost, but then Rosemont's jockey saw just enough of a hole, and Rosemont darted through. Splitting horses, he came flying while Seabiscuit's jockey felt the danger and went back to riding hard. They needed the official photograph to know for certain: Rosemont by a head.

This would remain Rosemont's greatest moment. The next day, his trainer told the press, "Rosy's feet are a little sore." He wouldn't be retired until 1939, but Rosemont wouldn't race often. His hooves weren't tough enough. Seabiscuit, growing stronger and stronger, would be voted America's champion older horse of the year 1937.

After the big race, Marion lingered in Southern California for a few days. If she visited Randy at his beach house, on a movie set, or somewhere else, her presence did not make the news. Of course, stealth was nothing new to Marion and her husband.

A reporter did infiltrate the set of *High, Wide and Handsome* that week and came away wishing he could have traded places with Randolph Scott. They were filming a scene of newlyweds: leading lady Irene Dunne asleep in bed, Scott breezing in with a branch of apple blossoms "dripping with raindrops." The reporter tantalized his readers with what he saw:

> Scott is in high good humor, shakes the wet apple blossoms over Miss Dunne's head, so that she is showered with pink petals and water. Then while she laughingly, weakly protests, he lifts her from the pillow, takes her in his arms, kisses her.
>
> Scott, however, doesn't seem to throw himself into the lovemaking with quite the warmth that [director Rouben] Mamoulian wants. We're wishing the director would call on us. Instead, he sits on the edge of the bed and holds quiet conference with his two players.
>
> "Make it more virile and vigorous," he tells his leading man. And to Miss Dunne, "keep it vibrant."

Randy would try, but the audience usually could see him trying. He always would be shy about filming love scenes. He could woo the camera with a delighted smile. He could tease his leading lady in a joking way without becoming too self-conscious. But he had trouble holding her gaze and showing anything that looked like need.

Did he see his wife that week? On her last night in Los Angeles, Marion wrote a note to her brother about her travel plans, using stationery from the Chapman Park Hotel on Wilshire Boulevard, perhaps writing from her own private bungalow within a Spanish garden courtyard. She did not say whether or not she was alone.

· · ·

Ten days before the 1937 Grand National, Marion might have thought that Battleship still had a shot. On very soft ground that he didn't especially like, he finished fourth in the prestigious National Hunt Handicap Chase at Cheltenham. Reg Hobbs, however, was not satisfied. He had seen Battleship barely clear the wide water jump, his front feet sinking into the earth only inches past the water's edge, his hindquarters tilted too high, his hind legs plunging forward like a cheetah's, trying to squeeze out a landing on a sliver of turf. Somehow, Battleship had done it. But Reg could not let him try this at Aintree. That week, when the final acceptances came due, he told Marion they were stopping. "He said the horse didn't have enough experience over the high jumps, that they wanted him to carry too much weight," Marion would recall. "He gave me 100 excuses." Several days after that decision, Marion opened a letter that she could not take at face value.

"I hated to scratch Battleship from the Grand National this year," Reg testified, "as he would have had a real good chance if he was only a bit bigger and had a little more scope, but he is inclined to jump on his head a little when landing over his fences in the heavy going in this country and that is the chief reason for my not running the little horse in the National this year, but it was a very great temptation."

Marion understood that given more time, her horse could be better prepared. Maybe he needed more fitness than this winter's bad weather had allowed. Maybe he needed to cope with the English racecourses for another season, absorbing their challenges into his muscles and his mind. Marion knew, however, that Battleship wasn't going to change very much. Now ten years old, he already had all the size and scope that he ever would have. When Reg said, "I hated to scratch Battleship from the Grand National this year, as he would have had a real good chance if he was only a bit bigger . . . ," he essentially was wishing that Battleship were a different horse.

Marion agreed to let it go, for now. But she may have perceived Reg's real temptation: securing a more promising National horse for Bruce.

And there was one in Reg's care, owned by Mrs. Ambrose Clark. Flying Minutes wasn't very big, but Reg thought he was safe—a gelding, who would get around Aintree without trying to protect the family jewels. Flying Minutes didn't have Battleship's brilliance, but Bruce had partnered him several times and could count on him for a solid performance. At age sixteen years and not quite three months, Bruce Hobbs was about to become one of the youngest riders in Grand National history.

"Riding for the first time at Liverpool is like crossing the equator," said steeplechase jockey turned mystery writer Dick Francis, "an experience to be looked forward to with awe, a graduation, a widening of horizons." All of this engulfed Bruce Hobbs when he walked onto the National course with his father and headed for the first fence. Bruce had entered a scene far bigger than peripheral vision. You would need a second pair of eyes to take in the full reach of this place. After sweeping his gaze across the immense space, Bruce set out to learn it one obstacle at a time. And he did have a second pair of eyes analyzing every approach, takeoff, and landing. He saw for himself. He saw even more through his father.

"Flying Minutes has a reasonable outside chance," Reg told a Liverpool reporter that week. "I am just a bit doubtful about him quite staying the four and a half miles." Reg also spoke of an entry he was sheltering for American horseman Bill Streett, who had decided to tackle Aintree this year. "What Have You has also an outside chance, as he is a great jumper," Reg told the press. "He has not been long enough over from America to have the necessary preparation for such a race, especially as he had a bad crossing and lost a lot of his condition on his way." Bill Streett, like Pete Bostwick a few years earlier, sounded more optimistic: "I believe my horse will give me a good ride, and with ordinary luck go near winning."

However they performed, it would be a royal occasion. King George VI, who would be crowned in mid-May, attended the Grand National with his queen. Caught up in the coronation spirit, the crowd surrounding the course swelled to an estimated four hundred thousand people. The traditional three cheers echoed as the royal couple arrived: "Hurrah! Hurrah! Hurrah!"

The king and queen saw the race from a magnificent viewpoint, the rooftop over Lord Derby's box. Making certain that their majesties wouldn't miss anything, Lord Derby even summoned a turf expert to interpret the action as it unfolded.

There were plenty of mishaps to describe. Only seven of the thirty-three starters would finish, and one barely began. As the field cantered past the grandstand and curved toward the starting place, the American-bred What Have You tried to escape and head back to his barn. Rider Bill Streett was able to keep him on the course and line up with everyone else, but when the flag fell, What Have You planted himself and bid everyone farewell. Only a couple of stablehands hitting him with their hats convinced What Have You to break away. And so Bill Streett began his Grand National a hundred yards behind his opponents. He might have thought they would be okay, anyway—more than four and a half miles for catching up—but What Have You took the first fence badly, would not jump the second, and that was it.

"I can't figure what got into him," Bill Streett puzzled afterward. A thoughtful spectator might just as easily wonder why Streett wasn't listening to his horse. Maybe the outrageously large crowd unsettled an animal who was used to racing past five or ten or twenty thousand people, not entering an arena where the sight and sounds of humanity made a dense wall in all directions. And maybe there was something about Aintree itself that made What Have You fear going out of his depth. "A great jumper," Reg Hobbs had called him. But here were great unknowns: thirty-two other horses around him, perhaps extra nerves jangling through his rider, then a massive hedge to leap and Lord knows what all coming after it.

"Aintree is no respecter of horses who try to skimp their work," said a Liverpool newspaper the next day. Dick Francis later added, "It is not a place for cowardly horses or bad jumpers, for even the brave and the bold sometimes fall there, and the others would do better to stay at home."

What Have You, despite his fine jumping, had not been ready. Bruce Hobbs was. In his dozen years of riding, his father had not given him any false sense of security or let him give in to beatable fears. When Bruce met Aintree, he recognized something unyielding but fair: the tone of life in his father's stable yard.

And when Bruce galloped Flying Minutes into the race, he started feeling the true meaning of these obstacles. "It's always amazing how those big fences look to be at an angle as you walk the course," he explained, "but when you ride over them, you meet them just right." Dick

Francis later had a similar feeling during his own National debut. "After two or three fences I began to enjoy my first excursion there," he recalled, "and there was nowhere afterwards that I liked better, as long as I was on a good horse."

Flying Minutes was a good horse. He had enough speed—perhaps a gift from his sire, Kentucky Derby winner Flying Ebony—to take Bruce up near the front and stay there. Second place over the water jump, wrapping up their first lap. Second place the second time over Becher's Brook, following a horse that the king might like: Royal Mail. Perhaps Flying Minutes was tiring as they trekked the second time through the country. Perhaps Reg Hobbs was right about the limits of his stamina. But Flying Minutes still was very much in the hunt, holding third place, when he fumbled over the third fence from home, a stout hedge with a wide open ditch on the landing side, and Bruce fell off.

Reporters praised the young rider for a good effort. Bruce thought that if only he had stayed on, he and Flying Minutes would have finished no worse than fourth.

Royal Mail dominated the second half of the race, bringing another victory to trainer Ivor Anthony, who had sent out Kellsboro' Jack not so long ago. The biggest threat had been a horse named Drim, who latched onto Royal Mail after losing his rider. After the victory, while mounted policemen escorted Royal Mail back to the paddock, Drim was not done with his newfound friend. He "tried his best," a reporter said, "to follow the winner to the saddling enclosure."

Snow flurries in South Carolina. Randolph Scott had come east in late March, and that is what he found, escorting his wife at Springdale Race Course on Carolina Cup day. Springtime at Springdale, horses racing through snowflakes and Marion in her element despite the strange weather. Will duPont joining them, along with Carroll and Jane Bassett. Jane would be hosting a buffet dinner for a big crowd afterward. Meanwhile, Carroll wasn't riding any races. Perhaps Randy hadn't been around enough to wonder if that, like South Carolina snow in springtime, was a little strange.

Marion may have confided in Randy, or she may have let him take things at face value and hoped for the best. Maybe today would be all smiles, but lately things hadn't been going well between Carroll and Jane. Decades later, acquaintances would remember how Carroll treated his wife and politely say that he had been "unkind." Maybe causes for his trouble were not hard to find. Among the racing crowd, almost everybody drank. Some drank staggering amounts. Partying at Bunree while his parents were away, Noel Laing once had led a few rounds of alcohol-inspired target practice, he and his friends shooting out all the glass panes of the house's three-sided sun porch. Rowdy, irresponsible fun. But now Noel was gone, and maybe that was part of Carroll's trouble. Hard-working, hard-playing Noel, his dear companion, forever out of reach. Of course Jane and her brother Andy, and Marion, and many others close to Carroll were grieving, too. It had been less than five months. They were navigating a racing season for the first time since Noel had died, feeling as if he should step in at any time.

And Carolina Cup day was supposed to be a great celebration. Someone counted license plates from more than twenty different states on the automobiles parked around Springdale racecourse. Also, this week Randy and Marion marked their first anniversary. They were able to be here together—wasn't that a good sign? And at long last, Marion soon would have her name changed from Marion duPont Somerville to Marion duPont Scott on every single stock certificate that she owned.

But while Marion could be feeling complete, her young friend Jane Fowler Bassett was torn. Jane had begged Carroll to give up drinking. If he could mend his ways, she would stay. Marion wanted Jane to stay, and perhaps Marion understood them both well enough to give wise advice. Or maybe Marion treated this situation in the same gently stubborn way she would train a young horse, giving a scared, confused, or angry animal many chances to succeed. But Carroll would seem to try, then fail. Whatever he needed was more than his wife—or anyone—could provide.

Marion could want Jane to tough it out, but maybe, this time, Marion wasn't being realistic. That spring, Jane watched her brother Andy Fowler happily preparing to get married. In late April, the difference between rosy new promises and her own dilemma confronted Jane while she served as a bridesmaid at her brother's wedding at a horsey estate in Gladstone, New Jersey. Not so long ago, it would have felt entirely natural for Carroll Bassett to serve as an usher for his good friend Andy. But Carroll was not there, and Jane was about to fly. Before Marion duPont Scott celebrated her birthday in early May, Jane had landed in Nevada to prepare for divorce.

What a strange set of images could be tumbling through Marion's mind. Carroll Bassett, somberly drinking. Jane Fowler Bassett, an unhappy Nevada refugee. And Randy Scott, plenty happy, not celebrating with Marion on May 3 but reveling at the May 1 birthday party in Santa Monica for William Randolph Hearst, a circus-themed bash for four hundred guests where gossip broadcaster Walter Winchell dressed up like a carnival barker and fiery actress Bette Davis portrayed a bearded lady. Marion, who had enjoyed gymnastics once upon a time, might have found a way to fit into the costumed crowd of would-be acrobats, clowns, and trick riders. Instead, there were only stories she might hear and pictures she might see, among them her husband parading in with Cary Grant and several other Hearst Castle weekend regulars, sporting matching pink-and-white satin trapeze costumes emblazoned with a red logo: "The Flying San Simeons."

Marion duPont Scott entered her forty-third year with a much less theatrical blaze of activity. Camden in mid-April, perhaps witnessing some of the final scenes between her dear friends the Bassetts. Then Montpelier, then Wilmington, then Montpelier again, where telegrams from Reg Hobbs tended to catch up with her.

Instead of Aintree in March, Reg had sent Battleship in early April to Bangor-on-Dee, a course that would become well known as a welcoming place for novice racers. Even so, the little horse didn't finish the course because the footing was bad. "Pulled up," the chart said. "Terribly deep and heavy," Reg wrote in his ledger. Later, Reg would look back with respect rather than disgust. "The times Battleship was beaten it tended to be very heavy ground, which he didn't like," said Reg. "He just pulled himself up; wouldn't go. A very brainy horse he was." Quite possibly, Battleship remembered the strain of his last American race—the Grand National at Belmont Park on boggy ground—and would not stress himself that way again.

But he was willing to work, and his first English springtime became like his Chicago summer: four races in five weeks. And Battleship seemed to be validating Reg's choice to save him for the park courses: a second place at Cheltenham, then a victory at Ludlow and another at Stratford-on-Avon. Battleship's triumph at Stratford in the Coronation Chase, only four days before the crowning of King George, was his final race before summer vacation. Reg's message to Marion included the compliment, "great performance by a great little horse," a validation that would keep Marion aiming for Aintree next year. Altogether, Battleship had scored five victories in thirteen English races. At age ten, entering middle age, he had completed the busiest campaign of his life.

Across the Atlantic, Battleship's former partner Carroll Bassett had stopped riding steeplechases. At age thirty-one, Carroll was young enough to keep going if he wished. But with his wife bound for Reno, he was grappling with the loss of what a friend described as a "one-in-a-lifetime love." Carroll could count on at least one thing: Marion's unwavering support. As another racehorse trainer who worked for Mrs. Scott would note, "The lady is very loyal. She's almost better when you lose than when you win." He was talking about the races, but he could have meant anything. Marion shepherded Carroll in late May, when her own notary public witnessed Carroll's Certificate of Attorney, hiring the Reno lawyer who would represent him when Jane brought her complaint to court on Monday, June 14.

Jane's case, like Marion's against Tom Somerville, would be locked away from the public. In a private hearing, Jane pleaded extreme cruelty "which caused [her] great unhappiness and injured her general health." Unlike Marion, she did not specify mental cruelty only. Like Tom Somerville, Carroll denied the cruelty charge but did not contest the divorce. The judge found in favor of Jane and sealed the evidence she brought forth.

Jane Fowler Bassett left Nevada as a single woman but still holding on to part of her past. She never stopped using Carroll's last name.

From then on, in steeplechasing, the name "Bassett" often went with one of Jane's horses rather than Carroll's exploits. And it fell far behind the name "Scott," which Marion planted like a horsey Johnny Appleseed: admiring her brother's design during opening day at Delaware Park, overseeing the Orange County Horse Show, gearing up for Saratoga. She may not have noticed when gossip queen Louella Parsons wrote, "Randy Scott denies those rumors that his long distance marriage is headed for the rocks, and since Mrs. Scott isn't saying anything, guess we'd better take Randy's word for it."

That summer, Randy's schedule revolved around the release of *High, Wide and Handsome:* the New York premiere, the Los Angeles premiere, and waves of charming publicity to offset some disappointing reviews. He found an ally in the gossip columnist Sheilah Graham, who enjoyed a luncheon party at Randy and Cary's beach house and told her readers, "Randy Scott performs beautifully on the diving board." Randy's guests that day also included the head of Paramount's publicity department, Bob Gillham, who rewarded Sheilah Graham with a bit of Hollywood naughtiness: the story of his first visit with Mae West. Living up to her raunchy image, West had shown Gillham her boudoir, complete with a big mirror above her bed. "Lie down," she told him with her famously suggestive drawl. "Now look up to the ceiling—that's how I do all my serious writing."

No wonder Bob Gillham had become a publicity chief. Nuggets like that would only help Mae West, whose empire depended on selling sex. At the same time, reporters might be distracted from wondering about Randy Scott, Cary Grant, and Randy's distant wife.

But in late August, Scott apparently did sit down with Sheilah Graham to talk about his marriage. "You see, it's like this," Randy reportedly said. "My wife has a career. Ever since she was a little girl she has been passionately devoted to horses—breeding them and racing them. It would be utterly selfish of me to expect her to give that up for the boredom of being a Hollywood wife. She'd have nothing to do out here except twiddle her thumbs." And so, their compromise. "We see each other one month out of every three—it's the best we can do until we figure something better," Randy explained.

How did did a healthy young man stand so much separation from his woman? Graham told her readers that "Scott spends a large part of his days at the Santa Monica Beach House, stifling his desire for Mrs. Scott's companionship with several rounds of golf, swimming and calisthenics in the studio gymnasium. The result is a tanned, exceedingly healthy

6-foot-2-inches (185 pounds) of handsome, nice, if slightly lonely, manhood." Graham politely added that "the evenings are less of a problem than they would be without the friendship of Mr. and Mrs. Fred Astaire and his housemate of his bachelor days and the present, Cary Grant."

Randy had learned that as a husband, he couldn't go out on the town very much. "It would be bad for my marriage to take out any girl here," he said. "I did it once—with bad results. A friend of mine wrote from New York that a girl he knew was coming to Hollywood, and would I do him a favor and show her a good time. I took her to Lamaze restaurant, and the next morning every newspaper and wire service had me getting a divorce. I won't do that again. I have more fun spending my evenings at Freddie's house. They have a projection room and show all the pictures we want."

Sheilah Graham had delivered a Randolph Scott interview that should satisfy his fans and the Paramount publicity department despite the fact that, as Graham noticed, "His chief—and only—aversion is discussing his off-screen self." Randy simply said, "My private life is not under contract to anybody."

But his private life *was* under contract, ever since he had slipped away to the county courthouse in Chester, South Carolina, and made a vow to Marion duPont. Their bond pulled Randolph Scott away from everything else when he opened a telegram on Friday, September 3. Randy had known that Marion was ill. But only now did he realize that she might die.

19

IT HURT TO BREATHE. THE MOST basic motion of being alive, and it hurt
her every time she drew air in, then let it out. She had just come back to
Montpelier, after visiting her brother at Bellevue, when it seemed as if she
might be catching cold. But then came fever, weakness, stabbing pains,
and it wasn't a cold, it was pneumonia. And the pneumonia wasn't simply
limping along, it was getting worse. Her lungs were inflamed. Tied up
with his movie work, Randolph Scott told himself that Marion would be
all right, she was getting the best of care. A special doctor flew down
from New York City. Then a telegram flew out to Hollywood. Scott
barely caught a red-eye flight from Los Angeles, racing on board only moments before takeoff.

He streaked through the atmosphere from Los Angeles to Washington, D.C., with no in-flight communications, no way to know whether
his wife was making it through the night. He caught his breath at D.C.,
where reporters told him that Marion was doing much better today and
had "a fine chance to live." Those words weren't melodramatic. Despite
promising research with antiviral and antibacterial serums, roughly
one in four pneumonia patients died. Scott's relief spilled out like an
apology for not being with her sooner: "I was so busy making trailers
and other publicity for my latest picture. It was a case of 'the show must

go on' and that sort of thing." Then Randolph Scott motored off to Montpelier, probably meeting a chauffeur sent to drive him there, perhaps meditating on his promise to support Marion "in sickness and in health. . . ."

Words couldn't prepare him for her pale vulnerability. If this was "considerably better," how bad had she been?! Pleurisy giving her constant pain, barely able to eat anything. The artificial comfort of an oxygen tent. The crisis had passed, the doctors told Scott, and yet a full day after Scott arrived, they still were thinking that she might need moving to the hospital at Charlottesville. Maybe Marion herself wanted otherwise. Wanting to stay home, the healthy home that her father had chosen; wanting her man nearby; needing the healing power of time.

On September 7, three days after Randolph Scott joined her, a Montpelier staffer was able to report that "Mrs. Scott had a very good night and shows considerable improvement this morning." She would not be strong enough for the September 11 Foxcatcher Hunt Ball at the Wilmington Country Club, which she and Randy had planned to attend together while Carroll Bassett went stag. But she could hear a radio broadcast from her brother's Fair Hill races on September 10, and right after that, her husband on the same radio network, talking about his movie career.

And along with his movie publicity, Marion let Randy go out and take up a social schedule that they had planned to share. The Foxcatcher National Cup Steeplechase at Fair Hill, the Foxcatcher Hunt Ball; then, not quite two weeks after rushing to Marion's side, Randy was playing golf at the Whitney family's course on Long Island and attending a debutante dance nearby, along with a Virginia foxhunting crowd. Returning south, he stopped at a couple of Virginia horse shows that Marion had to miss. His activities showed what a pleasant life they might have together, when she was well enough to travel again.

But togetherness was fleeting. As October began, Randy made a quick solo trip down to his old hometown of Charlotte, then briefly back to Marion before scooting off to Hollywood. Regaining some of her own mobility, Marion journeyed to Meadow Woods, her newly built Wilmington house, in mid-October. She would enjoy the company of her brother and his wife, gradually resuming her usual patterns, until she could be with her husband again.

She was getting stronger; he was gone.

Exactly one year after Noel Laing had died, Battleship ran his first race of the new season. He was a few days too late for the Aintree autumn meeting. Again he missed his chance to get acquainted with Becher's Brook and the Canal Turn and the Chair. Instead, Marion heard that her little horse ran fifth in a three-mile chase at Cheltenham, carrying the high weight but not distinguishing himself. She could only hope that this effort would knock the rust off. He would improve.

That same week, Marion threw her slowly reviving energy into launching a heartfelt tribute: the Montpelier Hunt Races would feature the first annual Noel Laing Memorial Steeplechase. The Warrenton Hunt had wanted to hold this event at their spring race meet, but Marion had spoken up. Her assertiveness could have seemed selfish. And yet the result was a model of generosity. Instead of donating a trophy all by herself, Marion invited all friends of Noel to contribute. However much or little they gave, each one was acknowledged. Together, they created what the *New York Times* called "one of the finest testimonials ever given to an amateur rider in this country," a trophy provided by friends of Noel, everyone from millionaires to stable boys. A trophy donated by nearly three thousand people.

Four thousand showed up at Montpelier for the race, including Noel's parents. Will duPont joined his sister, as usual, and supporting his wife on this great occasion, Randolph Scott flew in from California. Among Noel's racing friends, only Carroll Bassett was conspicuously absent. Brose Clark capped it all with a flourish when his horse Cadeau II easily won Noel's race by half a dozen lengths. So many feelings that Marion might not put into words found expression in this day. Even its place near the end of the year made the tribute to Noel feel even stronger, as if nothing would surpass him anytime soon—as the *New York Times* said, "a fitting close, to the hunts racing season."

And it may have felt like a beginning, after the crowd went home and

Mr. and Mrs. Scott could be alone. Nine days after the Montpelier races, Randy and Marion were together at Aiken, South Carolina, together for nothing but fun. Here, perhaps, they could blend Hollywood and horses. Here at Aiken, they were catching up with Randy's friend Fred Astaire—a longtime racing fan whose father-in-law was a prominent patron of the turf—while Fred vacationed with his wife and children at his in-laws' house, Prickley Pear. Perhaps, at this place, in this company, both Marion and Randy could find everything they needed.

Though Marion might wonder, seeing what happened when Fred Astaire stepped out from his in-laws' house and found himself ambushed by reporters. Fred took it well, smiling through an interview, allowing photographs, until the rest of his party emerged from the house and his wife said, "Come, Freddie, we must get going."

The reporters let him go—then tailed him. "Following close behind the car," one newshound proudly wrote, "it was noted that the handsome man at the wheel was trying to hide his identity. A chase ensued." And, although Marion was not their quarry, that drive from Prickley Pear to the Palmetto Golf Course became perhaps her worst experience of being hunted by newshounds.

The reporters were transported with delight when the handsome, evasive driver turned out to be Randolph Scott. They wanted an interview, but Randy said, "Not now. I drove 315 miles today to play this game of golf with Fred Astaire and we must get going."

Perhaps Randy and Marion had planned only a quick stop at Aiken. Or perhaps they were unsettled by the reporters giving chase. That evening, they drove up to Charlotte. They had not come back to Aiken when the town paper ran a front-page photo of Randy at the golf course and indiscreetly told all of its readers that Mr. and Mrs. Scott "are guests this week of Mr. and Mrs. Huston Rawls on Colleton Avenue."

And somewhere on her way back to Montpelier, news from Upper Lambourn reached Marion. Battleship had gone racing at nearby Newbury on December 2, a miserable day of rain and a bone-chilling wind. A reporter called the three-mile Cranborne Steeplechase "a good race to watch," however, because "none of the 17 starters fell." It was a good race in other ways, too. Battleship held the lead over the final two jumps, but near the finish Antipas drove ahead. Battleship lost by a length and a half, but he had been spotting Antipas thirteen pounds. Furthermore, Bruce Hobbs had learned something about his horse: when Battleship took the lead too soon, he might lose interest and weaken his finishing punch.

Bruce remembered this on December 11 at Hurst Park, beside the River Thames, in the important Lonsdale Steeplechase. Their opponents included Kellsboro' Jack, twelve years old and still looking like a champion. But Kellsboro' Jack was known to like harder ground underfoot. The betting public favored Battleship, who shouldn't mind softer footing and didn't have to give away much weight today.

This time, Bruce kept in touch with the leaders while biding his time. He didn't get ruffled when Battleship made a small mistake jumping a few furlongs from home. No hurry. Approaching the last fence, he finally sent Battleship up beside the leader, Belted Hero. The two horses leaped as a team, and Belted Hero gave the better-looking jump, but when they landed, Battleship flashed his speed. At the finish, Belted Hero could not get his head past Battleship's hip.

The result left racing experts torn between what they had seen and what they believed. The Lonsdale Chase was supposed to be a significant Grand National prep. But Battleship, the little American stallion, had won it. Noting that Battleship had started racing in England the previous year, the *Times* of London admitted that "he looks a better horse now than he did then." At the same time, the *Times* appeared to think that the horse should not be overrated, saying, "He owed not a little of his success on Saturday to the riding of B. Hobbs, who took him the shortest way round and must have saved many lengths. When Battleship made the one mistake that I noticed Hobbs gave him plenty of time to recover and he certainly sat down and rode him strongly from the last fence to the winning-post." In other words, although Battleship is a good horse, don't count on him for bigger challenges down the road.

Battleship's owner may have been wrestling with similar thoughts, though not about her horse. The week before Christmas, Randolph Scott was back in Aiken with Fred Astaire at Prickley Pear while Marion stayed at Montpelier, telling her brother, "hope to see you next week." On Christmas Eve, Walter Winchell would report that "those legends are around again—about Marion Dupont Somerville going to Reno—to give Randolph Scott his complete freedom." That was an interesting way to put it: presenting Randy's freedom as the issue that they needed to re-solve. And Marion certainly wasn't talking to reporters, so the notion must have been coming from Hollywood. The notion that Marion du-Pont was cramping Randolph Scott's style.

It was easy to write such things when you didn't know someone, didn't have to look her in the eye. Didn't have to inhabit her side of the question. Only had to sell "news." If Walter Winchell had known Marion, he would have seen toughness but also, right now, a lot of vulnerability. Surviving the pneumonia, she had pushed herself to be ready for the Montpelier races only a couple of months later. While her lungs healed, she couldn't do too much, too soon. At first, not walking very far with-out needing to sit down. Like Battleship with his injuries, rebuilding her strength gradually.

And at the same time, she carried recent emotional wounds: a long-distance marriage that flared up with unwanted intrusions when she and Randy did go out together. The emptiness where Noel Laing should have been, still painful after a year. The ruin of Carroll and Jane, who had be-come mainstays of Marion's life, only to fly apart.

If she couldn't keep the Bassetts together, maybe Marion at least could help Carroll recover. Maybe time and space would do him good. Accom-panied by his friend Ed Conklin, who became Marion's private airplane pilot, Carroll set out on a trip around the world.

With all of this on her mind as 1937 drew to a close, perhaps it was a good thing that Marion couldn't read Reg Hobbs's mind. On December 18, only seven days after his stellar Lonsdale Handicap win, Battleship ran tenth in the Sandown Handicap Chase. And although Reg didn't want Battleship to lose races, this resounding defeat provided some welcome ammunition. On the one hand, Reg liked Battleship and didn't want Marion to move him to another trainer. At the same time, he'd be damned if he would run that little stallion at Aintree. With Christmas a week away, Reg had decided—though he had not told Marion—that Battleship should not try Aintree come springtime. Or ever.

This would be no hardship for Bruce, Reg thought. Actually, quite the opposite. Flying Minutes, if he stayed sound, would give his boy a win-ning chance in the Grand National. And if Flying Minutes wasn't fit, Bruce was riding so well that he was sure to get other good offers. Reg's

private judgment looked solid when Battleship ran fifth at nearby Newbury on New Year's Eve. The 1937 National winner, Royal Mail, came in
third.

Bruce, meanwhile, was not worried about Aintree. The real challenge
for Bruce Hobbs, as 1938 began, was to keep rolling with the punches.
Not only the usual literal ups and downs of jump racing but also the
changes at home. Every so often he would pass through Leicestershire and
see his mother, but Bruce would come home from school, from the races,
from any outside activity, to a house without her. And while Bruce fortunately liked the family that his father had drawn closely into their lives
when he took up with Nellie Pratt, Nellie actually coming to live with
Reg and Bruce at Ronehurst was a jolt that Bruce didn't talk about. In a
way, the boy had circled back to that runaway ride with No Reckoning,
near the beginning of the whole affair—the ride where, Bruce said, "I just
sat and suffered."

Reg may have been sparing his son when he and Nellie got married
while Bruce was riding at a racing meet a hundred miles away. They
didn't put on a show, just a simple procedure at the Register Office in
Newbury on January 24, with Nellie's father serving as one of their witnesses. A new start for Reg, at age forty-one; a new phase for Nellie, a
first-time bride at age thirty-two, and more like a young aunt than a mum
to Reg's seventeen-year-old son.

In the face of such change, upholding their old patterns may have mattered more than ever to Reg and Bruce. Reaffirming, every time the father boosted his son into the saddle. Reconnecting, every time Reg
showed, by his purposeful criticisms and hard-earned praise, how much
he cared.

By the end of January 1938, Marion duPont Scott finally seemed free from
the lingering weakness of pneumonia. The illness had carved away any
traces of softness from her features. Parts of her face seemed to belong to
a handsome man: the naturally straight and solid eyebrows, not plucked
thin in beauty parlor style; the strong nose; the broad chin. At the same
time, there was a feminine gleam in her half-moon eyes and a sweet curve
to her mouth reminiscent of a young English actress who was going to

charm the world playing Southern belle Scarlett O'Hara in *Gone with the Wind*. This was the face that Marion carried forward into a life that she was fortunate to still have. Down in Camden, plainspoken relief poured out to her in a letter from her brother: "I am so glad to hear that you are feeling much better and that everything on your place looks well."

Marion would endure. And she had become a leader, not only on paper when hunt-racing wins were tallied every year, not only at Montpelier where she built upon traditions started with her father and her brother, but also now in Camden where she established herself. This year, she was going to hold the annual Camden Horse Show on her property. She accepted that burden at a time when she could have claimed weakness, a time when she certainly felt stabs of loneliness. This winter in Camden, two of her talented, popular friends would not be joining her for mornings on horseback and other amusements. Jane Bassett had flown nonstop farther south, not even pausing to foxhunt with Virginia friends. As the Middleburg newspaper put it, "Mrs. Jane Fowler Bassett, all excited about her health, was advised to go quickly to Florida's sunny clime and bask awhile." And, for the first time in decades, Carroll Bassett did not show his face at Goody Castle or at any of Camden's equine events. Jane would return in March, to ride in the Camden Horse Show. Carroll would come back someday but not this winter, not while the disgrace of his divorce was fresh.

Perhaps it was just as well that Battleship was looking like a better horse this year, that this winter Marion could look forward to adventuring across the sea. During January and February, the little stallion showed mild improvement—tenth, sixth, fifth—while carrying hefty weights and facing top competition. However, he also finished behind previous National winners Kellsboro' Jack, Golden Miller, and Royal Mail, as well as a new contender, Delachance. Honoring Marion's wishes, Reg Hobbs kept Battleship eligible for Aintree. He wouldn't tell her, not yet, that he had no intention of racing Battleship there. But he did tell her that Bruce was going to ride Flying Minutes in the Grand National again.

Marion honored Bruce's old commitment to her friend Mrs. Clark's horse. But in early March, something that Reg Hobbs had feared came true: Flying Minutes went lame. And Marion seized her chance to get the jockey she wanted for Battleship.

Her choice had received a Rover Ten Coupé sports car—known as "the Rolls-Royce of Light Cars"—for his seventeenth birthday and already had managed to wreck it. That one wild mistake made careful, patient, obedient Bruce Hobbs seem like a teenager, after all. Bruce remained, in his own words, "chased but chaste" when it came to girls and impeccably disciplined in his work. The racing stewards never had reason to reprimand him. What a strange thing for Bruce Hobbs, of all people, to turn up in court for causing a traffic accident. He had been hurrying home to Lambourn for tennis at the Pratts' house with his Jack Russell terrier, Budge, riding shotgun. "At the Challow crossroads," said Bruce, "I was apparently on the wrong side of the road, hit someone a right wallop and woke up lying on the verge with my dog sitting on top of me."

Bruce had been lucky. No broken limbs, unlike passengers in the car he hit. A father who was able to pay a big fine and get him off the hook. A father who hated any careless mistake but ultimately wanted his son to keep riding.

And Marion duPont Scott was counting on that boy, the jockey who best understood her horse—a good-natured boy, popular with the older jockeys even though he was earning more and more victories at their expense. Young Bruce Hobbs, in fact, hovered near the top of the winning list. Even with Flying Minutes out of the National, he was sure to pick up a mount with a winning chance. Offers included the bookies' second choice, Delachance, and the good French horse Takvor Pacha. But from a great distance, sight unseen, Marion made up her mind. Battleship ran well for Bruce. For the National, it *had* to be Bruce. She placed a transatlantic phone call.

"Oh, Mr. Hobbs," Reg heard through the line, "Bruce must ride Battleship." Reg hesitated, explaining that Bruce was "a free-lance jockey" with "the chance to ride four or five big horses."

"Oh, he must ride Battleship," Marion persisted. "Is it a question of business?"

Reg, the horse dealer's son, slipped into sales mode: "Now you're talking."

Marion cut to the bottom line: "You tell Bruce I'll give him twice as much as anyone else to ride my horse."

Reg gave in. And although he didn't think Battleship was a likely winner, Bruce felt satisfied. His father's strong concern for earnings had rubbed off on him, and Mrs. Scott's offer exploded the boundaries that Bruce knew. An ordinary steeplechase ride paid £3. The owners of Dela-chance, Takvor Pacha, and others would pay him £100 for a National ride. Twice that was a fortune.

And despite all the talk that Battleship did not look like an Aintree horse, the handicapper respected his class. The little stallion would be carrying 160 pounds. Only five Grand National nominees had been given more. All of Bruce's other prospects had been assigned at least eleven pounds less.

Furthermore, Bruce liked Battleship. Although Bruce now stood six foot one and the two of them looked stranger than ever together, Battle-ship was a friend. Enjoyed for his good qualities, forgiven his faults, trusted at the end of the day. Why not go around Aintree with him?

But first came Cheltenham, where Reg wanted Battleship to win the National Hunt Handicap Chase. He had the horse physically fit enough. But the little stallion had started to get "cunning," as Reg called it, exert-ing himself only when he thought it really mattered. Battleship always had been lazy about morning exercise; now he was slacking off in his races, too. Reg saw a smart, middle-aged horse deciding to conserve him-self. And so it would be back to the beginning for Battleship. He had started his racing career wearing blinkers, as a green young horse who did not understand enough. Now he would wear them again, as a wise older horse who understood too much.

Age. That was one more reason for thinking that Battleship was not a good Aintree hope. The stallion was now eleven years old. One racing correspondent tallied up the past seventy years of Grand National results and discovered that sixty-four of those seventy winners had ranged from five to ten years old. During those seventy years, only four eleven-year-olds had won. Not a very bright ray of hope, though Battleship had not reached the far edge of possibility. Two horses, Why Not and Sergeant Murphy, had won the National at age thirteen.

Seventeen days before the National, Bruce Hobbs and Battleship were go-ing to make their case. Battleship would have another chance to win the

National Hunt Handicap Chase at Cheltenham, where he had jumped precariously last year and convinced Reg that he couldn't handle Aintree. But today, surprisingly warm weather and firmer footing should suit Battleship, maybe rekindle the brilliance he had shown often in America and occasionally in the U.K.

First, however, Bruce partnered a horse who didn't seem to need to prove anything. Last year, the handsome gray Free Fare had won the prestigious Champion Hurdle Challenge Cup here at Cheltenham. Recently, with Bruce up, he had won a lesser race by fifteen lengths. Today, a reporter watching him warm up swore that Free Fare "has never looked better."

And Free Fare lived up to his looks. He was leading everyone with only two hurdles to go, with Bruce feeling plenty in reserve. Then a sudden awkward moment—starting gracefully as Free Fare "stood off" for a mighty jump—unraveling as the horse realized he had stood off too far. Free Fare "reached for his hurdle," Bruce would recall, "and just got his foreleg caught in the top bar, turning him over and breaking my nose."

The gray horse arose, unhurt. Bruce was not going to ride again today—doctor's orders—but Battleship was running in the very next race! Reg had only a few minutes to rustle up a substitute.

He hired a good one, Irish jockey Tommy McNeill. McNeill had to be bold and agile to handle the eccentric Airgead Sios—Gaelic for "ready money"—an Aintree favorite this year. But Airgead Sios was a very different character from Battleship: a horse who liked tearing away on the lead, a jumper who, as one reporter observed, "never takes off twice in the same way and . . . never looks like coming properly down." Somehow, Mc'Neill would stay on. Somehow, Airgead Sios would stay up and gallop on.

McNeill also could handle horses who lay off the pace. He didn't ride Battleship badly. But he didn't have him up beside the leader taking the final fence. Fred Rimell riding Teme Willow, last year's winner of this race, literally got the jump on McNeill and Battleship. Teme Willow cleared the final fence in first place, Red Knight and Battleship in pursuit, Battleship going faster than anyone else but running out of ground. Teme Willow beat Red Knight by three-quarters of a length; Battleship's hooded face didn't make it past Red Knight's ears.

Third place. But well behind Battleship was the well-regarded

Delachance, another horse whose Aintree hopes had seemed high. More important, Battleship had carried 169 pounds. Teme Willow toted only 159, and Red Knight only 143. A lot of weight to give away, but even so, Reg believed that with Bruce aboard, knowing exactly how to handle him, Battleship would have won. In his training diary he would write, "Very unlucky."

One of Reg's pals, Scottish bookmaker Johnny Maguire, thought so, too. "Bruce would have won with him," Maguire told Reg. "I think you can win the National. In fact, I'm going to back him." Reg told Maguire, "[You] should have more sense." Three miles over a park course did not resemble four and a half miles at Aintree. Only sentimental American bets would push Battleship's odds below fifty to one.

Instead of feeling encouraged by Battleship's strong performance, Reg now tried to distract Marion duPont Scott from actually running the little stallion in the Grand National. His chance came from a distinguished amateur who should have had more sense.

Hugh Lloyd Thomas, forty-nine years old, a British diplomat and former successful amateur jockey, owned a real Aintree horse: Royal Mail. Last year, Royal Mail had won the Grand National decisively. This year, he had been assigned top weight for the race and was favored over Airgead Sios in the early betting. But then Thomas activated his plan: this year, he was going to ride Royal Mail in the National himself.

He wouldn't be the first person to ride his own horse in the world's greatest 'chase, nor would he be the oldest jockey that the National had known. But no one as old as Hugh Lloyd Thomas ever had won, and no jockey had tried not only to come back to race riding after being away for three years, but also to be ready for Aintree within six weeks.

Thomas did know something about Aintree. He had ridden one of his horses to victory there in the 1932 Grand Sefton Chase, which covered one lap of the National course. A British journalist describing the situation to American horsemen called Lloyd Thomas "a first class horseman, with the admirable hunting seat that is an essential at Liverpool." At the same time, he wrote, "If the owner of Royal Mail can overcome the handicaps of his [nearly] 50 years and his lack of recent practice and win the world's greatest steeplechase next March, I shall not merely raise my hat to him—I shall go bareheaded for a twelvemonth."

In early February, the British hunt-racing world witnessed Mr. Thomas's return. His horse, Periwinkle II, fell with a mile to go. The next day, Mr. Thomas finished fourth in a two-mile 'chase with Royal Mail.

He raced Periwinkle again on February 22, and that was the end of Thomas's dream. Periwinkle fell upon landing at the final fence. Hugh Lloyd Thomas slammed into the ground headfirst and quickly died of a broken neck.

Dreaming of Aintree, he had taken leave from his regular job. Friends thought he had taken leave of his senses. Riding Royal Mail in the Grand National, was he trying to surpass his youthful glories and thought he had found the nearest thing to a sure thing? They had tried to tell him what a horseman should have known all along: there was no such thing.

There was now, however, an opportunity for Reg Hobbs. Royal Mail would be sold at auction in mid-March. Getting Royal Mail into his own stable would be like giving Bruce a Rolls-Royce Phantom III limousine instead of a Rover Ten Coupé. Royal Mail's weight assignment, 175 pounds, might be excessive; only four National winners had carried that much. On the other hand, maybe this grand-looking big horse was that good. The day after Bruce broke his nose, Reg sent a telegram to Marion:

BATTLESHIP FINISHED THIRD BIG CHASE YESTERDAY CHELTENHAM. RAN FINE RACE GAVE LOTS OF WEIGHT TO ALL RUNNERS BEATEN LESS THAN LENGTH FROM WINNER. HAS CHANCE IN NATIONAL IF HE JUMPS THE COURSE. ROYAL MAIL BEING SOLD PUBLIC AUCTION SATURDAY WITH GRAND NATIONAL ENGAGEMENT. HORSE FAVOURITE FOR RACE AT PRESENT. PLEASE CABLE AT ONCE IF YOU WOULD LIKE ME TO BID FOR YOU OR ANY OF YOUR FRIENDS. HOBBS.

Marion did not bid. She had not come this far with Battleship to change horses now.

But after reading Reg's cable, Marion did phone him "to make sure everything was going all right." *Has chance in National if he jumps the course.* What exactly did Reg mean? That Battleship had the class to keep up with the top contenders if he didn't fall? Was Reg hinting that Battleship *would* fall? Had something gone wrong?

Here was a challenge for Reg's relationship with Marion and his relationship with the truth. No matter what, he didn't want to lose such a good client or such a useful horse. But Aintree . . . how could he keep Battleship while getting out of that? What could he say that this smart, practical horsewoman wouldn't see through?

Reg did sincerely believe in Battleship's ability to race a long distance in top company. He had told Bruce that he thought the little horse could have won England's foremost flat race, the two-and-a-half-mile Ascot Gold Cup, if he had been in their stable as a four-year-old. And Reg had to admit to himself, and tell Marion, that Battleship was perfectly fit and healthy. Bringing her horse to this point, Reg had nearly completed the mission for which Marion had hired him. Privately, he still considered the chance of Battleship successfully jumping the Aintree course a tremendous *if*. But he could give her no undeniable reason to quit.

Reg swallowed his misgivings, and Marion took him at his word. Officially committed, barely more than two weeks from the race, she needed a boat from New York to Southampton, a London hotel, a ride to Liverpool, and seats at Aintree. Those things she could hurry into place . . . while maybe feeling a distant shiver for Great Britain, a target not that many miles from the uproar spreading out of Germany.

20

GOVERNING A NATION HAD A LOT in common with horseback riding. To get anywhere, rider and horse had to agree to go in the same direction. Much of the time, the horse might not care that much where the rider told him to go, as long as it wasn't too uncomfortable for too long. And many horses could be desensitized to things that at first seemed very strange when the leader, the rider, said with every ounce of his behavior that it all would work out.

Of course some horses were just plain spooky. Easily alarmed. Troubling the rider, disturbing the herd.

A strong leader could anticipate some such problems. Think of ways to minimize the spooking. Make the journey from one thing to another seem sensible, inevitable, part of the natural landscape. Once a horse trusted his rider, he would accept all sorts of things if the rider said so. He still might question or resist something that set off his alarms, but often the rider could reassure him, or rebuke him, and he would cooperate.

On March 11, negotiations between leader and follower—what felt safe, what felt unsafe—landed in Marion duPont Scott's backyard and also rippled toward England, toward the land that held the world's greatest steeplechase, toward the honor that Marion dreamed of making her own. The possibilities traveled simultaneously with Jane Fowler Bassett riding a chestnut mare into a show ring at Marion's Camden property, and with Hitler's followers taking control of Austria.

Jane was competing in a class for ladies' hunters, horses who were supposed to be especially well behaved. But the mare that Jane was showing for someone else distrusted the obstacle Jane wanted her to jump. The mare slammed on the brakes. Jane became a missile, flung over the fence, crunching to the ground. Her hope for victory dissolved into a hospital visit, X-rays, and recovery outside the public eye.

Storm troopers on the march should have seemed more threatening than a slender young woman insisting on taking a jump. And yet much of Austria behaved very differently from Jane's horse. In another time zone, the American journalist William L. Shirer tried to witness all the changes happening that afternoon and literally overnight: crowds in the streets of Vienna singing Nazi anthems, city police uniforms sprouting swastika armbands. "Young toughs were heaving paving blocks into the windows of the Jewish shops," Shirer recorded in his journal. "The crowd roared with delight." But it didn't seem completely real, somehow, until the reporter pushed his way to the Congress of Vienna building. "Twenty storm troopers are standing on one another before the building, forming a human pyramid," Shirer wrote. "A little fellow scampers to the top of the heap, clutching a huge Swastika flag." The American reporter found himself outnumbered and overwhelmed, while the little soldier fastened the flag along the balcony rail, then let it unroll.

In Camden, spectators had been horrified when Jane Bassett took a bad fall. In Vienna, they cheered the spectacle of an entire nation falling down.

The American reporter tried to send his daily radio broadcast, as usual, to New York City. Nazi soldiers would not allow it. For someone who would not sing the Nazi songs, would not wear the emblem or salute the swastika flag, it was time to leave. If possible. Already, the Gestapo had control of the airport. In the morning, Shirer was lucky to catch a flight to Berlin, then continue to Amsterdam. He wrote, while flying from Amsterdam to London:

Vienna was scarcely recognizable this morning. Swastika flags flying from nearly every house. . . . I bought the morning Berlin newspapers. Amazing! Goebbels at his best, or worst! Hitler's own newspaper, the

Völkische Beobachter, on my lap here. Its screaming banner-line across page one: GERMAN-AUSTRIA SAVED FROM CHAOS. And an incredible story out of Goebbels's evil but fertile brain describing violent Red disorders in the main streets of Vienna yesterday, fighting, shooting, pillaging. It is a complete *lie.* But how will the German people know it's a lie?

And would the American people care? They were full of their own pains—their own stubbornly high unemployment rate, their own fears, their own arguments about individual rights versus socialism—and the Atlantic Ocean seemed to separate them so neatly from the rest of the world. They might not *like* the Nazis, but it was so easy not to care. So easy to keep doing whatever was convenient. And Austria going over to Hitler wasn't such a stretch, was it? Two German-speaking nations unifying. Maybe they would form a peaceable future together.

And so when Marion duPont Scott needed a fast boat from New York to England, first class, in time for the Grand National, she didn't hesitate to book the German ocean liner *Europa*—recently advertised as "the Choice of 149,322 Trans-Atlantic Travelers in 1937." The chic and speedy *Europa,* which had been flying a Nazi flag for nearly five years, ever since Hitler had come into power.

While Marion made a convenient choice, the atmosphere at her destination started shifting. The British parliament could no longer ignore the ambitions emanating from Berlin, fewer than six hundred miles by airplane from London. Even the cautious prime minister, Neville Chamberlain, who had thought that he could bargain for peace, now strongly hinted that Britain should begin preparing for war. Member of parliament Winston Churchill put the question more bluntly: "Why should we assume that time is on our side?"

While Britons debated how to handle their national defense, Marion duPont Scott made homier plans. Her brother's wife wanted to buy a dog, an English beagle. When Marion visited England for the Grand National, could she have a look at a particular dog that Will's wife had in mind? Of course she could.

. . .

According to many Grand National experts, Marion Scott sending Battleship to Aintree was like taking a knife to a gunfight. She had a good
weapon, but was it the right one? British racing fans gave her little horse a
nickname based on limitations. They called him "Pocket Battleship."

The nickname was complimentary and confining at the same time.
The pocket battleship was Germany's answer to the Treaty of Versailles,
the World War I settlement slashing the size of German warships. The
new German vessels were small. They weren't supposed to have enough
power to threaten full-size battleships. And yet they were so cleverly engineered that, as the *New York Times* noted in 1937, experts "hailed [them] as
more than a match for any warship afloat outside the true battleship class."

Pocket Battleship. The racing fans liked him. And even his critics
thought that he was good, perhaps very good. They simply thought that in
the toughest fight, he wouldn't measure up. Seeing how Aintree champions such as Royal Mail and Kellsboro' Jack towered over Battleship, some
commentators called him "the American pony." When discussing Aintree,
British turf experts usually left him out of the conversation. One who did
mention him simply noted that, among the higher-weighted entries, the
mare Pontet and Battleship "do not fill the eye as National winners."

Reg Hobbs heartily agreed. And yet he honored his contract with
Marion, continuing to make Battleship as fit as possible. On the morning
of Thursday, March 17, eight days before the race, Reg sent Battleship for
a mile-and-a-half gallop with a workmate and thought that he did "wonderfully well." Marion, meanwhile, had left Camden and arrived in New
York. She was meeting her two companions for her transatlantic voyage,
recently back from their round-the-world trip: her private airplane pilot,
Ed Conklin, and her friend Carroll Bassett.

It had to be Carroll, still handsome in his slightly fractured way. Carroll, who had urged her that Battleship was the one. Carroll, finally living
up to the emblem on his father's coat of arms, functioning like the rafter
of a house, supporting a great endeavor.

And it felt momentous, boarding the ship that would carry them to
England, toward their supreme adventure, boarding on a Friday night
with *Europa* lit up like a nightclub, preparing for her customary midnight
departure. The passengers might feel a bit like youngsters having a slum-
ber party, liberated from their normal bedtime. But there was even more

this time. Tonight, Marion and her companions joined a celebration in progress—their ship saluting Austrian and German unity. *Europa* flying her pennants, along with her Nazi flag; her crew wearing their best uniforms. And there might be a feeling of intrigue among the passengers, while settling in and noticing the crew. Last month, a young German woman working aboard *Europa* as a hairdresser had been arrested by the FBI and had confessed to being a spy, carrying secrets stolen from the U.S. military. Perhaps no one in Marion's group gave this a thought. But anyone making this voyage might look at the crew and wonder.

In any case, Marion was happy to discover her friends Walter and Sarah Jeffords among the first-class passengers. She knew them as fellow steeplechasing enthusiasts. The racing world at large knew them best for their close connection with Man o' War. Mr. and Mrs. Jeffords owned many Man o' War offspring and were England-bound for that reason: eager to see Battleship represent his sire at Aintree.

Meanwhile, more than four million people on several continents anticipated the Grand National for a far different reason: they had bought tickets to enter the Irish Hospitals Sweepstakes, a charitable fund-raising lottery that tied its payouts to the National results. Throughout Saturday and Sunday, while Marion began her transatlantic voyage, giant rotating barrels set up inside the lord mayor of Dublin's mansion shuffled and reshuffled millions of paper slips. On Monday morning, March 21, the sweepstakes drawing took place. Attractive nurses in uniform pulled hundreds of random slips from the huge drums, matching several batches of ticket holders with the name of each horse entered in the Grand National. Those matched with Battleship had no idea how close they came to having no horse in the race.

With the National only three days away, Reg sent Battleship out for a strong gallop—his final tune-up before traveling to Aintree. Knowing that Battleship would loaf unless he had another horse to beat, Reg gave him a workout partner and expected a good show. But instead, Battleship "was listless," Reg said. "He wouldn't take the bit and go." Reg didn't see any physical problem. Like a confident poker player, he decided to call Battleship's bluff.

A little later that morning, Battleship went back out to the gallops with a fresh workmate beside him and a blinker hood on his head. Reg had chosen "open cups" that offered a fairly wide range of vision, but his message was clear: win this race. This time, Battleship came alive. Not only challenging his fresh workmate but, Reg said, "he nearly ran away from that horse."

With Battleship beautifully fit, Reg finalized his arrangements for Aintree. He had even had special reins put on Battleship's racing bridle, reins eighteen inches longer than usual, so that Bruce wouldn't be pulled out of the saddle if—or *when*—Battleship tipped his hips up over those drop fences and came down on his nose. Reg made everything as ready as he knew how. The next day, Wednesday, they would travel to Aintree. But there is a saying that racehorses are like strawberries: they can spoil overnight.

Wednesday morning, Reg's head lad brought an unwelcome message from the stable: Battleship was "set fast." Those words would make any racehorse trainer groan. In America, they called it "tying up" because the horse's stiff back and hindquarter muscles looked as if they were tightly tied in place. The symptoms could be so mild that they were hard to diagnose or so severe that they could cause kidney damage, even death.

Set fast. Reg would fight past a sick feeling and probably ask, *How bad is he?* Hear the response while going to see for himself. Tying up could happen to a dehydrated horse; it could happen from a protein overload, such as eating too many oats. Or it could come from lactic acid cramping the muscles after hard exercise. Battleship had galloped twice on Tuesday, and although his first gallop wasn't rigorous, maybe the excitement of that second gallop, where he wanted to run off at true racing speed, had thrown his electrolytes out of balance.

Stepping into Battleship's stall, Reg saw that "his kidneys were tied up, across his back." Definite symptoms, but not the worst. Maybe they still could make Aintree. Keep Battleship standing up, massage his tight muscles, then blanket him to keep those muscles warm, and keep offering him sips of water. Sometimes dissolving a box of baking soda in water and pouring it down the horse's throat helped, because baking soda could neutralize acid.

They gave him as much time as they could spare before setting out to Aintree. Finally, that afternoon, they needed either to lead him into the motor van or leave him at home. Battleship emerged from his stall walking, as Reg put it, "like a man of ninety." Maybe that description was unfair to many a ninety-year-old man, but it captured the difference between Battleship the athlete with a big, easy stride and unwell Battleship taking short, halting steps, making painfully slow progress. Climbing the short, sloping ramp into the traveling horse box became a struggle, the kind of situation where strong men might link arms behind the horse's rump and practically push him up. But they could not do this unless the horse agreed to enter a space that often meant heading out to the races.

Battleship did it. He was giving them a chance. Reg, his mind racing through all that he knew about horses, grabbed an idea that might strengthen their chance. Hating to use strong medicine only two days before a race but feeling that he had no choice, he chose a large purgative pill made by Cupiss, a leader in equine medicines. He pushed the pill back past Battleship's tongue, held the horse's muzzle up high, waited for him to swallow, then let go.

Reg the gambler was taking a shot. The pill would make Battleship relieve himself over and over again. Maybe this would correct the unhealthy imbalance in the little horse's system and give Battleship a chance to heal himself.

The horse van rolled on its way, taking Battleship and War Vessel to Aintree at last. Then Reg and Bruce, with their stable clothing and Bruce's racing gear, their proper race-day suits and their formal wear for celebration parties, set out for their second National together.

It would be almost like turning back time, to the days when it was Reg and Bruce against the world. To the days when Margery Hobbs could not make herself watch her son risking his neck but would be waiting at home. Here was Reg's new wife seeing them off, wishing them success with all her heart, then Reg and Bruce together for the ride, no one else inside the space that held their questions and their dreams.

As always, Reg tried to be ready for anything, even though there was no way to know, as they drove north, whether they should have any hope. So much depended upon how Battleship came off that van.

Several hours later, here came the horse box rolling up at the Aintree stable yards. The van stopping, the lads hopping out. The ramp falling. The horse walking out.

And he was the horse that Reg and Bruce knew. A little horse whose hind legs swung well under him as he moved. A high-headed horse taking in his new surroundings, a small horse with a big attitude. If he wasn't one hundred percent quite yet, he was within reach.

It looked as if Reg had won his gamble. He and Bruce could check into their hotel knowing that Battleship might well make the race less than two days away. But was that a good thing? Reg, who understood so much about horses and what abilities lay within them, still didn't know.

They were safe in the heart of Liverpool that Wednesday night. Bruce had gone up to bed already, locked away within the limestone and marble walls of the elegant Adelphi Hotel. Downstairs, Reg mingled with friends and cohorts in a lounge designed for the kind of patrons who would have sailed first class on the *Titanic* twenty-six years ago.

They were a cheerful crowd, these horsemen and bookmakers from all over England, Scotland, Wales, Ireland, and beyond, gearing up for the world's richest steeplechase. A spirited group, in fact, even during ordinary race days when the jockeys joked about being paid "one pound a mile" to ride a three-mile 'chase. Although he couldn't share their drinking sessions at the bar, Bruce Hobbs treasured the lightheartedness that his fellow riders brought into his life. "They used to say that if you looked into a race-train you could tell the difference between the jump-jockeys' compartment and the flat-race jockeys'," Bruce would look back and laugh. "The jumping lads would be playing cards, gambling with each other, enjoying themselves, whereas their flat counterparts would be just counting their cash!"

This week, the Grand National fraternity would be counting their cash—much higher fees and purses than usual. Being among them should have lifted Reg's spirits. He settled in at the bar with a group including his close friend Jack Anthony, a former jockey who knew Aintree extremely well. Jack had ridden the Grand National twelve times. Three times, he had won.

Sitting there with a healthy middle-aged man who had survived a dozen National rides should have been reassuring. But Reg ached with doubt. In his Aintree adventures, Jack Anthony hadn't been riding a little stallion who lifted his hips and landed on his nose. Drinking with Jack and other friends, surrounded by the merry crowd, Reg kept picturing Battleship falling end over end. Reg sat there "worried," he said, "about my boy getting killed."

The possibility that Reg had kept pushing away when Bruce was much younger, smaller, weaker would not leave him now. All the horseback dangers that Reg had made Bruce face growing up were the types of things that Reg had survived as a child. Reg *knew* that Bruce, like himself, could make it. But he never had imagined Bruce attempting Aintree with a horse like this, a horse who should *not* be there.

A voice broke into his thoughts. A well-known voice, belonging to someone Reg liked but heavy with sarcasm tonight. Percy Thompson, a bookmaker from London, had seen a likely target.

"Reg, do you fancy that skin you have on Friday?" Thompson was insulting Battleship, goading Reg for daring to bring him to Aintree. "Skin" meant the horse was nothing, an empty threat, like calling a person an empty suit.

And for all his doubts, Reg knew that Battleship was more than that. He didn't want anyone ridiculing the horse or his own predicament. "I shan't tell you what my reply was," Reg later told an interviewer, "except to say it was short and to the point." Perhaps Reg needed only seven letters.

Unruffled, Thompson made his real point: "I'll lay you a good price on Battleship."

"Don't be daft," Reg snorted, picturing his little horse meeting the tallest obstacle on the course. "He won't even be able to see over the Chair!"

Thompson's reply made Reg think again: "You can have a hundred to one."

What if . . . *what if* . . . Every so often Reg had been remembering his bookmaker friend Johnny Maguire at Cheltenham, after Bruce broke his nose and Battleship finished an unlucky third with a last-minute rider, Johnny Maguire saying, *Bruce would have won with him. I think you can win the National. In fact, I'm going to back him.*

Reg juggled the odds and couldn't resist. All right, then, he would lay 100 shillings on Battleship, 50 to win, 50 to place—"In case," Reg announced, "I have to buy the champagne!"

Everyone could have a laugh at that. Percy Thompson took the rough equivalent of $25, reckoning he had scored a nice little profit. Reg supported his horse but did not change his mind.

That same night, Marion duPont Scott, Ed Conklin, and Carroll Bassett should have been checking into London's Berkeley hotel. Perhaps Marion had pictured some small celebration there—a telegram waiting, a transatlantic phone call—marking her second wedding anniversary with Randolph Scott. Instead, any communications would be ship to shore. The *Europa* had been stalled by rough weather. So much for "Swift dependable crossings" and "punctual arrivals." Marion might contact Randy from her awkward distance, eight hours farther along in her day than his in Hollywood. She could fret away the evening with Carroll and other friends, feeling that they *had* to make Aintree, uncertain when or if their ship would be able to dock.

Marion had thought she could be at Aintree that Thursday afternoon, watching War Vessel race in the Stanley Steeplechase. Instead, she and the other *Europa* passengers were climbing into small boats and being lowered onto the waves, the turbulent waves that were keeping ocean liners from safely docking at Southampton today. Instead of gliding into port, they fought their way to shore.

About two hundred miles north, Reg Hobbs donned an immaculate suit and saddled War Vessel as planned. Ordinarily, Bruce would have had the mount, but Reg did not let him ride any races today. Reg had learned the hard way—his own broken leg only a few days before he would have ridden the Grand National in 1933. Reg understood what the late Hugh Lloyd Thomas, dreaming of triumph riding Royal Mail, had tried to brush away: that bad accidents, as well as good, could happen anytime to anyone.

As it turned out, Bruce didn't miss a great deal. War Vessel looked promising about halfway through the race, but he faded and finished far back.

Tomorrow, they would know about Battleship.

That night, with Bruce abed in his hotel room, Reg put on an evening suit and went celebrating with the Stanley Steeplechase winners and friends. Around midnight, the jolly group decided that walking the Grand National course in the moonlight would be a lovely idea. Out on the turf, they gave in to a temptation that had beckoned many a partygoer: the water jump. With champagne and other libations urging them on, it didn't look so bad. A man could jump it! One of them, tonight, who would do it best? They ran toward it in their tuxedo shoes, or if they decided to spare their shoes, the frosty grass crunched under their bare feet. An Olympic broad jumper might have cleared the fifteen-foot span. Reg and his companions splashed down in the middle.

Reg spent the night washing away fear. In a few hours, he would be back at the stable with Battleship, ready to supervise the final exercise before the ultimate test. Come morning, he would meet Mrs. Scott here at Aintree—and persuade her to see things his way.

21

SHE HAD BEEN TRAVELING ALL NIGHT. The little boat into Southampton, the trains to London, then to Aintree. Making progress uncomfortably, so that she could meet with Reg Hobbs early on Grand National morning, Friday, March 25, at Aintree Racecourse. And in the middle of it all she faced a womanly problem: what to wear.

She knew the general guidelines: a tweed suit, to insulate her against the wind and rain that were massaging Aintree today, and practical accessories like the ones that a Liverpool newspaper recently had described. "Do wear sensible shoes," a lady journalist had urged. "It's no good trekking off to look at a jump in a pair of stilts." Of course not. And yet, in honor of the greatest race, Marion wanted to look especially sharp. She chose shoes with Cuban heels, low enough for comfortable walking but set on at a fashionable slant. She topped her outfit with a jaunty "Robin Hood" hat, somewhat triangular with a couple of feathers swooping up from one side. A secure hat, unlikely to blow away. "There is nothing a man hates more," the Liverpool lady had written, "than having to be a kind of porter with the girl-friend's race card, field glasses, shooting stick, and what not, because she has a whole-time job clinging to her headgear." Suited up for whatever would come, Marion picked up her new alligator-skin clutch purse and went forth on her mission.

At the racecourse she found her trainer, dapper in his bowler hat and overcoat, smiling, eager to please his patron. It was about 7:00 A.M., and Reg already had been busy. There had been a hard frost overnight, now dissolving under the rainfall, and Reg figured that the going might be a bit slippery. He didn't want Battleship's hind feet sliding when he pushed off to jump, so Reg had summoned a blacksmith. A couple of small screws underneath each of Battleship's hind shoes would, as Reg said, "help him get more grip."

With his haunches blanketed against the chilly rain, Battleship came out for a short gallop, a brief burst of aerobic exercise that horsemen call a pipe-opener. He seemed bright and well. Someone who didn't know that he had "tied up" only a couple of days ago would not guess that anything had been wrong.

Reg did not seem worried about that, but he was eager to drive home another point. Maybe his message would become clear to Marion as they walked the immense Grand National course. Stepping onto the turf felt almost like stepping toward infinity. A definite path inside uncommonly wide horizons, encompassed by a limitless gray sky.

They hiked to the first fence, four and a half feet tall, the second an inch higher, the third a full five feet high with a six-foot-wide ditch on its takeoff side. Was Marion getting the message? Two more high, sturdy fences, then Becher's Brook, with its serious drop on the landing side, where a horse needed to come down more than five and a half feet past the hedge to be sure of not sliding down into the brook.

Owner and trainer did not say where they stopped and talked in the falling rain. Maybe here at Becher's, maybe the Canal Turn, maybe somewhere out in the country beside the canal. Somewhere within these escalating challenges, Reg could not stifle his feelings any longer. "He was dying," said Marion, "for me to agree to take Battleship out of the race."

Reg would gladly forfeit the extravagant jockey fee that Marion had promised his son, along with his own modest wager. He assured Marion that Battleship would continue doing well on the English park courses this season and next. That, not this, would be their best hope. He waited for her to agree.

Marion, reticent Marion, often paused to collect her thoughts. If a pause made Reg think he had prevailed, it soon was his turn to be taken aback. *Hobbs isn't going to down me again, a second straight year,* Marion thought. "No," she told Reg. "Battleship is going back to Virginia next week."

It would be the National or nothing. Reach for everything, today, or simply stop. Marion saw no purpose in making Battleship repeat well-worn routines, perhaps settling for minor awards as his interest in racing faded and his body inevitably aged. *Here* was his last significant chance. Not the park courses, never again.

Reg looked at the woman who was small but game, like her horse, a woman who actually wouldn't be able to see over the Chair unless she wore very high heels. Expert horse dealer that he was, he saw that this was her final offer. All of his best salesmanship could not change her mind.

He gave in. Reg could not reject such an important client. He would do everything he could imagine to give Battleship and Bruce their best chance—not to win, that seemed too remote, but to avoid catastrophe.

That afternoon, less than an hour before joining Battleship in the Aintree paddock, Bruce received a telegram in the jockeys' weighing room. It came to him from someone who knew how it was to fly over the turf with Battleship and feel what the horse needed, someone who couldn't take his mother's place but had become family. Bruce opened the slip of paper from someone who had helped make Battleship as good as possible for this race, fit for carrying Bruce's life. He read:

```
WISHING YOU THE VERY BEST LUCK TODAY
NELL
```

They were late for the unveiling. Marion did not say why. Maybe there had been a delay with Carroll and Ed. Maybe she had left the course to freshen up after her early walk with Reg and then had trouble getting back in time. Near midafternoon, with the sun out now, Marion and her companions reached the paddock where the thirty-six National starters were being saddled—and they found the gates firmly shut. Even as an owner, she was too late to go inside.

And so they saw the unveiling as members of the public, from outside the fence. Not one of Carroll's sculptures, but a living horse, uncovered now. A horse they thought they knew extremely well, but somehow they had not realized just how he would look in this setting. The scale seemed all wrong.

That winter, from a distance, Marion had known that little Battleship would be carrying a higher weight today than most of his opponents. But seeing him now, walking among these grand, big horses, his challenge became tangible. Uncovered for the race, Battleship appeared thinner than Marion ever had seen him. Surely he weighed less than a thousand pounds! Compared with his opponents, he looked, Marion thought, "like a Shetland pony."

All these years, she had been seeing beyond appearances. She had believed in Battleship's character, but now it struck her: what if she had gotten it wrong? She thought of Reg Hobbs, convinced that Battleship was a "park horse," urging her to agree. She had hired Hobbs in the first place because he was a damn fine trainer. What if he indeed was right?

At least the sun had chased away the rain about an hour ago. And at least Battleship looked more enthusiastic than last year's winner, Royal Mail. But the winner on looks was probably one of the well-fancied Irish horses, seven-year-old Royal Danieli, who had run second in a November race over part of the National course. That experience should help him today. And wasn't he a grand-looking fellow, big and blooming, rather like Kellsboro' Jack.

And now Carroll Bassett, Marion's accomplice, Battleship's cheerleader, did not help. Sizing up the situation, Carroll told Marion that he thought they had "overstepped their enthusiasm."

But Marion had insisted on the ultimate test, and now every gear she had cranked into motion would sweep Battleship into action.

The jockeys streamed out of their changing room, the tallest one striding over to the smallest horse. Bruce Hobbs, carrying Marion's old rose, French blue, and silver silks above the crowd, stopping near his father and absorbing his words. "Go down the middle on the outside, not the inside," said Reg, "and when you start jumping the water, if you're still in, you can start riding the race." He didn't have to explain what "riding the race" meant. As Reg later noted, "Bruce knew Battleship so well, there was nothing else to say."

Bruce knew how competition motivated his horse: *Join the leaders at the last fence—then kick on for home.*

The call came for riders up. Slender, tall Bruce Hobbs, reminding one friend of a telephone pole, stepped forward for the leg up on his so-called pony. Reg Hobbs, caught between loving and dreading this moment, boosted his son into the saddle. Battleship, ears up, head up, peered brightly from his blinker hood, felt the familiar presence settle onto his back, and strode forward with purpose, ready to take a crack at anybody.

To watch her second Grand National, Marion had to become one of the crowd. Her friends Walter and Sarah Jeffords, who were sending some of their horses to one of England's most powerful flat-racing trainers, shared a private box. But Marion had put off making reservations, and Battleship racing in the National itself didn't make up for that. There weren't any seats to give her. Even Reg Hobbs had no box to share with her—there were no seats reserved for National trainers, so Reg had to find his own standing room. And so Marion and Carroll and Ed climbed a narrow staircase to the County Stand roof.

Standing on the concrete bleachers, she took a lesson from her du Pont ancestors who had handled physical challenges alongside their employees. Even with Carroll and Ed on each side, Marion was buffeted by the tightly packed crowd. Her alligator-skin purse, eye-catching but impractical, slipped from her hands and fell among strangers. When at last she got it back, Marion handed the rogue accessory to Ed Conklin. She could not trust herself with it. She had come here knowing that, ultimately, racing luck and chaos would have their way with her horse. She had not reckoned how her own insulation also would be stripped away.

It was all she could do to simply stand here, craning to see the horses, while tall Ed Conklin clamped her purse under one arm and helped support a woman on his other side who was, Marion thought, "trying to faint."

Meanwhile, out on the turf that felt perfectly springy underfoot, Bruce cantered Battleship leftward past the grandstands, then back to the right, toward the start. Beside him, the supersized gelding What Have You made Battleship appear, as one reporter put it, "even smaller than usual and hardly worth considering." And yet he had something in common with another American horse who had paraded here a decade ago. Like Billy Barton, Battleship looked small compared with his rivals; also like

Billy Barton, he had a remarkably long stride. This might not make him faster than the other horses, but he wouldn't burn extra energy simply keeping up.

Cantering past the County Stand, Battleship was like a small clue to a big mystery, hiding in plain sight. As the track announcer's comments floated out over the public address system, Marion heard his proper British voice compliment and dismiss her horse: "Little Battleship, a great favorite with the crowd, has bitten off more than he can chew today." But had he? Battleship carried with him something the public could not see: his time with Noel Laing among the hills of Rappahannock County, where fox and hounds took unpredictable courses, where the ground was uneven but you still sometimes jumped without seeing exactly what was on the other side.

He carried his history to the starting post, where thirty-six horses lined up, and who could tell which ones had everything they would need to get around? The crowd hushed. Then a flag fell and the crowd roared, as thirty-six horses joined a chase that had begun when Queen Victoria was young and Charles Dickens was publishing *Oliver Twist*.

For a quarter mile they sorted themselves out before meeting the first fence, Airgead Sios blazing the way, near the inside rail, with well-regarded Royal Danieli not far behind. Near the leaders came two favorites which Bruce might have ridden if Marion had felt differently: Royal Mail and Delachance. Battleship settled into midpack, jumping well but hiking his hips up over the brush. As Reg feared, the drop landings would show whether or not the little stallion could handle this course. And the first drop was the most infamous: Becher's Brook.

One, two, three, four, five fences, and here it came. Reaching Becher's the first time, Bruce knew what to expect. Battleship did not. Bruce guided him toward the middle, where the landing drop and the course's left turn would be less severe. Even so, when Battleship crested the hedge and saw what he was in for, his neck shot forward in surprise.

A leap into the unknown, but Noel Laing was with him, and Shirley Banks, and Reg Hobbs, as the extralong reins went sliding through Bruce's hands, all the way to the buckle that made two strips of leather work as one. A lifeline connecting father and son as Battleship landed and his nose "was gouging the floor," Bruce said, "and without the extra rein I'd have been over his head."

And then a sensation that Bruce had relied upon—Battleship gathering, balancing, finding that extra leg and propelling them on with the race.

The seventh fence looked innocent, several inches shorter than Becher's, on level ground. But it had one subtle trick up its sleeve: a straightforward jump, then a slight hitch to the left as the course kinked toward the Canal Turn. Bruce knew this quirk—he had handled it twice with Flying Minutes last year. He did not think that his horse would be quicker than his own thoughts.

But Battleship was reading the path ahead and following the leaders. He leaped and landed well, then instantly swiveled five degrees left. His quick shift flung Bruce to the right, and suddenly Bruce was falling off. An undeniable force knocked him sideways. "No argument!" said Bruce later, "I was gone."

And then Bruce's character saved him. His good-natured attitude when the older riders kidded him, his willingness to help them when he could, his modesty, his competence. When Battleship swiveled, a smug young rider might have found nothing between himself and the ground. But as he lurched sideways, Bruce felt the strong hand of his friend Fred Rimell—a jolly comrade in the jockey house, a leading competitor on the racecourse—grabbing the seat of his pants, yanking him back into the saddle while calling out, "Where do you think you're going, matey?"

He gave Bruce just enough help to balance himself for the next jump, the Canal Turn—where Fred's horse fell. Fred's race was over. Battleship and Bruce cleared the five-foot hedge, turned a sharp left, and galloped on.

They were into the farthest reaches of the course, facing four fences in a row, each five feet high. Airgead Sios still showed the way, leading Royal Danieli by daylight over Valentine's Brook. Nine fences he had cleared in his catlike, devil-may-care, spectacular style. Then Airgead Sios took off too far from number ten, knocking into the top of the close-packed brush, flopping down onto his side, becoming one of sixteen starters who would not finish the first lap.

Finish with a rider up, that is. With an empty saddle, Airgead Sios arose and ran onward with the pack. Like Takvor Pacha, who had jettisoned his jockey at Becher's Brook, Airgead Sios would gallop the entire four miles, 856 yards, instead of stopping to nibble some grass or running back to his barn.

Rounding the far turn, they raced back to where Marion could see them well again. Royal Danieli led them over the Chair, with its gaping ditch on the takeoff side. And here came Battleship, near the middle of the pack, leaping higher than his own shoulders, safely across. Now twenty horses getting over the water—but almost immediately the crowd saw one of them, the handsome gray Rock Lad from Canada, collapse and lie still. Nearly halfway through the National, he had died of a heart attack. He would lie there for the rest of the race, his jockey kneeling beside him . . . a mournful sight right in front of Marion's perch.

A hundred yards beyond, Battleship completed the first circuit. Bruce began riding a race.

Heading back into the country, the little stallion had been rating in seventh place. Now, Bruce let him stretch. Battleship rolled past Delachance and ranged up to Royal Danieli, finding room between the tall Irish gelding and the inside rail, taking the lead. Bruce was saving ground but no longer playing it safe. Now that they were racing rather than scouting their way around, he left his father's instructions—*Go down the middle on the outside, not the inside*—behind.

Nearing Becher's the second time, Battleship still hugged the inner track. With Royal Danieli at Battleship's right flank, offering him no room to change his path, Bruce coolly aimed for the most difficult spot. First of everyone, Battleship arced up and past the famous "B" flag fluttering above the fence. Two hooves, two ankles, two cannon bones swathed in thick cotton, led the way over the massive hedge. Battleship crested Becher's with his neck beautifully arched this time, perfection in flight. Then his shoulders tipped down, his forefeet reaching for earth. His neck pitched low, his hips jerked up. Matching his own balance with Battleship's extreme angle, Bruce leaned his long torso backward until his shoulder blades almost touched the steeply raised haunches. His long legs stayed nearly vertical, almost as if they could be standing upon the ground. His arms extended low and straight, stretching to keep contact with the bit in Battleship's plunging mouth. His hands steadied the last inch of rein.

They took the longest drop of anyone, more than six feet to the ground, and Battleship had not stopped protecting his undercarriage. He leaped

Becher's so high that several inches of sky showed between his loins and the brush while the two big Irish geldings stalking him, Royal Danieli and Workman, rustled their bodies across. And yet Battleship was not caught off guard this time. His nose did not quite touch the ground as his feet touched down. Landing far past the deep-cutting brook, he bounced up and on.

And this time there was no problem at the little fence after Becher's. Bruce and Battleship swiveled together alongside the inner rail, galloped slightly uphill to the Canal Turn, handled the sharp left turn, and raced into the country. Meanwhile, the horse that Reg had hoped Marion would buy for Bruce to ride came to a halt. Royal Mail was bleeding from his respiratory tract. Even a proven Aintree winner could not compete if he could not properly breathe.

Entering Aintree's long backstretch, Battleship and Royal Danieli took each other's measure. Galloping side by side now, they looked like model racehorses built on two entirely different scales, Battleship's rump several inches lower than his rival's, his body fitting like a nesting doll within Royal Danieli's outline.

They took Valentine's Brook together, with Workman and Delachance close behind. Any one of those four would win, a London reporter thought. Over fence twenty-six they went, now twenty-seven with its open ditch on the takeoff side, now galloping to fence twenty-eight, where Bruce had fallen from Flying Minutes last year. The little stallion took it alongside Royal Danieli—and then Royal Danieli flashed ahead. All of the reporters— "and they were many," one Londoner said—who believed that Battleship would tire out in a four-and-a-half-mile race figured that he was done. They hadn't seen him make what Bruce later called "his one real mistake."

Battleship had taken off too close to fence twenty-eight. His body hit the brush. Bruce heard his horse give a heavy sigh—"it fairly knocked the stuffing out of him, poor little mate"—and felt him almost fall as they landed, mercifully clearing the open ditch that lay in their way.

Bruce could see Royal Danieli pulling away from them, and Workman cruising by to join the leader. He could see the race seemingly floating out of reach. He could feel Battleship struggling like a swimmer caught in a riptide, and without even thinking, Bruce knew not to fight it. Breathe. That's all he could do. Let Battleship breathe.

The big Irish horses opened a gap while rounding the final bend, near-ing the final two fences and the long homestretch. But Bruce would come to feel that Battleship had made his mistake in the best possible place. The space between fences twenty-eight and twenty-nine was one of the lon-gest flat gallops in the race. Battleship's lungs and legs began working fuller and faster. And he had a target now, the big horses up ahead. Bruce later would say that this mistake gave Battleship a better chance—a rea-son to take a breather, a reason to finish strong.

Delachance had fallen back. He, not Battleship, was the American hope who didn't want four and a half miles. The race was between Royal Danieli and Workman, it appeared. But complications were arising as the Irish horses rose to the second-to-last fence. Behind them, a little horse gaining steam, moving less like a battleship than a locomotive. Beside them, a loose horse: Takvor Pacha ducking into Workman while Work-man landed the jump. Workman's rider stayed in the saddle while his horse took the bump, but they had no time for a breather—only a few strides to the final fence.

Riderless Takvor Pacha got there first but avoided the jump, crossing in front of Royal Danieli and scooting out around the obstacle. Royal Danieli made a handsome leap, landing clear and keeping his three-length lead. Marion saw Battleship take aim, with Bruce sitting relaxed as a man in an easy chair, and sail past the place where Billy Barton ten years ear-lier had rolled to the ground. She saw Workman fade out of contention—the final jump, so soon after bumping at the second-to-last, had deflated him. She saw that Battleship had only one horse to catch, but that horse was running strong. After more than four miles, after thirty jumps, it would come down to speed in the final five hundred yards.

Royal Danieli held the inner rail. Bruce wanted to come up beside him, but riderless Takvor Pacha veered back onto the homestretch and decided to visit Battleship. Bruce didn't like that idea. Momentum meant everything now. He couldn't let anything break their stride. He steered Battleship far to the right, almost reaching the outer rail, and hunkered down to ride. No whip, just body and hands, urging all, encouraging all, while Battleship chopped away at the gleaming giant's lead, like a scrappy Galloway pony reminding England of its motley racing roots.

And British as well as Americans were cheering him now, a little horse sprinting the end of a long race "with," said the London *Times,* "a courage almost beyond praise." His chance was here, and Marion's chance of her life, and she could barely tell what was happening while the crowd churned around her and Ed Conklin, cheering, dropped her troublesome pocketbook. Irish fans hollered for Royal Danieli; bookmakers who had nothing to lose if Battleship won yelled for the "American pony" who still had half a length to find, but he wasn't done, he was surging. Two Thoroughbreds passed the finish in a blur, nearly the course width apart. Only the judges, positioned exactly on the line, could tell for certain who had come in first. For a moment, a quarter million people fell silent. Then they burst into riotous motion and sound.

Far back from the finish line, Marion knew only that it was close. Nearby, a policeman tried to marshal the swarming spectators down the narrow stairs. Carroll spoke up for her: "I wonder if we might get through? We might have won this race." The bobby told Marion, "Oh, madam, let me try."

"He helped us through the jostling," Marion noted, "but the stands were open bleachers with three-foot steps." One of her stylish Cuban heels came down wrong and broke off, bouncing away. Pulled along by Carroll and Ed, Marion literally hopped down the stairs and back toward the paddock, to find out what her horse had done. She could not see Bruce and Battleship returning, pausing to meet up with Reg, then walking on.

Marion, Carroll, and Ed finally neared the area where the first three National finishers stepped into high-walled stalls for unsaddling. "There were two steps going up to the building," Marion would recall, "and I couldn't see anything." They could keep fighting the crowd, or they could pause and get the answer now. In the next moment, Marion was not a forty-three-year-old matron; she was the girl who had once attacked a tumbling act. Carroll and Ed linked hands; Marion stepped onto their palms, steadying her light body as the men boosted her up, lifting her face and shoulders above the crowd. There she saw the stalls numbered 3, 2, 1, a pair of horse ears visible above each wall. Marion saw brown, brown, and chestnut—the only chestnut—her Battleship, in number one.

Bruce Hobbs was the first to know, or at least believe, that Battleship had finished first. "The last ten yards," he said, "I was convinced I'd won."

Photographs developed later, taken from various angles, would show Marion's horse in front, but Aintree had no photo-finish camera. After conferring for several minutes, the judges announced that Battleship had won by a head. Royal Danieli's jockey swore that, "By Jesus, if there'd been a photo-finish, I think there'd a'been a dead-heat." Bruce later kindly said, "Well, you know, if I had been second, I'm sure I'd have said much the same thing." But as he passed the finish and eased Battleship down to a canter, a jog, a walk, he felt certain: "I thought I'd won half a length."

And Battleship clearly felt that he had done enough. He had given all that his rider wanted; he also knew the way back to his stable, and *that* was where he decided to go. Moments after winning the Grand National, Bruce found himself nearly as powerless as he had been as a small boy, unable to make a stubborn pony carry him out of his father's stable yard. With every step, Battleship tried to go home. With every step, Bruce told him, *No, not yet, we have one more place to go.* The boy was barely keeping his little horse moving toward the paddock, toward the winner's unsaddling stall, when his father and the policemen took control.

Even before the official result, the world began converging on Bruce and Battleship. Reg sprinting over, asking, "Did you win?" Bruce saying, "Yes!" while the mounted policemen charged with protecting the winner surrounded them, anticipating the news. Soon Reg would be telling reporters, "It is the greatest day of my life." But as he led Battleship back to the paddock, Reg shot his son the same question he would have given any jockey after a less-than-perfect trip: "What was that trouble after Becher's first time?"

While Bruce explained how Fred Rimell had rescued him, Reg noticed blood running from Battleship's nose and feared he might be bleeding internally, then realized no. These were scratches from the steep landings where the little stallion had scraped his muzzle on the ground while finding that extra leg.

Reg and Marion both had been right. Battleship had the wrong jumping style for Aintree; but he was a true National horse.

They squeezed through masses of people, with friends calling, "Good old Bruce! Good old Reggie!" Then the relief, for Battleship, of 160 pounds gone from his back. Bruce stepped onto a scale, his saddle draped over one arm, proving that Battleship had carried his assigned weight all the way, while steam rose from Battleship's body into the chilly air and a groom began seeing to his comfort.

And then someone saw Marion. Newspapers would say that she had been "too excited" to lead her horse into the winner's enclosure, but in fact she had been lost in the crowd. Now Reg went to her, ushered her in, and introduced her to his son.

For nearly two years, the woman and the boy had been like legends to each other—distant, separate, expert forces aiming toward a common goal. Now her blue-gray eyes looked up into his gray eyes. So different in age and life experience, so similar in knowing how it was to want to go somewhere with a horse. All the way from Shetland ponies to Battleship.

They could not fit their whole alliance into words. Bruce had needed Marion's horse, but Marion, in a way, had needed Bruce as an extension of herself. She thanked the boy for his wonderful ride. He realized that she was tenacious but also seemed very shy. Then Bruce, eager to join Battleship back at the stable, hurried off to change from his dirty silks, breeches, and boots into a tailored suit and bowler hat that would meet his father's exacting standards.

Marion stood there in her broken shoe, fulfilled and remarkably contained. Later that night she would call this a "most exciting win," but her feelings did not bubble out in front of everyone. While Reg Hobbs could not stop smiling, a reporter at the scene called Marion "the most composed person on the course" and said that she accepted the great victory "without, as far as one could see, the slightest tremor of excitement."

She was wearing her public armor. But the excitement was there. Just not in ways that anyone who didn't know her well would understand.

As the flurry of official procedures and spontaneous celebrating began to subside, a British journalist asked Marion for an interview. He was astonished when she turned to Reg Hobbs and escaped with six words: "Let's go and see the horse."

She had done it—and she had done few of the things that people expected a Grand National winning owner to do. She had not claimed the honor of leading her horse back to be unsaddled. She took tea at the racecourse with Mrs. Ambrose Clark, two American women quietly celebrating Battleship and Kellsboro' Jack. Then Marion boarded a train for London, with Carroll and Ed, while Reg and Bruce and dozens of racing folk stormed Liverpool for a lavish celebration dinner at the Adelphi Hotel.

"The truth was," Marion later claimed, "I hadn't had nerve enough to bring along a special dress for such a party. We hardly expected to win."

While Marion slipped away, the first father-and-son combination to win the Grand National climbed into evening attire. In his hotel room, Bruce saved a telegram that had been sent about twenty minutes after he and Battleship passed the winning post, sent from the town of Melton Mowbray, their old stomping ground of the Quorn Hunt and Warwick Lodge. She wasn't there to hug him, but she did so with her words:

```
HEARTIEST CONGRATULATIONS
DELIGHTED
FONDEST LOVE
MUMMY
```

Perfectly groomed, father and son made their way to the Adelphi's grandest banquet room and began working their way through an expensive menu. Reg silently worried that he would be stuck with a tremendous bill—"I knew the party was going to cost at least a thousand quid"—because Marion had left without mentioning it. Shortly before midnight, someone handed him a telegram from London:

```
SORRY MISS PARTY AFTER MOST EXCITING WIN PLEASE EXTEND ALL
POSSIBLE HOSPITALITY
MARION SCOTT
```

She was picking up the tab. Said Reg, "I enjoyed the rest!"

Marion retired to her room at The Berkeley, her English home away from home. Evidence of her triumph met her at the door to her suite: a pile of telegrams needing to be gathered up before she could step inside. Mostly congratulations and also, said Marion, "some charity hospitals trying to make a touch." The hotel, like an old friend or doting mother, even had a cake waiting for her, "with two horses jumping on top."

She lingered in England for a few days while American newspapers blossomed with tributes to the latest great son of Man o' War, pictures of Bruce and Battleship, pictures of herself and of Randolph Scott, and stories of the fourteen Americans who held tickets on Battleship in the Irish Sweepstakes, winning $150,000 each—a single ticket paying more than three times Battleship's first-place purse. The media celebrated his unlikely success, but to one journalist, it seemed inevitable: "An American horse that came from the home of James Madison in the one hundred and fiftieth anniversary year of the ratification of the Constitution of the United States couldn't help but whip the British."

The British, truth be told, had been good sports. Sticking to their Stud Book rules, they would give Marion a beautiful golden trophy engraved with BATTLESHIP, H.B.—"half-bred." But genuine joy filled the traditional parade through the National winner's hometown, with Battleship walking behind a bass drummer through the main street of Lambourn; and respect shone through such tributes as a headline in *Country Life* magazine: "A Memorable Grand National: Gallant Little American Horse."

The good feelings lingered. Three weeks after the National, Reg and Bruce Hobbs participated in a live radio broadcast celebrating Man o' War's twenty-first birthday. The program began at Big Red's Kentucky stud barn with a crowd of visitors singing, then broadcaster Clem McCarthy interviewing several dignitaries and fruitlessly hoping that Man o' War himself would give a snort or a neigh.

Then a switch to a BBC studio in London. Suddenly America heard Reg Hobbs, with his charming voice that was not exactly common but not quite posh; and Bruce, sounding strikingly like his father, only with the higher, lighter tones of youth. They read prepared statements, the father speaking first. Reg choked back laughter while explaining that he had thought little Battleship winning the National would be "a physical impossibility." Bruce gave a jockey's highest praise: "I have never ridden a gamer horse, and I know I never shall."

22

Some people assumed that he would keep going. Finishing the course in 9 minutes, 29 and 4/5 seconds, Battleship had won the fourth-fastest Grand National in history. If Marion would bring him back next year, maybe he could win two in a row.

It was a sweet and fleeting temptation, like the feeling Charles Lindbergh had experienced thirty hours into his epic flight from New York to Paris. "Judging from the nose tank," Lindbergh thought, "I have enough fuel to reach Rome. I can certainly go that far if this tail wind keeps blowing."

But what if it didn't? Lindbergh considered everything that needed to go right if he pushed past his original goal. He remembered the detailed planning and flashes of good fortune that had brought him this far and realized that crossing the ocean to Paris was plenty. Despite temptation, he would stick with the plan.

And so would Battleship. Before long, Marion announced that he would retire to stud at Montpelier, although her husband out in Hollywood had received an interesting offer. Randy's studio was producing a racetrack movie starring real-life racehorse owner Bing Crosby. The director wondered, could Scott get Battleship to appear in *Sing, You Sinners*, portraying "Uncle Gus"?

Marion didn't care for that idea. The role went to Bing Crosby and Lin

Howard's colt Ligaroti, who already lived nearby and would gain fame that summer in a match race with Seabiscuit. Crosby, a part owner of Southern California's Del Mar racetrack, believed in horse racing as an entertainment business and was happy to drum up publicity. But Marion was thinking only of what would be good for Battleship. He didn't need a trip to Hollywood. Bringing him home to Virginia was enough.

Battleship did travel home like a movie star. He sailed back to the United States aboard the SS *Manhattan,* one of the fastest transatlantic liners, because the voyage to England had upset him and his people wanted this trip to be as short and comfortable as possible. The shipping line custom-built a spacious fourteen-by-fourteen-foot stall within an air-conditioned room belowdecks "ordinarily used," *The New Yorker* magazine reported, "for shipping canaries and tropical birds."

Reg and Bruce Hobbs accompanied Battleship, seeing to his well-being while others pampered them. Marion was going to reward them with a long visit at Montpelier, after they attended special events near New York; but first, out at sea, they were treated like celebrities by their fellow passengers and crew. The youngest rider ever to win the Grand National! The first all-American horse! The tallest rider ever to win, and one of the smallest horses! It seemed as if everyone on the ship wanted to congratulate them and also see the horse. Several times daily, Reg and Bruce welcomed visitors at Battleship's stall. Bruce especially remembered women climbing the ladder into the hold wearing pajama pants under their skirts, for modesty's sake. He collected a small fee, or tip, from each tourist, but not for himself. After the voyage, Bruce donated the money to the Red Cross.

They entered New York Harbor on June 9, and none too soon. Midway through the voyage, Battleship had become so agitated that he grabbed the back of Reg's coat in his teeth and ripped it apart. Soon he would reach his old paddock at Montpelier and shake off the cabin fever, but first he had to walk into a shipping crate, be hoisted down to the pier, and enter a horse van that would take him to a railroad car. And Bruce was unhappy to see that all this wouldn't happen quietly. As their ship docked and he and his father disembarked, an explosion of noise and motion honored them: cheering spectators, a brass band playing, sirens wailing, and harbor tugboats spouting great arcs of water from their fire hoses, while New York's mayor Fiorello LaGuardia came forward to personally congratulate them. For Bruce, this hoopla was more daunting than riding the National course. Overwhelmed by the display, he worried about Battleship.

"The water squirted out, flags waved, the horse came up in a special crate," said Bruce, "and there was I, the National hero, frightened to death while my father stood there with tears streaming down his face." It was like so many moments of his childhood: Reg relishing the glory; Bruce grappling with fear.

Marion duPont Scott avoided the sirens and hoses. Instead, Randolph Scott had crossed the United States to represent her at the docks. It was his last public appearance on her behalf. Two days later, back in Hollywood, Scott confirmed that he and Marion had separated. Their parting could not have been more friendly, Scott said; their East Coast–West Coast lives simply could not be reconciled. Marion acknowledged that this was true, while adding that they had not made any plans to get a divorce.

But it didn't take long for rumors to bloom. Perhaps that was inevitable, when a married woman sailed to England and back with a man who was not her husband. Some newspapers said that Marion was going to divorce Randolph Scott and marry Carroll Bassett. When a reporter pressed her about this, she said only, "I have no comment to make."

Marion went racing at Saratoga with Carroll, as in years past, but she did not act like someone eager to shake off one marriage and enter another. That autumn, the gossip columnist Sheilah Graham reported that "Randolph Scott is asking his blue-blood wife for a divorce, but she says 'No.' Randy says there is not another woman in the case—he just wants to be free." In late October, Randy visited Montpelier and even sat down for an interview with twelve-year-old Joyce Craig, a daughter of Marion's longtime farm secretary Hugh Boyd Craig. Perhaps with an editor's help, Joyce reported that "you could not find a better mannered, more friendly person anywhere. As he shook my hand, that smile and friendly twinkle in his eye made me feel as if I had known him for years." Young Joyce also repeated a point that Scott often made: "Randy (as I have learned to call him) told me that you could never believe what you read. He has read articles about him that had not the least truth in them, and sometimes people quote him as saying things he never heard of."

Randy and Marion remained friends but also stayed separated. Eventually, they divorced so quietly that newspapers couldn't even pinpoint the date. Randolph Scott and Cary Grant continued sharing their Santa Monica beach house until Grant married the heiress Barbara Hutton in the summer of 1942. All in all, Grant would marry five times, finally for keeps. Eventually, his daughter, Jennifer, would write a warm and candid book about her loving father and observe that "Dad somewhat enjoyed being called gay. He said it made women want to prove the assertion wrong." Jennifer Grant also recognized a universal attractiveness in her father's nature and manner. "Dad treated men and women very similarly," she reflected. "Perhaps he flirted with no one, or perhaps he flirted with everyone."

Although movie stardom could be a form of flirting with everyone, Randolph Scott seemed less provocative in his private life. Early in 1944, he married Marie Patricia Stillman, an attractive young lady from a prominent New York family. Several years later, they adopted a boy and a girl. During the 1950s, his own middle age, Randolph Scott enjoyed the comforts of family life and also the peak of his movie career. Westerns were his greatest strength, after all.

He always respected his first wife. When Marion died, five decades after he and she had secretly married, Randy sent flowers in her honor to Montpelier. Marion had kept his last name for the rest of her life.

Bruce Hobbs seemed as if he would keep winning steeplechases until rising weight forced him out of his jockey career. But he never rode another Grand National. Perhaps he would have had several more chances before growing too heavy if World War II had not shut down the National from 1941 through 1945. But something else stopped him much more quickly. In mid-November 1938, Bruce broke his back in a racing fall. He endured a bone graft and many weeks wrapped in a hard cast. The doctors hoped there would be no permanent paralysis but could not guarantee it. His mother faithfully kept him company, as she had done after his concussion ten years before. "As soon as she heard of my accident," Bruce recalled, "she moved down from Melton, found herself digs in Oxford and spent every single hour of every single day by my bedside." As she had done when he was small, Margery helped Bruce believe that he would be all right, that he could hang on.

His mother apparently was not allowed to stay beside him while, finally, a medical team removed his body cast—"and I was told," Bruce said, "that I had got to lie absolutely still because I had to learn to walk again. They were going to teach me." Then, not counting on a jockey's restless spirit, the hospital staff briefly left Bruce alone in his room. The boy who had scrupulously obeyed orders while his father and fellow riders pursued adult amusements couldn't help it: he began to move. He sat up—felt dizzy—slid his legs over the side of the bed and pressed his feet against the floor. A nurse found him turning back toward the bed, not steady enough to travel more than a couple of steps. While she berated him, tucking him back into place, Bruce couldn't contain his joy: "Nurse, I can walk. I can walk!" Decades later—after serving with British cavalry in the Middle East during World War II and receiving a Military Cross for bravery under fire; after coming home to a brief and winning return as a jockey; then marriage, fatherhood, and a distinguished career training Thoroughbred racers—Bruce Hobbs treasured this moment of getting onto his feet again, the transition toward so much that followed. Nearly fifty years later, he said, "That was probably the best day of my life."

Battleship and the Grand National also kept a fond place in his heart. Over time, Bruce saw the National course made less hazardous. Bowing to public outcry against horse injuries, Aintree management made many of the obstacles easier to jump. Bruce thought that this only would create other problems. "If they soften those fences still further," he reckoned in the early 1980s, "they're going to have some real carnage." In his experience, jockeys believing that they had an easier way through a tough course did not help them handle it better.

In his later years, Bruce also wondered whether overcautiousness might overtake society at large, undermining human confidence and competence. "Of course I'm all for safety," he declared, "but I think we are so safety-conscious nowadays that very soon you'll have to wear a crash helmet to cross the road!"

Bruce did understand how nostalgia can distort a person's perceptions. "We all like to think that in our day things were a lot tougher than they are now," he said nearly forty years after his Aintree win with

Battleship. "Still, I do think anybody now who rode [the Grand National] in those days would admit that those fences were slightly stiffer than they are today . . . and they were absolutely straight up! There was no guideline—no belly at the takeoff. It was tough. A horse Battleship's size had to be awfully good to win it."

Battleship enjoyed lifelong retirement at Montpelier. He sired only fifty-eight offspring, but eleven of them became stakes winners—an astounding 19 percent, nearly five times the average rate for a Thoroughbred stallion. He did not win great fame as a sire, however, because many of these racers were doing what Battleship himself had done best: excelling over jumps. His sons Shipboard and War Battle became steeplechase champions in the United States, with Shipboard winning many important 'chases for Marion duPont Scott. But Shipboard, like Battleship's other top racing sons, was a gelding, and his daughters did not excel as broodmares. There would be no generations of Battleship descendants beating a path to Aintree.

There was simply Battleship, unique, the American pioneer. For twenty years after his grand achievement he impressed Montpelier visitors with his presence that seemed larger than his body. Farrier Lee Rose observed, "He was a very secure horse. He knew who he was."

Keeping fit with a daily hour of exercise under saddle during much of his retirement, Battleship thrived into his thirty-first year. He was like a person who stayed mentally sharp and physically mobile well into his nineties. Eventually, his eyesight faded away, and Marion saw that he was declining. "Just old age," she said, "he could not get around." On September 12, 1958, she had Battleship humanely put down and buried near his barn, near Annapolis, who had died the previous year.

It came to her, a few years later, how to better honor them. She would move Battleship and Annapolis to one side of Montpelier's front lawn, about half a furlong from the house. Battleship was laid to rest on a path of particular honor, set along a straight line to James Madison's meditation temple and Montpelier's front door.

She never held a trainer's license, but Marion duPont Scott personally directed the early training of her Thoroughbreds until she was eighty-eight years old. And while Marion eventually campaigned champion flat racers as well as jumpers, she always gave special attention to producing steeple-chasers. She started many of her young horses schooling over jumps but recognized that "either it's natural for them, or it isn't." If it wasn't, she wouldn't force them.

Well into the 1960s, Carroll Bassett often joined her at the stables and in the fields of Montpelier, a slender man with a surprisingly deep voice, talking slowly and directly like the petite woman who ran the show. Until his death in 1972, Carroll made his home at the Montpelier cottage that Marion had put up for him and Jane Fowler Bassett. Its mid-1930s mod-erne style had much in common with Marion's Red Room.

Some people believed that Marion and Carroll were romantically in-volved, but others close to them swore that was not so. Carroll and Mar-ion shared several passions: horses, gardening, game fowl, dogs. They shared a wealth of memories, of course, and also the habit of thoughtful silence, taking time to speak and saying exactly what they meant. Their alliance lasted until Carroll died in 1972. A few years later, Marion pub-lished a book called *Montpelier* and dedicated it "To Carroll and Noel," the friends who had brought the greatest joy to her racing life.

For nearly a decade after Carroll was gone, Marion kept on supervis-ing the training of her yearlings and two-year-olds at Montpelier. Every morning, even during unpleasant weather, she entered the landscape that she had redesigned as a young woman with her father and her brother. Sometimes she directed exercises at Montpelier's dirt track, but her young horses often worked out in the fields or up and down hill. The varied ter-rain strengthened their bodies in several different ways, while the open countryside freed their minds from the speed craziness of the track.

Well into her seventies and eighties, Marion would drive a blue-and-white Oldsmobile station wagon out into the middle of a field, then climb up and sit on the roof of the car. She would call out instructions with a solemn face and a firm voice, but every so often, during a training session or back at the barn, something would make her giggle.

In her final years, as her defenses weakened, she would become more obviously upset when something went wrong with a horse. One day in the big house at Montpelier, her housekeeper Mae Helen Corbin came downstairs and saw that Mrs. Scott was crying. Mae Helen didn't know what to do or say, so she simply went over and put her arm around her employer. It turned out that one of Marion's horses had died. They were, said Mae Helen, like her children.

All of the workers at Montpelier knew that they were under Marion's wing, as well. To her face, they called her "ma'am" or "Mrs. Scott." Out of her hearing, they called her "Mama." A person who kept them in line—but also cared for their well-being.

Even as her body became frail, Marion kept the habit of looking out for the people who looked out for her. Late in her life, when walking became difficult, she and Mae Helen Corbin developed a routine for getting around the house: Mae Helen linking arms with Marion while Marion used her cane with her other hand. One day while they were slowly walking down a hallway, Mae Helen felt an unwelcome spasm taking over her own body.

"Oh Mrs. Scott," she gulped, "I've got hiccups." Mrs. Scott didn't say anything. They slowly walked several more steps. Suddenly, Marion swung her cane up in a high arc while a vigorous sound came forth from the tiny, quiet lady: *"Woooooo!"*

Mae Helen didn't know what was happening. Was Marion falling down?! But no, she was perfectly fine.

"Oh, Mrs. Scott," Mae Helen gasped, "you gave me such a fright!"

And she got the logical response of the expert horsewoman, the executive, Mama.

"You don't have the hiccups anymore, do you?"

Despite her physical limitations, Marion had solved the problem. "No, ma'am," Mae Helen answered, relieved, "I don't!"

Visiting the du Pont family graveyard at Wilmington, seeing the monuments to her great-grandparents and other kin, Marion may have noticed how engravings on stone can start to disappear after a century or so. Perhaps with this in mind, she had the letters and numbers on Battleship's simple headstone carved deeply enough to last a thousand years.

But could she do the same for Montpelier? An entity much more complicated than a chunk of granite. An estate holding many parts: the historic main house, the facilities for several types of animals, the fields of grain and a granary for storing it, the gardens, the greenhouses, an electrical plant, a sawmill churning out boards to repair fences, an ingenious system of water towers so that the farm wouldn't be held hostage by drought. Longtime employee Mike Clatterbuck said, "I never did see a contractor come in. Everything she needed was here."

She had come to manage it all through the will made by her father in 1928, expecting that Montpelier eventually would go to William Jr.'s children or their heirs if Marion died childless. And yet the place had another distinct legacy that lingered in her mind. Late in 1963, her brother responded to some of her musings. "You were talking at one time about restoring Montpelier as James Madison had it," Will duPont wrote. "If you wish, you could do it out of tax-free dollars. Then if you gave the place—which I would join with you—to some historical society whatever the value of the place would again be deductible. However, this is only something to play with in thought."

Marion did not change the house, kept it as her home, and outlived her brother by nearly eighteen years. On September 4, 1983, Montpelier received her final breath. Her last will and testament revealed a painful decision for her nieces and nephews to grapple with but perhaps, ultimately, a rewarding one. Marion wanted the National Trust for Historic Preservation to own the property. She left an endowment for making Montpelier a public destination, like Mount Vernon and Monticello. She suggested that, if the Trust thought it fitting, the mansion house might be restored to its form from the James and Dolley Madison years.

She had willed her own answer to a question posed by *Time* magazine in 1923, asking how the children of rich Americans would choose to serve their country, an answer that *Time* had thought would come from the sons of famous families, "who can, if they like, win Grand Nationals."

But it wasn't a son. It was a daughter. And her gift did not stop with winning the world's toughest horse race. In the end, she was a gardener, trusting the regenerative power that springs up from deep roots. The roots of a nation reached up from her home. Marion duPont Scott let them reconnect with the public, opening the way to James Madison's Montpelier.

Acknowledgments

There's a saying in the horse world: you can bring a horse to a top competition, but it's better when the horse takes you there. That's what Battleship did with this book, nudging his way past other possible subjects and saying, *What about me?* He had been waiting in the background ever since 1970-something, when I read every C. W. Anderson book of racehorse stories in the library and first heard of "the American pony." Battleship reintroduced himself at Saratoga in 2001, when the National Museum of Racing and Hall of Fame's *Hall of Fame Heroes* exhibit featured his Grand National trophy and his corrective shoe. It's an outlandish-looking hunk of metal that makes you wonder: How the *heck* did he go from wearing that thing to winning the toughest Thoroughbred horse race in the world?

After leaping back into my thoughts, Battleship waited a few more years while I researched his dad. There was no plan to write *Man o' War* and then "Son of Man o' War." But when you finally finish a book, the windows of your mind that were trying to contain one subject spring open again. That's when Billy Barton strolled in—the gallant loser of the world's biggest chase—and I thought, *Why not?* Why does the hero always have to win? Then Battleship stepped up, asserting his rightful place, the one who finished what Billy had begun. So I began pulling at threads, and they weren't single threads, they were a tapestry.

Sadly, Bruce Hobbs had died on November 21, 2005, soon after Battleship asserted himself. And a Battleship book wasn't a full-fledged project then, anyway. *Man o' War* publication and publicity dominated the next two years. But during 2007, I learned of a new program that made all the difference.

A John F. Daniels Fellowship from the National Sporting Library in Middleburg, Virginia, made this project possible. Being granted many weeks to immerse myself in their wonderful collection of periodicals, books, and special materials let this steeplechasing rookie get off the ground. I am deeply grateful to the Fellowship Committee, Director Nancy Parsons, subsequent Director Rick Stoutamyer, and Librarian Lisa Campbell. Board member and Red Fox Fine Art director F. Turner Reuter Jr. went out of his way to gather information about Carroll Bassett. Elizabeth Tobey, director of Communications & Research, went above and beyond with support and suggestions. Curatorial Assistant Brenna Elliott cheered me by discussing discoveries about Marion duPont Scott and saying, "I *like* this woman!" Many thanks to fellow "Fellow" Elisabetta Deriu for her good company, feedback about riding sidesaddle, and help with the history of Quarantaine; and to office manager Judy Sheehan and summer intern Allison Frew for buoying me with smart and jolly conversations.

During the fellowship and other Sporting Library visits, several people in the Middleburg area offered perspective and hospitality. Thank you again to Alice Porter for good discussions and the rides with King and Nipper; to Jim Whitner, who, in conversation during the 2009 Hunt Country Stable Tour, lit up with admiration for Bruce Hobbs's riding in the Grand National with Battleship, explaining how hard it is for a tall rider to jump tall fences with a small horse (Hobbs must have had "perfect balance"); and to Margaret Worrall for talking about Trouble Maker. Special thanks to farrier Lee Rose, who remembered seeing Battleship at Montpelier in the 1950s and interpreted several types of corrective shoeing.

Several friends encouraged me over the bridge from having a new book idea to inhabiting its world. Special thanks to my sister, Linda Ours, for a lifetime of storytelling adventures; to Joan Meyer and Diana Zipperer for the experience of running a 5K race (and thus relating to racehorses in training in a whole new way); to Nina Quinn and the horses of

Heyday Farm for their inspiration and wisdom; and to Laura Hillen-
brand, who read the *Battleship* outline, used the word "lyrical," and helped
me feel free to sing a new song.

Because Battleship and Carroll Bassett are Hall of Fame members, the
National Museum of Racing in Saratoga Springs, New York, keeps files
and other materials relating to them. Curator Beth Sheffer went out of
her way to supply additional information and insight. Historian Allen
Carter chased down some pesky details. The late Dick Hamilton, retired
communications officer and former racing steward, remembered seeing
Marion duPont Scott at the races and always amused me by calling steeplechasing "up and over the furniture."

As usual with research involving Thoroughbred racing, Kentucky
made vital contributions. Mark and Mary Simon generously shared resources from the files of *Thoroughbred Times,* along with their exception-
ally good company. Keeneland Library remains a world-class resource.
Edward L. Bowen, president of Grayson–Jockey Club Research Foundation, supported my interest in the John H. Daniels Fellowship and asked
useful questions about this project.

Research quickly made it clear that without Marion duPont Scott,
there would be no Battleship story to rediscover because he never would
have landed at Aintree or in the Hall of Fame. Vital resources came from
the region where her life began, at Wilmington, Delaware. Many boxes
of papers from the William du Pont Sr. and William du Pont Jr. collections at the Hagley Museum and Library gave an indispensable link to
this remarkable woman and the strong family that produced her. Conversations with Lucas Clawson, reference archivist at Hagley, deepened my
understanding of the DuPont Company origins and the family's bravery.
Visiting Bellevue Hall at Bellevue State Park during early May and hearing a presentation by Martha du Pont opened more windows into the
world of William and Annie du Pont.

Although Battleship never ran in the Maryland Hunt Cup, walking
that course and seeing that race made Trouble Maker's experiences there
three-dimensional. Special thanks to Joe Clancy of *Steeplechase Times* (now
Mid-Atlantic Thoroughbred) and photographer Lydia Williams for taking
this rookie under their wings; and to a passing horsewoman who, when

the gigantic third fence stopped me cold during the course walk, said, "Just climb it like a ladder." Thanks also to Patrick Smithwick Jr. for his encouragement and the enlightenment of his wonderful memoir, *Flying Change: A Return to Steeplechasing.*

Retracing Battleship's steps led me to Camden, South Carolina, where Springdale Race Course still stretches out majestically among the tall pines. Many thanks to Hope Cooper, executive director of the National Steeplechase Museum, for guiding me through their collections and also around Camden, sharing local and Battleship-related history. Kristin Cobb, executive director at Fine Arts Center of Kershaw County, welcomed me to their beautiful Bassett Room. The Kershaw County Library and the Camden Archives and Museum yielded important resources. Farther up the road, the Robinson-Spangler Carolina Room at the Charlotte Mecklenburg Library (Charlotte, North Carolina) supplied unique and reliable material about Randolph Scott.

Other necessities arrived by email and telephone. David Levesque, technical services librarian/archivist at Ohrstrom Library, verified Will duPont's presence and activities at St. Paul's School, September 1910–June 1911. Amanda Langendoerfer, head of Special Collections & Archives, Pickler Memorial Library, Truman State University, rounded up dozens of Walter J. Salmon documents from the Harry H. Laughlin Papers. Cathy L. Eberly, director of Marketing and Communications, delved into Randolph Scott's student days at Woodberry Forest School. Joan Roberts-Coleman, records service coordinator, UNC–Chapel Hill, directed me to the Louis Round Wilson Special Collections Library, where Morgan Elizabeth Jones, Graduate Research Assistant, illuminated Randolph Scott's brief time as a student there.

Several people in Nevada shed light on the Reno divorces of Marion duPont Somerville and Jane Fowler Bassett. Jacque Sundstrand, manuscripts and archives librarian, University of Nevada, found an especially informative newspaper article; Sue Anne Monteleon of the Nevada State Museum put me in touch with Mella Rothwell Harmon, M.S., who contributed vibrant descriptions of the Winters Ranch; Chris Matthews, county webmaster, washoecounty.us, helped me contact someone who could determine whether any Somerville or Bassett records were available; and Amanda Croghan at the Washoe County Courthouse located the files and delivered more information than I ever expected would surface from cases with sealed testimony. Terri B. Zion, deputy probate judge, at the Chester County Courthouse, South Carolina, cleverly found the Marion duPont Somerville/George Randolph Scott marriage license filed under "Su," confirming various details of their secret wedding.

And, although Battleship had been gone for more than fifty years when I seriously began seeking out his story, Virginia remembered him. Meeting Noel Laing's nieces and nephew, Dr. Aileen Laing, Susan Laing, and Noel Laing, and receiving Dr. Laing's many thoughtful responses to ongoing questions, ranks among the very best experiences in this great journey. Through them, quiet Noel with his "very quiet hands" seemed to step out from photographs and become unfrozen from time. The past also began speaking through documents held by the Orange County Courthouse and knowledge shared by Atwell Somerville. And this book could not have come to life without James Madison's Montpelier, where horses still race over the hedges planted by the du Pont family and they still run the race named for Noel Laing.

Among those connected with Montpelier, Martha Strawther, executive director, Montpelier Hunt Races, boosted me time and again with pertinent insights, introductions, and humor. Jack Strawther added to my store of local lore. Cheryl Brush (now retired) expertly introduced me to the Marion duPont Scott scrapbooks and Tiffany Cole, assistant curator for Research & Documentation, cheerfully continued the journey. Raymond G. Woolfe Jr., whose father was a dear friend of Carroll Bassett and trained horses for many years for Mrs. Scott, helped me sense their personalities and see Montpelier as it was in their day. Mike Clatterbuck shared wonderfully vivid memories of Mrs. Scott the expert horsewoman directing morning exercise and also of her generosity. Mae Helen Corbin thoughtfully helped me glimpse Marion duPont Scott as a very caring person as well as an efficient boss, someone who is fondly remembered and missed even after all these years.

Among those connected with Montpelier through the du Pont family, I am grateful to Mary Carter McConnell for sharing her perceptions of William and Annie du Pont as "a strong couple" and to Susan McConnell for perspective about history versus privacy. I am especially grateful to James H. T. "Jamie" McConnell for pointing out several common myths about the du Pont family, his great-aunt Marion, and her stable; and to Bill du Pont for kindly sharing personal observations about his aunt Marion.

Naturally, Battleship's story required a leap across the Atlantic. Michael More-Molyneux graciously responded to my questions about Loseley Park. Central Library in Liverpool yielded important details about the 1933 and 1938 Nationals. Aintree Racecourse bridged a chasm simply by still existing and allowing racegoers to walk most of the National course. And I am immensely grateful to three ladies whose support improved this book immeasurably. In chronological order: Sue Forsey, whose discovery of outstanding 1938 Grand National newsreel footage, involvement with National Hunt racing, and observations enriched this project; Jane Clarke, curator and founder of the Aintree Grand National Museum, whose passionate expertise steered me right in so many ways; and Mrs. Robert Leader, who so considerately shared memories and materials relating to her parents, Reginald and Nellie Hobbs, and her brave older brother, Bruce.

Everyone who read any part of the manuscript made the final result better in some way—starting with my agent, John Ware, whose perspicacity elevated the original outline, and concluding with my editor, Marc Resnick, whose enthusiasm and keen insight always help this writer find "another leg." Ann M. Ours, Letitia Grant, and Sally Grant all helped me consider, reconsider, and strengthen the approach. Dr. Robert M. Ours perceptively discussed world history and American football. Finally, extra credit to Michelle Tonkin for reading every word, using great analogies when something didn't add up, and cheering for parts that gave her chills. No writer could receive a better gift.

After Aintree, Bruce Hobbs swore that Battleship seemed to know where the finish line was and made sure to get up in time. The little horse has done it again. Though I did not consciously plan it, he got us to the finish in time for the seventy-fifth anniversary year of his epic Grand National win.

Dorothy Ours
Morgantown, West Virginia

Notes

Listing every source that contributed somehow to this book would consume so many pages that, like Carroll Bassett moving the inner "rail," I tried to take a shortcut.

Basic data on when, where, and how Battleship and other horses competed comes from *Daily Racing Form* chart books, *Record of Hunt Race Meetings in America*, *Racing Up-to-Date* (UK), and *Ruff's Guide to the Turf* (UK).

Unless otherwise noted, Hobbs family quotes and stories are drawn from *No Secret So Close: The biography of Bruce Hobbs, MC* by Tim Fitzgeorge-Parker, and Marion duPont Scott quotes and childhood descriptions are from *Montpelier: The Recollections of Marion duPont Scott* by Gerald Strine.

The William du Pont Sr. (1855–1928) Papers and William du Pont Jr. (1896–1965) Papers (Accession 2317) held at the Hagley Museum and Library (Wilmington, DE) provided a tremendous amount of primary material, including a vast number of letters and receipts, numerous news clippings, and various legal documents.

As well as providing a landscape of Mrs. Scott's life, James Madison's Montpelier (Montpelier Station, VA) houses the Marion duPont Scott scrapbooks (property of the National Trust for Historic Preservation) and a reconstruction of her famous Red Room. One can pay respects at

Battleship's grave; and I even was able to visit Battleship's barn and step inside his former stall.

Fellow researchers will find many of my sources within the Battleship, Carroll Bassett, and Marion duPont Scott files in the National Museum of Racing and Hall of Fame's library (Saratoga Springs, NY); National Sporting Library (Middleburg, VA); Robinson-Spangler Carolina Room, Charlotte Mecklenburg Library (Charlotte, NC); Bassett Room, Fine Arts Center of Kershaw County (Camden, SC); National Steeplechase Museum (Camden); and Liverpool Public Library (Liverpool, England).

Online archives yielded a tremendous amount of material, including birth records, census records, passport information, and passenger lists through Ancestry.com, plus a wealth of historical newspapers accessed through Genealogy Bank, Newspaper Archive, the *New York Times* digital archive, and the *Times* of London digital archive. DigitalNC (digitalnc .org) proved especially useful for information about Noel Laing, through *The Pilot* newspaper from Southern Pines, North Carolina. *Daily Racing Form* digital archives (kdl.kyvl.org/drf) and hard copies found in the Keeneland Library's extensive *DRF* collection (Lexington, KY) yielded much data and many useful articles. Online resources such as MapQuest and Google helped me with geography on both sides of the Atlantic. YouTube and other online sources provided newsreels of the 1928, 1933, and 1938 Grand Nationals at Aintree. James Madison's Montpelier holds especially good 1938 National footage, including Bruce Hobbs getting a leg up from his father and Battleship looking ready to take a crack at anyone.

To shorten the notes as much as possible, I use the following abbreviations.

PEOPLE AND HORSES

ARdP	Annie Rogers (Zinn) du Pont
B	Battleship
BB	Billy Barton
BH	Bruce Hobbs
CKB	Carroll Kinney Bassett
JFB	Jane Fowler Bassett
KJ	Kellsboro' Jack

MdPS	Marion duPont (Somerville) Scott
NL	Noel Laing
RH	Reginald Hobbs
RS	Randolph Scott
THS	Thomas H. Somerville
TM	Trouble Maker
WdP Jr.	William duPont Jr. (Willie or Will duPont)
WdP Sr.	William du Pont Sr.
WJS	Walter J. Salmon

INSTITUTIONS AND PUBLICATIONS

AR 1938	*American Race Horses, 1938.*
BBR	*The Bloodstock Breeders' Review,* London.
Blood-H	*The Blood-Horse,* Lexington, Kentucky.
DRF	*Daily Racing Form,* Chicago.
FAC	Fine Arts Center of Kershaw County.
FAClark	F. Ambrose Clark Scrapbook, 1933, National Sporting Library.
Hagley	Hagley Museum and Library, Middleburg, Virginia.
MdPS SB	Marion duPont Scott Scrapbooks (James Madison's Montpelier).
NMR	National Museum of Racing, Saratoga Springs, New York.
NSL	National Sporting Library, Middleburg, Virginia.
NSM	National Steeplechase Museum, Camden, South Carolina.
NYT	*New York Times.*
RTD	*Richmond Times-Dispatch.*
TR	*Thoroughbred Record,* Lexington, Kentucky.

For more information about books referenced by author, title, within these notes, see the bibliography.

PRELUDE

1 Hobbs family information primarily from Fitzgeorge-Parker, *No Secret So Close.*
1 Details of BH and B jumping Becher's Brook from several photographs in MdPS SB and in periodicals collection of the NSL.

2   RH riding like "a bat out of hell": "Aintree Still a Thrill for Oldest National Survivor Hobbs," *Independent* (London), April 2, 2003.

CHAPTER 1

4   F. Ambrose Clark description: Fitzgeorge-Parker, *No Secret So Close.*

4   Clark "one of the most skillful and daring" riders: "Amateurs in Flat Race," *NYT,* April 13, 1904.

5   Grand National course (Aintree) circa 1928 and earlier, Rubio (1908 winner): Munroe, *The Grand National.*

5   Tubed horses: "Silver Tubes for 'Roarers,'" *NYT,* March 1, 1896.

5   Pulling plug from tube: Captain H. S. Wilkins, Ord. Dept., "Billy Barton," *Field Artillery Journal,* November 1928.

6   Cork in pocket: "This Season's Fixtures: Fife," Northern Area Point to Point Website (UK), 2008.

6   Transatlantic phone hookup in Baltimore: "Baltimore Fans Hear How Billy Barton Ran," *NYT,* March 31, 1928.

6   Billy Barton's name: *Under the Lilacs,* Louisa May Alcott, 1878.

6   BB banned: "Billy Barton Owes Success to Temper," *NYT,* March 31, 1928; Tom Keyser, "A Lifetime of Stories Itching to Be Told: A Walking History Book of Local Racing, George Mohr . . . ," *Baltimore Sun,* August 22, 2000.

7   Howard Bruce, Master of the Elkridge Hounds: Anderson, *A Touch of Greatness.*

7   BB greeted handlers with pruned ears: Michael Ball, "Billy Barton and the Grand National," pookieschmookie.com/billy-barton.

7   BB never refused a jump: "Life-Sized Bronze Statue of Billy Barton Unveiled at Laurel," *Frederick (MD) News Post,* March 21, 1952.

7   BB begins steeplechasing (1926), wins three classics in three weeks: Anderson, *A Touch of Greatness*; Brown, *Aintree.*

7   BB prep races in England, BB (16.1 hands) one of smallest horses in the National: Captain H. S. Wilkins, Ord. Dept., "Billy Barton," *Field Artillery Journal,* November 1928.

8   1928 Grand National cloudy weather, Lord's Prayer: "Sport: Grand National," *Time,* April 9, 1928.

8   "Yankee horse leading," "Come on, Billy Barton!": Allen Raymond, "Billy Barton Falls, but Runs Second in Grand National," *NYT,* March 31, 1928.

9   Whistling sound from Tipperary Tim's tube: "Tracheotomy on a Horse," *NYT,* April 21, 1888.

9   Tim "never falls down": John Cottrell, "A Great Day at Aintree—and in Tipperary," *Sports Illustrated,* June 22, 1970.

9   BB falls at final fence: newsreel of 1928 Grand National at Aintree, YouTube.

9   Tipperary Tim took outside path: W. P. Dutton, "Amazing Scenes at the Grand National," *Pheon,* June 1928.

10   Easter Hero and BB at Canal Turn: "Billy Barton Jumped Fence and Horse, Too," *NYT,* April 6, 1928; Brown, *Aintree.*

11   The Jersey Act, Lexington blood "impure": major sources including J. B. Robertson, "American Mares: Their Breeding Value," *BBR,* April 1912; *Blood-H:* "The Jersey Act," November 1, 1930; "None So Blind—," June 13, 1936; Salvator [John

L. Hervey], "The Background of the Jersey Act," March 2, 1946; Salvator, "Setting the Stage for the Act," April 6, 1946; Salvator, "We Accept the Act Without a Fight," April 13, 1946.

12 Bill Tilden's Wimbledon: "Tilden Wins Tennis Title of Britain," *NYT*, July 4, 1920.

12 Walter Hagen's British Open: "Walter Hagen Wins British Open Title," *NYT*, June 24, 1922.

12 Stephen Sanford and Sergeant Murphy, American-bred and -owned horse "may carry off the Grand National": "Comment on Current Event in Sports: Turf," *NYT*, March 26, 1923.

12 Charles Schwartz and Jack Horner: "Grand National Won by American's Horse," *NYT*, March 27, 1926.

12 "The problem of aristocracy": "Sport: The Grand National," *Time*, March 31, 1923.

CHAPTER 2

See Bibliography, "du Pont History." Lucas R. Clawson (reference archivist, Hagley) shared perspectives on the DuPont Company's early days, including the family's commitment to facing danger alongside its employees. Primary material from Hagley includes letters written by WdP Sr. to his father, correspondence between WdP Sr. (England) to Charles King Lennig (United States), and letters to WdP Sr. from Louisa Gerhard du Pont and Ellen du Pont Irving. "An Afternoon with Martha duPont Remembering the duPonts of Bellevue" (Bellevue State Park, Wilmington, DE, May 15, 2011) added perspective on WdP Sr., ARdP, and their time at Bellevue Hall. James H. T. McConnell (grandson of WdP Jr.) shared the "du Pont vs. duPont" telephone book observation and punctured various myths.

13 MdPS shyness, WdP Sr. taking his children to cockfights: Raymond Woolfe Jr. interviewed by F. Turner Reuter Jr. for the NSL, December 4, 2009.

13 Numerous other sources calling MdPS "shy" include "The Year in Review," *Steeplechasing in America*, 1972, in which Snowden Carter said, "She is a quiet, shy lady."

14 The phrase "excruciating beauty": confidential source to the author, 2011.

19 Annie Rogers marriage to George Zinn (June 22, 1876), WdP Sr. and ARdP marriage (June 1, 1892), and death of Mary Rogers Zinn at age fifteen (January 19, 1893): Ancestry.com.

20 South Dakota divorce colony sources include "A Great State for Divorces," *NYT*, July 26, 1891; "The 'Colony' Must Go," *NYT*, December 24, 1892.

21 Arborfield Hall: Arborfield Local History Society.

21 WdP Sr. and ARdP 1893 return to U.S.: receipts, WdP Sr. Papers, Hagley.

23 Loseley Park information: owner Michael More-Molyneux email and loseleypark.co.uk.

25 "Virginia Farms Campaign," receipt for pony Bonnie Bell: WdP Sr. Papers, Hagley.

26   "We can cut through the back of Montpelier," polo ponies or hunt club: Strine, *Montpelier*.

26   View from Montpelier front door: author visits, 2008–2012.

26   Owner demanded $100 per acre: WdP Sr. Papers, Hagley.

26   What an average Virginia farm would cost: 1910 Virginia Census, Records Project: Virginia Census Record Information Online. For $74,000. Montpelier was his, WdP Sr. renovates: MdPS SB; Montpelier guided tour, 2008.

27   George Vanderbilt's Biltmore estate: biltmore.com.

27   William C. Whitney's Tudor mansion: "The Manse/William Collins Whitney Estate," Old Long Island (website), May 29, 2008.

28   Montpelier's mustard yellow stucco, "willow gate": MdPS SB.

29   Marie Antoinette foxhunting wearing breeches, "If you are riding like a man": "Marie Antoinette's Revolution in Equestrian Attire," Ingrid Mida, *Fashion Is My Muse* blog, October 16, 2008.

29   "Straddling a saddle I regard as an abomination," tricycle riding: "To the Editor: Cycling and Cycling," signed "Progress," *New York Herald*, August 1, 1893.

29   "Such violent exercise as riding," "parents do not appreciate what the results may be": De Hurst, *How Women Should Ride*.

30   "If the horse was as recent an invention as the bicycle": Dr. Samuel Caldwell, July 1901, quoted in *High Country News*, April 1, 2002.

CHAPTER 3

MdPS SB is a source for: Paper titled "Tumbling," MdPS with dogs, WdP Jr. marries Jean Liseter Austin, MdPS looked like a rock star, essay: "The Love of a Dog," and poem "Out in the Fields," by Elizabeth Barrett Browning.

34   MdPS riding astride: *The Official Horse Show Blue Book* (New York: J. W. Waring, 1915), NSL; MdPS SB.

35   The 1915 National Horse Show: "Horse Show to See Girls Riding Astride," *Ogden (UT) Standard*, October 30, 1915; "National Horse Show Season Here," *NYT*, November 6, 1915; "Star Horses in Ring," *Washington Post*, November 6, 1915; "'Gossip' Wins at the Horse Show," *Middletown (NY) Daily Times-Press*, November 8, 1915; "Jumping Thrills Horse Show Crowd," *NYT*, November 9, 1915; "Mounted Police Perform in Garden," *NYT*, November 10, 1915; "Championship Day in Horse Show," *NYT*, November 13, 1915.

37   Twenty-four Karat "perfect," Gossip "faulty" in championship: "Foremost Horses Compete for Championship Before Brilliant Crowd in Final Session of Garden Show," *New York Herald*, November 13, 1915.

37   Dallas Watson and his mule: "Foxcatcher," Alexander Mackay-Smith Papers, Box 1, NSL.

38   "A secure seat, light hands, a cool head": De Hurst, *How Women Should Ride*. MdPS "might chatter nervously or flinch away": Martha du Pont, Bellevue Hall, 2011.

38   MdPS "absolute confidence" with horses: Reuter, Raymond Woolfe Jr. interview, 2009.

39   MdPS grandfather Boss Henry and his dogs: Mosley, *Blood Relations*.

39   William duPont Jr.: "Obituary: William Du Pont, Jr.," St. Paul's School *Alumni Horae*, Spring 1966, Vol. 46, issue 1 (archives.sps.edu); William Bradford Williams, "The Ball Grain Explosives Co.," in *Munitions Manufacture in the Philadelphia Ordnance District* (Philadelphia: A. Pomerantz, Printers, 1921).

40   Altama: "Buys Land for Game: Senator du Pont's Brother to Have Georgia Preserve," *Washington Post*, March 4, 1914.

40   Marion duPont to her father re dogs, cattle, horses, and farm management issues of Montpelier: WdP Sr., Papers, Hagley.

CHAPTER 4

WdP Sr. Papers, Hagley, is the source for: MdPS on lookout for a good horse, tennis, billiard parties, "Want to school my race horse," doodled hearts on telephone pad, "Meeting of the Del[aware] Trust Co[mpany]," "I went down to the garden," WdP Sr. cartoon from 1925, MdPS "picked out a place for the flat track," "My bay mare is schooling so well with me," MdPS and THS at Pimlico Futurity, "big Parker gun," and "send some carnations."

43   1925 Nursery stud auction: many January–May 1925 articles from *DRF* and *NYT*; "The Nursery Sale" and "Turf Notes," *TR*, May 23, 1925. Other details in photo "Fair Play: $100,000," taken by Judge G .B. Kinkead, University of Kentucky, Kentuckiana Digital Library, kdl.kyvl.org.

44   Walter J. Salmon bio, Mereworth Farm: "Walter J. Salmon, Realty Man, Dead," *NYT*, December 26, 1953; report by Landmarks Preservation Commission, December 14, 2010: 500 Fifth Avenue Building, nyc.gov/html/lpc/downloads/pdf/reports/2427.pdf; "Turf Notes," *TR*, March 22, 1924; "Turf Notes," *TR*, November 29, 1924; Bowen, *Legacies of the Turf*.

47   Genetics research supported by WJS: "Carnegie Bureau to Mark 25th Year," *NYT*, May 26, 1929; Waldemar Kaempffert, "Mathematical Formula Based on Records of Thoroughbreds Is Devised for Rating Their Ability," *NYT*, May 6, 1934.

47   WJS and Harry H. Laughlin (HHL) correspondence: HHL Papers, Pickler Memorial Library, Truman State University, Kirksville, MO.

47   "Better analysis of the breeding of Thoroughbred Horses than anyone has yet succeeded in developing": HHL to WJS, September 23, 1924, HHL Papers.

49   WdP Jr. and Jean duPont farm near Rosemont, PA: Michael Yockel, "Last Hurrah for Historic Liseter Hall Farm," *Maryland Thoroughbred*, September 2005.

49   Replica of Montpelier at Newtown Square: Martha du Pont, Bellevue Hall, 2011.

49   MdPS first racehorse (Safety Catch): T. Beverly Campbell, "Saddle Horse Competition Feature at Orange Today," *RTD*, July 30, 1925.

50   MdPS mourned her favorite servant: Margaretta Fox gravestone.

50   Somervilles with five brothers: U.S. census.

50   Thomas Hugh Somerville: "Children of Samuel Wilson Somerville and Jennie Albert (Somerville) Hamilton," Rootsweb; 1920 U.S. census, World War I draft registration cards, 1917–1918; marriage license, Orange County, Virginia, Courthouse,

December 27, 1925; author interviews with Atwell Somerville, 2009, and Mae Helen Corbin, 2012.

51   Shopping for MdPS wedding to THS: receipts, WdP Sr. Papers, Hagley.

51   Best man Randy Scott: photo of MdPS wedding to THS (Mae Helen Corbin); wedding date not announced: "Virginia Weddings and Engagements," *RTD*, December 18, 1925.

52   RH travel and personal data: New York passenger lists, 1820–1957; England & Wales Marriage Index, 1916–2005; U.K. incoming passenger lists, 1878–1960.

54   WdP Sr. popular with workmen who renovated Montpelier: MdPS SB.

55   WdP Jr. creating Fair Hill, developing racecourses at Montpelier: WdP Sr. Papers, Hagley.

56   Phenolax (laxative and horse): Stephanie Winnett, "Take two Dover's and call me in the morning . . . ," *Industrious Historian* blog, September 29, 2010; "Their Past Performances: Entire Racing Career of Every Horse Named to Take Part in the Running of This Year's Kentucky Derby," *DRF*, April 18, 1920; "Phenolax Judged Champion Hunter," *NYT*, June 2, 1929; Strine, *Montpelier*.

56   WdP Jr. racing stable: "The Satrap Arrives Here," *NYT*, November 2, 1926; "Mars Beats Peanuts in the Washington . . . Fair Star Takes Selima," *NYT*, October 31, 1926; "Fair Star Is Winner of Pimlico Futurity," *NYT*, November 6, 1926; "Kentucky Derby Prospects," *DRF*, April 4, 1927.

57   ARdP wintered in London, "Merry Xmas to you Marion Tom," "Everything seems to be in order to go South": WdP Sr. Papers, Hagley.

57   Death of ARdP: "Obituary: Mrs. William du Pont," *NYT*, January 23, 1927; WdP Sr. Papers, Hagley; laid to rest in du Pont family cemetery: author visit to location.

CHAPTER 5

WdP Sr. Papers, Hagley, is a source for: "Sires heavy boned colts hunter types," horses at Montpelier, construction of Greenville (DE) house, THS "I've put aside some money," Safety Catch hurt, Drogheda "unsatisfactory," "I can't stand Miss Lee any longer," "Manton Manor," billiard room completed, making Montpelier racetrack permanent, hoping no frost, bring pajamas, long, newsy letters from MdPS to her father, WdP Sr. hospitalized with myocarditis, "My sincere wishes for an early recovery" (RS), and Hildreth Scott letter to WdP Sr. and his reply.

WdP Jr. Papers, Hagley, and The Satrap: several *DRF* articles, April 1–23, 1927, are sources for: Foxcatcher Farms certificate of incorporation, MdPS registered Montpelier Hunt, Crusader and WdP Jr. stud farm, WdP Jr. correspondence with Victor E. Schaumburg re Saratoga, and MdPS chose two fillies.

61   Transatlantic flight: Lindbergh, *The Spirit of St. Louis*.

64   Taking off into a tailwind: challengers101.com/Tailwind.html.

61   Man o' War's sire record: Faversham, *Great Breeders and Their Methods*.

62   Maurice Éphrussi, "landowner": Edmund de Waal, *The Hare with Amber Eyes: A Family's Century of Art and Loss* (New York: Farrar, Straus, 2010).

62   Éphrussi stable during war: *Annuaire de la Chronique du Turf* (Paris), 1914–1918.

62   Frousse: "Press Pack IV A Real Wonderland," Éphrussi de Rothschild Villa & Gardens, villa-ephrussi.com/en/home.

63   Quarantaine as broodmare in France: "Mères de Vainquers classées par Étalons" and "Liste Alphabêtique des Poulinières," *Revue des Éleveurs de Chevaux de Pur Sang*, 1920–1924; "Quoi Wins French Oaks," *TR*, June 9, 1923; "Important Races in France," *BBR*, 1923.

63   Quarantaine as broodmare in U.S.: *AR 1938*.

63   Famously hygienic foaling stalls: Thos. B. Cromwell, "Mereworth Stud," *Blood-H*, March 8, 1930.

67   WdP Jr. "mile-eating stride": Michael Yockel, "Last Hurrah for Historic Liseter Hall Farm," *Maryland Thoroughbred*, September 2005.

72   Death of WdP Sr.: "William Du Pont Dies in Georgia," *NYT*, January 21, 1928; "Retired Head of Duponts Is Dead," *San Antonio Express*, January 21, 1928; "Wm. Dupont, Wealthy Manufacturer, Dies While Reading Paper," *Danville (VA) Bee*, January 21, 1928.

72   MdPS 40 percent included Montpelier: Last Will and Testament of William du Pont, January 3, 1928 (draft in WdP Sr. Papers, Hagley; filed at Orange County, Virginia, Courthouse).

CHAPTER 6

WdP Jr. Papers, Hagley, is the source for: MdPS Thoroughbred race-horses circa 1929, MdPS "life racing colors," MdPS returned to Altama, WdP Jr. builds Saratoga stable, form letters with "Dear Sir" printed at the top, farrier Joseph E. Bell, Lost Agnes summer 1929 earnings, and "How you should word the letter."

74   Inventory of Montpelier (1928): WdP Jr. Papers, Hagley (filed at Orange County, Virginia, Courthouse).

74   ARdP jewelry value: WdP Sr. Papers, Hagley. "Washington Hopeful of Acquiring Madison Home at Montpelier as Show Place," *Elyria (OH) Chronicle-Telegram*, April 17, 1928.

78   Lost Agnes "sprang right to the front": "McLean Silks First as Nymph King Beats Folking," *NYT*, April 18, 1929.

78   Phenolax at Devon: "Phenolax Judged Champion Hunter," *NYT*, June 2, 1929.

80   DuPont Company prospers: "Du Pont Income Up $1,000,000 a Month," *NYT*, October 23, 1929.

80   Battleship "small and immature": *AR 1938*.

80   Wall Street crash "hurricane of liquidation": "Premier Issues Hard Hit," *NYT*, October 29, 1929.

80   DuPont dropped from 150 points to 70: "Financial Markets; Further Fall of Extreme Violence in Stocks," *NYT*, October 30, 1929.

81   DuPont diversification: "Diversifying Grows in Many Companies," *NYT*, November 24, 1929.

CHAPTER 7

84   Record low temperatures, morning snow flurries: "City Shivers in Grip of Its Coldest April 23," *NYT*, April 24, 1930.

84   MdPS fashion sense: photos in MdPS SB, *Polo* magazine, and other publications.

84   MdPS liked sapphires: jewelry insurance notes, WdP Jr. Papers, Hagley.

84   MdPS blue-gray eyes: Mae Helen Corbin; color photographs, Strine, *Montpelier*.

84   Havre de Grace horse auction (April 23, 1930): "Paddock Sale," *Blood-H*, May 3, 1930.

84   The company of two attractive young men: photos from many sources, including *Montpelier* and MdPS SB.

85   "Hell-raisers": author interview with NL nephew Noel Laing, 2011.

85   MdPS occasional soft words: friends and relatives, including Bill duPont; Charles Hatton, "Mrs. Scott an 'Old School' Devotee of Racing, Breeding" (Scrap Book, NSM Library).

85   NL no races to ride that week, CKB few tracks in the racing world: *Polo* magazine hunt-race schedules and results.

85   NL and CKB at home with silences, made a few words count: author interviews with Laing family members, 2011; Mike Clatterbuck, 2012; Raymond Woolfe Jr., 2012.

85   Laing family history from Ballina, Ireland, to United States; rolling hills reminded him of Ireland; "stealing peas from the garden"; charisma drew people near (characteristic of NL and his brother Douglas); college "a waste of time"; "very quiet hands": Dr. Aileen Laing.

87   Nicknamed him "Mouse": Pawling School yearbook via Dr. Aileen Laing. Additional Laing family records through Ancestry.com.

87   Ballast II rehabilitation: Katharine Lamont Boyd, "Obituary: Noel Laing," *Horse & Horseman*, December 1936 (also printed as "*Sans Peur et Sans Reproche*," *Southern Pines (NC) Pilot*, November 20, 1936).

88   The 1928 Warrenton Hunt Cup: "The Amateur Racing Season Ends," *Polo*, January 1929.

88   Goody Castle history: Sidney N. Shurcliff, "Sporting Estates at Camden, South Carolina," *The Sportsman*, June 1933.

88   "One may begin the day in the frosty dark": Smith, *Life and Sport in Aiken and Those Who Made It* (quoting David Gray).

89   Carroll Phillips Bassett biography: "Obituary: Carroll Bassett, 88, Consulting Engineer," *NYT*, January 10, 1952; a "quiet philanthropist," Beacon Hill mansion: "The History of the Bassetts" and "History of the 'Beacon,'" beaconhillclub.org.

89   Bassett coat of arms: John Burke, Esq., and John Bernard Burke, Esq., *Encyclopædia of Heraldry* (London: Henry G. Bohn, 1844); *Report of the Proceedings of the First Reunion of the Bassett Family Association of America*, 1897, digitized by Boston Public Library, archive.org.

89 Kinney coat of arms: Burke, *Encyclopædia of Heraldry*; James Parker, *"A Glossary of Terms Used in Heraldry,"* heraldsnet.org/saitou/parker/Jpglossf.htm#Finches.
89 CKB sat beautifully straight in rocking-horse saddle: photo in Bassett Room, FAC.
89 Westminster School yearbook profile: CKB Hall of Fame file, Library, NMR.
90 Colleges: Reuter, *Animal & Sporting Artists in America*.
90 Sculpture: displayed at FAC.
90 Inaugural Carolina Cup: "Carolina Cup Inaugural Drew Large Attendance," *Camden (SC) Chronicle*, March 28, 1930; "Ballast II Wins the Carolina Cup," *NYT*, March 23, 1930.
90 Springdale Racecourse (Camden): "Clem Visits Springdale," *Blood-H*, March 29, 1930; author visit, 2012.
91 MdPS hired NL: *AR 1938*.
91 CKB's unexpectedly deep voice: Mike Clatterbuck, 2012.
91 Roguish, gap-toothed grin: many photos, including MdPS SB and FAC.
91 Havre de Grace history: "All About Havre de Grace, MD," havredegracemd.com/pdf/History.pdf; "Gunning the Flats," Havre de Grace Decoy Museum, decoymuseum.com/exhibits.html.
91 Houseboat *Bugaboo*: "Death of a Racetrack," Bob Moore, Bowie racetrack file, NMR.
92 B "wouldn't have won the head-over-the-stall-door contest": Mason Grasty, quoted in Joe Clancy, "Battleship's Amazing Blast from the Past," *Mid-Atlantic Thoroughbred*, January 2008.
92 MdPS many trips looking at horses: 1918–1927 letters, WdP Sr. Papers, Hagley.

CHAPTER 8
93 American Flag and Crusader bigger than B: "Old Rosebud, Odds and Ends," *Blood-H*, January 4, 1930; Hervey, *Racing in America*.
93 Will Rogers at Preakness: Bryan Field, "Dr. Freeland Wins Preakness Stakes," *NYT*, May 11, 1929.
94 Arabians, Barbary and Turkish chargers, Irish Hobby horses, and Galloway ponies: Mackay-Smith, *Speed and the Thoroughbred*; Willett, *An Introduction to the Thoroughbred*; J. B. Robertson, "American Mares: Their Breeding Value," *BBR*, April 1912.
95 U.S. Vice President Curtis at Bowie races: "Sandy Ford First in Roslyn at Bowie," *NYT*, November 28, 1929.
95 Charles Curtis biography: "Charles Curtis, 31st Vice President (1929–1933)," senate.gov/artandhistory/history/common/generic/VP_Charles_Curtis.htm.
95 Battleship racing debut: "Sandy Ford First in Roslyn at Bowie," *NYT*, November 28, 1929.
96 Bayard, Florida, description: "Florida: Keeney," *Blood-H*, January 4, 1930.
96 Frank A. Keeney starts Keeney Park: "Marcus Loew Buys Brooklyn Theatres," *NYT*, June 10, 1926.
96 Betting on horse races illegal in Florida: "Turf Season Opens in Florida Today," *NYT*, December 14, 1929.
96 The envelope system: "Betting Methods in East," *DRF*, March 9, 1915.
97 Keeney Park opening day, legal action: "Four Records Set at Keeney Park," *NYT*, December 15, 1929.

97   B races at Keeney Park: "2 New Track Marks Set at Keeney Park," *NYT,* December 18, 1929.

97   Track shut down: "Seeks Writ to Stop Keeney Park Racing," *NYT,* December 17, 1929; "Officials Cancel Keeney Park Meet," *NYT,* December 21, 1929.

98   Track kitchens closed: "By-Product," *Blood-H,* February 22, 1930.

98   Dreary Christmas, Keeney "as popular . . . as the Mediterranean fruit fly": "Florida: Keeney," *Blood-H,* January 4, 1930.

98   "I believe that Florida should be the playground": "2 Florida Tracks Sure of Opening," *NYT,* December 22, 1929.

98   Joseph E. Widener investing in Hialeah, "the highest class of animals": "Miami," *Blood-H,* February 1, 1930.

98   MdPS and THS at Altama, WdP Jr. Papers, Hagley.

99   Hialeah racetrack description, winter 1930: "Hialeah Wasn't Much in 1925, But Look at It Now!" Hialeah racetrack file, NMR.

99   B races at Hialeah (Miami): "Rain or Shine Wins by 4-Length Margin," *NYT,* January 19, 1930.

99   Wasting energy at the starting line ("on his bad behavior, as usual, at the barrier"): "Battleship Wins Rowe Memorial," *Syracuse Herald,* April 6, 1930.

100 Florida Derby Trial: "Son of Man o' War Wins in Derby Test," *NYT,* March 5, 1930; "shades of the immortal Man o' War": "Man o' War's Son Runs Fine Race," *Massillion (OH) Evening Independent,* March 5, 1930. Florida Derby, "Battleship was dead": "Titus, 7 to 1, Takes Derby at Hialeah," *Syracuse Herald,* March 9, 1930. "what inferior cattle his opponents were": "Some General Items," *Blood-H,* March 22, 1930.

101 Woodlawn Vase: "Turf," *Time,* May 20, 1929.

101 Bowie racetrack description: Frances L. S. Dugan, "A Little Visit to Bowie," *Blood-H,* November 29, 1930.

101 James Rowe Memorial Handicap: "Battleship Wins Rowe Memorial: 20,000 Cheer Man o' War Colt Victory," *Syracuse Herald,* April 6, 1930; "Battleship Wins Bowie Park Purse," *Port Arthur (TX) News,* April 6, 1930.

103 Small woman framed by big fur collar (MdPS at Chesapeake Trial Purse): deduced from photos of MdPS at wet and chilly racing meets during this era.

103 Early starting gates (stall gate): Hervey, *Racing in America.*

103 Waite gate: "New Orleans: Lighter Construction," *Blood-H,* March 8, 1930; Old Rosebud, "Odds and Ends," *Blood-H,* June 7, 1930.

103 Rattling Waite gate at Havre de Grace (circa 1930): G. F. T. Ryall, "How About Starting Gates?" *Polo,* November 1935.

103 B damaged coronet band: *AR 1938.*

104 Recuperated at Mereworth Farm: "Chronicle Cover," *Chronicle of the Horse,* October 17, 1958.

104 Gallant Fox, Sande, and whip: William Braucher, "Veteran Jockey Sure to Give Woodward Colt a Great Ride," *Syracuse Herald,* May 4, 1930.

104 Sande received ten percent of Gallant Fox earnings: Audax Minor, "The Race Track," *New Yorker,* May 24, 1930.

104 WJS would sell MdPS "one in one season, the other on the next": "Mrs. Scott an 'Old School' Devotee of Racing, Breeding," Charles Hatton (Scrap Book, NSM Library).

105 TM failed as two-year-old at Havre de Grace: *DRF* charts.

105 Randolph Ortman greatly enjoyed riding TM out hunting: R. T. Corbell, "Horses and Hounds," *RTD*, February 2, 1930.

105 1930 Virginia Gold Cup: Myzk, *History and Origins of the Virginia Gold Cup.*

105 Ballast stepped in a hole, NL walked back to Bunree: Dr. Aileen Laing.

105 Wagon wheel rut, NL made Ballast lie down: "Accident Robs Noel Laing of Gold Cup Win," *Southern Pines (NC) Pilot,* May 9, 1930.

106 Drought, horses subsisted on hay, beef cattle shipped to market early: "The Drought," *Blood-H,* August 2, 1930.

106 MdPS, THS, Jennie and Hamilton Somerville to England, occupation "housewife": Passenger lists, Ancestry.com.

106 RMS *Mauretania,* "Wedding Cake": *Mauretania,* tyneandweararchives.org.uk/ mauretania/index.htm.

106 Eleanor Roosevelt article: Mrs. Franklin D. Roosevelt, "What Is a Wife's Job Today?" *Good Housekeeping,* August 1930.

107 MdPS offering a friend's favorite dishes: Mae Helen Corbin, 2012.

107 WdP Jr. expensive yearling: "Buys Top Colt," *Blood-H,* September 20, 1930; "Leg Broken, $35,000 Gone," *Blood-H,* November 15, 1930.

107 Max Hirsch "I just don't know what to say": WdP Jr. Papers, Hagley.

108 The 1930 Montpelier Hunt Races (Annapolis, TM): "Steeplechase Summaries: The Montpelier Meeting," *Polo,* December 1930.

108 Shipped down to Southern Pines: "Laing Horses Arrive for Southern Pines Season," *Southern Pines (NC) Pilot,* October 24, 1930.

108 B lameness: *AR 1938.*

108 X-ray history: including Alexi Assmus, "Early History of X Rays," *Beam Line,* Summer 1995; "The X Ray," *Logansport (IN) Pharos-Tribune,* May 24, 1924. January 1931 X-ray demonstration, diagnosis, and treatment: "American Year: Story of the Winner," *Blood-H,* April 2, 1938; "Veterinarians Convene at U.K.," *Lexington (KY) Herald,* January 30, 1931.

109 Shoeing to alleviate ringbone: *AR 1938;* "On the Case," with Farrier Ernest Woodward and Veterinarian Mark Silverman, April 25, 2012, hoofcareblogspot .com/2012/04/on-ringbone-case-one-piece-california.html.

CHAPTER 9

110 WJS opens 500 Fifth Avenue: "Brick Work Finished at 500 Fifth Avenue," *NYT,* September 7, 1930; "New Skyscraper Opened by Salmon," *NYT,* March 1, 1931.

110 "Government appropriations ten times as big": "By-Products: We Have Grown," *NYT,* March 8, 1931.

111 "Worse than the present world-wide depression": "Bruening Attacks German Fascists," *NYT,* March 9, 1931.

112 Annapolis "worth going miles just to look at": Stuart Rose, "The Spring Steeplechases," *Polo,* May 1931.

112 The 1931 Warrenton Hunt Cup (Grenadier Guard, Bluemont), "practically unbreakable fences," maybe timber racing heading in the wrong direction, "not much fun in having a horse killed," 1931 Billy Barton Steeplechase, "a better ride

than most of the entrants," eighteen horses "far too many for that small infield at Pimlico": Stuart Rose, "America's Great Steeplechase," *Polo*, June 1931.

112 BB demonstrated "that it is possible to fly timber jumps as if they were hurdles": Stuart Rose, "The Autumn Race Meetings," *Polo*, November 1930.

113 Montpelier Hunt's "rough and hilly country": "Montpelier Hunt," *The Sportsman*, October 1933.

114 Letter from MdPS: "The Horseman's Forum—Steeplechase Charts," *Polo*, June 1931.

114 "Sorry to tell you that 'Veronique' is dead": WdP Sr. Papers, Hagley.

114 Annapolis sculpture: "Horses in Bronze: Carroll K. Bassett," *Polo*, March 1932.

115 Ram's Head Stable (CKB and J. Spencer Weed): "Hall of Fame, Jockey: Carroll K. Bassett," National Museum of Racing, racingmuseum.org.

115 Ram's Head Stable silks: Bassett Room, FAC.

115 B arrives in Chicago: "Salmon Horses Coming," *DRF*, June 3, 1930; "Large Field for American Derby," *DRF*, June 16, 1931.

115 Workouts: *DRF*, June 16–26, 1931.

117 Leading money winner Sun Beau: "Sun Beau Triumphs, Passes Money Mark Set By Gallant Fox," *DRF*, August 2, 1931.

117 Hawthorne Handicap: "Plucky Play Victor, with Sun Beau Next," *NYT*, August 9, 1931.

118 Great Lakes Handicap: "Hygro Triumphs over Liberty Limited in $13,850 Hawthorne Juvenile Handicap," *NYT*, August 23, 1931.

118 "A great stretch run": "Battleship First in the Manos Purse," *NYT*, September 1, 1931.

119 Improving with age: "Man o' War's Kid Okay," *Galveston Daily News*, September 1, 1931.

119 Thoroughbred yearling market, WJS stallion roster for 1932: "Stud News," *Blood-H*, September 5, 1931.

119 Bayview Claiming Handicap: Bryan Field, "Gold Prize, 5 to 1, First by a Length," *NYT*, September 26, 1931.

119 Edgemere Handicap: "Widener's Curate and Woodward's Faireno Win Closing Features at Aqueduct," *DRF*, October 4, 1931.

119 "Raced well in spots and came again at the end": *DRF* chart.

119 MdPS buys Battleship: *AR 1938*; Strine, *Montpelier*.

120 Grasslands Steeplechase: Durham, *Grasslands*; "The Grasslands 'Chase," *Blood-H*, December 12, 1931; "Sport: Who Won," *Time*, December 14, 1931.

121 Safety: "40 Players Killed in Football Season," *NYT*, December 6, 1931.

121 Brüning radio address, situation in Germany: German Propaganda Archive, Calvin College, Grand Rapids, MI, calvin.edu/academic/cas/gpa/hitleranbruening .htm; "Answer Given Hitler Group," *Bradford (PA) Era*, December 9, 1931; "Mass Meetings Are Banned in Germany Until Jan. 3, 1932," *Oshkosh Daily Northwestern*, December 9, 1931.

CHAPTER 10

WdP Jr. Papers, Hagley, is a source for: MdPS and THS quail hunting with WdP Jr., WdP Jr. family illnesses, Altama (game birds retreated into the swamps, deer poachers, "absentee landholder," decision to sell).

123 WJS could breed five mares to B: *AR 1938*.

123 MdPS sent B to Montpelier: Strine, *Montpelier*; NL ledger, courtesy of Dr. Aileen Laing.

123 Special shoeing for B by Joseph E. Bell: *AR 1938*; Strine, *Montpelier*.

124 B corrective shoe: viewed while on loan to "Hall of Fame Heroes," NMR.

125 Essie Seavey Lucas paintings (including MdPS with Phenolax and hounds at Montpelier): Worthpoint.com/worthopedia.

125 Illness and death, "a nervous breakdown": obituary, *The Horse*, March–April 1932, p. 23.

125 Oconomowoc Health Resort, "a homelike atmosphere": Henry M. Hurd, et al., *The Institutional Care of the Insane in the United States and Canada*, Vol. 3 (Baltimore: Johns Hopkins University Press, 1916).

125 MdPS "a very compassionate person": Mae Helen Corbin, 2012.

127 Carolina Cup emblem and motto: Ernie Trubiano, *The Carolina Cup: 50 Years of Steeplechasing & Socializing* (Columbia, SC: Ernie Trubiano, 1982); Hope Cooper, NSM.

127 1932 Carolina Cup and Springdale Steeplechase: "Carolina Cup Won by Trouble-maker," *NYT*, March 27, 1932; Stuart Rose, "The Hunt Races," *Polo*, May 1932. "Two or three times his speed nearly sent him to the ground," "It's all in the game," "one of the hardest and fastest three miles," "the most surprised man in the world," Fox Movietone newsreel camera: "Thousands of Horse-Lovers See Troublemaker Win Cup," *Camden (SC) Chronicle*, April 1, 1932.

128 "An occasion of unusual brilliance": "Hotels Were Filled for Annual Races," *Camden Chronicle*, April 1, 1932.

129 1932 Maryland Hunt Cup: "Troublemaker Captures Maryland Hunt Cup in Record Times Before a Crowd of 28,000," *NYT*, May 1, 1932.

129 MdPS had attended Maryland Hunt Cup several times: MdPS SB. "Larger fields starting in the Maryland; but none better," Downey Bonsal's shoulder went out during the race, Downey flicked a look to the right, NL "sat down to ride for his life," NL felt he could get by Brose Hover anytime: Stuart Rose, "Maryland's Great Race," *Polo*, June 1932.

130 Bonsal riding "heavily bandaged": Rossell, *The Maryland Hunt Cup*.

130 Third fence nicknamed "Union Memorial": several sources, including William B. Streett, "The Hunt Race Meetings," *The Sportsman*, June 1933.

131 NL tying a jaunty scarf around his throat: trophy presentation photo.

132 1932 Maryland Hunt Cup triptych by CKB: displayed at FAC.

132 Red Room: photos and background in Strine, *Montpelier*; "Christmas at Montpelier," *Fredericksburg (VA) Free Lance-Star*, December 23, 2001; actual (relocated) room on display at the Visitor Center, James Madison's Montpelier.

133 1932 Billy Barton Steeplechase: "Billy Barton Chase Annexed by Tereus," *NYT*, May 13, 1932; photo of mud-soaked CKB, FAC.

133 MdPS "dressed in her racing colors" at Brookline: "Tack Room Talk," *Boston Herald*, June 16, 1932.

133 CKB consulted WdP Jr.: WdP Jr. Papers, Hagley.

133 NL and Annapolis fall in Saratoga race: Bryan Field, "Speed Boat, 8 to 1, Victor by a Length," *NYT*, August 26, 1932.

134 TM sailed for England: photo caption for ". . . Troublemaker, who sailed for England August 12 . . . ," "News of the Horseman's World," *Polo,* September 1932.

134 That April, B had moved from Montpelier up to Bunree: NL ledger, Dr. Aileen Laing.

CHAPTER 11

135 Description of B's barn at Bunree Farm, NL would jump horses over pasture fences: Dr. Aileen Laing.

135 B feisty with strangers but pleasant with familiars: *AR 1938.*

136 Grand National born from real conditions: Bird, *A Hundred Grand Nationals.*

136 Plowed land dwindled to a ceremonial strip: "Course at Aintree Hardest in World," *NYT,* March 31, 1928.

136 Qualifying hunters: "Hunter's Qualifications" blank certificate, circa 1931, Alexander Mackay-Smith Papers, Box 8, NSL.

136 Story of Trillion, "I will give you a certificate," "keep behind a hundred yards or so": "Qualifying Hunters," Harry Worcester Smith Papers, Box 7, NSL.

137 NL's training process, "fairly hunted" his racehorses: Dr. Aileen Laing.

137 Captain Sterling Loop Larrabee biography, "Why in hell don't you go up in Rappahannock": "The History of Old Dominion Hounds," as remembered by Sterling Larrabee, MFH, old-dominion-hounds.com/wp/about-odh-2/.

137 "If you want to hunt in the bushes": General William Mitchell, "A Tribute to Sterling Loop Larrabee, Master of the Old Dominion Foxhounds," *Polo,* January 1935.

138 "After about seven miles of state road": Donald Scott Sharpe, "The Happy Hunting Grounds," *Saddle and Bridle,* n.d. [after 1934], Sterling Larrabee Papers, NSL.

138 Old Dominion Hounds' obstacles and terrain: "Chronicle Cover," *Chronicle of the Horse,* October 17, 1958; "History" and "The Old Dominion Country," Gordon Smith Files, NSL.

138 "For the most part, these obstacles are stiff": Sterling Larrabee, "Virginia Hunting . . . Old Dominion Runs Featured by Faster Pace, Better Fox and Stiffer Fences," *Washington Times,* September 20, 1933.

138 TM had done nothing much for several weeks: "Topics of English Turf: Crack U.S. 'Chaser Arrives," *Singapore Straits Times,* September 6, 1932 (dateline August 23).

138 NL departure for England: photo titled "To Ride in 'National,'" clipping from unknown newspaper via Dr. Aileen Laing.

139 Shirley Banks: age, "Mulatto," father's farm ownership, able to read and write: 1920 U.S. census. "Trainer—S. Banks": [Harry] Kirkover Papers, NSM Library.

139 Handling B while NL in England: *AR 1938. Maybe* Banks could have ridden behind the hunt as a groom: speculation by Dr. Aileen Laing.

139 CKB racing record, autumn 1932: "Joint Race Meeting of the Foxcatcher Hounds and Montpelier Hunt," *Polo,* December 1932; Crawford Burton, "The Hunt Races," *Polo,* December 1932; various *Polo* result charts.

139 River Club description: "River Club Interests Society," *NYT,* May 4, 1930; Michael Henry Adams, "Great Houses of New York: The River Club," huffingtonpost.com, October 27, 2009.

139 Jane Fowler age: Social Security Death Index.

139 Jane Fowler debut: "Dinner Dance Given for 2 Debutantes," *NYT*, November 27, 1932.

139 Jane Fowler physical description: photos including "Society Folk at Opening Day of Country Club Races," *Boston Herald*, June 16, 1933; "Miss Jane Fowler to Become Bride," *NYT*, May 13, 1934; "Miss Jane Fowler Wed in New Jersey," *NYT*, July 27, 1934; photo walking beside Carroll Bassett, FAC.

140 B's late arrival at Southern Pines: "The Week at Southern Pines," *Southern Pines (NC) Pilot*, December 16, 1932.

140 "Guard rails have not been erected": Virginius Dabney, "New Skyline Drive Opened in Virginia," *NYT*, November 13, 1932.

140 MdPS gives Mt. Athos to THS, bought in 1929 for $25,000 cash: Orange County, Virginia, Courthouse.

141 "I am now settled on Altama," MdPS activities in England: WdP Jr. Papers, Hagley.

141 *Berengaria* history: ocean-liners.com/ships/imperator.asp; liverpoolmuseums .org.uk/maritime/collections/liners/berengaria/.

141 Somervilles' travel details and occupations: Passenger lists, Ancestry.com.

141 MdPS investments: finding aid for WdP Sr. Papers, Hagley.

141 Themes of *The Divorcee* and *Week-end Marriage*: author viewings.

142 TM racing in England: "American-Bred Nag Far Back in Test," *San Antonio Light*, January 17, 1933; "Trouble Maker Finishes Last in Derbyshire Handicap Chase," *NYT*, February 22, 1933.

142 "Was still jumping the last fence" and "racing with his ears pricked": Charles A. Smith, "12 U.S. Entries at Aintree," *Chester (PA) Times*, February 22, 1933.

142 "Trouble Maker is not doing well": Delmege Trimble, "Trouble Maker Feared out of Grand National," *RTD*, March 10, 1933.

CHAPTER 12

Dozens of United Kingdom and Irish newspaper clippings, magazine articles, and photographs describing the 1933 Grand National are found in the F. Ambrose Clark Scrapbook (1933) at the National Sporting Library. Other sources include "Pete Bostwick, Tossed at Famous Becher's Brook, Tells of Thrills," *RTD*, March 25, 1933; Charles Sumner Bird Jr., "The Grand National Steeplechase, 1933," *The Sportsman*, May 1933; "National 25 to 1 Winner's Record Time," *Liverpool Echo*, March 24, 1933; "Kellsboro Jack Wins National," *Lowell (MA) Sun*, March 24, 1933; "Thought Horse Unlucky," *NYT*, March 25, 1933.

144 CKB asked Banks to school B, "probably 16½ minutes over each fence": *AR 1938*.

145 B "noble-looking," "as classy a ride as a horse could wish": "Ray Wolfe [sic], Riding Hotspur, Winner for a Second Time," *Camden (SC) Chronicle*, February 24, 1933.

145 Spectators laughing: Strine, *Montpelier*.

145 Woolfe glanced over and saw B's belly: Reuter, Raymond Woolfe Jr. interview, 2009; author, 2012.

146 Mrs. F. Ambrose (Florence) Clark's appearance: *London Evening Standard,* March 25, 1933; photos from FAClark SB, NSL.

146 Managing her own steeplechasing stable: Bryan Field, "Mrs. Clark, Noted Sportswoman, Personally Directs Own Stable," *NYT,* March 25, 1933.

146 Buying Kellsboro' Jack, credited Mr. Clark himself: "American Woman's 'National' Win," *Daily Telegraph* (London), March 25, 1933.

146 Mr. B. M. Slocock pointed out this particular Jackdaw colt: "Kellsboro' Jack on View at Melton Hunt," *Daily Mail* (London), March 31, 1933; "The Early History of Kellsboro' Jack and His Dam," *Sporting Life,* April 8, 1933.

146 BH belief that RH found KJ: Fitzgeorge-Parker, *No Secret So Close.*

146 Leaping bullock fences: "Kellsboro' Jack Visits His Bedridden Trainer," *Nottingham Evening News,* March 31, 1933.

146 Dudley Williams had partnered KJ to all of his wins so far: "Bostwick Keen over Mount in Grand National," *Otsego (NY) Farmer & Republican,* February 10, 1933.

146 Pete Bostwick biography: Bryan Field, "Players of the Game: Pete Bostwick— Grand National Aspirant," *NYT,* January 26, 1932.

146 Weighed 125 pounds: "G. H. Bostwick Back from Races Abroad," *NYT,* January 14, 1932.

146 "World's best amateur rider," KJ faltered and Pete began looking elsewhere: S. W. Cousans, "Aintree Gives Mrs. Clark Her Heart's Desire," *Spur,* May 1933.

147 Schooled KJ: "Bostwick Keen over Mount in Grand National," *Otsego (NY) Farmer & Republican,* February 10, 1933.

147 Dud Williams made sure the trainer knew: "Fencing Errors of Golden Miller . . . Faith in His Mount," *Sporting Life,* March 25, 1933.

147 RH named as Chadd's Ford rider, injured less than a week before the National: "Grand National Acceptors," *Singapore Straits Times,* March 16, 1933.

148 Dusty Foot "safe jumper of the slow, but sure, type": *DRF,* March 24, 1933.

148 "I anticipate a thrilling ride": "Trouble Maker Held Lightly," *Poughkeepsie Eagle-News,* March 23, 1933.

148 TM "doubtful" starter: Bryan Field, "Strong U.S. Entry in Grand National," *NYT,* March 19, 1933.

148 NL's parents arrived in London: Passenger lists, Ancestry.com.

148 NL "didn't honestly know": "Two Rated at 9–1 for Aintree Race," *NYT,* March 22, 1933.

149 Pete Bostwick says, "They're big—even bigger than I thought," Dusty Foot at sixty-six to one and TM as high as two hundred to one, "not all will finish": "American Mount Aintree Favorite," *Poughkeepsie Eagle-News,* March 24, 1933.

149 "Mingled shoulder to shoulder": "A Ladies' Event," *Liverpool Echo,* March 24, 1933.

153 TM "climbed over the last fence on his nerve": Paul Brown, "The Grand National," *Polo,* May 1933.

154 KJ a couple years younger than average National winner: "The average age of the ninety-five winners of the Grand National since 1839 was eight years, ten months,"

Charles Sumner Bird Jr., "The Grand National Steeplechase, 1933," *The Sportsman*, May 1933.

154 KJ never would enter the Grand National again: "Kellsboro' Jack to Rest on His Laurels; Will Never Run in 'National' Again," *Swindon Evening Advertiser*, April 6, 1933.

155 KJ at Melton War Memorial Hospital: "Kellsboro' Jack Visits His Bedridden Trainer," *Nottingham Evening News*, March 31, 1933; "Kellsboro' Jack," *Birmingham Gazette*, April 1, 1933; "Kellsboro' Jack's Hospital Visit," *News Chronicle* (London), April 1, 1933.

CHAPTER 13

William B. Streett, "Brookline and Raceland: The Hunt Race Season Climax," *The Sportsman*, July 1933, is the source for: Bryan Trophy, Ladies' Race, Andy Fowler bought Peacock, Rosy Covert busted through hedge, CKB charged B at man holding tape, Annapolis racing twice in one afternoon ("This is something I had heard of"), "Annapolis ran a corking good race both times," and CKB won the draw.

156 Malvern Hill Steeplechase: "Entries for Deep Run Hunt Club Races at Curles Neck," *RTD*, April 7, 1933; "The Hunt Races," *Polo*, May 1933; Delmege Trimble, "Jumping Jack Leads Throughout to Win Deep Run Hunt Cup" and "Mrs. Somerville Scores a Triple Victory in First Three Starts," *RTD*, April 9, 1933; Delmege Trimble, "Deep Run Race Chart," *RTD*, April 9, 1933.

157 "A pony, very powerful," what chance he had: Dr. John M. Hughes, "Keeping Up with Joncs," *RTD*, July 17, 1938.

158 Preston Morris Burch: Bowen, *Masters of the Turf.*

158 "He was a teacher": Oscar Otis, "Trainer Burley Parke Recalls His Early Days on Race Track," *DRF*, June 27, 1964.

158 Linstead Steeplechase: "Senado Wins Steeplechase," *DRF*, May 2, 1933; "Pimlico Results," *Oakland (CA) Evening Tribune*, May 2, 1933.

158 The 1933 Billy Barton Steeplechase: "Hunt Set Out in Force," *DRF*, May 12, 1933; "Mrs. T. H. Somerville Captures Third Billy Barton 'Chase in Row," *Boston Herald*, May 12, 1933; "Battleship Wins Chase at Pimlico," *NYT*, May 12, 1933.

158 BB as grand as a king: William B. Streett, "The Other Hunt Races," *The Sportsman*, July 1933.

159 MdPS beautiful stationery, helping her brother finance work relief projects: WdP Jr. Papers, Hagley.

159 Wedding of Harriet Hildreth Scott: "Four Weddings of Prominent Richmonders Climax Past Week's Social Events," *RTD*, June 11, 1933.

159 Alice Cole: "Miss Alice Cole Will Be Bride of John Hughes," *RTD*, June 4, 1933; Mary Binford Hobson, "Richmonders Sail June 10 for England," *RTD*, June 6, 1933.

160 Racing at The Country Club: "Old Racetracks Around Boston," September 27, 2010, hubtrotter.blogspot.com/2010/09/old-racetracks-around-boston.html; massmoments.org/moment.cfm?mid=18, tcclub.org/club/scripts/public/public.asp.

160 "Two great horses which stand out prominently": P. J. Cullen, "Man o' War Get in Races Here," *Boston Herald*, June 9, 1933.

160 NL would handle MdPS timber horses: *AR 1938*.

160 CKB weighing less than 140 pounds: Wilf P. Pond, "Turf, Field and Show Ring," *Spur*, April 1933 (gives CKB weight as 136 pounds).

160 Jane Fowler at The Country Club races: "Society Folk at Opening Day of Country Club Races," *Boston Herald*, June 16, 1933.

160 "What would be the feelings": Curtiss and Heard, *The Country Club*.

161 MdPS wouldn't wear slacks: photos in MdPS SB and Strine, *Montpelier*, plus Mae Helen Corbin testimony ("I never saw a pair of pants in her closet").

161 "Automobile road" across Country Club racecourse: "Tack Room Talk," *Boston Herald*, June 16, 1933.

162 National Hunt Cup finish photo: "Highlights in Thrilling Opening Day Races at Brookline," *Boston Herald*, June 16, 1933.

162 "One of the most thrilling finishes": P. J. Cullen, "Battleship and Spar Win National Hunt and Chamblet Memorial Chases," *Boston Herald*, June 16, 1933.

163 "Raising Thoroughbreds": William C. Phillips, "Virginia Breeding Farm Home of Mrs. Scott," *Morning Telegraph* (now *DRF*), August 1, 1957.

164 Best liniment for Racketeer's legs: WdP Jr. Papers, Hagley.

164 The 1933 Saratoga yearling sales: "Gallant Fox Colt Draws Top Price," *NYT*, August 12, 1933.

164 Eastern Horse Club Hunters' Steeplechase Handicap "very deep in mud": Bryan Field, "Sun Celtic, 4–1, Beats Some Pomp; Battleship Takes Chase," *NYT*, August 24, 1933.

165 Meadow Brook Hunt Cup, NL fell ill: "Meadow Brook Cup to Trouble Maker," *NYT*, October 1, 1933; William B. Streett, "Autumn Blood and Thunder," *The Sportsman*, November 1933.

165 Erdenheim Cup, Bedminster Chase, MdPS America's leading hunt racing owner: *Record of Hunt Race Meetings in America, Vol. III*.

165 Man o' War tensing his abdominal muscles: " 'Blowing Up' a Girthing Myth," *Equus*, 2012.

166 RS sailed to England with a buddy: Passenger lists, Ancestry.com.

166 Groom became ill: "Cary Grant Has Operation," *Dallas Morning News*, December 15, 1933; "Cary Grant Returns from Visit to England," *Boston Herald*, February 24, 1934.

166 RS spends Christmas week at Montpelier: "Gordonsville," *RTD*, December 24, 1933.

166 Visit in Augusta, Georgia: "Personal Mention," *Augusta Chronicle*, April 5, 1931.

166 "A Thrilling Drama!": ad for *Women Men Marry*, *Springfield (MA) Daily Republican*, April 30, 1931.

166 No plans to marry Vivian Gaye: George Shaffer, "Hot from Hollywood," *Seattle Daily Times*, January 21, 1934.

166 Joke about his struggles: numerous 1930s RS interviews.

167 "Social lion" from Woodberry Forest School: *Fir Tree* (yearbook), quoted by Cathy L. Eberly, director of marketing and communications, Woodberry Forest School.

167 MdPS rents handsomely simple Camden house: WdP Jr. Papers, Hagley.

167 St. Augustine golf tournament: "M'Carthy Defeats Dann in Club Golf," *NYT*, January 31, 1934; "M'Carthy Upsets Aycock by 2 and 1," *NYT*, February 1, 1934.

167 MdPS sidesaddle on racehorse Wild Son: photo, *Record of Hunt Race Meetings in America*, 1933.

169 "Swashbuckling gentlemen jockeys," unclaimed since inaugural Maryland Hunt Cup, "Up, gentlemen, please": Charles Houston, "The Sport Critic," *RTD*, April 27, 1934.

169 "It was a perfect day," blood trail back to fence thirteen, "as big as your two hands and deep": Stuart Rose, "The Greatest Maryland," *Polo*, June 1934.

169 Running of the Maryland Hunt Cup: William B. Streett, "The Maryland Hunt Cup and the Hunt Races," *The Sportsman*, June 1934; Robert F. Kelley, "Maryland Hunt Cup Won by Captain Kettle," *NYT*, April 29, 1934.

169 Surprised backward glance: MdPS SB.

170 Hustled TM to a nearby barn: "Sewing up Trouble Maker—Heisers Barn M.H.C. '34," Paul Brown, *Ups and Downs* (New York: Scribner, 1936).

170 Plastic surgeon: Rossell, *The Maryland Hunt Cup*.

170 "Put a few stitches in this thing" through "He's sewing up Trouble Maker": "Notes on Horses and Horsemen," *Polo*, July 1934.

170 MdPS at age forty: summer 1934 photographs; Emily Post, "Good Taste Is Discussed by Mrs. Emily Post; Women of Forty Resent the Implication That They Are Old," *RTD*, May 25, 1934.

171 Billy Barton Steeplechase: "Our Friend Furnishes Upset," *DRF*, May 11, 1934; "Post and Paddock: At the Big Tracks," *Polo*, July 1934.

171 Jane Fowler agreed to marry CKB: "Miss Jane Fowler to Become Bride," *NYT*, May 13, 1934.

CHAPTER 14

172 Memorial Day 1934 (New York Harbor): "Fleet Will Steam up Bay Thursday," *NYT*, May 27, 1934.

172 "Greatest assemblage of naval vessels," "The sight of the warships," "a deep bass roar": Charles W. Hurd, "Roosevelt Stirred as Ships Pass; Signals 'Well Done' to the Navy," *NYT*, June 1, 1934.

173 Navy signal lights: "22,000 Bluejackets Swarm into City," *NYT*, June 1, 1934.

173 Roslyn Steeplechase with sailors "having a fairly enjoyable time": J. C. Cooley, "Post and Paddock," *Polo*, July 1934.

173 B an "old campaigner": "Cito, 6–1, Scores in Bowman Chase," *NYT*, June 2, 1934.

174 A photograph told everything: MdPS SB.

174 "Only second- or third-raters": Frederick Stuart Greene, "Post and Paddock: At the Big Tracks," *Polo*, July 1934.

174 Aiken Hunters' Steeplechase: *AR 1938*.

174 Inception "ripe" to win today: Touch and Go, "Horse Shows and Hunts," *New Yorker*, June 16, 1934.

175 Challenge trophy unclaimed for nineteen years: Arthur Siegel, "Schooling of 75 Horses Begins Today at The Country Club Just About Time Average Citizen Is Ready to Rise," *Boston Herald*, June 14, 1934.

175 "You ask them 'What horse is that?'," CKB delayed by fog: "Tuckerman Irked by Incognitos," *Boston Herald*, June 15, 1934.

175 MdPS looked summery, "Succeeded Where Men Failed": photo captioned "Succeeded Where Men Failed," *Boston Herald*, June 17, 1934.

175 CKB "tucked the tips of his ears": Ed Costello, "Liverpool Magnet at The Country Club; Mrs. Somerville Has Corner on Silver," *Boston Herald*, June 17, 1934.

175 JFB and her cousin watched: Marion Lyndon, "Smart Throng at Clyde Park," *Boston Herald*, June 17, 1934.

175 The National Hunt Cup: Arthur Siegel, "Battleship Wins National Hunt," *Boston Herald*, June 17, 1934; "Battleship Wins Brookline Chase," *NYT*, June 17, 1934.

176 B "fenced beautiful": *Record of Hunt Race Meetings in America*, Vol. IV, chart.

176 NL "dazed for about an hour": "Battleship Wins National Hunt," *Boston Herald*, June 17, 1934.

176 West family hosting a special guest, "because the rider wore a brown shirt": "Harvard Will Not Award Degree to Dr. Hanfstaengl," *Boston Herald*, June 19, 1934.

176 Hanfstaengl needed special permission, fifteen hundred protesters, "Down with Hitler," protesters "mostly Communists": "Hanfstaengl Here, Avoids Foes at Pier," *NYT*, June 17, 1934.

176 Posters sprouted in Harvard Yard, "will be normal before long" through "propelled him out of the yard": "Honors Are Denied for Hanfstaengl," *NYT*, June 19, 1934.

177 "What did you think of your welcome?," six Boston policemen: "Hitler's Aide Arrives Here; Met by Police," *Boston Herald*, June 18, 1934.

178 CKB only rider with four wins in one day at Brookline: Arthur Siegel, "Carroll Bassett, Sculptor-Horseman, Rides Four Winners at Country Club," *Boston Herald*, June 19, 1934; "Four Hunt Victors Ridden by Bassett," *NYT*, June 19, 1934.

178 MdPS and CKB "had a heart-to-heart talk": Arthur Siegel, "Carroll Bassett, Sculptor-Horseman, Rides Four Winners at Country Club," *Boston Herald*, June 19, 1934.

179 CKB "smoking a huge cigar": "Post and Paddock: Eastern Horse Club," *Polo*, July 1934.

179 CKB and JFB wedding: "Miss Jane Fowler Wed in New Jersey," *NYT*, July 27, 1934; "Recent Activities of Boston Society," *Boston Herald*, July 31, 1934.

179 Orange County Horse Show, Dr. John Hughes and wife Alice Cole at Montpelier: "Orange Show to Take Place on July 27–28," *RTD*, July 12, 1934.

179 THS and MdPS stayed with Dr. and Mrs. Hughes: "Miss Richard to Lead Hunt Ball," *RTD*, April 1, 1934.

179 MdPS at Saratoga: WdP Jr. Papers, Hagley.

179 WdP Jr. racing meet at Fair Hill: "America's Great Course," *Polo*, October 1934.

179 "It is impossible to say too many good things," "as near perfect as possible": William B. Streett, "Hunt Racing's Good Fortune: William du Pont, Jr., Opens a Magnificent New Course at Fair Hill, in Maryland," *Polo*, October 1934.

180 "The course of tomorrow": William B. Streett, "The Fall Hunt Races," *Polo*, November 1934.

180 Humphrey Finney visits MdPS, "My highly competent guide" through "the Hackney world of the past": H. S. Finney, "Montpelier (Little Visits to the Studs)," *Blood-H*, September 15, 1934.

181 Grand National at Belmont Park: Cornelia Prime, "Eastern Gossip," *TR*, September 1934.

182 B's forelock, mane, and tail neatly braided, his neck lathered: published photos plus MdPS SB. "Frivolous" objection: "Battleship's Grand National," *Blood-H*, September 22, 1934.

183 Futurity and Jockey Club Gold Cup: Cornelia Prime, "Eastern Gossip," *TR*, September 22, 1934; Bryan Field, "Chance Sun, 8–1, Defeats Balladier by 4 Lengths in the $98,330 Futurity," *NYT*, September 16, 1934; "Chance Sun Captures Belmont Futurity Race," *Springfield (MA) Republican*, September 16, 1934; Thomas H. Noone, "Rich Race Won by Chance Sun," United Press, September 16, 1934.

183 CKB told MdPS "you've got to run this horse in England": Reuter, Raymond Woolfe Jr. interview, 2009.

184 Meadow Brook Cup, "worst day one could possibly imagine": William B. Streett, "The Fall Hunt Races," *Polo*, November 1934.

184 TM thought over the hill, "Trouble Maker is no antique yet": "Noel Laing Rides Old Trouble Maker to Win," *Southern Pines (NC) Pilot*, November 2, 1934.

184 B's tendon injury, Burch knew that MdPS would want best for B, after a month B's leg cool and firm, expert from Baltimore line-fired B, Dr. McCarthy said, MdPS debated the problem: *AR 1938*.

185 B not ridden for a year: Burch, *Training Thoroughbred Horses*.

185 THS's ailing father died: "S. W. Somerville's Funeral Is Held," *RTD*, December 11, 1934.

185 Galloping steeplechasers at private training track with CKB and JFB, MdPS riding Billy Bozo: Bert Clark Thayer photo, "A Day in Camden," *Polo*, March 1935.

CHAPTER 15

187 *"National Velvet"* a Book-of-the-Month Club selection: "Wunderkind," *Time*, April 29, 1935.

187 A wispy, dark-eyed girl: newspaper photos of Mary Hirsch, April 1935.

187 Applied for Jockey Club license, "No express prohibition in the rules": Bryan Field, "Miss Hirsch Asks Jockey Club for a License to Train Horses," *NYT*, February 8, 1933.

188 Licensed in Illinois: "License to Miss Hirsch Upsets Racing Precedent," *NYT*, July 29, 1934.

188 Max Hirsch best breakfast at Saratoga: "Trainer," *Time*, April 15, 1935; Stanley D. Petter Jr., Field Horne interview, 2010.

188 "Certainly, no opposition": "Miss Hirsch Licensed as Trainer by Stewards of the Jockey Club," *NYT*, April 3, 1935.

188 MdPS a worthy candidate: "Woman Pioneers New Field and Wins Recognition as Trainer," *Zanesville Signal*, April 7, 1935.

188 Remarked upon by the *Wall Street Journal*, "There she goes, always fixing her horses" through "a thorough sportswoman": "With Sportsmen Afield and Afloat," *Wall Street Journal*, September 30, 1927 (WdP Sr. Papers, Hagley, and MdPS SB).

189   "Worst weather in the history of" Deep Run races: "Deep Run Cup Goes to Drinmore Lad," *NYT*, April 7, 1935.

189   "At Aintree the fences are brush" through "cooked": "Maryland Cup Course Tougher than Aintree," *Piqua (OH) Daily Call*, April 16, 1935.

189   Walk the Maryland Hunt Cup course: Robert F. Kelley, "Maryland Chase Draws Fine Field," *NYT*, April 27, 1935.

189   Fences "looked like one mountain after another," "We were all settled in our stride," "Charlie White still had a good hold," "the black sheep of the lot," "It does seem strange," "I can't tell you how much more pleasant," TM buried at the seventeenth: William B. Streett, "The Maryland and Other Races," *Polo*, June 1935.

189   "A superb day," TM "sailed the famous big third fence": "Hotspur II Takes Maryland Chase," *NYT*, April 28, 1935.

189   "Go ride him for me today": Charles Houston, "The Sport Critic: No More Troubles for Trouble Maker," *RTD*, April 29, 1935.

190   No such thing as level ground: author's observation from 2011 course walk.

191   TM took off too far away, his other end pitched and twisted in midair: MdPS SB.

191   Hurled NL off with a violent somersault, NL in tears: Rossell, *The Maryland Hunt Cup*.

192   NL at TM's head: Anderson, *Black, Bay and Chestnut*.

192   MdPS wasn't finished with timber racing: hunt-race results from autumn 1935 and spring 1936.

193   Sir Barton's half brother: "Sir Martin Dead," *Blood-H*, August 2, 1930.

193   Dropped dead at a dinner party: "William Streett, Ex-Amateur Rider," *NYT*, July 6, 1940 (died July 5).

193   Seeing a loose horse at fence seventeen: conversation with Margaret Worrall, 2009; James Reynolds, "Death of a Great Heart: Trouble Maker," *Ghosts in American Houses* (New York: Farrar, Straus, 1955).

193   MdPS rarely talked about TM, speaking of him made her cry: Strine, *Montpelier*.

194   MdPS looked vibrantly well: MdPS SB.

194   MdPS gave CKB a string of horses to train: WdP Jr. Papers, Hagley.

194   MdPS lunch with JFB and Selby Burch: "Gov. Earle Takes Saratoga Baths," *NYT*, August 7, 1935.

195   "Whereas unfortunate disagreements and differences": Agreement signed by MdPS and THS, August 12, 1935, filed Washoe County, Nevada, Courthouse.

195   MdPS and THS, along with his brother Hamilton: "Notables Throng Saratoga Track," *NYT*, August 18, 1935.

195   By Tuesday MdPS was twenty-seven hundred miles away: based on October 1 hearing, which required six-week residency.

195   Ensconced at Rancho del Sierra: WdP Jr. Papers, Hagley.

195   "Every one seems to see it": WdP Sr. Papers, Hagley.

195   "Reno-vated": early sources include "Walter Winchell 'On Broadway,'" *Nevada State Journal*, March 20, 1932.

196   AP reported MdPS to Reno, collared THS at Montpelier: "March of Events: City, State, National and Foreign News in Review," *RTD*, September 8, 1935.

196   WdP Sr.'s first wife died when MdPS was thirty-three years old: "Senator Saulsbury's Widow Dies," *NYT*, May 8, 1927.

196 Description of Rancho del Sierra house: National Register of Historic Places Inventory: Nomination Form, July 30, 1974; "The Winters Ranch (Rancho Del Sierra)," nevada-landmarks.com/wa/shi94.htm.

196 Silver and blue landscape: "Winter's Ranch," April 22, 2011, chrisdufferhoffman .blogspot.com/2011/04/winters-ranch.html.

197 "The du Pont Company gave an extra 65¢" through "anything I can do for you": WdP Jr. Papers, Hagley.

197 Details of MdPS and THS property settlement, "any and all claims," "neither party shall molest the other": Agreement signed by MdPS and THS, August 12, 1935, filed Washoe County, Nevada, Courthouse, October 1, 1935.

197 NL breaks collarbone: Arthur J. Daley, "Connecticut Cup Taken by Lucier," *NYT*, September 8, 1935.

198 Before the county clerk's office opened, 9:30 A.M. closed hearing, MdPS testimony sealed: "Du Pont Heiress Divorced Today," *Reno Evening Gazette*, October 1, 1935.

198 "Extreme cruelty," "That for cause of divorce": Complaint, No. 51021, filed by L. D. Summerfield, Attorney for Plaintiff, in the Second Judicial District Court of the State of Nevada, in and for the County of Washoe, October 1, 1935.

198 Did not yet recognize "irreconcilable differences": Daniel Clement, Clement Law Firm, "Irreconcilable Differences in New Jersey One Year Later: What Was the Fuss About?" June 1, 2008.

198 THS denied: Answer to Complaint, filed Washoe County Courthouse, October 1, 1935.

198 THS "is so changeable," "warn him ahead of time": MdPS to Earl Edinger, 1941, WdP Jr. Papers, Hagley.

199 "Annapolis won as he pleased": "America's Greatest Steeplechase," *Polo*, October 1935.

199 His first steeplechase of the year: "More Hunt Races: Monmouth," *Polo*, November 1935.

199 "Coming around the last turn," CKB was *furious*, "We were all rather surprised": William B. Streett, "The Autumn Hunt Race Meetings," *The Sportsman*, December 1935.

199 Annapolis disqualified in Shrewsbury Steeplechase: Albert P. Stauderman, "Fugitive Is First in Gold Cup Chase," *NYT*, October 20, 1935.

200 CKB threaded Wild Son through traffic: Bryan Field, "Mrs. Somerville's Wild Son Captures Feature at Pimlico," *NYT*, November 8, 1935.

200 Montpelier Hunt Races committee: "Montpelier Hunt Opens Saturday at Orange," *RTD*, November 17, 1935.

201 MdPS leading owner fourth year in a row: Montfort Amory, "Winners at the Hunt Race Meetings," *Horse & Horseman*, January 1936.

201 MdPS, CKB, and JFB sailed to England, arrived five days before Christmas, MdPS return to United States: Passenger lists, Ancestry.com.

201 BH rode a horse named Seaway: "Full Returns of All Meetings Under National Hunt Rules from January 1, 1935, to December 31, 1935," *Ruff's Guide to the Turf, 1936*.

202 RH developing BH through careful steps: "Full Returns of All Meetings Under National Hunt Rules from January 1, 1936, to December 31, 1936," *Ruff's Guide to the Turf, 1937*.

201 "From the first moment," older riders looked after BH, "There was a grand spirit," "always overfacing me," "would stand with her back turned," only a fiber skullcap through "that was the end of him": Fitzgeorge-Parker, *No Secret So Close.* American Liberty League: sources including "Nye Sees in Letter by Raskob 'Birth' of Liberty League," *NYT,* December 21, 1934.

202 "To combat radicalism": "League Is Formed to Scan New Deal, 'Protect Rights,'" *NYT,* August 23, 1934.

202 Not nearly so large as loans made by some other du Ponts: "Democrats Report $1,008,840 Spent: Liberty League Report," *NYT,* September 12, 1936.

203 National Advisory Council members: *Facts About the American Liberty League,* pamphlet dated May 29, 1935.

CHAPTER 16

204 George Grant Scott most influential CPA: "Charlotte Builders," *Charlotte Observer,* July 4, 1922; cmhpf.org/s&rr/RScott.html.

204 George Randolph Scott, no record of his birth in Orange County: author research at Orange County, Virginia, Courthouse.

204 "I solemnly swear that I was born at CHARLOTTE": U.S. passport application approved September 29, 1922.

204 "Randy Scott is a complete anachronism," suffered a back injury, toured Europe after college, golfing with Howard Hughes, extras for *Sharp Shooters,* dialogue coach for Gary Cooper, held out for Paramount offer: Gene Ringgold, "Randolph Scott: Embodied Everyone's Idea of a Southern Gentleman," *Films in Review* (Carolina Room, Charlotte Public Library).

205 Tipping his hat to autograph seekers at Montpelier races: Jamie McConnell, 2012.

205 Five older sisters and a brother seven years his junior: Ancestry.com.

205 Everything from football to glee club: *Fir Tree* (Woodberry Forest School yearbook), quoted by Cathy L. Eberly, director of marketing and communications.

205 Details of RS friendship with Harriss family; military aspirations, training, and service with Andrew Harriss, "I always felt that Scotty": Gen. Andrew H. Harriss, "Recalling Randolph Scott '17," *Woodberry Forest* alumni magazine, Summer 1988.

206 Sgt. RS nominated to West Point, to be "exempted": R. E. C. Bryant, "Charlotte Youth Overseas Nominated for West Point," *Charlotte Observer,* July 24, 1918.

206 Marion du Pont served on committee: "Society," *Washington Post,* August 25, 1918.

207 RS returned to United States in early June 1919: "Personal," *Charlotte Observer,* May 30, 1919.

207 Catching up with Virginia friends: "Personal," *Charlotte Observer,* September 6, 1919.

207 RS disliked profanity: examples such as Sheilah Graham, "Shirley Temple's milk fund—supported by contributions of 10 cents every time a naughty word is said in her hearing—has shrunk considerably since Randolph Scott became her leading man . . . ," *Cleveland Plain Dealer,* November 9, 1937.

207 Heisman disliked profanity, "wherever Mrs. Heisman wishes to live": "John Heisman," RamblinWreck.com.

207 RS second-string end: "Battleship Owned by Former Jacket," *The Technique* (Georgia Institute of Technology student newspaper), No. 21, April 1, 1938.

208 "Fine nerve": Mrs. J. P. Caldwell, "One Minute Interviews—Randolph Scott," *Charlotte Observer,* November 9, 1919.

208 "Special student" at UNC, stayed only a year: "The School of Commerce—Curricula," and Wilson Library Archives, University of North Carolina.

208 Charter member of the Civitan Club: "Organizations: Civic, Social, Patriotic, Miscellaneous," cmstory.org/history/hornets/organize.htm.

208 Joined Charlotte's most prominent Freemason lodge: Walter J. Klein, 32°, K.C.C.H., "The Accountant on West Tenth Street," *Scottish Rite Journal of Freemasonry,* Southern Jurisdiction, USA, October 2002.

208 "Ineffable Degrees": scottish-rite-mn.org/degrees.htm.

208 Best man at several weddings: North Carolina society news. "Probably the most destructive hurricane": Stuart McIver, "1926 Miami: The Blow That Broke the Boom," *Fort Lauderdale Sun-Sentinel,* September 19, 1993.

209 "Always look for the good in all": "Spes mea in Deo est" (my hope is in God), 32°, "Scottish Rite," Supreme Council of the United States, westernsupremecouncil.org.

209 Francis Jackson Heath data: Social Security Death Index.

209 Same mold as Bobby Jones: "Heath-Ehle Meet for Title Today," *RTD,* June 25, 1927.

209 Jack's older half brother eloped with RS's sister Virginia: Mrs. Margaret Kelly Abernethy, "Society—Prominent Young Couple Quietly Married in York," *Charlotte Observer,* August 26, 1921.

209 Studied at Georgia Tech and at UNC, running a car dealership in Charlotte: Obituary, *Kentucky New Era (Hopkinsville),* July 22, 1975; Charlotte, North Carolina, city directory, 1926.

209 Hollywood trip a "vacation": many sources, including Inez Wallace, "A Vacation to Fame," *Cleveland Plain Dealer,* March 21, 1937.

209 Introduction letter to Ella Rice Hughes: Hedda Hopper, "Looking at Hollywood—Randy Scott, Boxoffice Ace, in Films in Spite of Himself," *Omaha World Herald,* August 31, 1952.

209 RS an uncredited extra or bit player: "Randolph Scott (1898–1987)," imdb.com.

210 Cooper earning $3,400 a week: "Biography for Gary Cooper," imdb.com.

210 Lived in a rented room, "one bed that you won't kick the foot off," "carted his comfortable bed": Inez Wallace, "A Vacation to Fame," *Cleveland Plain Dealer,* March 21, 1937.

211 Studio publicity called him "young": for example, Amos Parrish, "What's in Fashion?" *New Orleans Times-Picayune,* November 2, 1931.

211 "Gentle, understanding sweetheart," "nonchalant young libertine": "Movie Review: *Hot Saturday*—Malicious Gossip," *NYT,* November 5, 1932.

211 Sharing a West Hollywood house, rented Santa Monica beach house in March 1935: "Cary Grant and Randolph Scott," Gerald Clarke, *Architectural Digest: Hollywood at Home* (New York: Harry N. Abrams, 2005).

211 CG "scripts full of little notes," "You never saw any fear in him": Nelson, *Evenings with Cary Grant.*

212 "It's just publicity": "Actor Says Story He Loves Lupe Velez Is 'Publicity,'" *Tampa Morning Tribune,* April 1, 1932.

212 Author's note: Although William Mann's book *Wisecracker* makes a well-researched and compelling case for their being more than friends, direct evidence

that Randolph Scott and Cary Grant were lovers has not surfaced. Articles and books published after they died rely on speculation and quotes gathered from second- and thirdhand sources that can't be authenticated and may not be reliable. Some photos circa 1935—from staged shoots where dozens of images would be taken—appear suggestive but prove nothing. For example, one shot of Scott sitting behind Grant on a diving board shows RS's hand apparently about to brush against CG's arm, while CG sits with his arms crossed and looks somewhat uncomfortable. We know that the two men were close friends. We don't know *why* Scott made that gesture at that moment.

212 William Haines biography, "I'm already married," RS and CG parade of girlfriends: Mann, *Wisecracker*.

213 "Facts don't interest people": Nelson, *Evenings with Cary Grant*.

214 Female stars pestering Paramount to borrow RS: "Scott in Demand," *San Diego Union*, July 29, 1935.

215 RS camped out at Malibu Lake: "*So Red the Rose* Is Latest Outstanding Production Laid in Sylvan Grandeur," *San Diego Union*, July 5, 1935.

215 MdPS back to Virginia while RS in Hollywood: WdP Jr. Papers, Hagley.

215 RS grandfather Tarlton Woodson Scott a Confederate veteran: Ancestry.com.

215 RS visited N.C. state Department of Revenue, "chorus of nervous giggles": "Atwitter," *Greensboro (NC) Record*, January 28, 1936.

215 WdP Jr. and MdPS took a train to Southern California: WdP Jr. Papers, Hagley.

215 Rosemont in 1935 Santa Anita Handicap: "Top Row Wins $104,600 Race," *Tampa Sunday Tribune*, February 23, 1936.

216 George Grant Scott died: "Randolph Scott's Father, Employe [sic] of N.C., Stricken," *Burlington (NC) Daily Times-News*, March 5, 1936; "Dies After Heart Attack in Raleigh," *Greensboro (NC) Record*, March 5, 1936.

216 RS retreated to his beach house: "Actor's Father Dies," *Nevada State Journal*, March 5, 1936.

216 RS flew east on Friday: "Screen Actor Flies East to Attend Father's Funeral," *Riverside (CA) Daily Press*, March 6, 1936.

216 MdPS revised her divorce agreement: MdPS and THS signed March 7 (CKB witness); CKB got papers notarized March 9, 1936, in Kershaw County; Order Modifying Decree filed March 12, 1936, in Washoe County.

216 RS starring as Hawkeye: Louella O. Parsons, "Cooper Tale Headed for Screen," *San Antonio Light*, March 9, 1936.

217 Details of MdPS and RS wedding: marriage license issued by Chester County, South Carolina, Courthouse, March 23, 1936.

217 Could legally wed without any waiting period: Terri B. Zion, Deputy Probate Judge, 2012.

217 RS would not tell his own mother: "Film Star Wed 5 Months Ago; Wedding Is Surprise to Randy's Friends," *Charlotte Observer*, August 13, 1936.

217 RS back to Hollywood: "Hollywood Roundup," *Trenton Evening Times*, March 28, 1936.

217 "Because you thought you were being loyal": Inez Wallace, "Inez Writes an Open Letter to Randolph Scott About His Divorce from Rich Socialite," *Cleveland Plain Dealer*, August 21, 1938.

218 Auto insurance made out to MdPS: WdP Jr. Papers, Hagley.

218 NL's saddle had slipped: Bryan Field, "Indigo, 2–5, Takes Carolina Cup Race," *NYT*, March 29, 1936.

218 NL looked like a jockey: spring 1936 photos.

218 Rubber suit, sometimes "wouldn't eat": Dr. Aileen Laing.

218 NL serving on committees and promoting horse sports at Southern Pines: numerous articles from *Southern Pines (NC) Pilot*.

218 "It takes years of heady and courageous riding": "Noel Laing Captures Virginia Gold Cup," *Southern Pines (NC) Pilot*, May 8, 1936.

219 "Fishing trip," the Mayo Clinic: Dr. Aileen Laing, from her father, Douglas Laing.

219 Shirley Banks a licensed jockey: "Our Friend First in Hunts Contest," *NYT*, October 6, 1935.

219 B working under saddle again: "Chronicle Cover," *Chronicle of the Horse*, October 17, 1958.

219 Annapolis "had to have things his own way," B "would take a crack at anybody": Strine, *Montpelier*.

219 B "a big little horse": Lee Rose, 2009, and others.

219 "At least one fine horseman close to him": *AR 1938*.

220 Advice of Irish-born rider and trainer Jim Ryan: Strine, *Montpelier*.

220 Fifteen-year-old BH rode his second winner: *Ruff's Guide to the Turf, 1937*.

220 BH still called RH "Daddy": Fitzgeorge-Parker, *No Secret So Close*.

CHAPTER 17

221 Athletes on their way to the Olympic Games, "Boycott Hitler Germany": "United States' Olympic Team, 334 Strong, Embarks for Berlin Contests," *NYT*, July 16, 1936.

221 Two sons of Man o' War sailed July 24: *AR 1938*.

222 At her brother's request (stallion Blenheim II), RH at London Docks, "The leg that was fired": Strine, *Montpelier*.

222 Importation of Blenheim II: "U.S. Syndicate Buys Blenheim for $250,000," *Springfield (MA) Daily Republican*, July 6, 1936.

222 MdPS wrote a big check, Delaware Park being built: WdP Jr. Papers, Hagley.

223 MdPS at resort hotel: "George Bull Gives Party in Saratoga," *NYT*, August 17, 1936.

223 Gideon Putnam Hotel designed "to produce restful reactions": H. I. Brock, "Saratoga Spa Opens," *NYT*, July 21, 1935.

223 MdPS accompanied by CKB and JFB: Bryan Field, "Granville Beats Sun Teddy by Head in Travers at Spa," *NYT*, August 16, 1936.

223 WdP Jr. announced that his sister had been married: "Mrs. Somerville Is Wed," *NYT*, August 13, 1936.

223 RS corroborated the news, explained that they delayed: "Screen Actor Announces He Married Months Ago," *Fitchburg (MA) Sentinel*, August 13, 1936.

223 Flabbergasted Hollywood, MdPS from Montpelier, Vermont?: "Actors Pass Up Filmland for the '400,'" *Portsmouth (OH) Times*, September 27, 1936.

223 Mariona?: including "The New American Royalty Who Save Our Heiresses from Foreign Ignoblemen," *Albuquerque Journal*, September 27, 1936.

224 MdPS at Travers Stakes: Bryan Field, "Granville Beats Sun Teddy by Head in Travers at Spa," *NYT*, August 16, 1936.

224 MdPS hired a contractor, RS met MdPS at Wilmington: WdP Jr. Papers, Hagley; "Actor Takes Trip East," *Edwardsville (IL) Intelligencer*, September 16, 1936.

224 Orange County friends celebrated them: Nellie Smith, "Mr. and Mrs. John Walker of Woodberry Forest Entertain Tonight," *RTD*, September 29, 1936.

224 MdPS had Montpelier's basement floor lowered: Sarah Booth Conroy, "The Once and Future Montpelier," *Washington Post*, July 16, 1989.

224 NL home to Bunree, telephone beside his bed; NL relied upon Shirley, Andy, and his own father: Dr. Aileen Laing. Extra-powerful X-ray treatments, "X-ray dosage five times as great": "Former Bluffs Doctor Tells Cancer Treatment," *Omaha World-Herald*, May 13, 1936.

225 BH had felt awestruck, description of gallops near Mann Down and Hobbs workout schedule: Fitzgeorge-Parker, *No Secret So Close*.

225 "Battleship is a fine mover," B "went and jumped beautifully," "Both horses are going on very well," B "a useful horse": Strine, *Montpelier*.

226 Nellie Pratt biography, B fussing with his riders, Nellie Pratt's perfect posture and gentle hands: info and photo from Mrs. Robert Leader, 2012.

226 RS and MdPS at Fair Hill: Morgan Photo Services, "Foreign: American Year," *Blood-H*, April 2, 1938.

226 "A tall, handsome collar-ad": Stewart Atkins, "Through the Keyhole," *Gastonia (NC) Daily Gazette*, October 7, 1936.

227 An eighteen-foot-tall pin oak, wanted Montpelier a national shrine: "Oak Tree Planted in Madison Square," *NYT*, October 7, 1936.

227 NL good-bye to Bunree Farm ("a patient in the Emergency Hospital in Washington since October 10th"): "Noel Laing Gravely Ill in Washington, D.C.," *Southern Pines (NC) Pilot*, November 6, 1936.

227 "As if they gathered there for reassurance": Katharine Lamont Boyd, "Obituary: Noel Laing," *Horse & Horseman*, December 1936.

228 B first race in two years, "a real nice school," "a bit troublesome," "I feel sure he will get over all that," "jumping wonderfully": Strine, *Montpelier*.

228 BH wild ride with No Reckoning, RH relationship with Nellie Pratt, BH choosing to live with his father, BH not yet needing to shave: Fitzgeorge-Parker, *No Secret So Close*.

229 Fred Pratt felt mortified: Fitzgeorge-Parker, *No Secret So Close*, and Mrs. Robert Leader, 2012.

230 NL accepted sedation, unlikely to recover: "Noel Laing Gravely Ill in Washington, D.C.," *Southern Pines (NC) Pilot*, November 6, 1936.

230 RH scratched B from National: William Leggett, "Youth Will Have Its Day," *Sports Illustrated*, October 4, 1976.

230 "I have decided not to run Battleship," RH dreaded what might happen: Strine, *Montpelier*.

230 "Marriage tackle": "Aintree Still a Thrill for Oldest National Survivor Hobbs," *Independent* (London), April 2, 2003.

231 B lost his rider in his next race: "Performances of Battleship," Strine, *Montpelier*.

231 Andy Fowler visited NL on Tuesday night, NL made Andy promise that they would race, NL funeral, his horses ran: "Launch Move to Honor Memory of Noel Laing," *Southern Pines (NC) Pilot,* November 27, 1926.

231 NL's parents and brother Doug keeping vigil: "Noted Amateur Rider Succumbs," *Aiken (SC) Standard and Review,* November 20, 1936.

231 RS would fly to Texas: "Good-Will Dinner Marks Opening of U.D.C. Convention," *Dallas Morning News,* November 17, 1936.

231 "Dear Mr. Edinger": WdP Jr. Papers, Hagley.

232 NL's father left the horse business, mother never really got over losing him: Dr. Aileen Laing.

232 NL headstone: Findagrave.com.

233 BH taller than his father, his toes could nearly touch B's elbows: various photos.

233 "You're shutting out the light!": Fitzgeorge-Parker, *No Secret So Close.*

233 Practically no margin for error: author conversation with Jim Whitner, Middleburg, VA; "7 Horses Entered from America for English National," *Middleburg (VA) Chronicle,* January 21, 1938 (Flying Minutes and B both "are bold, chunky and short coupled and the most difficult sort to sit over Aintree. It won't be if they can jump, for both are fully capable of the trying obstacles, but it will be more if their jockeys can sit with them.").

233 "He's got five legs, Daddy, not four": Strine, *Montpelier.*

233 B and BH debut together: "Sandown Park Meeting: Success of Victor Norman," *Times (London),* December 12, 1936.

233 Two and a half miles might be too short, "Mr. Hobbs charged the last fence," "very little room," "It is no exaggeration": "Success of Battleship," *Times (London),* December 14, 1936.

234 "So my last two rides as an amateur": Fitzgeorge-Parker, *No Secret So Close.*

235 MdPS to California for Christmas: "Visits Hollywood," *RTD,* December 27, 1936.

235 "Waves do everything but wash the breakfast dishes": Frank Cunningham, "Stars over Hollywood: Randolph Scott," *RTD,* December 20, 1936.

235 "Reaching a domestic compromise," be a "gentleman farmer": Willa Okker, "The Hollywood Parade," *San Mateo (CA) Times and Daily News Leader,* December 29, 1936.

235 MdPS stopped at Charlotte: WdP Jr. Papers, Hagley.

CHAPTER 18

236 BH alone in a five-star hotel room, "You'll be all right now," sometimes fell asleep on a couch, "instead of arriving at Oxford," "It's always amazing," BH walks National course with RH, BH fell off Flying Minutes, BH thought he would have finished in top four: Fitzgeorge-Parker, *No Secret So Close.*

237 Fosse Chase, "Whether Battleship will ever stay the [Grand National] distance": "Battleship Wins," *Times (London),* January 6, 1937.

237 BH pulled up his horse: *Ruff's Guide to the Turf, 1938.*

237 MdPS training track at Camden: "Start Work on Track Jan. 4," *NYT,* December 24, 1936.

237 WdP Jr. "I know I will be unable," MdPS using Chapman Park Hotel stationery: WdP Jr. Papers, Hagley.

238 MdPS at Sea Island Beach, Georgia: "Notes of Social Activities in New York and Elsewhere," *NYT*, February 11, 1937.

238 JFB won a blue ribbon: "Hunter Trial Goes to Easter Morning," *NYT*, February 22, 1937.

238 WdP Jr. showed up with his wife: "Notes of Social Activities in New York and Elsewhere," *NYT*, February 22, 1937.

238 Rosemont's Santa Anita Derby: Bryan Field, "50,000 Watch Race; Rosemont's Spurt Wins Santa Anita Handicap in Photo Finish," *NYT*, February 28, 1937; "Favorite Noses out Seabiscuit," Robert Myers, *San Diego Union*, February 28, 1937; Ted Steinmann, "Rosemont Wins Santa Anita Handicap," *San Diego Union*, February 28, 1937.

238 "Rosy's feet are a little sore": "Santa Anita Handicap Winner Not to Run in Closing Feature of Coast Meet," *NYT*, March 1, 1937.

239 Wishing he could trade places with RS, "dripping with raindrops," RS "in high good humor": J. D. Spiro, "On the Lots with the Candid Reporter—Damp Posies," *Rockford (IL) Register-Republic*, March 6, 1937.

240 B barely cleared National Hunt Handicap Chase water jump: "News of the Day Told in Pictures," *Springfield (MA) Republican*, March 20, 1937.

240 "He said the horse didn't have enough experience," "I hated to scratch Battleship from the Grand National": Strine, *Montpelier*.

241 "Riding for the first time at Liverpool," "After two or three fences": Francis, *The Sport of Queens*.

241 "Flying Minutes has a reasonable outside chance," "What Have You has also an outside chance," "I believe my horse": "Stable Fancies for the National," *Liverpool Echo*, March 15, 1937.

241 "Hurrah! Hurrah! Hurrah!," What Have You's antics, Streett "I can't figure what got into him," reporters praised BH, Drim "tried his best to follow the winner": "U.S.-Owned Horses Fail to Finish Grand National Chase Won by Royal Mail," *NYT*, March 20, 1937.

241 Lord Derby summoned a turf expert, "Aintree is no respecter," reporters praised BH: Bee, "How Royal Mail Won a Grand Race," *Liverpool Echo*, March 19, 1937.

243 Snow flurries in Camden, RS attended with MdPS, license plates from more than twenty states: Fred Van Ness, "Fugitive, 3–1, Wins Carolina Cup Race, with Indigo Next," *NYT*, March 28, 1937.

243 JFB hosting buffet dinner: "Notes of Social Activities in New York and Elsewhere," *NYT*, March 26, 1937.

244 CKB "unkind" to JFB: Hope Cooper, NSM.

244 NL's alcohol-inspired target practice: Dr. Aileen Laing.

244 Marion duPont Scott on every single stock certificate: WdP Jr. Papers, Hagley.

244 JFB had begged CKB to give up drinking, MdPS wanted JFB to stay: told to Raymond Woolfe Jr. by his father, Raymond G. Woolfe, Reuter interview, 2009.

244 MdPS giving a scared, confused, or angry horse many chances to succeed: author interview with former Montpelier exercise rider Mike Clatterbuck, 2012.

244 JFB bridesmaid at her brother's wedding, CKB not there: "Genevieve Brady New Jersey Bride," *NYT*, April 24, 1937.

245 William Randolph Hearst birthday party: "Hollywood Circus Party Honors Randolph Hearst," *San Antonio Light*, May 3, 1937; matching pink and white satin tra-

peze costumes: Phyllis-Marje Arthur, "Hollywood on the Air—I Crash a Party," *Lowville (NY) Journal and Republican,* May 27, 1937.

246 Telegrams from RH, "The times Battleship was beaten," "terribly deep and heavy," "great performance by a great little horse," "The lady is very loyal": Strine, *Montpelier.*

246 CKB-JFB "one-in-a-lifetime love": Reuter, Raymond Woolfe Jr. interview, 2009.

246 MdPS notary Chester C. Hazard witnessed CKB's Certificate of Attorney, May 28, 1937: JFB divorce papers, Washoe County, Nevada, Courthouse.

246 Extreme cruelty, "which caused [her] great unhappiness," did not specify mental cruelty only: JFB Complaint, filed June 14, 1937, Washoe County, Nevada.

246 "Bassett" often went with one of JFB's horses: hunt-racing results circa 1937–1938.

247 RS "denies those rumors": Louella O. Parsons, "Warners, Up to Old Tricks," *San Antonio Light,* July 10, 1937.

247 RS "performs beautifully on the diving board" through "all my serious writing": Sheilah Graham, "Hollywood in Person," August 17, 1937.

247 "You see, it's like this" through "show all the pictures we want," "His chief—and only—aversion," "My private life is not under contract to anybody": Sheilah Graham, "Hollywood in Person: Scott's Matrimonial Problem," August 27, 1937.

248 Telegram on September 3, barely making it on board: "Husband Races to Wife's Side," *Reno Evening Gazette,* September 4, 1937.

248 RS had known that MdPS was ill: "Randolph Scott Flies to Wife Ill in Virginia," unidentified newspaper (possibly Warrenton, VA) from Dr. Aileen Laing.

CHAPTER 19

249 It hurt to breathe: "Your Good Health: Pleurisy Brings Agony," *Baton Rouge Morning Advocate,* October 9, 1937.

249 After visiting her brother at Bellevue: WdP Jr. Papers, Hagley.

249 Special doctor flew down from New York City, "I was so busy": "Randolph Scott Flies to Wife Ill in Virginia," unidentified newspaper (possibly Warrenton, VA) from Dr. Aileen Laing.

249 MdPS ill with pneumonia and pleurisy, reporters told RS that MdPS had "a fine chance to live": "Wife of Film Star Ill," *Cleveland Plain Dealer,* September 5, 1937.

249 Roughly one in four pneumonia patients died: "Science's Century-Old Fight Against Pneumonia Continues as March Peak Drawing Near," *Dallas Morning News,* February 18, 1937.

250 RS motored to Montpelier: "Wife of Movie Star Recovers from Illness," *Nevada State Journal,* September 7, 1937.

250 Barely able to eat anything, hospital at Charlottesville, crisis had passed: "May Take Scott's Wife to Hospital," *Danville (VA) Bee,* September 6, 1937.

250 Oxygen tent: Margaret Leonard, "Sciences: Exhibit Here to Illustrate 200 Years," *RTD,* May 11, 1937; also, oxygen tent used at WdP Jr. home during William Henry duPont's illness, 1932.

250 "Mrs. Scott had a very good night," Foxcatcher Hunt Ball, MdPS to Meadow Woods: WdP Jr. Papers, Hagley.

250 Radio broadcast from Fair Hill, RS on same network: "Radio Roundup," *RTD,* September 10, 1937.

250 RS golf and debutante dance: "Town and Country Gossip," *Middleburg (VA) Chronicle*, September 24, 1937.

250 RS at Virginia horse shows: "Northern Part of State Begins Gay Fall of Parties, Hunts," *RTD*, September 26, 1937.

250 RS quick solo trip, briefly back to MdPS: "Screen Actor Returns Here," *Greensboro Record*, October 2, 1937.

251 Warrenton Hunt had wanted to hold NL memorial race: Nina Carter Tabb, "Steeplechase to Center Interest at Middleburg," *RTD*, November 18, 1937.

251 Invited all friends of NL to contribute: WdP Jr. Papers, Hagley. "One of the finest testimonials," trophy donated by nearly three thousand people: "Laing Chase Saturday," *NYT*, November 17, 1937.

251 Montpelier Hunt Races attendees, "a fitting close": Fred Van Ness, "Cadeau II Annexes Noel Laing Chase," *NYT*, November 21, 1937.

252 RS and MdPS together at Aiken, Fred Astaire ambushed by reporters, "Come Freddie, we must get going," "Following close behind the car," "Not now": "Two Movie Stars Pay Visit to Sports Center of South," *Aiken (SC) Standard and Review*, December 1, 1937.

252 Front-page photo of RS, "guests this week of Mr. and Mrs. Huston Rawls": "Here on Vacation," *Aiken (SC) Standard and Review*, December 3, 1937.

252 Cranborne Steeplechase, "a good race to watch": "A Day of Rain," *Times (London)*, December 3, 1937.

253 Lonsdale Steeplechase, "He looks a better horse now": "Racing Notes: The Ring and the Totalisator; Hurst Park Meeting," *Times (London)*, December 13, 1937.

253 RS back in Aiken: "Miniature Hollywood in Aiken These Days," *Aiken (SC) Standard and Review*, December 17, 1937.

253 "Hope to see you next week": WdP Jr. Papers, Hagley.

253 "Those legends are around again": Walter Winchell, "Broadway: The Man About Town Discovers Who's Whose," *Wisconsin State Journal*, December 24, 1937.

254 CKB trip around the world: Strine, *Montpelier*.

255 BH fortunately liked the Pratt family: Fitzgeorge-Parker, *No Secret So Close*, and Mrs. Robert Leader, 2012.

255 Details of Reg Hobbs and Nellie Pratt wedding: Entry of Marriage, registered at Newbury, Berkshire, England, January 24, 1938.

255 BH riding "a hundred miles away" at Birmingham: *Ruff's Guide to the Turf, 1939*.

255 Carved away any softness: spring 1938 photos of MdPS. "I am so glad to hear": WdP Jr. Papers, Hagley.

256 Camden Horse Show on MdPS property: "Two Blue Ribbons to Royal Reveler," *NYT*, March 12, 1938.

256 JFB "all excited about her health": "Casualty List," *Middleburg (VA) Chronicle*, January 21, 1938.

256 CKB did not show his face: absence from winter-spring 1938 Camden sporting and social news.

257 With Christmas a week away RH had decided, BH wrecked his car, "chased but chaste," stewards never had reason to reprimand him: Fitzgeorge-Parker, *No Secret So Close*.

256 BH to ride Flying Minutes in National: The Briton, "English Turf Topics," *Blood-H,* March 5, 1938 (listed W. B. Street [*sic*] as rider for Battleship).

256 Flying Minutes lame, BH felt satisfied with B, ordinary steeplechase ride paid £3, owners would pay £100 for a National ride, BH now stood six foot one, Free Fare "reached for his hurdle," BH under doctor's orders: Fitzgeorge-Parker, *No Secret So Close.*

257 "Rolls-Royce of Light Cars": rover-freunde.de/rffzh110dt.html.

257 "Oh, Mr. Hobbs" through "twice as much as anyone else to ride my horse," B started to get "cunning," B "Very unlucky," "Bruce would have won with him" (at Cheltenham), "I think you can win the National," "[You] should have more sense": Strine, *Montpelier.*

258 B always lazy about morning exercise: *AR 1938.*

258 During those seventy years, only four eleven-year-olds had won: The Briton, "English Turf Topics," *Blood-H,* February 12, 1938.

259 1938 Champion Hurdle Challenge, Free Fare "never looked better," National Hunt Handicap Chase, B's rider moves too late: "The National Hunt Meeting: Our Hope Wins," *Times (London),* March 9, 1938.

259 B running in the next race: "Cheltenham Results," *Times (London),* March 9, 1938.

259 Airgead Sios "never takes off twice in the same way": "Manchester Meeting: Airgead Sios Wins," *Times (London),* January 3, 1938.

260 Hugh Lloyd Thomas biography: The Briton, "English Turf Topics," *Blood-H,* January 22, 1938.

260 "A first class horseman," "overcome the handicaps": "Foreign: Grand National Acceptances," *Blood-H,* February 12, 1938.

261 Periwinkle II fell with a mile to go, finished fourth in a two-mile 'chase with Royal Mail, died of a broken neck: The Briton, "English Turf Topics," *Blood-H,* March 5, 1938.

261 Friends thought he had taken leave of his senses: "Thrown by Horse, British Envoy Dies," *NYT,* February 23, 1938.

261 RH sent telegram ("Battleship finished third big chase"), MdPS phoned "to make sure everything was going all right," RH thought B could have won Ascot Gold Cup: Strine, *Montpelier.*

261 MdPS didn't bid on Royal Mail: Fitzgeorge-Parker, *No Secret So Close.*

CHAPTER 20

264 JFB competing in a class for ladies' hunters: "Two Blue Ribbons to Royal Reveler," *NYT,* March 12, 1938.

264 William L. Shirer tried to witness all the changes . . . : Shirer, *Berlin Diary.*

265 "The Choice of 149,322 Trans-Atlantic Travelers in 1937": advertisement, *Springfield (MA) Republican,* January 31, 1938.

265 Flying a Nazi flag for nearly five years: "dual flag law" cited at en.wikipedia.org/wiki/SS_Bremen_(1929); "Travel aboard the Nazi-flagged SS *Europa* in 1936," at youtube.com/watch?v+0rUUc_Jy8W4.

265 "Why should we assume that time is on our side?": Ferdinand Kuhn Jr., "Chamberlain Grim: Hints at Conscription of Some Kind in Bidding All to Join National Effort," *NYT,* March 15, 1938.

265 Could MdPS look at a particular dog: WdP Jr. Papers, Hagley.

266 They called him "Pocket Battleship": "Grand National Steeplechase—'Pocket' Battleship Wins by a Head," *BBR*, 1938; Strine, *Montpelier*.

266 "More than a match for any warship afloat": *"Admiral Scheer* a Powerful Ship," *NYT*, May 30, 1937.

266 "The American pony": sources including Anderson, *Twenty Gallant Horses*.

266 "Do not fill the eye as National winners": The Briton, "English Turf Topics: Grand National, Last Guess," *Blood-H*, March 19, 1938.

266 B goes "wonderfully well" in gallop, two companions for MdPS transatlantic voyage, B "wouldn't take the bit and go," "nearly ran away from that horse," reins eighteen inches longer than usual, "worried about my boy getting killed," "Reg, do you fancy that skin," "I shan't tell you what my reply was," "I'll lay you a good price on Battleship," "You can have a hundred to one," MdPS climbing into small boat, RH splashed down in the middle: Strine, *Montpelier*.

267 *Europa* saluting Austrian and German unity: "Ship Fetes 'Anschluss,'" *Oregonian*, March 19, 1938. German spy aboard *Europa:* "German Girl and Two Men Held in Spy Case," *Springfield (MA) Republican*, February 27, 1938.

267 Jeffords among the first-class passengers: Strine, *Montpelier*.

267 Irish Hospitals Sweepstakes, ticket drawing: "Counterfoils in the Irish Sweep, Bringing Fortunes to Many, Thoroughly Mixed," *Gleaner* (Jamaica, West Indies), March 19, 1938; "Americans Share in Lottery Prize," *Kingsport (TN) Times*, March 21, 1938; "Grand National," *Time*, March 29, 1937.

268 B "set fast," B was the horse that RH and BH knew: Fitzgeorge-Parker, *No Secret So Close*.

268 Tying up symptoms and treatments: "Tie-Up," *Blood-H*, January 22, 1938; Stacey Oke, "Fact Sheet: Tying-Up in Horses," TheHorse.com.

268 "His kidneys were tied up," "like a man of ninety," RH pushed the pill back past B's tongue: Strine, *Montpelier*.

269 Purgative pill from Cupiss company: Fitzgeorge-Parker, *No Secret So Close*; Strine, *Montpelier*; and franciscupiss.co.uk/med.htm.

270 Adelphi Hotel description: author visit, 2012; en.wikipedia.org/wiki/Britannia_Adelphi_Hotel; bbc.co.uk/liverpool/localhistory/journey/lime_street/adelphi/hotel.shtml.

270 Jockeys were paid "one pound a mile," "They used to say that if you looked into a race-train," RH at bar with a group including his close friend Jack Anthony, "Don't be daft," "In case I have to buy the champagne!," RH did not let BH ride any races, Around midnight the jolly group decided: Fitzgeorge-Parker, *No Secret So Close*.

270 Jack Anthony bio: Bee, "How Royal Mail Won a Grand Race," *Liverpool Echo*, March 19, 1937.

272 RH bet 100 shillings on B, 50 to win, 50 to place: "Winner of Big Feature Nearly Watched Race," *Fairborn (OH) Daily Herald*, March 26, 1938.

272 "Swift dependable crossings" and "punctual arrivals": advertisement, *Springfield (MA) Republican*, January 31, 1938.

272 War Vessel faded and finished far back: "Blue Shirt to Win National," *Liverpool Echo*, March 24, 1938.

273 The frosty grass: "There was a sharpish frost overnight" (RH), Strine, *Montpelier*.

CHAPTER 21

274 MdPS traveling all night: "Winner of Big Feature Nearly Watched Race," *Fairborn (OH) Daily Herald,* March 26, 1938.

274 Tweed suit, "Robin Hood" hat: "Sport: 11-Year-Old Stallion," *Time,* April 4, 1938.

274 "Do wear sensible shoes": "Are You Going to the National This Year?" Elizabeth Inglis, *Liverpool Echo,* March 9, 1938.

274 Cuban heels, alligator-skin clutch purse: Strine, *Montpelier.*

274 MdPS met RH early on Grand National morning, walked the course, might be a bit slippery . . . "help him get more grip," a pipe-opener, B thinner than MdPS had seen him, MdPS thought of RH convinced that B was a "park horse," "overstepped their enthusiasm," "Go down the middle on the outside," join the leaders at the last fence, Mr. & Mrs. Jeffords shared private box, RH had to find his own standing room, pocketbook slipped from her hands, handed it to Ed Conklin, "trying to faint," "Little Battleship, a great favorite with the crowd," BH wanted to come up beside Royal Danieli, bookmakers cheered for B, crowd burst into riotous motion and sound, "I wonder if we might get through," heel broke off and bounced away, "The last ten yards," "By Jesus, if there'd been a photo-finish," "Well, you know, if I had been second," "I thought I'd won half a length," RH feared B might be bleeding internally, MdPS tea with Mrs. Ambrose Clark, "The truth was I hadn't had nerve enough," "I knew the party was going to cost," pile of telegrams, "two horses jumping on top": Strine, *Montpelier.*

275 Exercise about 7:00 A.M., Royal Mail "rather listless in the Paddock," ground perfectly springy underfoot for the National: Our Racing Correspondent, "Sporting News—Racing: The Grand National," *Times (London),* March 26, 1938.

275 B's haunches blanketed: common practice, photos of B in England tacked up for workouts.

275 Within the falling rain: "Sporting News: Racing—The Grand National," *Times (London),* March 26, 1938.

276 Nell Hobbs to BH, Margery Hobbs ("Mummy") to BH, a "most exciting win," "Sorry miss party": telegrams courtesy of Mrs. Robert Leader.

276 MdPS too late to go inside paddock, BI reminding one friend of a telephone pole, all the way to the buckle, find "another leg," swiveled five degrees left, "No argument!," his friend Fred Rimell, "Where do you think you're going, matey?" Battleship's "one real mistake," BH knew not to fight it, mistake gave Battleship a better chance, "Did you win?," "What was that trouble after Becher's first time?": Fitzgeorge-Parker, *No Secret So Close.*

277 B weighed less than a thousand pounds: *AR 1938* (upon returning to the United States, B "looked extremely well, weighed 1,040 lbs., possibly 50 lbs. over his weight in the National paddock").

277 Winner on looks probably Royal Danieli: The Briton, "English Turf Topics: Grand National, Last Guess," *Blood-H,* March 19, 1938.

278 Narrow staircase to County Stand roof: "Mrs. Scott's Evening," *Blood-H,* July 1, 1974; Aintree historian Jane Clarke. B looked "even smaller than usual," Rock Lad jockey kneeling by his horse, B tried to go to stable, "Good old Bruce! Good old Reggie," MdPS "the most composed person on the course": "American Millionairess and Wife of a Film Star Wins Grand National," *Liverpool Echo,* March 25, 1938.

278 B like BB had a remarkably long stride: Anderson, "Billy Barton: A Gallant Rogue";
     Strine, *Montpelier.*
279 Size of Grand National obstacles circa 1937–1938: "Course at Aintree Severest in
     Sport," *NYT,* March 19, 1937.
279 Running of 1938 Grand National: Our Racing Correspondent, "Sporting News—
     Racing: The Grand National," *Times (London),* March 26, 1938; Our Racing Cor-
     respondent, "Sporting News—Racing: Grand National Film—Some Revised
     Opinions," *Times (London),* March 29, 1938.
280 B's nose "gouging the floor . . . I'd have been over his head": "Aintree Still a Thrill
     for Oldest National Survivor Hobbs," *Independent* (London), April 2, 2003.
280 Airgead Sios flopping down onto his side, would gallop the entire four miles 856
     yards, any one of those four would win, "and they were many," riderless Takvor
     Pacha ducked into Workman, Takvor Pacha avoided final jump: Our Racing Cor-
     respondent, "Sporting News—Racing: Grand National Film—Some Revised
     Opinions," *Times (London),* March 29, 1938.
281 Rock Lad heart attack, Royal Mail bleeding: "Sporting News: Racing—The
     Grand National," *Times (London),* March 26, 1938.
281 B over Becher's perfection in flight . . . several inches of sky: photo, Strine, *Mont-
     pelier.*
281 BH long legs nearly vertical: *Life* magazine photo archive.
283 BH sitting relaxed: photo in "The Grand National: Victory for American Horse,"
     Times (London), March 26, 1938.
284 "A courage almost beyond praise": Bird's-Eye, "A Memorable Grand National:
     Gallant Little American Horse," *Country Life,* April 2, 1938.
284 BH heard B give a heavy sigh, crowd fell silent right after the finish, "Let's go and
     see the horse": "Grand National Steeplechase—'Pocket' Battleship Wins by a
     Head," *BBR,* 1938.
285 RH "It is the greatest day of my life": "Winning Jockey: Hobbs Delighted With
     His Success," *Liverpool Echo,* March 25, 1938.
286 MdPS "too excited" to lead in her horse: Robert P. Post, "Battleship, Man o' War's
     Son, Wins Grand National by a Head," *NYT,* March 26, 1938; Associated Press re-
     ports from Aintree, March 25, 1938.
286 RH found MdPS: "Battleship Wins Grand National," *Fitchburg (MA) Sentinel,*
     March 25, 1938.
286 BH gray eyes: T. O'R, "Horse Shows and Hunts: A Jockey of Size," *New Yorker,*
     June 18, 1938.
287 Perfectly groomed, father and son at banquet: RH and BH photo, "Grand Na-
     tional," *Horse & Horseman,* May 1938.
287 "I enjoyed the rest!": Fitzgeorge-Parker, *No Secret So Close.*
288 "An American horse that came from the home of James Madison": "Blood Will
     Tell," *Moravia (IA) Union,* April 14, 1938.
288 Radio broadcast including RH and BH quotes: "Man o' War Birthday Celebra-
     tion," NBC Blue network, hosted by Clem McCarthy, March 29, 1938 (shelf RWA
     3119 B1-2, Library of Congress).

CHAPTER 22

289 Assumed B would keep going: "Winner of Big Feature Nearly Watched Race," *Fairborn (OH) Daily Herald,* March 26, 1938.

289 "Judging from the nose tank": Lindbergh, *The Spirit of St. Louis.*

289 MdPS announced that B would retire: "Mrs. Scott to Place Battleship in Stud at Montpelier Farm," *RTD,* April 5, 1938.

289 Portraying "Uncle Dudley [sic] (actually "Uncle Gus")": Richard E. Hays, "Amusements Along Film Row," *Seattle Daily Times,* April 13, 1938.

289 Role went to Ligaroti: "Bing's Best Racer Makes Film Debut," *Seattle Daily Times,* September 15, 1938.

290 Sailed on the SS *Manhattan,* spacious fourteen-by-fourteen-foot stall, "ordinarily used for shipping canaries," grabbed the back of RH's coat in his teeth: T. O'R., "Horse Shows and Hunts: A Jockey of Size," *New Yorker,* June 18, 1938.

290 Long visit at Montpelier after special events near New York: Fitzgeorge-Parker, *No Secret So Close.*

290 BH collected a small fee, or tip, donated money to Red Cross, horse van would take B to railroad car, RS represented MdPS: Strine, *Montpelier.*

291 East Coast/West Coast lives could not be reconciled: "Randolph Scotts Part," *NYT,* June 12, 1938.

291 No plans to divorce: "Mrs. Randolph Scott Confirms Separation," *RTD,* June 12, 1938.

291 Rumor MdPS to divorce RS and marry CKB: Sam Woolford, "Glenda That Way About Randolph Scott," *San Antonio Light,* July 18, 1938.

291 "I have no comment to make": "Mrs. Scott Silent on Divorce Move," *Chester (PA) Times,* June 21, 1938.

291 RS "asking his blue-blood wife for a divorce": Sheilah Graham, "Hollywood in Person: Bill Gets Taste of Home Life," September 26, 1938.

291 "You could not find a better mannered, more friendly person": Joyce Craig, age twelve, "Randolph Scott Tells Joyce About the Life of Movie Star," *RTD,* October 30, 1938.

292 RS and CG continued sharing their beach house: sources including 1940 U.S. census

292 "Dad somewhat enjoyed being called gay" through "perhaps he flirted with everyone": Grant, *Good Stuff.*

292 RS adopted a boy and a girl: "Service Held for Randolph Scott," *Bend (OR) Bulletin,* March 5, 1987.

292 RS sent flowers to Montpelier: Mae Helen Corbin, 2012.

292 BH broke his back in a racing fall, "Of course I'm all for safety": Fitzgeorge-Parker, *No Secret So Close.*

293 BH "We all like to think": Strine, *Montpelier.*

294 B sired nearly five times the average number of stakes winners: thoroughbred times.com/stallion-directory/media/resources/averages-for-the-breed.pdf.

294 "He was a very secure horse": author interview with Lee Rose, 2009.

294 Daily hour of exercise under saddle: *AR 1938.*

294 "Just old age": "Chronicle Cover," quoting MdPS letter to the editor, *Chronicle of the Horse,* October 17, 1958.

294 Buried near his barn, near Annapolis, B and Annapolis graves moved: MdPS SB.

295 CKB often joined MdPS at stables, until she was eighty-eight years old, details of MdPS training yearlings and two-year-olds at Montpelier, CKB's surprisingly deep voice, "I never did see a contractor come in": Mike Clatterbuck, 2012.

295 CKB talking slowly and directly: author interviews with Mike Clatterbuck, 2012, and Raymond Woolfe Jr., 2012.

295 Bassett Cottage style had much in common with Marion's Red Room: Mary Carter McConnell, 2012.

295 Others close to them swore that was not so: notably Raymond Woolfe Jr. ("It was an absolute platonic relationship": Reuter interview, 2009.

295 Mrs. Scott was crying, "I've got hiccups": Mae Helen Corbin, 2012.

296 They called her "Mama": Mike Clatterbuck and other Montpelier employees, 2012.

297 Will made by WdP Sr. in 1928: filed at Orange County, Virginia, Courthouse.

297 "You were talking at one time about restoring Montpelier": WdP Jr. Papers, Hagley.

297 MdPS wanted National Trust for Historic Preservation to own Montpelier: Will of Marion duPont Scott, filed at Orange County, Virginia, Courthouse.

297 "Who can, if they like, win Grand Nationals": "Sport: The Grand National," *Time*, March 31, 1923.

Selected Bibliography

du Pont History

Du Pont: The Autobiography of an American Enterprise: The Story of E. I. Du Pont de Nemours & Company Published in Commemoration of the 150th Anniversary of the Founding of the Company on July 19, 1802. Wilmington, DE: E. I. Du Pont de Nemours & Company, 1952.

Gates, John D. The du Pont Family: An Inside Look at One of America's Most Fascinating and Private Dynasties. Garden City, NY: Doubleday, 1979.

Mosley, Leonard. Blood Relations: The Rise and Fall of the du Ponts of Delaware. New York: Atheneum, 1980.

Williams, William Bradford. Munitions Manufacture in the Philadelphia Ordnance District. Philadelphia: A. Pomerantz & Co., 1921.

Aintree and the Grand National

Bird, T. H. A Hundred Grand Nationals. New York: Scribner, 1937.

Brown, Paul. Aintree: Grand Nationals—Past and Present. New York: Derrydale Press, 1930.

Francis, Dick. The Sport of Queens: The Autobiography of Dick Francis. New York: Harper, 1969.

Graham, Clive, and Bill Curling. The Grand National: An Illustrated History of the Greatest Steeplechase in the World. New York: Winchester Press, 1972.

Munroe, David Hoadley. The Grand National, 1839–1930. New York: Huntington Press, 1930.

Assorted History

De Hurst, C. (pseud.). How Women Should Ride. New York: Harper, 1892.

Gerson, Noel B. The Velvet Glove: A Life of Dolly [sic] Madison. Nashville: Thomas Nelson, 1975.

Hervey, John. *Racing in America, 1922–1936*. New York: Jockey Club, 1937.

Land, Barbara, and Myrick Land. *A Short History of Reno*. Reno: University of Nevada Press, 1995.

Lindbergh, Charles A. *The Spirit of St. Louis*. New York: Scribner, 1953.

Shirer, William L. *Berlin Diary: The Journal of a Foreign Correspondent, 1934–1941*. New York: Knopf, 1941.

Smith, Harry Worcester. *Life and Sport in Aiken and Those Who Made It*. New York: Derrydale Press, 1935.

Steeplechasing

Blood-Horse. *A Quarter-Century of American Racing*. Silver Anniversary Supplement to the Blood-Horse of August 30, 1941. Lexington, KY: American Thoroughbred Breeders Association, 1941.

Curtiss, Frederic H., and John Heard. *The Country Club: 1882–1932*. Brookline, MA: Privately Printed for the Club, 1932.

Durham, Walter T. *Grasslands: A History of the Southern Grasslands Hunt and Racing Foundation, 1929–1932*. Franklin, TN: Providence House, 2010.

Myzk, William. *The History & Origins of the Virginia Gold Cup*. Warrenton, VA: Piedmont Press, 1987.

Rossell, John Ellis, Jr. *The Maryland Hunt Cup: Past and Present*. Baltimore: Sporting Press, 1975.

Smithwick, Patrick. *Flying Change: A Year of Racing and Family and Steeplechasing*. Baltimore: Chesapeake Book Company, 2012.

Streett, William B. *Gentlemen Up*. New York: Derrydale Press, 1930.

Racing Biographies

Anderson, C. W. "Troublemaker: The Gallant" and "Battleship: A Chip of [sic] the Old Block." In *Black, Bay and Chestnut: Profiles of Twenty Favorite Horses*. New York: Macmillan, 1939.

————. "Billy Barton: A Gallant Rogue." In *A Touch of Greatness*. New York: Macmillan, 1945.

————. "Battleship: A Chip off the Old Block" and "Troublemaker: The Gallant." In *Twenty Gallant Horses: Illustrated Stories of the Great Turf Champions of All Time*. New York: Macmillan, 1965.

Bowen, Edward L. "Mereworth Farm." In *Legacies of the Turf: A Century of Great Thoroughbred Breeders*. Ed. Walter J. Salmon Vol. 1. Lexington, KY: Blood-Horse Publications, 2005.

————. "Preston Burch." In *Masters of the Turf: Ten Trainers Who Dominated Horse Racing's Golden Age*. Lexington, KY: Eclipse Press, 2007.

Burch, Preston M. *Training Thoroughbred Horses*. Lexington, KY: Blood-Horse Publications, 1953.

Fitzgeorge-Parker, Tim. *No Secret So Close: The Biography of Bruce Hobbs, MC*. London: Pelham Books, 1984.

Hervey, John. "Steeplechasers." In *American Race Horses, 1938*. New York: Sagamore Press, 1938.

Reuter, F. Turner, Jr. *Animal & Sporting Artists in America*. Middleburg, VA: National Sporting Library, 2008.

Strine, Gerald. *Montpelier: The Recollections of Marion duPont Scott.* New York: Scribner, 1976.

Thoroughbred Bloodlines

Faversham, Rommy. *Great Breeders and Their Methods: Samuel Riddle, Walter Jeffords and the Dynasty of Man o' War.* Neenah, WI: Russell Meerdink, 2005.

Mackay-Smith, Alexander. *Speed and the Thoroughbred: The Complete History.* Lanham, MD: Derrydale Press, 2000.

Willett, Peter. *An Introduction to the Thoroughbred.* London: Stanley Paul, 1975.

Foxhunting

Menzies, Mrs. Stuart. *Women in the Hunting Field.* London: Vinton & Company, 1913.

Reeve, J. Stanley. *Fox-Hunting Formalities.* New York: Derrydale Press, 1930.

Simpson, Charles. *Leicestershire & Its Hunts: The Quorn, the Cottesmore, & the Belvoir.* New York: Knopf, 1926.

Hollywood

Astaire, Fred. *Steps In Time: An Autobiography.* New York: Harper, 1959.

Grant, Jennifer. *Good Stuff: A Reminiscence of My Father, Cary Grant.* New York: Knopf, 2011.

Mann, William J. *Wisecracker: The Life and Times of William Haines, Hollywood's First Openly Gay Star.* New York: Viking, 1998.

Nelson, Nancy. *Evenings with Cary Grant: Recollections in His Own Words and by Those Who Knew Him Best.* New York: William Morrow, 1991.

Rense, Paige, ed. "Cary Grant and Randolph Scott." In *Architectural Digest: Hollywood at Home.* New York: Harry N. Abrams, 2005.

Index